Grade 7

Currency and Coins Photos courtesy of United States Mint, Bureau of Engraving and Houghton Mifflin Harcourt

Printed in the U.S.A.

ISBN   978-1-328-95180-9

7 8 9 10 0607 28 27 26 25 24 23 22

4500849414   r11.21

Dear Students and Families,

Welcome to *Into Math*, Grade 7! In this program, you will develop skills and make sense of mathematics by solving real-world problems, using hands-on tools and strategies, and collaborating with your classmates.

With the support of your teacher and by engaging with meaningful practice you will learn to persevere when solving problems. *Into Math* will not only help you deepen your understanding of mathematics, but also build your confidence as a learner of mathematics.

Even more exciting, you will write all your ideas and solutions right in your book. In your *Into Math* book, writing and drawing on the pages will help you think deeply about what you are learning, help you truly understand math, and most important, you will become a confident user of mathematics!

Sincerely,
The Authors

Authors

Edward B. Burger, PhD
President, Southwestern University
Georgetown, Texas

Matthew R. Larson, PhD
Past-President, National Council
of Teachers of Mathematics
Lincoln Public Schools
Lincoln, Nebraska

Juli K. Dixon, PhD
Professor, Mathematics Education
University of Central Florida
Orlando, Florida

Steven J. Leinwand
Principal Research Analyst
American Institutes for Research
Washington, DC

Timothy D. Kanold, PhD
Mathematics Educator
Chicago, Illinois

Consultants

English Language Development Consultant

Harold Asturias
Director, Center for Mathematics
Excellence and Equity
Lawrence Hall of Science, University of California
Berkeley, California

Program Consultant

David Dockterman, EdD
Lecturer, Harvard Graduate School of Education
Cambridge, Massachusetts

Blended Learning Consultant

Weston Kiercshneck
Senior Fellow
International Center for Leadership in Education
Littleton, Colorado

STEM Consultants

Michael A. DiSpezio
Global Educator
North Falmouth, Massachusetts

Marjorie Frank
Science Writer and
Content-Area Reading Specialist
Brooklyn, New York

Bernadine Okoro
Access and Equity and
STEM Learning Advocate and Consultant
Washington, DC

Cary I. Sneider, PhD
Associate Research Professor
Portland State University
Portland, Oregon

Proportional Relationships

Build Conceptual Understanding   Connect Concepts and Skills   Apply and Practice

MODULE 2 Proportional Reasoning with Percents

Unit 2 Rational Number Operations

Sioux City, IOWA

−5 °F

Build Conceptual Understanding   Connect Concepts and Skills   Apply and Practice

© Houghton Mifflin Harcourt Publishing Company

Model with Expressions, Equations, and Inequalities

Build Conceptual Understanding   Connect Concepts and Skills   Apply and Practice

MODULE 8 Solve Problems Using Inequalities

© Houghton Mifflin Harcourt Publishing Company • **Image Credits:** (dog) ©GK Hart/Vikki Hart/Getty Images; (house) © irina88w/iStock/Getty Images Plus/Getty Images; (cat) © Stockdisc/Getty Images

Build Conceptual Understanding   Connect Concepts and Skills   Apply and Practice

© Houghton Mifflin Harcourt Publishing Company • Image Credit: ©Todd Gipstein/Corbis Documentary/Getty Images

MODULE 11 Analyze Surface Area and Volume

© Houghton Mifflin Harcourt Publishing Company • **Image Credits:** ((l) © leezsnow/iStock/Getty Images Plus; (r) Houghton Mifflin Harcourt

Unit

5 Sampling and Data Analysis

MODULE 12 Proportional Reasoning with Samples

MODULE 13 Use Statistics and Graphs to Compare Data

Build Conceptual Understanding   Connect Concepts and Skills   Apply and Practice

© Houghton Mifflin Harcourt Publishing Company • Image Credit: © ewastudio/iStock/Getty Images Plus/Getty Images

Unit 6 Probability

Build Conceptual Understanding   Connect Concepts and Skills   Apply and Practice

My Progress on Mathematics Standards

The lessons in your *Into Math* book provide instruction for Mathematics Standards for Grade 7. You can use the following pages to reflect on your learning and record your progress through the standards.

As you learn new concepts, reflect on this learning. Consider inserting a checkmark if you understand the concepts or inserting a question mark if you have questions or need help.

	Student Edition Lessons	My Progress
Domain: RATIOS & PROPORTIONAL RELATIONSHIPS		
Cluster: Analyze proportional relationships and use them to solve real-world and mathematical problems.		
Compute unit rates associated with ratios of fractions, including ratios of lengths, areas and other quantities measured in like or different units.	1.3, 1.6	
Recognize and represent proportional relationships between quantities.	1.1 See also below.	
• Decide whether two quantities are in a proportional relationship, e.g., by testing for equivalent ratios in a table or graphing on a coordinate plane and observing whether the graph is a straight line through the origin.	1.2, 1.4	
• Identify the constant of proportionality (unit rate) in tables, graphs, equations, diagrams, and verbal descriptions of proportional relationships.	1.1, 1.2, 1.4, 1.5	
• Represent proportional relationships by equations.	1.2	
• Explain what a point (x, y) on the graph of a proportional relationship means in terms of the situation, with special attention to the points (0, 0) and (1, r) where r is the unit rate.	1.4	
Use proportional relationships to solve multistep ratio and percent problems.	1.5, 1.6, 2.1, 2.2, 2.3, 2.4, 2.5, 6.3, 14.2, 14.3, 14.4, 15.1, 15.2, 15.3, 15.4	

Interactive Standards

Domain: THE NUMBER SYSTEM		
Cluster: Apply and extend previous understandings of operations with fractions to add, subtract, multiply, and divide rational numbers.		
Apply and extend previous understandings of addition and subtraction to add and subtract rational numbers; represent addition and subtraction on a horizontal or vertical number line diagram.	3.1, 3.2, 3.3, 4.1, 4.2, 4.3, 4.4 *See also below.*	
• Describe situations in which opposite quantities combine to make 0.	3.3	
• Understand $p + q$ as the number located a distance $|q|$ from p, in the positive or negative direction depending on whether q is positive or negative. Show that a number and its opposite have a sum of 0 (are additive inverses). Interpret sums of rational numbers by describing real-world contexts.	3.1, 3.2, 3.3, 4.1	
• Understand subtraction of rational numbers as adding the additive inverse, $p - q = p + (-q)$. Show that the distance between two rational numbers on the number line is the absolute value of their difference, and apply this principle in real-world contexts.	4.2, 4.3	
• Apply properties of operations as strategies to add and subtract rational numbers.	4.4	
Apply and extend previous understandings of multiplication and division and of fractions to multiply and divide rational numbers.	*See below.*	
• Understand that multiplication is extended from fractions to rational numbers by requiring that operations continue to satisfy the properties of operations, particularly the distributive property, leading to products such as $(-1)(-1) = 1$ and the rules for multiplying signed numbers. Interpret products of rational numbers by describing real-world contexts.	5.1, 5.2, 5.4	
• Understand that integers can be divided, provided that the divisor is not zero, and every quotient of integers (with non-zero divisor) is a rational number. If p and q are integers, then $-\left(\frac{p}{q}\right) = \frac{(-p)}{q} = \frac{p}{(-q)}$. Interpret quotients of rational numbers by describing real-world contexts.	5.1, 5.3	

• Apply properties of operations as strategies to multiply and divide rational numbers.	5.1, 5.2, 6.1	
• Convert a rational number to a decimal using long division; know that the decimal form of a rational number terminates in 0s or eventually repeats.	5.3	
Solve real-world and mathematical problems involving the four operations with rational numbers.	4.3, 5.2, 5.3, 5.4, 6.1, 6.2, 6.3	

Domain: EXPRESSIONS & EQUATIONS

Cluster: Use properties of operations to generate equivalent expressions.

Apply properties of operations as strategies to add, subtract, factor, and expand linear expressions with rational coefficients.	7.2	
Understand that rewriting an expression in different forms in a problem context can shed light on the problem and how the quantities in it are related.	2.2, 7.1, 7.2	

Cluster: Solve real-life and mathematical problems using numerical and algebraic expressions and equations.

Solve multi-step real-life and mathematical problems posed with positive and negative rational numbers in any form (whole numbers, fractions, and decimals), using tools strategically. Apply properties of operations to calculate with numbers in any form; convert between forms as appropriate; and assess the reasonableness of answers using mental computation and estimation strategies.	5.4, 6.1, 6.2, 6.3, 7.4, 10.1, 10.2, 10.3, 10.4, 11.2, 11.3, 11.4, 14.4, 15.3	
Use variables to represent quantities in a real-world or mathematical problem, and construct simple equations and inequalities to solve problems by reasoning about the quantities.	7.3, 8.2 *See also below.*	
• Solve word problems leading to equations of the form $px + q = r$ and $p(x + q) = r$, where p, q, and r are specific rational numbers. Solve equations of these forms fluently. Compare an algebraic solution to an arithmetic solution, identifying the sequence of the operations used in each approach.	7.4, 7.5	
• Solve word problems leading to inequalities of the form $px + q > r$ or $px + q < r$, where p, q, and r are specific rational numbers. Graph the solution set of the inequality and interpret it in the context of the problem.	8.1, 8.3	

Interactive Standards

Domain: GEOMETRY		
Cluster: Draw, construct, and describe geometrical figures and describe the relationships between them.		
Solve problems involving scale drawings of geometric figures, including computing actual lengths and areas from a scale drawing and reproducing a scale drawing at a different scale.	1.6	
Draw (freehand, with ruler and protractor, and with technology) geometric shapes with given conditions. Focus on constructing triangles from three measures of angles or sides, noticing when the conditions determine a unique triangle, more than one triangle, or no triangle.	9.1, 9.2, 9.3, 9.4	
Describe the two-dimensional figures that result from slicing three-dimensional figures, as in plane sections of right rectangular prisms and right rectangular pyramids.	10.3, 11.1	
Cluster: Solve real-life and mathematical problems involving angle measure, area, surface area, and volume.		
Know the formulas for the area and circumference of a circle and use them to solve problems; give an informal derivation of the relationship between the circumference and area of a circle.	10.1, 10.2	
Use facts about supplementary, complementary, vertical, and adjacent angles in a multi-step problem to write and solve simple equations for an unknown angle in a figure.	7.5	
Solve real-world and mathematical problems involving area, volume and surface area of two- and three-dimensional objects composed of triangles, quadrilaterals, polygons, cubes, and right prisms.	10.4, 11.2, 11.3, 11.4	

Domain: STATISTICS & PROBABILITY		
Cluster: Use random sampling to draw inferences about a population.		
Understand that statistics can be used to gain information about a population by examining a sample of the population; generalizations about a population from a sample are valid only if the sample is representative of that population. Understand that random sampling tends to produce representative samples and support valid inferences.	12.1	
Use data from a random sample to draw inferences about a population with an unknown characteristic of interest. Generate multiple samples (or simulated samples) of the same size to gauge the variation in estimates or predictions.	12.2, 12.3	
Cluster: Draw informal comparative inferences about two populations.		
Informally assess the degree of visual overlap of two numerical data distributions with similar variabilities, measuring the difference between the centers by expressing it as a multiple of a measure of variability.	13.1, 13.2, 13.3	
Use measures of center and measures of variability for numerical data from random samples to draw informal comparative inferences about two populations.	13.1, 13.2, 13.3	
Cluster: Investigate chance processes and develop, use, and evaluate probability models.		
Understand that the probability of a chance event is a number between 0 and 1 that expresses the likelihood of the event occurring. Larger numbers indicate greater likelihood. A probability near 0 indicates an unlikely event, a probability around $\frac{1}{2}$ indicates an event that is neither unlikely nor likely, and a probability near 1 indicates a likely event.	14.1	
Approximate the probability of a chance event by collecting data on the chance process that produces it and observing its long-run relative frequency, and predict the approximate relative frequency given the probability.	14.2, 14.4, 15.1, 15.3	

Interactive Standards

Develop a probability model and use it to find probabilities of events. Compare probabilities from a model to observed frequencies; if the agreement is not good, explain possible sources of the discrepancy.	15.1 *See also below.*	
• Develop a uniform probability model by assigning equal probability to all outcomes, and use the model to determine probabilities of events.	15.1, 15.3	
• Develop a probability model (which may not be uniform) by observing frequencies in data generated from a chance process.	14.2	
Find probabilities of compound events using organized lists, tables, tree diagrams, and simulation.	*See below.*	
• Understand that, just as with simple events, the probability of a compound event is the fraction of outcomes in the sample space for which the compound event occurs.	14.3, 15.2	
• Represent sample spaces for compound events using methods such as organized lists, tables and tree diagrams. For an event described in everyday language (e.g., "rolling double sixes"), identify the outcomes in the sample space which compose the event.	14.3, 15.2	
• Design and use a simulation to generate frequencies for compound events.	14.3, 15.4	

Proportional Relationships

Astronomer

Michael E. Brown is a professor of planetary astronomy at the California Institute of Technology and the author of the book *How I Killed Pluto and Why It Had It Coming*. Brown and his team discovered a number of objects in our solar system farther away than Neptune. One of these objects, the dwarf planet Eris, is more massive than Pluto (shown above). This discovery resulted in The International Astronomical Union demoting Pluto to a dwarf planet.

STEM
POWERING INGENUITY

STEM Task:

We often use ratios to describe scale models. If a model rocket has a scale 1 inch = 12 feet, that means for every part of the model that measures 1 inch the corresponding part of the rocket measures 12 feet. Use this scale to calculate the height of a rocket if the model is 26 inches tall. Explain your reasoning.

Learning Mindset

Perseverance Collects and Tries Multiple Strategies

Perseverance is the ability to stick with a task, even if it is difficult. Have you ever noticed that you are able to manage your time on tasks better than before or that you are able to identify study skills that are effective for you? Those are signs that your ability to persevere is growing. Here are some tips for helping you persevere through difficult tasks.

- Get rid of distractions, like your cell phone, while you are working. Your brain is less effective when you attempt to multi-task. All human brains are! That's because multi-tasking isn't really doing two things at once. Your brain is actually shifting attention between the activities, and that slows you down. It can also make the quality of your work decrease.

- Divide complex tasks into smaller steps. This helps you focus your efforts. It also makes it easier to spot mistakes.

- Even if your effort is unsuccessful, look at what you can learn from each attempt and adjust your strategy.

- Check for a fixed-mindset voice in your head telling you that you're not good with certain content or with certain tasks. Activate your growth-mindset voice telling you that you can learn more about the content and get better at the tasks.

Reflect

Q What are some strategies you used to manage your time while working on the STEM Task?

Q How have you kept yourself on task in the past? What is your plan for improving your ability to stay focused as you face math challenges?

Identify and Represent Proportional Relationships

WHICH RATIO DOES NOT BELONG?

Express each ratio of apples to oranges shown below in words and as a fraction. Share with a partner or a small group.

A.

B.

_____

C.

Apples	Oranges
8	18
32	72
56	126

_____

_____

_____

D.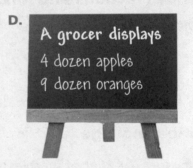

A grocer displays
4 dozen apples
9 dozen oranges

_____

_____

_____

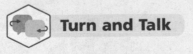 **Turn and Talk**

- Explain how the ratios are related and how they are different.

- Which ratio does not belong? Explain why.

Are You Ready?

Complete these problems to review prior concepts and skills you will need for this module.

Solve One-Step Equations

Solve the equation.

1. $8x = 56$ _____   **2.** $4a = 23$ _____

Ordered Pairs on the Coordinate Plane

Write the ordered pair for each point.

3. A _____   **4.** B _____

Plot and label the ordered pairs on the graph.

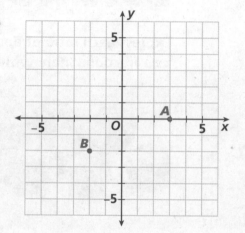

	Point	(x, y)
5.	C	(−3, 2)
6.	D	(1, −2)

Divide Fractions and Mixed Numbers

Divide.

7. $\frac{3}{4} \div \frac{3}{5}$ _____   **8.** $7\frac{1}{2} \div \frac{5}{8}$ _____

9. $\frac{3}{8} \div \frac{1}{2}$ _____

Ratio Language

10. Jasper has a jar of marbles. Complete the table to show the ratios of marbles.

blue:red	
blue:yellow	
red:blue	
yellow:red	

Name _____

Explore Relationships

(I Can) recognize when relationships presented in tables, diagrams, and verbal descriptions can be represented by a constant unit rate.

Spark Your Learning

These salsas are made for a competition.

On Fire!

2 tablespoons peppers; 5 tablespoons tomatoes

Blazin'

4 tablespoons peppers; 12 tablespoons tomatoes

Kickin'

6 tablespoons peppers; 15 tablespoons tomatoes

Feel the Burn

3 tablespoons peppers; 6 tablespoons tomatoes

If peppers and tomatoes are the only ingredients in the salsas and the names are based on taste, which two salsas should have the same name? Show your work and explain.

Turn and Talk Using the ratios described in the salsa recipes, describe which recipe is most hot and which recipe is most mild.

Build Understanding

1 ▶ The table shows how many ounces of salsa you get when buying small jars of salsa.

Small jars of salsa	4	8	12	16	
Ounces of salsa	32	64	96		

A. Describe a pattern you see in the rows of the table.

_____

_____

B. Describe a pattern you see in the columns of the table.

_____

_____

C. Use your patterns to extend the table.

D. You previously learned that a **unit rate** is a rate in which the second quantity in the comparison is one unit, such as 4 ounces per 1 serving. Describe the relationship between ounces of salsa and small jars of salsa using a unit rate.

_____

_____

E. The diagram shows how many ounces of salsa you get when buying medium jars of salsa. Describe the relationship using a unit rate.

48 ounces

_____

_____

 Turn and Talk Is the relationship represented in the table the same as the relationship represented in the diagram in Part E? Why or why not?

2 ▸ The tables show the prices and weights of avocados.

Avocados	Price
1	$1.25
2	$2.50
3	$3.75
4	$5.00
5	$6.25

Avocados	Weight
1	7 oz
2	13 oz
3	20 oz
4	26 oz
5	34 oz

An avocado is classified as a fruit, and in particular, as a one-seeded berry.

A. Can the relationship between the price and the number of avocados be described with a constant rate? Explain.

_____

_____

_____

B. Can the relationship between the weight and the number of avocados be described with a constant rate? Explain.

_____

_____

_____

Check Understanding

1. A 2-pound package of hamburger costs $7.00, and you pay $10.50 for a 3-pound package of hamburger. Complete the table. Then decide whether it makes sense to use a constant rate to describe the relationship. Explain.

Weight (lb)	2	3	4	5
Cost ($)	7.00		14.00	17.50

_____

_____

2. The table shows the total costs of different numbers of tickets. Decide whether it makes sense to use a constant rate to describe the relationship. Explain.

Number of tickets	6	8	10	14	25
Total cost ($)	34.50	44.00	52.50	73.50	131.25

_____

_____

On Your Own

3. **(MP) Reason** Flo measures the amount of water her high pressure sprayer uses and finds that it uses 20 gallons of water in 4 minutes and 30 gallons in 6 minutes. Complete the table. Then decide whether it makes sense to use a constant rate to describe the relationship. Explain.

Time (min)	2	4		10	18
Water (gal)	10		30	50	90

_____

_____

_____

For Problems 4–5, use the given information.

Ken rode his bike on Monday and Tuesday. Each table shows the distance that he was from home at various times.

Monday	
Time (min)	Distance (km)
20	5
40	10
60	12
80	14
100	16

Tuesday	
Time (min)	Distance (km)
20	4
40	8
60	12
80	16
100	20

4. Can the relationship in Monday's table be described by a constant unit rate? Explain.

_____

5. Can the relationship in Tuesday's table be described by a constant unit rate? Explain.

_____

 **I'm in a Learning Mindset!**

What can I apply from previous work with ratios and rates to recognize when a relationship between two quantities can be described by a constant unit rate?

_____

_____

© Houghton Mifflin Harcourt Publishing Company • Image Credit: ©Larry Metayer/Dreamstine

Explore Relationships

1. The amount of money Chaz earned for walking dogs is given in the table. Can the relationship be described by a constant rate? Explain.

Dogs walked	6	8	11
Money earned ($)	112.50	150.00	206.25

_____

2. **STEM** The diagram shows the structure of a molecule of sulfur dioxide. The ratio of oxygen atoms to sulfur atoms in sulfur dioxide is always the same. How many oxygen atoms (O) are there when there are 6 sulfur atoms (S)? Explain how you got your answer.

_____

3. (MP) **Reason** Three different sizes of sports–drink mix are shown with their prices. Can the relationship between price and volume (in grams) be described by a constant rate? Explain.

_____

For Problems 4–5, use the values in the table.

Servings of cereal	Cups of cereal	Cups of milk
16	12	4
24	18	6

4. Can the relationship between cups of milk and cups of cereal be described by a constant ratio? Why or why not?

_____

5. Can the relationship between cups of cereal and servings of cereal be described by a constant rate? Why or why not?

_____

Test Prep

6. Jane is saving to buy a cell phone. She is given a $100 gift to start and saves $35 a month from her allowance. So after 1 month, Jane has saved $135. Does it make sense to represent the relationship between the amount saved and the number of months with one constant rate? Why or why not? Explain your answer.

_____

_____

_____

_____

7. Raj is mixing different colors of paint. The table shows the amount of each color paint Raj uses for each mixture.

Raj's Paint Mixtures		
Mixture	Red (ounces)	Blue (ounces)
1	2	1
2	7	3.5
3	4.5	2
4	5.5	2.5

Select the two mixtures that will produce the same color.

Ⓐ mixtures 1 and 2

Ⓑ mixtures 3 and 4

Ⓒ mixtures 1 and 3

Ⓓ mixtures 2 and 4

Spiral Review

8. At 1:00 p.m., a diver's elevation is −30 feet relative to sea level. At 2:00 p.m., the diver's elevation is −45 feet. At which time is the diver farther from sea level?

_____

9. A share of stock costs $83.60. The next day, the price increases $15.35. The following day, the price decreases $4.75. What is the final price?

_____

Name

Recognize Proportional Relationships in Tables

(I Can) identify proportional relationships in tables and equations, identify the constant of proportionality, and write the associated equation.

Spark Your Learning

For which tables can you predict the cost of 100 units of the item? Explain why you can make that prediction for some of the tables and not for others. For the tables that let you predict the cost of 100 units, find the cost.

Peanut butter (oz)	Total cost ($)
8	3
16	4
40	6

Binder clips	Total cost ($)
12	2
36	5
50	6

Trail mix (lb)	Total cost ($)
2	6
8	24
12	36

Shower sponges	Total cost ($)
4	8
8	16
10	20

 Turn and Talk What characteristic of the table allows you to predict the cost of any number of items?

Build Understanding

1 Maxine walks dogs to earn extra money. The table of values shows the proportional relationship between the number of dogs Maxine walks and the amount of money she earns.

Dogs walked	2	4	6
Amount ($)	7	14	21

A. Show that the ratio of dogs walked to amount earned is a constant ratio.

_____

B. Show that the ratio of amount earned to dogs walked is a constant ratio.

_____

C. What is the unit rate of dogs walked per dollar earned? Does it make sense? Explain.

_____

_____

D. What is the unit rate of dollars earned per dog walked? Does it make sense? Explain.

_____

_____

_____

E. What is the constant of proportionality k in this situation?

_____

F. Describe what the unit rate k represents in this situation.

_____

_____

Turn and Talk In a table of values that represents a proportional relationship, how can you find the constant of proportionality?

Step It Out

2 ▶ Two relationships are represented in the tables. Which table shows a proportional relationship, and which does not? Explain.

Table 1

Windows washed, x	3	6	7
Amount earned ($), y	36	72	84

Table 2

Windows washed, x	4	5	8
Amount earned ($), y	48	55	64

Table 1

The ratios $\dfrac{\text{amount earned ($), } y}{\text{windows, } x}$ are:

$$\frac{36}{\square} = \square \qquad \frac{\square}{6} = \square \qquad \frac{\square}{7} = \square$$

The ratios $\frac{y}{x}$ are / are not equivalent. Therefore, the relationship shown in this table is / is not proportional.

Table 2

The ratios $\dfrac{\text{amount earned ($), } y}{\text{windows, } x}$ are:

$$\frac{48}{\square} = \square \qquad \frac{\square}{5} = \square \qquad \frac{\square}{8} = \square$$

The ratios $\frac{y}{x}$ are / are not equivalent. Therefore, the relationship shown in this table is / is not proportional.

3 ▶ The number of students whom Malcolm tutors is proportional to the amount earned. The calendar shows Malcolm's earnings from tutoring in one week.

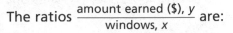
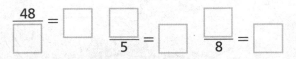

Tutoring Schedule

Mon	Tue	Wed	Thu	Fri
Clive	Justice	Rance	Molly	Janis
Bray	Krissy	Kimee	Rick	$30
Jen	Eve	Yuri	Sharona	
Haley	Nolan	$90	Mikay	
$120	Armond		Paco	
	Landree		$150	
	$180			

A. Complete the table.

Number of students, x		3		5	
Amount earned ($), y	30		120		180

B. Find the constant of proportionality k.

$$k = \frac{y}{x} = \frac{\square}{\square} = \square$$

C. The **equation** for a proportional relationship is $y = kx$, where k is the constant of proportionality. Use the value of k you found in Part B to write an equation for this proportional relationship.

$$y = \square\, x$$

4 The equation $y = 12x$ represents the number of inches y in x feet.

A. The equation $y = 12x$ | does / does not | represent a proportional relationship. If so, what is the constant of proportionality? How do you know?

_____

_____

B. Use the equation to complete the table of values for the relationship between inches and feet.

Feet, x	0	1	2			5
Inches, y				36	48	

 Turn and Talk When would it be better to use an equation to represent a proportional relationship? When would it be better to use a table?

Check Understanding

1. There are 4 quarters in $1.00.

A. Make a table of values to represent this relationship.

Dollars, x					
Quarters, y					

B. Is this a proportional relationship? If so, identify k and explain what it represents. If not, explain why not.

_____

C. Write an equation for the situation. _____

2. The equation $y = 7x$ gives the cost y of x pounds of chicken at the grocery store. Complete the table for the given weights of chicken.

Weight (lb), x	1	2	5	8
Cost ($), y				

3. Is the relationship in the table proportional? If it is, write its equation.

x	1	2	3	4
y	5	10	15	20

On Your Own

4. 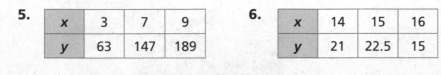 **Model with Mathematics** Reanna is making a scrapbook which holds 14 photos on each 2-page spread. Make a table of values to represent this relationship. Write an equation for the situation.

2-page spreads, x				
Photos, y				

Tell whether each table represents a proportional relationship. If it does, identify the constant of proportionality.

5.

x	3	7	9
y	63	147	189

6.

x	14	15	16
y	21	22.5	15

7. Determine whether the table represents a proportional relationship. If it does, find the constant of proportionality and use it to write an equation to represent the table of values.

x	1	2	3	4	5
y	7	14	21	28	35

8. The equation $y = 8x$ gives the number of slices y in x pizzas. Make a table of values using the equation. Identify the constant of proportionality. Then complete each sentence.

Pizzas, x				
Slices, y				

There are _____ slices in 3 pizzas.

There are 16 slices in _____ pizzas.

9. 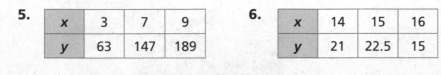 **Reason** The table shows the relationship between the number of workers painting apartments in an apartment building and the number of days it takes to paint all 50 apartments. Determine whether the relationship is proportional. Explain your reasoning.

Workers, x	5	10	15	20	25
Duration of job (days), y	60	30	20	15	12

(MP) **Model with Mathematics** For Problems 10–12, use the description of a proportional relationship to make a table. Then identify the constant of proportionality, and write an equation for the situation.

10. A 2-cup serving of chicken noodle soup has 1.5 ounces of noodles.

Cups of soup, x	Ounces of noodles, y

11. Rick is exercising at a constant pace.

126 steps every 3 minutes

Time (min), x	Steps, y

12. Colin is preparing equal-sized care packages. He placed 34 items in 2 care packages he made.

Packages, x				
Items, y				

13. The equation $y = 100x$ gives the number of centimeters y in x meters. Make a table of values using the equation. Identify the constant of proportionality. Then complete each sentence.

Meters, x				
Centimeters, y				

$k = $ _____ ; There are _____ centimeters in 3 meters. There are 200 centimeters in _____ meters.

 I'm in a Learning Mindset!

What strategies do I use to decide if a relationship displayed in a table is proportional? How do I know when I am finished?

_____

_____

Recognize Proportional Relationships in Tables

Tell whether each table represents a proportional relationship. If it does, identify the constant of proportionality.

1.

x	2	5	7
y	18	45	63

2.

x	3	4	5
y	42	60	80

_____   _____

3. Math on the Spot Determine whether the table represents a proportional relationship. If it does, find the constant of proportionality and use it to write an equation to represent the table of values.

Number of lawns, x	1	2	3	4
Amount earned ($), y	24	48	72	96

_____

_____

4. The equation $y = 6x$ gives the cost y of x of the tickets shown. Make a table of values. Identify the constant of proportionality. Then complete each sentence.

Tickets, x					
Cost ($), y					

_____

It costs _____ for 5 tickets.

It costs $24 for _____ tickets.

Ⓜⓟ **Model with Mathematics** Use the description of a proportional relationship in each table. Identify the constant of proportionality, then write an equation to represent the situation in the table.

5. Alison earned $24 by stocking shelves at the grocery store for 3 hours.

Time (h), x	1	2	3	6
Total pay ($), y	8	16	24	48

_____

6. Each cooler holds 18 water bottles.

Coolers, x	1	2	4	7
Water bottles, y	18	36	72	126

Test Prep

7. Which table represents a proportional relationship?

Table 1			
Carrots (lb)	2	3	4
Number of carrots	23	33	43

Table 2			
Deli meat (lb)	2	3	4
Total cost ($)	23	34.50	46

8. Use the proportional relationship in the table.

Milk (gal), x	2	4	8
Servings, y	32	64	128

A. Write an equation for the relationship.

_____

B. There are 4 quarts in a gallon and 4 cups in a quart. How many cups are in one serving? _____

C. There are 8 fluid ounces in a cup. How many fluid ounces are in one serving? _____

9. What is the meaning of the constant of proportionality in this situation?

Rocking chairs, x	2	3	5
Time to build (h), y	48	72	120

_____

10. Describe a method for determining whether a table represents a proportional relationship.

_____

_____

_____

11. Kevin uses $\frac{2}{3}$ cup of flour to make 2 servings of biscuits. How many cups of flour are there per serving? How many cups of flour should Kevin use to make 7 servings?

- Ⓐ $\frac{1}{3}$ cup; $2\frac{1}{3}$ cups
- Ⓑ $\frac{2}{3}$ cup; $2\frac{1}{3}$ cups
- Ⓒ $\frac{2}{3}$ cup; $4\frac{2}{3}$ cups
- Ⓓ $1\frac{1}{3}$ cups; $4\frac{2}{3}$ cups

Spiral Review

12. Donya ran a 3k race at a constant speed in 21 minutes 30 seconds. At this speed, how long does it take her to run 1k?

_____

13. It costs $20 for 4 play tickets and $35 for 7 play tickets. Is cost per ticket constant? Why or why not?

_____

Name

Compute Unit Rates Involving Fractions

(**I Can**) compute unit rates associated with ratios of fractions.

Spark Your Learning

Rick and Tina hiked at different constant rates. Rick hiked $\frac{1}{2}$ mile every 15 minutes, or $\frac{1}{4}$ hour. It took Tina 10 minutes to hike $\frac{1}{4}$ mile. Find the distance each hiked in 1 hour.

Rick

Tina

Turn and Talk How can you use the distance they each hiked in 1 hour to write a rate for the distance they each would hike in 2 hours?

Build Understanding

1 ▷ Jessie loves to go hiking on rustic trails through trees and along rivers. One day in 20 minutes of hiking, she hiked 1 mile. If Jessie hiked at a constant rate, what would that rate be?

   A. Write Jessie's hiking rate in all the ways you can think of from the information given.

   B. Complete the statements below to show how to write Jessie's hiking rate as a unit rate in miles per hour.

   $$\frac{1 \text{ mile}}{20 \text{ minutes}} = \frac{1 \text{ mile}}{\frac{1}{3} \text{ hour}} = \frac{1 \text{ mile} \times \boxed{}}{\frac{1}{3} \text{ hour} \times \boxed{}} = \frac{\boxed{} \text{ miles}}{1 \text{ hour}}$$

   You have to multiply $\frac{1}{3}$ hour by _____ to make the second quantity in

   the unit rate _____ hour, so multiply the first quantity by _____ as well.

   C. Amiya prefers hiking on more hilly trails. One time Amiya reached the mile marker pictured in 20 minutes hiking at a steady pace. Show how to find the unit rate in minutes per mile.

   $$\frac{20 \text{ min}}{\boxed{} \text{ mi}} =$$

$\frac{1}{2}$ mile

 Turn and Talk Compare the rates "minutes per mile" and "miles per minute." Give an example of each rate.

Step It Out

2 ▶ A recipe says to use $\frac{2}{3}$ cup of milk to make $\frac{4}{5}$ serving of pudding. How many cups of milk are in 1 serving?

A. Recall that **reciprocals** are two numbers whose product is 1. Explain how reciprocals are used to find the unit rate.

$$\frac{\frac{2}{3} \text{ cup of milk}}{\frac{4}{5} \text{ serving of pudding}} \qquad \frac{\frac{2}{3} \times \frac{5}{4}}{\frac{4}{5} \times \frac{5}{4}} = \frac{\frac{5}{6}}{1}, \text{ or } \frac{5}{6} \text{ cup of milk per serving}$$

_____

_____

B. How can you use division to find this unit rate?

_____

> **Turn and Talk** How can you find the number of servings of pudding for every cup of milk?

3 ▶ Jaylan makes limeade using $\frac{3}{4}$ cup of water for every $\frac{1}{5}$ cup of lime juice. Rene's limeade recipe is different. He uses $\frac{2}{3}$ cup of water for every $\frac{1}{6}$ cup of lime juice. Whose limeade has a weaker flavor?

A. What do you need to know to solve this problem?

_____

B. Compute the unit rate of water to lime juice in each limeade.

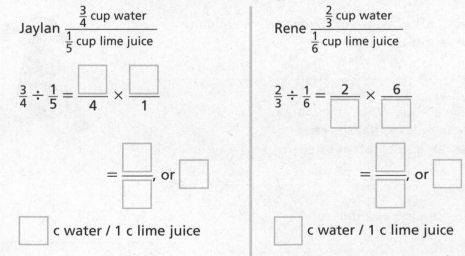

Jaylan $\dfrac{\frac{3}{4} \text{ cup water}}{\frac{1}{5} \text{ cup lime juice}}$

Rene $\dfrac{\frac{2}{3} \text{ cup water}}{\frac{1}{6} \text{ cup lime juice}}$

$$\frac{3}{4} \div \frac{1}{5} = \frac{\square}{4} \times \frac{\square}{1}$$

$$\frac{2}{3} \div \frac{1}{6} = \frac{2}{\square} \times \frac{6}{\square}$$

$$= \frac{\square}{\square}, \text{ or } \square$$

$$= \frac{\square}{\square}, \text{ or } \square$$

$\square$ c water / 1 c lime juice

$\square$ c water / 1 c lime juice

C. Whose limeade has a weaker flavor? Explain.

_____

_____

4 The moon has a weaker gravitational pull than Earth, so objects weigh less on the moon. For example, Jaxon weighs $30\frac{5}{6}$ pounds on the moon and 185 pounds on Earth. Viola weighs 135 pounds on Earth and $22\frac{1}{2}$ pounds on the moon.

A. Show that the relationship between weight on the moon and weight on Earth is proportional.

Jaxon: $\dfrac{30\frac{5}{6}}{\boxed{}} = 30\frac{5}{6} \div \boxed{} = $ _____

Viola: $\dfrac{\boxed{}}{135} = \boxed{} \div 135 = $ _____

The constant of proportionality for $\dfrac{\text{moon weight (lb)}}{\text{Earth weight (lb)}}$ is _____ .

B. Let x represent the weight on Earth. Let y represent the weight on the moon. Write an equation for the proportional relationship. Use it to find the weight of a 20-pound dog on the moon.

The equation is _____ .

On the moon, the dog would weigh about _____ pounds.

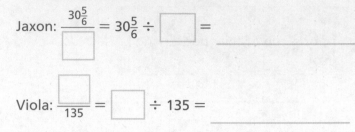

Turn and Talk What would a dog that weighs 12 pounds on the moon weigh on Earth?

Check Understanding

1. A faucet leaks $\frac{5}{8}$ quart of water in 15 minutes. How many quarts does the faucet leak per hour?

   _____

2. Toni ran $\frac{4}{5}$ mile in $\frac{1}{5}$ hour. Write an equation for the distance in miles y that she ran in x hours if she ran at a constant rate.

   _____

3. Write $\frac{3}{4}$ cup per $\frac{1}{2}$ serving as a unit rate.

   _____

4. Write $2\frac{1}{4}$ miles in $\frac{3}{4}$ hour as a unit rate.

   _____

© Houghton Mifflin Harcourt Publishing Company • Image Credits: (t) ©Okea/Dreamstime/Harcourt; (b) ©Alexstar/Dreamstime

On Your Own

5. **Health and Fitness** Jorge measured his heart rate after jogging. He counted 11 beats during a 6-second interval. What was the unit rate for Jorge's heart rate in beats per minute? _____

6. Chen bikes $2\frac{1}{2}$ miles in $\frac{5}{12}$ hour. What is Chen's unit rate in miles per hour?

_____

7. Amal can run $\frac{1}{8}$ mile in $1\frac{1}{2}$ minutes.

   A. If he can maintain that pace, how long will it take him to run 1 mile?

   _____

   B. How long would it would take Amal to run 3 miles at that pace?

   _____

   C. Naomi can run $\frac{1}{4}$ mile in 2 minutes. Does Amal or Naomi run faster? How do you know?

   _____

   _____

8. **Open Ended** When both quantities in a rate are fractions, what strategy do you use to write the rate as a unit rate?

   _____

   _____

   _____

9. (MP) **Reason** What is the ratio of dried fruit to sunflower seeds in the granola recipe? If you need to triple the recipe, will the ratio change? Explain.

   _____

   _____

Granola

2 cups old-fashioned oats	**3** tablespoons honey
2/3 cup raw nuts	**2** tablespoons sunflower oil
1/8 cup sunflower seeds	**1/2** teaspoon vanilla
1/2 cup dried fruit, chopped	**1/8** teaspoon salt

Preheat oven to 300 °F. Combine and mix ingredients in a bowl. Spread on baking sheet. Bake for 10 minutes. Cool. Store in closed container in the refrigerator.

10. The table shows the numbers of packages of peanut butter crackers y that can be made using various amounts of peanut butter x.

Peanut butter (tbsp)	$\frac{1}{2}$	$\frac{5}{8}$	$\frac{3}{4}$	$\frac{7}{8}$
Cracker packages	2	$2\frac{1}{2}$	3	$3\frac{1}{2}$

A. Show that the relationship is proportional.

_____

B. Write an equation to represent the relationship, and find the amount of peanut butter used to make 25 cracker packages.

_____

11. The relationship between adult dog weight x in pounds and the daily recommended amount of dog food y in cups is proportional.

Dog weight (lb)	10	40	50	100
Dog food (cups)	$\frac{1}{6}$	$\frac{2}{3}$	$\frac{5}{6}$	$1\frac{2}{3}$

Write an equation for the relationship. How much dog food is recommended for a 25-pound adult dog?

_____

For Exercises 12–15, find each unit rate.

12. $\frac{5}{8}$ mile in $\frac{1}{4}$ hour

_____

13. $68 for $8\frac{1}{2}$ hours

_____

14. $1\frac{1}{4}$ cup of flour per $\frac{1}{8}$ cup of butter

_____

15. $2\frac{1}{2}$ miles in $\frac{3}{4}$ hour

_____

I'm in a Learning Mindset!

What did I learn from peers when they shared their strategies with me for writing a unit rate?

_____

_____

© Houghton Mifflin Harcourt Publishing Company • Image Credit: ©Eric Isselee/Shutterstock

Name _____

Compute Unit Rates Involving Fractions

1. **STEM** Density is a unit rate measured in units of mass per unit of volume. The mass of a garnet is 5.7 grams. The volume is 1.5 cubic centimeters (cm^3). What is the density of the garnet?

   _____

2. **Math on the Spot** Jen and Kamlee are walking to school. After 20 minutes, Jen has walked $\frac{4}{5}$ mile. After 25 minutes, Kamlee has walked $\frac{5}{6}$ mile. Find their speeds in miles per hour. Who is walking faster?

   _____

3. (MP) **Reason** Maria and Franco are mixing sports drinks for a track meet. Maria uses $\frac{2}{3}$ cup of powdered mix for every 2 gallons of water. Franco uses $1\frac{1}{4}$ cups of powdered mix for every 5 gallons of water. Whose sports drink is stronger? Explain how you found your answer.

   _____

   _____

   _____

4. (MP) **Model with Mathematics** Serena estimates that she can paint 60 square feet of wall space every half-hour. Write an equation for the relationship with time in hours as the independent variable. Can Serena paint 400 square feet of wall space in 3.5 hours? Why or why not?

   _____

5. Cheri paid $6.50 for the bunch of grapes with the weight shown on the scale. What was the price per pound?

   _____

Find the unit rate.

6. $\frac{1}{4}$ kilometer in $\frac{1}{3}$ hour

7. $\frac{7}{8}$ square foot in $\frac{1}{4}$ hour

8. $6.50 for $3\frac{1}{4}$ pounds of grapes

9. $49.50 for $5\frac{1}{2}$ hours

10. 247 heart beats in $6\frac{1}{2}$ minutes

11. $8\frac{1}{2}$ miles in $\frac{1}{2}$ hour

Test Prep

12. Select all the rates equivalent to the rate $\frac{3}{4}$ cup per pound.

    (A) $\frac{3}{8}$ cup per $\frac{1}{2}$ pound

    (B) $\frac{1}{4}$ cup per $\frac{1}{2}$ pound

    (C) 3 cups for every 2 pounds

    (D) $1\frac{1}{2}$ cups for every 2 pounds

    (E) 0.1875 cup for every 0.25 pound

13. Jordan cooked a $16\frac{1}{5}$-pound turkey in $5\frac{2}{5}$ hours. How many minutes per pound did it take to cook the turkey? Express your answer as a unit rate.

    _____

14. Mr. March sells popcorn at his theater. He uses $3\frac{3}{4}$ cups of unpopped corn to make 15 bags of popped corn. Write an equation for the number of bags of popcorn b that can be made with c cups of unpopped corn.

    _____

15. Lucia uses 3 ounces of pasta to make $\frac{3}{4}$ serving of pasta. How many ounces of pasta are there per serving? How many ounces of pasta should Lucia use to make 5 servings?

    (A) 3 ounces; 15 ounces   (C) 6 ounces; 30 ounces

    (B) 4 ounces; 20 ounces   (D) 9 ounces; 40 ounces

Spiral Review

16. John left school with $8.43. He found a quarter on his way home and then stopped to buy an apple for $0.89. How much money did he have when he got home?

    $ _____

17. Arian is making bracelets. For each bracelet, it takes $\frac{1}{10}$ hour to pick out materials and $\frac{1}{4}$ hour to braid it together. How many bracelets can Arian make in 5 hours?

    _____

18. For a game, 3 people are chosen in the first round. Each of those people chooses 3 people in the second round, and so on. How many people are chosen in the sixth round?

    _____

Name

Recognize Proportional Relationships in Graphs

(**I Can**) decide whether a relationship shown in a graph is proportional and explain the connection between the constant of proportionality and the point (1, *r*) on the graph.

Spark Your Learning

Jake makes custom–painted sneakers. He makes 6 pairs in 4 hours. On a graph of this proportional relationship, what point would represent 6 pairs in 4 hours? Justify your answer with a description or model.

x	y

 Turn and Talk How did you decide which axis represents which variable? Explain.

Build Understanding

1 ▸ The table shows the proportional relationship between pairs of sneakers Jake makes to sell at a craft fair and the revenue from selling them.

Sneakers

Pairs of sneakers, x	0	1	2	3	4	5
Revenue ($), y	0	40	80	120	160	200

A. How do the data in the table show a proportional relationship? How do you know?

_____

B. Write the data in the table as ordered pairs and graph them.

_____

C. Do the points all lie along a straight line? _____

D. Does the graph pass through the origin? _____

> **Turn and Talk** Describe the characteristics of the graph of a proportional relationship.

2 ▸ Maya sells homemade spice mixes in different sizes at the craft fair. The graph shows the proportional relationship between teaspoons of cumin and teaspoons of chili powder in one recipe.

A. What does the origin represent?

_____

_____

B. What are the coordinates of the point at $x = 1$, and what do they represent?

_____

_____

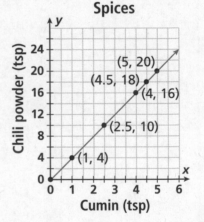

Spices

C. Explain why the graph shows a proportional relationship.

_____

_____

D. Why is the graph a solid line?

_____

_____

Step It Out

3 Parker sells lemonade at the craft fair. The relationship between the number of servings and cups of water used is shown.

Servings, x	2	3	6	8
Water (c), y	1	$1\frac{1}{2}$	3	4

A. Graph the relationship, and tell whether it is a proportional relationship. Explain how you know.

_____

_____

_____

B. The graph of the line should be solid / dashed because x and y can be any nonnegative numbers.

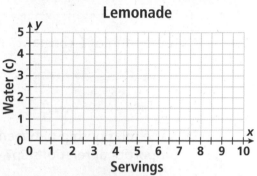

C. What is the constant of proportionality? Write an equation for the relationship.

_____

4 Angel was in charge of ordering graphic T-shirts for the craft fair. The graph shows the relationship between the number of boxes of T-shirts Angel ordered x and the total number of T-shirts y.

A. Is the relationship in the graph a proportional relationship? Explain how you know.

_____

_____

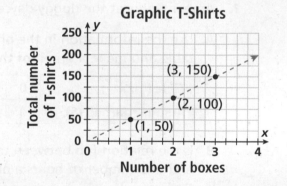

B. What is the constant of proportionality? How do you know based on the graph?

_____

C. Write an equation to represent the relationship.

_____

D. Why is the graph dashed rather than solid?

_____

Alonso pays a fee of $4 plus a percentage of his sales to participate in the crafts fair. The table shows the amount Alonso pays in relationship to his sales.

Sales ($), x	10.00	20.00	35.00	45.00	50.00
Fee ($), y	4.50	5.00	5.75	6.25	6.50

A. Graph the relationship.

B. What does the point (0, 4.00) represent?

_____

_____

C. Is the ratio of $\frac{y}{x}$ constant? Justify your answer.

_____

_____

D. Is the relationship between the total fees and the amount of sales a proportional relationship? Explain.

_____

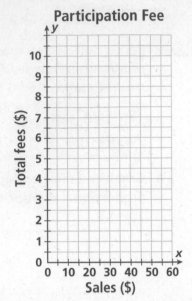

Participation Fee

Check Understanding

1. Amber works at the doggy daycare after school.

A. Use the information in the photograph to complete the table and make a graph of the data.

Time (h), x	0	1	2	3		5
Amount earned ($), y	0				32	

B. Is the relationship between the amount Amber earns and the number of hours a proportional relationship? Explain.

_____

_____

C. What point represents the constant of proportionality?

_____

D. What is the ratio $\frac{y}{x}$ for each point on the graph?

_____

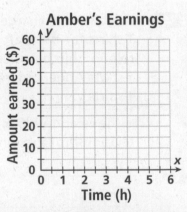

Amber's Earnings

$8 PER HOUR

On Your Own

2. **(MP)** **Model with Mathematics** The table shows the amounts of cherries (in cups c) used to bake pies.

   Make a graph of the data. Tell whether the relationship between the amounts of cherries and the number of pies is a proportional relationship. Explain. If the relationship is proportional, write an equation for the relationship.

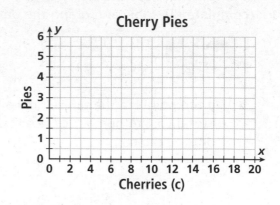

Cherry Pies

Cherries (c), x	4	8	12	16
Pies, y	1	2	3	4

_____

_____

_____

3. The graph shows the distance x Yazmin jogs and the amount of time y that it takes her.

   A. What is the meaning of the point (1, 16) on the graph?

   _____

   _____

   B. Does the graph show a proportional relationship? If so, what is the constant of proportionality k? What is the equation of the graph? Explain your reasoning.

   _____

   _____

   _____

   _____

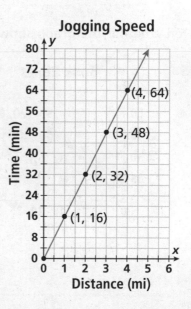

Jogging Speed

(4, 64)
(3, 48)
(2, 32)
(1, 16)

   C. **Open Ended** Describe how the graph would be different if Yazmin's jogging rate were a different constant.

   _____

   _____

   _____

4. **(MP) Model with Mathematics** Henry goes to the town fair. Use the prices on the photograph to complete the table and graph the data.

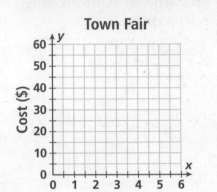

$10 entry fee and $6 per ride

Rides, x	1	2	3	4
Cost ($), y	16	22		34

A. Do the points in the table show a constant ratio of total cost to number of rides? Give an example from the table.

_____

_____

B. Does the graph show a proportional relationship? Why or why not?

_____

_____

_____

Town Fair

[Graph with y-axis "Cost ($)" from 0 to 60, x-axis "Rides" from 0 to 6]

Tell whether the graph shows a proportional relationship. Explain.

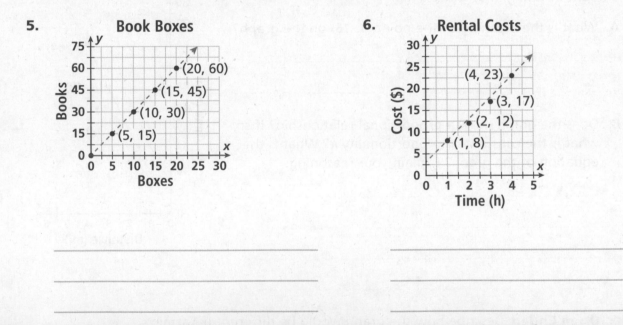

5. **Book Boxes**

[Graph with y-axis "Books" from 0 to 75, x-axis "Boxes" from 0 to 30, points (5, 15), (10, 30), (15, 45), (20, 60)]

_____

_____

6. **Rental Costs**

[Graph with y-axis "Cost ($)" from 0 to 30, x-axis "Time (h)" from 0 to 5, points (1, 8), (2, 12), (3, 17), (4, 23)]

_____

_____

I'm in a Learning Mindset!

How can I make the process of writing a proportional relationship for a graph more efficient?

_____

_____

Recognize Proportional Relationships in Graphs

1. The graph shows the area y that can be covered by a given amount of paint x when using a paint sprayer.

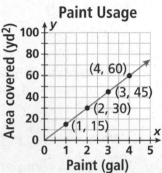

A. Does the graph show a proportional relationship? Explain.

_____

_____

_____

B. Using the point (3, 45), find the constant of proportionality k and write an equation that describes the proportional relationship.

_____

Paint Usage

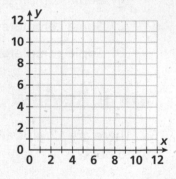

2. (MP) **Construct Arguments** Graph the data from the table.

x	2	4	6	8	10
y	4	6	8	10	12

Does the graph show the relationship is a proportional relationship? Does the relationship have a constant of proportionality? Justify your answer using any two points from the table.

_____

_____

_____

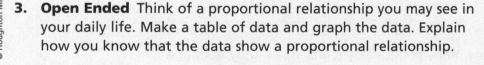

3. **Open Ended** Think of a proportional relationship you may see in your daily life. Make a table of data and graph the data. Explain how you know that the data show a proportional relationship.

Test Prep

4. The table shows the costs of books at the library book sale. Select all the ordered pairs that would be on the graph of this relationship.

Books, x	2	4	6	8	10
Cost ($), y	5	10	15	20	25

Ⓐ (3, 7.5)

Ⓑ (12, 33)

Ⓒ (9, 22.5)

Ⓓ (11, 27)

Ⓔ (5, 12.5)

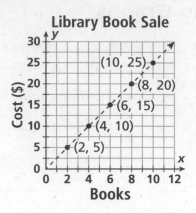

Library Book Sale

5. Sonia plays a computer game and completes puzzles during levels of the game. The data are shown in the graph.

What does the point (1, 3) on the graph represent?

Ⓐ Sonia completes 1 puzzle every 3 levels.

Ⓑ Sonia completes 3 puzzles on each level.

Ⓒ Sonia completes 1 puzzle on level 3.

Ⓓ Sonia completes puzzles 1 to 3.

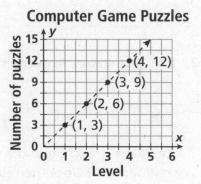

Computer Game Puzzles

Spiral Review

6. There are 12 girls and 14 boys in class today. What is the ratio of girls to boys?

_____

7. A bakery charges $14.00 for 4 croissant sandwiches. What is the unit rate?

_____

8. The table shows how many pages Andy reads. Does Andy read at a constant rate? Explain.

Time (min), x	10	20	30	40	50
Pages, y	4	9	10	15	20

_____

_____

Name _____

Use Proportional Relationships to Solve Rate Problems

(I Can) identify the constant of proportionality and write an equation for a proportional relationship presented in various forms and use them to solve multistep ratio problems.

Step it Out

1 ▸ The bar diagram shows how many inches a garden snail travels over time. At this rate, how many feet would the snail travel in 0.75 hour?

1.32 in.

1 sec   1 sec   1 sec

0.44 in.   0.44 in.   0.44 in.

A. What is the unit rate in inches per second? Use conversion factors to convert the unit rate to feet per hour.

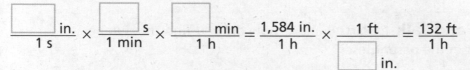

$$\frac{\boxed{}\ \text{in.}}{1\ \text{s}} \times \frac{\boxed{}\ \text{s}}{1\ \text{min}} \times \frac{\boxed{}\ \text{min}}{1\ \text{h}} = \frac{1{,}584\ \text{in.}}{1\ \text{h}} \times \frac{1\ \text{ft}}{\boxed{}\ \text{in.}} = \frac{132\ \text{ft}}{1\ \text{h}}$$

B. Write an equation for the number of feet y the snail travels in x hours, and use it to solve the problem.

$y = kx$

$y =$ _____ x

$y =$ _____ (_____) = 99 feet in 0.75 hour

C. What is the unit rate in miles per hour? Write an equation for the number of miles y the garden snail travels in x hours. (5,280 ft = 1 mi)

$$\frac{\boxed{}\ \text{ft}}{1\ \text{h}} = \frac{0.025\ \text{mi}}{1\text{h}} \qquad y = \underline{}\ x$$

Turn and Talk Explain how you converted the unit rate to miles per hour.

2 The graph shows the number of gallons of water used over time in one lane of a car wash. At this rate, how much water would be used if the lane were used continuously from 8:00 a.m. to noon?

Water Use

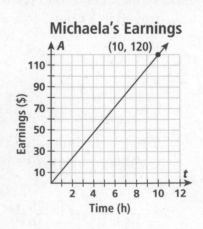

A. What is the unit rate in gallons per minute? Use conversion factors to convert the unit rate to gallons per hour.

$$\frac{\boxed{} \text{ gal}}{1 \text{ min}} \times \frac{\boxed{} \text{ min}}{1 \text{ h}} = \frac{\boxed{} \text{ gal}}{1 \text{ h}}$$

B. Write an equation for the number of gallons of water y used in x hours, and use it to solve the problem.

$y = kx$

$y = \underline{\qquad} x$

$y = \underline{\qquad} (\underline{\qquad}) = 1{,}200 \text{ gallons}$

C. How much water would be used during the hours of 7:30 a.m. to 3:45 p.m.?

$y = \underline{\qquad} x$

$y = \underline{\qquad} (\underline{\qquad}) = 2{,}475 \text{ gallons}$

Turn and Talk In Parts B and C, how did you find the number to put in the parentheses?

3 The graph shows Michaela's earnings over time. Marcus's hourly rate is represented in the table. Who has a greater rate of pay, and how much more than the other will that person earn in 40 hours of work?

Michaela's Earnings

(10, 120)

Marcus's Earnings					
Time (h)	2	4	5		
Earnings ($)	19.00			57.00	76.00

A. Complete the table, write an equation, and graph Marcus's earnings A over time t.

$k = \dfrac{19}{2} = \underline{\qquad}$ $A = \underline{\qquad}$

B. Use the graph to determine who is earning a greater rate of pay. Explain how you know.

_____

_____

C. What information do you still need in order to solve the problem? Solve the problem and show your work.

I still need: _____

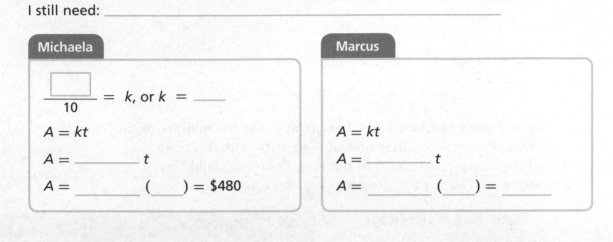

Michaela

$$\frac{\boxed{}}{10} = k, \text{ or } k = \underline{\quad}$$

$A = kt$

$A = \underline{\quad\quad} t$

$A = \underline{\quad\quad} (\underline{\quad}) = \$480$

Marcus

$A = kt$

$A = \underline{\quad\quad} t$

$A = \underline{\quad\quad} (\underline{\quad}) = \underline{\quad}$

_____

_____

 Turn and Talk What happens to the difference in their earnings over time?

Check Understanding

1. Solve the problems using the diagrams.

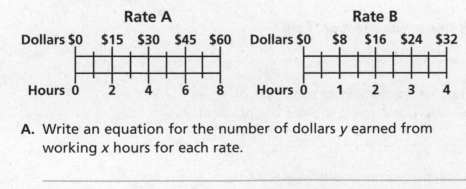

Rate A

Dollars $0 $15 $30 $45 $60

Hours 0   2   4   6   8

Rate B

Dollars $0 $8 $16 $24 $32

Hours 0   1   2   3   4

A. Write an equation for the number of dollars y earned from working x hours for each rate.

_____

B. What is the difference between total dollars earned from 40 hours of work for these rates? Show your work.

_____

On Your Own

2. Use the diagram of distance traveled at a constant rate.

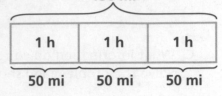

A. What is the unit rate?

_____

B. Convert the rate to feet per minute.

_____

C. Convert the rate to inches per second.

_____

3. (MP) **Model with Mathematics** The graph shows the number of cubic feet of water used over time at a water park that is open during the hours in the table. At this rate, how many cubic feet of water would be used at the water park on a Sunday?

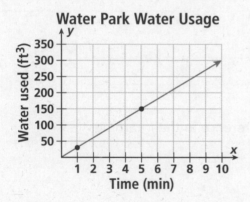

Water Park Hours of Operation	
Days	Hours
Monday to Thursday	11:00 a.m. to 7:30 p.m.
Friday and Saturday	11:00 a.m. to 9:00 p.m.
Sunday	12:00 p.m. to 6:00 p.m.

A. What is the unit rate in cubic feet per minute?

_____

B. What is the unit rate in cubic feet per hour?

_____

C. Write an equation for the number of cubic feet of water y used in x hours, and use it to solve the problem.

_____

D. How many cubic feet of water would be used at the water park on a Tuesday?

_____

4. **MP** **Model with Mathematics** The distance Dan jogged over time is shown in the graph. Pattie's constant jogging speed is represented in the table. Who has a faster jogging speed? How much more distance will that jogger have traveled with a total of 22 hours jogging?

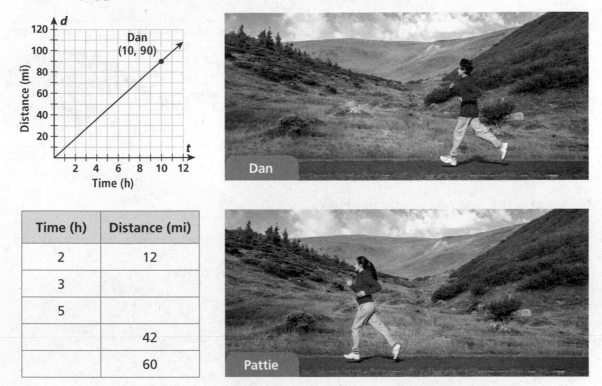

Dan
(10, 90)

Distance (mi)

Time (h)

Dan

Time (h)	Distance (mi)
2	12
3	
5	
	42
	60

Pattie

A. Use the table to find Pattie's jogging speed k. Complete the table.

_____

B. Write an equation for the distance in miles d that Pattie jogs in t hours. Graph the equation on the grid with Dan's graph.

_____

C. Solve the problem and show your work.

5. A cheetah, the world's fastest land animal, cannot maintain its top speed for very long. This bar diagram shows a cheetah's top speed, in feet per minute. Suppose a racecar is driven at the cheetah's top speed. How many miles would it travel in 3 hours?

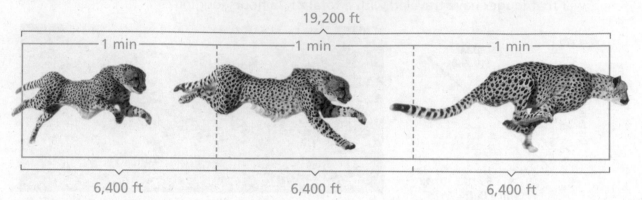

19,200 ft
1 min · 1 min · 1 min
6,400 ft 6,400 ft 6,400 ft

A. What is the unit rate in feet per hour?

_____

B. What is the unit rate in miles per hour, to the nearest tenth?

_____

C. Write an equation for the number of miles *y* that the racecar travels in *x* hours, and use it to solve the problem.

_____

6. Rhoni reads at a rate of 75 pages per hour. The number of pages Rie reads over time is shown in the table.

Time (h)	3	5	9	10
Pages	195	325	585	650

A. Who has a greater rate of reading?

_____

B. At these rates, what is the difference in the number of pages they will read in 4 hours?

_____

C. How long will it take each student to read a book with 780 pages? Show your work.

_____

_____

Name _____

Use Proportional Relationships to Solve Rate Problems

ONLINE
Video Tutorials and Interactive Examples

Give each rate in miles per hour. Round to the nearest tenth.

1. Dev jogs $8\frac{1}{2}$ miles in $1\frac{1}{2}$ hours.

2. Caroline walks $9\frac{1}{2}$ inches per second.

3. Dhruv jogs 8 feet per second.

4. Rachel jogs 20 feet in 3 seconds.

5. A bald eagle flies 43.2 meters in 3 seconds. The graph shows the distance a typical peregrine falcon flies over time. At these rates, what is the difference in the distances flown by these two birds after 3 hours of flight? Show your work.

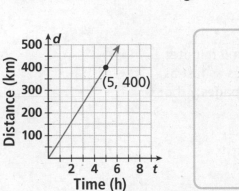

6. Two water tanks are leaking. Tank A has leaked $\frac{1}{16}$ of a gallon in $\frac{1}{12}$ minute, and Tank B has leaked $\frac{3}{80}$ of a gallon in $\frac{1}{30}$ minute. Which tank is leaking faster?

7. (MP) **Model with Mathematics** Write an equation for each boat-rental company that gives the cost in dollars y of renting a kayak for x hours. What is the difference in cost between the company that charges the most and the one that charges the least for 4 hours? Show your work.

Company B The cost y of renting a kayak for x hours is $9.00 for each half hour.

Company C The cost y of renting a kayak is $14.25 per hour.

Company A	
Hours	Total cost ($)
2	$33.00
3	$49.50
4	$66.00
5	$82.50

© Houghton Mifflin Harcourt Publishing Company • Image Credit: ©Sergey Uryadnikov/Dreamstime

Test Prep

8. James walked at a constant rate for 3 hours as shown in the graph. Jaycee walked 14.5 miles in 3 hours at a constant rate. Who walked farther, and how much farther? Explain.

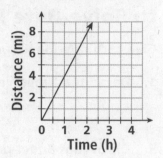

_____

_____

_____

9. A squirrel can run a short distance at a rate of $4\frac{3}{4}$ miles in 15 minutes. A fox can run a short distance at a rate of 21 miles in half an hour. Which is faster, and how much faster in miles per hour?

(A) the squirrel; 23 miles per hour

(B) the fox; 23 miles per hour

(C) the squirrel; 2 miles per hour

(D) the fox; 2 miles per hour

10. Joelle can read 3 pages in 4 minutes, 4.5 pages in 6 minutes, and 6 pages in 8 minutes. Paxton can read 3 times as fast as Joelle. Which is the equation for the number of pages y that Paxton can read in x minutes?

(A) $y = \frac{9}{4}x$

(B) $y = \frac{6}{5}x$

(C) $y = \frac{3}{4}x$

(D) $y = \frac{1}{4}x$

Spiral Review

Compare. Write < or >.

11. −3 _____ −15

12. $-\frac{5}{8}$ _____ $-\frac{1}{4}$

13. List the numbers in order from least to greatest.

−2, 8, −15, −5, 3, 1

_____

Graph each number on the number line. Then use your number line to find the absolute value of each number.

```
◄─┼──┼──┼──┼──┼──┼──┼──┼──┼──┼──┼──┼──┼──┼──┼──┼──┼──┼──┼──┼─►
 −10 −9 −8 −7 −6 −5 −4 −3 −2 −1  0  1  2  3  4  5  6  7  8  9 10
```

14. 2 _____

15. −8 _____

16. −5 _____

Name _____

Practice Proportional Reasoning with Scale Drawings

(I Can) make scale drawings and use them to find actual dimensions.

Step It Out

The scale on a scale drawing can be shown in the same unit or in different units.

Connect to Vocabulary

A **scale** is a ratio between two sets of measurements.

A **scale drawing** is a proportional two-dimensional drawing of an object.

1 ▶ Mario's school is building a basketball court from the scale drawing.

Drawing length (in.)	Actual length (ft)
0.6	12
2.1	42

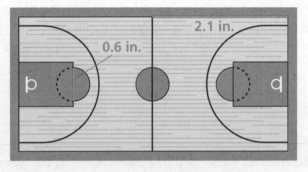

A. The table shows some lengths from the drawing and the corresponding lengths on the actual court. How can you tell this is a scale drawing?

_____

_____

B. What is the scale of the drawing in inches to feet? _____

C. Write an equation for the proportional relationship between the actual length in feet x and the drawing length in inches y. _____

D. Use your equation from Part C to find the actual length represented by a scale drawing length of 1.5 inches, and to find the scale drawing length that represents an actual length of 70 feet.

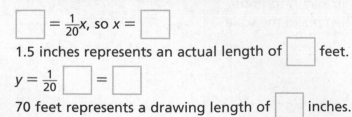

$\boxed{} = \frac{1}{20}x$, so $x = \boxed{}$

1.5 inches represents an actual length of $\boxed{}$ feet.

$y = \frac{1}{20}\boxed{} = \boxed{}$

70 feet represents a drawing length of $\boxed{}$ inches.

2 What is the relationship between area in the scale drawing and area on the actual basketball court?

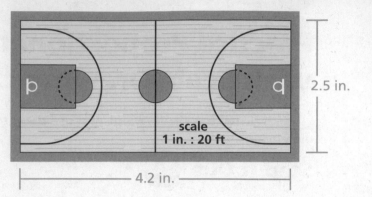

scale
1 in. : 20 ft

2.5 in.

4.2 in.

A. Show how to find the area of the court in the scale drawing.

_____

B. Show how to find the length and width of the actual court.

_____

C. What is the area of the actual basketball court? Show your work.

_____

D. Is the ratio of actual area to drawing area the same as the ratio of actual lengths to drawing lengths? Explain.

_____

_____

_____

 Turn and Talk Is there a relationship between the scale for area and the scale for length? If so, describe the relationship.

3 Mario's school is also planning to make a rectangular garden 60 feet wide by 70 feet long. On the grid provided, make a scale drawing of the rectangular garden using the scale given.

3 units:20 ft

A. Write an equation for the actual length *y* based on a drawing length *x*.

_____

_____

B. Use the equation you wrote in Part A to find the scale drawing lengths. Then make the scale drawing.

_____

_____

 Turn and Talk How could you write an equation for the drawing length *y* based on an actual length *x*?

4 Mario's school is also planning a smaller rectangular area as a sitting spot. A scale drawing of the sitting spot is shown. Redraw the sitting spot on the grid at a scale of $\frac{1 \text{ grid unit}}{4 \text{ feet}}$.

A. Write and simplify the ratio of the new scale to the original scale.

$$\frac{\text{new scale}}{\text{original scale}} = \frac{\boxed{}}{\frac{1 \text{ grid unit}}{2 \text{ ft}}} = \boxed{}$$

1 unit:2 ft

B. Each side of the new drawing will be | longer / shorter | than the corresponding side of the original drawing.

C. Draw the rectangle for the new scale.

 Turn and Talk What is another way you could have found the dimensions of your new scale drawing?

Check Understanding

1. The dimensions of an Olympic swimming pool are shown. A scale drawing of the swimming pool has dimensions of 50 centimeters by 100 centimeters and a diagonal that is about 112 centimeters long.

   A. What is the scale of the drawing in centimeters to meters? _____

   B. What is the actual length of the diagonal of the pool? _____

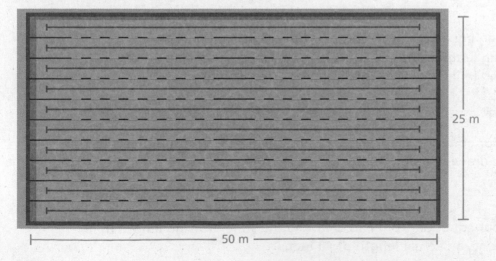

25 m

50 m

2. A different scale drawing of the same Olympic pool uses a scale of $\frac{5 \text{ cm}}{1 \text{ m}}$. What are the dimensions of the drawing? _____

On Your Own

3. (MP) **Use Structure** Veronica's town is building a tennis court using the scale drawing below. Find the scale between the drawing and the actual court. Then use the scale to show how a given length on the drawing represents a length on the tennis court, and how a given length on the tennis court is represented in the drawing.

A. The table shows some lengths in the drawing and the corresponding lengths on the actual court. Explain how you can tell from the table that the drawing is a scale drawing.

Drawing length (in.)	Actual length (ft)
2	10
3	15
5	25
10	50

B. What is the ratio between the actual length and the drawing length as a unit rate?

C. Write an equation for the proportional relationship between the drawing lengths and the court lengths, where x is length in the drawing in inches and y is length on the court in feet.

D. Use your equation from Part C to find the actual length represented by a scale drawing length of 3.5 inches.

E. Use your equation from Part C to find the scale drawing length that represents an actual length of 40 feet.

© Houghton Mifflin Harcourt Publishing Company

4. What is the relationship between area in the scale drawing and area on the actual tennis court?

scale
1 in. : 5 ft

7.2 in.

15.6 in.

A. Show how to find the area of the scale drawing of the tennis court.

B. Show how to find the length and width of the actual court.

C. Show how to find the area of the actual tennis court.

D. (MP) **Attend to Precision** What is the ratio of the area of the actual court to the area of the drawing (as a unit rate)? Is it the same as the ratio of the length of the actual court to the length of the drawing? How do you know?

5. The students in Suzanne's school are painting a rectangular mural outside the building that will be 15 feet by 45 feet.

    A. Write the unit rate for the proportional relationship between lengths on the mural *y* and lengths in the scale drawing *x*.

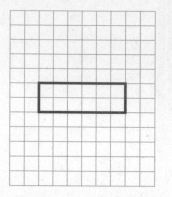

    B. 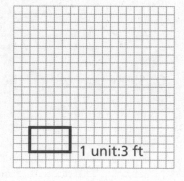 **Model with Mathematics** Write an equation that relates *x* and *y*. The diagonal of the scale drawing is approximately 6.3 units. Estimate the length of the diagonal of the mural.

6. The students at Suzanne's school are also going to paint a smaller mural inside the building. A scale drawing of the mural is shown on the grid.

    A. Redraw the inside mural on the grid using a scale of 1 unit:1 foot.

    B. How many grid units are there for every 3 feet of mural in the original scale? How many grid units are there for every 3 feet of mural in the new scale?

1 unit:3 ft

    C. What is the length of your scale drawing compared to the length of the original scale drawing?

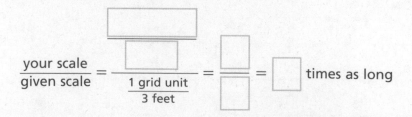

$$\dfrac{\text{your scale}}{\text{given scale}} = \dfrac{\boxed{}}{\dfrac{1\ \text{grid unit}}{3\ \text{feet}}} = \dfrac{\boxed{}}{\boxed{}} = \boxed{}\ \text{times as long}$$

    D. How does the area of your drawing compare to the original area?

Practice Proportional Reasoning with Scale Drawings

1. (MP) **Model with Mathematics** Martine's town is building a volleyball court based on a scale drawing that is 40 centimeters by 80 centimeters and uses the scale 1 cm:22.5 cm.

    A. Write an equation for the proportional relationship between drawing court lengths x in centimeters and court lengths y in centimeters.

    _____

    B. What are the length and width in meters of the actual court? Show your work.

    _____

    _____

    C. Write the ratio of the area of the actual court to the area of the court in the scale drawing.

    _____

2. The students in Roberto's school are painting a mural that will be 8 feet by 15 feet. First they make a scale drawing of the mural with a scale of 2 feet:5 feet.

    A. Write an equation for the proportional relationship between drawing mural lengths x in feet and mural lengths y in feet.

    _____

    B. What are the length and width of the scale drawing in feet? Show your work.

    _____

    _____

    C. **Open Ended** Choose a different scale and use it to make a scale drawing of the mural that will fit on a piece of graph paper.

    _____

3. **Geography** A map has a scale of 1 in.:10 mi. Find the distance on the map between two cities that lie 147 miles apart. Show your work.

    _____

    _____

Test Prep

4. Ricardo draws a scale model of the floor plan of his house. His house is 60 feet long and 40 feet wide. He uses the scale $\frac{1 \text{ inch}}{4 \text{ feet}}$ to draw his model. Which statements are true? Select all that apply.

Ⓐ The equation $\ell = \frac{1}{4}(60)$ can be used to find the length of the scale model.

Ⓑ The equation $w = (4)(40)$ can be used to find the width of the scale model.

Ⓒ The width of the scale model is 10 inches.

Ⓓ The length of the scale model is 240 inches.

Ⓔ The scale means that 1 inch in the model represents 4 feet in the house.

5. A scale drawing of an elephant shows the animal as 6 inches high and 10.8 inches long. The scale used for the drawing was 3 in.:5 ft. What are the height and length of the actual elephant?

Height: _____ feet   Length: _____ feet

6. Town planners are planning a 500–foot by 700–foot parking lot by making a scale drawing that is 90 inches by 126 inches. What is the scale of inches in the drawing to inches in the actual object?

Ⓐ 3:200   Ⓑ 1:300   Ⓒ 2:30   Ⓓ 1:200

Spiral Review

7. A machine produces parts at a steady rate of 160 parts in 8 hours. Complete the table for this relationship.

Hours	2		5	8
Parts		60		160

8. The table shows possible numbers of basketball teams in a league and the number of jerseys needed for the number of teams.

A. Graph the relationship between the number of teams in the league and the number of jerseys needed.

B. Is the relationship between the number of teams and the number of jerseys proportional? Explain.

Teams, x	Jerseys, y
3	36
4	48
5	60
6	72
7	84
8	96

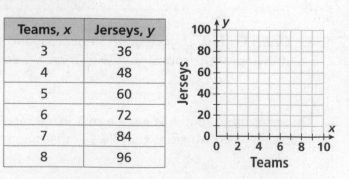

_____

_____

Review

Vocabulary

Choose the correct term from the Vocabulary box.

Vocabulary
constant of proportionality
proportional relationship
ratio
scale
scale drawing
unit rate

1. the quantity k in a relationship described by an equation of the form $y = kx$

_____

_____

2. a rate in which the second quantity is one unit

_____

3. a relationship between two quantities in which the rate of change or the ratio of one quantity to the other is constant

_____

Concepts and Skills

4. Which ratio is equivalent to the scale 3 in.:1 ft?

Ⓐ $\dfrac{\frac{1}{4}\text{ in.}}{\frac{2}{3}\text{ ft}}$ Ⓑ $\dfrac{2\text{ in.}}{\frac{2}{3}\text{ ft}}$ Ⓒ $\dfrac{4\text{ in.}}{\frac{5}{6}\text{ ft}}$ Ⓓ $\dfrac{5\text{ in.}}{6\text{ ft}}$

5. (MP) **Use Tools** A news radio program has 3 commercial breaks per half-hour of programming. What is the unit rate of commercials to hours of programming? State what strategy and tool you will use to answer the question, explain your choice, and then find the answer.

_____

_____

6. A recipe calls for 2 cups of sugar for $\frac{1}{4}$ cup of butter. What is the unit rate for sugar to butter? _____

7. Jana and Jenn are training to run a race. Jana runs 3 miles in $\frac{1}{3}$ hour. Jenn runs 5 miles in $\frac{3}{4}$ hour. Who runs faster, and what is the unit rate of her speed in minutes per mile? _____

8. A scale drawing of a rectangular mural has the dimensions 2 inches by 3 inches. The scale is 0.5 inches:5 feet. Find the actual dimensions of the mural. Then find the dimensions of another scale drawing with the scale 0.25 inches:10 feet. _____

9. Which of the following tables represents data that have a proportional relationship?

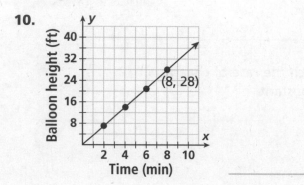

(A)

x	y
0	0
1	1.5
3	3.5
6	6.5
8	8.5

(B)

x	y
0	0
1	1.5
3	4.5
6	9.0
8	12.0

(C)

x	y
0	0.5
1	1
3	3
6	6
8	8

(D)

x	y
0	0
1	0.5
3	1.5
6	3
8	5

Write an equation of the form $y = kx$ for the relationship shown in the graph or table.

10.

Balloon height (ft) vs Time (min)

(8, 28)

_____

11.

x	6	10	12
y	45	75	90

_____

12. Use the graph from Problem 10. What is the value of r at the point with coordinates (1, r)? What does this point mean in terms of the proportional relationship shown in the graph?

_____

_____

13. A store sells beans for 80¢ per pound.

A. Graph the proportional relationship that gives the cost y in dollars of buying x pounds of beans.

B. Write an equation of the form $y = kx$ to represent this relationship.

_____

C. A farmers' market sells organic locally grown beans for $1.25 per pound. How much more would it cost to buy 3 pounds of beans at the farmers' market than at the store?

_____

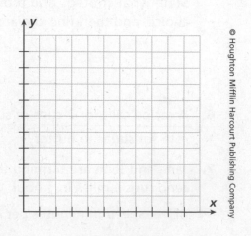

Proportional Reasoning with Percents

THE **CASE** OF THE MISSING **DIAGRAM**

The Bounceville Table Tennis Club holds a 50-game tournament each year.

The shaded portion of each diagram represents the games won by a table tennis team during the tournament.

Write a sentence for each diagram that describes the percent of the whole that is shown. The first one is done for you.

A. Team Dachshunds: 10% of 50 is 5.

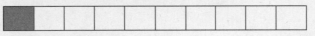

B. Team Ferrets _____

C. Team Tigers _____

D. Team Honey Badgers _____

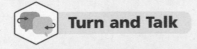 **Turn and Talk**

What diagram do you think is missing from the sequence of figures above? Explain your reasoning using a diagram.

Are You Ready?

Complete these problems to review prior concepts and skills you will need for this module.

Multiply Decimals by Whole Numbers

Find each product.

1. 0.3(12) _____ **2.** 0.75(68) _____ **3.** 1.25 · 40 _____

Find a Percent or a Whole

Solve each problem.

4. What is 60% of 120? _____ **5.** Find 8% of 65. _____

6. 50% of what number is 27? _____ **7.** 63% of what number is 252? _____

8. Carl scored 35% of his basketball team's 40 points during a game. How many points did Carl score?

_____

Use Ratio and Rate Reasoning

Solve each problem.

9. The ratio of fish to snails in an aquarium is 3 to 2. There are 18 fish in the aquarium. How many snails are in the aquarium?

_____

10. Irina ran 0.25 mile in 2 minutes. At this rate, how many minutes will it take her to run 2 miles?

_____

11. A painter mixes gray paint by using 1 gallon of black paint for every 7 gallons of white paint. How much black paint and how much white paint will the painter need to mix 20 gallons of gray paint?

_____

_____

Name

Percent Change

(I Can) solve multi-step problems involving percent change.

Step It Out

1 ▷ When a quantity increases or decreases, you can use number sense and proportional reasoning to compare the amount of change to the original amount.

A. Janis earns $7.00 per hour at Pizza King. After 6 months, her hourly rate of pay increased to $7.70 per hour. What is the percent increase in her hourly rate of pay?

The original amount is $_____.

The new amount is $_____.

The amount of change is $_____.

Write the ratio as a percent. Note that the original amount is 10 times the amount of change.

$$\frac{\text{amount of change}}{\text{original amount}} = \frac{0.7}{7} = \frac{1}{\boxed{}} = \frac{\boxed{}}{100}$$

Her rate of pay increased by _____%.

B. Pizza King decided to decrease the price of a large pizza, as shown on their sign. What is the percent decrease in the cost of a large pizza?

The original amount is $_____.

The new amount is $_____.

The amount of change is $_____.

$$\frac{\text{amount of change}}{\text{original amount}} = \frac{4}{16} = \frac{1}{\boxed{}} = \frac{\boxed{}}{100}$$

The cost decreased by _____%.

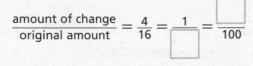
Turn and Talk How can you use number sense to write $\frac{1}{8}$ as a percent?

2 A population of cheetahs has decreased 30% over the last 18 years. If there were originally about 12,000 cheetahs, how many cheetahs are there now?

A. What is the percent decrease in the cheetah population? What was the original population?

_____

B. Find the change in the number of cheetahs. Write the percent as a decimal.

Percent decrease × Original amount = Decrease amount

_____ × _____ = _____

C. How many cheetahs are there now?

_____ − _____ = _____, so there are about _____ cheetahs now.

Turn and Talk Can you find another way to determine how many cheetahs there are now?

---

3 Chasidy is changing the size of the garden shown to fit more vegetables. She plans to increase the width by 25%.

A. What will the new width be?

Increase in width: 8 × ☐ = ☐ feet

New width: 8 + ☐ = ☐ feet

B. How much greater is the new area?

Original area: 8 × 12 = ☐ ft² New area: ☐ × 12 = ☐ ft²

The new area is ☐ square feet greater.

C. Chasidy plans to add 5 more plants. If each vegetable plant requires a minimum of 1.25 square feet, will Chasidy's plan work for the new dimensions of her garden?

Area needed for new plants: ☐ × ☐ = ☐ ft²

Will Chasidy's plan work? Why or why not?

_____

_____

4 A machine cuts lumber into 8-foot planks. Company regulations allow the lengths to vary by $\frac{1}{2}$%, which can be either an increase or decrease of $\frac{1}{2}$% of the intended length. Find the range of values allowed by the company's regulations.

A. How do you express $\frac{1}{2}$% as a decimal?

$$\boxed{} \div 100 = \boxed{}$$

B. What is the length, in feet, that the planks are allowed to vary? Remember, the · indicates multiplication.

$$\boxed{} \cdot \boxed{} = \boxed{} \text{ foot}$$

C. What is the length of the shortest allowable plank and the longest allowable plank cut by the machine?

Shortest: $8 - \boxed{} = \boxed{}$ feet

Longest: $8 + \boxed{} = \boxed{}$ feet

Check Understanding

1. Peggy earned $20 for each lawn she mowed last summer. This summer, she raised her price to $23 per lawn. What is the percent increase of Peggy's charges?

_____

2. Robert is inspecting a shipment of 22-inch pipes. The lengths of the pipes may vary by 1%. What is the range of allowable lengths of the pipes?

_____

3. When Bart bought his car, it averaged 28 miles per gallon of gas. Now, the car's average miles per gallon has decreased by 14%. What is the car's average miles per gallon now? Round your answer to the nearest mile per gallon.

_____

4. A number changes from 50 to 76. What type of percent change is this? Calculate the percent change.

_____

5. The data plan for Shawn's phone has 32,000 megabytes of storage for photos. She wants to increase the amount of data by 4%. If each photo uses 5 megabytes, will she have enough new memory for 200 additional photos? Explain.

_____

_____

On Your Own

6. The population of deer in a protected area is 225. If the population increases at a rate of 24% per year, how many deer will be in the area next year?

_____

7. There are 75 students enrolled in a camp. The day before the camp begins, 8% of the students cancel. How many students actually attend the camp?

_____

8. Two years ago, a car was valued at $24,000. This year, the value of the car is $23,160. What was the percent decrease in the value of the car?

_____

9. Mr. Milton had $1,200 in his savings account at the beginning of the year. If his account has a balance of $1,230 at the end of the year, what is the percent increase of his balance?

_____

10. Last year, 140 people in a community had cell phones. This year, the number of people in the community with cell phones has increased by 65%.

A. What is the percent of increase?

_____

B. What is the change in the number of people with cell phones?

_____

C. How many people in the community have cell phones this year?

_____

11. A library has 300 feet of shelves for books. The library will increase the number of feet of shelves by 18%.

A. How many feet of shelves are being added?

_____

B. How many feet of shelves will the library have after the new shelves are installed?

_____

C. The library plans to add 1,000 books to its collection. If the library can fit 15 books on each foot of shelving, will the library have enough room on the new shelves for all the new books? Explain.

_____

_____

12. A village parking lot is 120 feet wide by 180 feet long, and it has room for 75 cars. The village plans to increase the length by 30%.

A. What will be the new length of the parking lot?

_____

B. How much greater is the new area?

_____

C. (MP) **Construct Arguments** If each car needs about 288 square feet in a parking lot, will the new parking lot be able to fit 20 more cars than the original parking lot? Explain.

_____

_____

For Problems 13–20, find each percent change. State whether it is an increase or decrease.

13. From 50 to 22

_____

14. From 50 to 43

_____

15. From 20 to 35

_____

16. From 112 to 140

_____

17. From 40 to 38

_____

18. From 60 to 36

_____

19. From 28 to 42

_____

20. From 80 to 128

_____

21. A display for rolls of tape indicates that each roll contains 150 yards of tape. If the actual length of tape can vary by 2.5% of that amount, what is the range for the length of tape on a roll?

_____

_____

22. An airline states that an airplane flight between two cities takes 2.5 hours. The airline also says that the actual flying time can change by up to 15% of that amount. What are the shortest and longest times for the airplane flight? Round your answers to the nearest tenth of an hour.

_____

_____

For Problems 23–28, find the range of allowable values based on the given information. Round to the nearest tenth.

23. 15; can vary by 2%

_____

24. 24; can vary by 3.5%

_____

25. 31; can vary by 7%

_____

26. 44; can vary by 4.2%

_____

27. 49; can vary by 8.1%

_____

28. 50; can vary by 30%

_____

29. Last year, one model of a gasoline-powered car had a gas tank that holds 22 gallons of gas. This year, the carmaker is going to increase the capacity of the gas tank by 15%. The car's mileage both last year and this year, is 23 miles per gallon. Will this year's model be able to travel 100 miles farther on a single tank of gas? Explain.

_____

_____

_____

30. During a job fair last year, an employer spent 200 minutes interviewing people for jobs. This year, the employer wants to interview at least 4 more people than last year. The company will increase the amount of interviewing time by 40%. If each interview, both last year and this year, takes about 15 minutes, will the employer meet its goal? Explain.

_____

_____

_____

_____

31. Martin is building a rectangular fire pit in his backyard. He dug a hole 30 inches by 30 inches. He decides to make each side of the pit 6 inches longer. What is the percent increase in the area of the fire pit?

_____

32. (MP) **Attend to Precision** A peanut butter company is changing its packaging. The current container holds 16 ounces of peanut butter. The new container will hold 14 ounces. What is the percent decrease in volume for the new package? Round your answer to the nearest tenth.

_____

LESSON 2.1
**More Practice/
Homework**

ONLINE

Video Tutorials and
Interactive Examples

Percent Change

1. Five years ago, an average model 70" TV cost about $2,400. Now a similar TV costs approximately $1,680. What is the percent decrease in TV price?

   _____

2. Antoine made $33,284 last year. He received a 4.5% annual raise. What will his new salary be for the coming year?

   _____

   > The number of bacteria has increased by 40%.

3. **STEM** A scientist observes and counts 155 bacteria in a culture. Later, the scientist counts again and finds the number has increased as shown. How many bacteria are there now?

   _____

4. The number of veggie burgers sold at a restaurant in Houston, Texas, was 425 in April. The number sold in May was 16% less than the number sold in April. How many veggie burgers were sold in May?

   _____

5. A warehouse worker fills 150 orders per day on average. From day to day, the number of orders varies by 2%. What is the range of the number of orders the worker fills each day?

   _____

6. Find the percent change from 96 to 93. State whether it is an increase or decrease.

   _____

7. Find the percent change from 32 to 60. State whether it is an increase or decrease.

   _____

8. Find the range of allowable values based on a measure of 130 inches if the values can vary by 1.4%.

   _____

9. (MP) **Attend to Precision** In Cary's basketball career, he's made 80% of his free throws, plus or minus 5%. If he attempts 200 free throws this season, what is the range of successful free throws he can expect to make? Show your calculation.

   _____

Test Prep

10. A collector bought a rare coin for $30. The coin is now valued at $37.50.

Select all the true statements.

Ⓐ The scenario represents a percent increase.

Ⓑ The scenario represents a percent decrease.

Ⓒ The percent of change was 20%.

Ⓓ The percent of change was 25%.

Ⓔ The percent of change was 75%.

11. A coffee machine dispenses 8-ounce cups of coffee automatically. The amount of coffee may vary by 3%. What are the least and greatest number of ounces the coffee machine may dispense?

Least number: _____ ounces   Greatest number: _____ ounces

12. A German shepherd puppy weighed 25 pounds at 4 months old and 31 pounds at 5 months old. What is the percent increase or decrease of its weight?

Ⓐ 24% increase   Ⓒ 35% increase

Ⓑ 35% decrease   Ⓓ 54% decrease

13. The butterfly population at Glen Arbor Farms was 250 last year. This year there are 100 butterflies. What is the percent increase or decrease?

Ⓐ 50% decrease   Ⓒ 60% decrease

Ⓑ 50% increase   Ⓓ 60% increase

Spiral Review

14. There is a proportional relationship between time in hours and time in days.

A. What is the constant of proportionality?

_____

B. What equation describes this relationship?

_____

15. A triangle has a base length of 10 inches and a height of 4 inches. What is the area of the triangle?

_____

© Houghton Mifflin Harcourt Publishing Company

Name _____

Markups and Discounts

(I Can) calculate markups and markdowns.

Step It Out

1 ▶ Music Enterprise buys digital downloads of music albums for $5.00. This $5.00 is called the **cost**. The markup rate is 30%. How much will you pay for an album, not including tax?

A. The markup rate is _____%. As a decimal, it is _____.

B. The original amount, or cost, is _____.

C. Calculate the amount of the markup added to the cost.

$\boxed{} \times 5 = \boxed{}$ The markup amount is $_____.

D. Calculate the retail price after markup.

$5.00 + \$\boxed{} = \$\boxed{}$ The retail price is $_____.

E. Write the ratio of the retail price to the cost of the download. Express this ratio as a percent.

$\dfrac{\boxed{}}{\boxed{}} = \boxed{}\%$

So the retail price after markup is $\boxed{}$% of the cost. In other words:

original amount + markup = retail

$100\% + \boxed{}\% = \boxed{}\%$

After New Year's Day, Music Enterprise marks down their retail prices as shown. What will be the new retail price after this markdown?

F. The retail price is $\boxed{}$. The markdown is $\boxed{}$%.

G. Calculate the amount of the markdown.

$\boxed{} \times 6.50 = \$\boxed{}$

H. Calculate the retail price after markdown.

$6.50 - \$\boxed{} = \$\boxed{}$

> **Connect to Vocabulary**
>
> **Markup** is the amount of increase in a price. The markup rate is similar to percent increase but more specific to selling items.
> **Retail price** is the amount an item is sold for after a company adds the markup.
> **Markdown** is the amount of decrease in a price.

Limited Time Only
40%
DISCOUNT
On album downloads!

Turn and Talk Explain why the final retail price is lower than the original cost.

2 You can also use equations to solve problems involving markups, markdowns, and discounts.

Penelope buys bracelets in bulk at a cost of $8 each to sell at her store. She uses a markup rate of 125%, which is added to the bracelet cost. What is the retail price of a bracelet?

A. The markup rate is _____. The markup rate in decimal form is _____.

B. The equation $m =$ _____ x gives the markup amount m in dollars for the bracelets in terms of the original cost x in dollars.

C. Use the equation to find the markup amount for a bracelet.

$m = \boxed{} \times \boxed{} \qquad m = \boxed{}$

The markup amount is $_____.

D. Calculate the retail price of the bracelet.

cost + markup = retail price

$\$8 + \$\boxed{} = \$\boxed{}$

The retail price is $_____.

E. The markup amount is _____ x. An equation for the retail price r in dollars in terms of the original amount x in dollars is
$r =$ ___ $x +$ _____ $x =$ _____ x.

Penelope marked down the price of necklaces in her store as shown. Find the markdown rate of the sale price.

F. Write the ratio of the sale price to the original retail price. Express this ratio as a percent.

$$\frac{\text{sale price}}{\text{retail price}} = \frac{\$\boxed{}}{\$\boxed{}} = \boxed{} = \boxed{}\%$$

G. Think of the original retail price of the necklace as 100%. How does the sale price compare to the retail price of the necklace? What does this tell you about the markdown rate?

_____

_____

H. What is an equation in the form $y = kx$ that relates the sale price to the retail price x? _____

 Turn and Talk Discuss how you find the markup and markdown amounts. Which concept did you find more challenging to understand, and why?

3 A sporting goods store uses a markup of 87.5% for baseball bats. What is the price the store should display for a baseball bat with an original cost of $40?

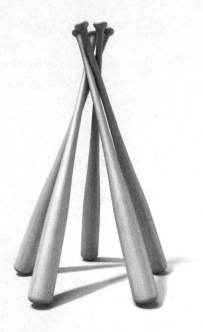

A. Use words to complete the equation you should use to find the amount of the markup.

$$\boxed{} = \text{percent} \times \boxed{}$$

B. Because the store marks up the original cost, the price will ⟨decrease / increase⟩. The percent change is _____%.

C. Write an equation that gives the retail price y of a bat with an original cost of x.

$$y = \boxed{}\, x + \boxed{} \qquad x = \boxed{}\, x$$

D. To find the price that the store should display, substitute _____ for x in the equation in Part C. The store should display a price of $ _____.

Check Understanding

1. This weekend the hardware store is having a blowout sale, where everything is discounted 40%. A weed eater originally sells for $145. How much will the weed eater cost during the blowout sale?

_____

2. A grocery store buys organic apples for $0.75 per apple. The grocery store marks up the cost of each apple by 18%. To the nearest cent, how much will one organic apple cost at the grocery store?

_____

3. A hailstorm caused damage at a car lot. A compact car usually sells for $27,500, but the damaged cars are discounted to $17,875. What was the percent discount on a damaged compact car?

_____

4. A store is selling all toaster ovens at 15% off. Write an equation in the form $y = kx$ to represent the sale price y in dollars of a toaster with an original retail price of x dollars. Then find the amount Jill paid for a toaster with an original retail price of $40.

_____

On Your Own

5. A hobby store marks up remote-controlled cars 20%. The original price was $35. What is the retail price to purchase a remote-controlled car at the hobby store?

_____

6. Organic hot dogs at the grocery store cost $2.00 each. At a major league baseball game, an organic hot dog costs $6.50. By what percent does the baseball field mark up its organic hot dogs?

_____

7. The Bakers want to sell their house for $145,500. After 2 months, the Bakers decided to mark down the price of their house 8% to sell more quickly. How much are the Bakers selling their house for now?

_____

8. Shelly's Boutique had a Labor Day sale featuring 25% off any item. Tammy wanted to buy a blouse that originally sold for $21.99. To the nearest cent, how much will it cost her, before tax, to buy the blouse during the sale?

_____

9. The pair of shoes shown had a sale price of $76.50. What was the retail price?

_____

10. (MP) **Model with Mathematics** A convenience store sells prepaid mobile phones. It purchases them for $12 each and uses a markup rate of 250%.

A. What is the markup rate in decimal form? _____

B. The markup rate is the constant of proportionality in the equation $y = kx$. Write an equation that can be used to find the markup on the cost x of a phone.

_____

C. Using the equation, calculate the markup amount.

_____

D. What is the retail price of a phone?

_____

Next week the store is going to reduce the price to $31.50.

E. Calculate what percent the sale price is of the retail price. Show your work.

_____

F. Think of the retail price of the phone as 100%. How does the sale price compare to the retail price? What does this tell you about the markdown rate?

_____

_____

_____

G. What is an equation in the form $y = kx$ that relates the sale price to the retail price x?

_____

For Problems 11–13, find the new price for the markup, markdown, or discount given. Round to the nearest cent if necessary.

11. $12.99 marked down 25%

_____

12. $3.00 marked up 72%

_____

13. $125.49 discounted 30%

_____

14. The thrift store is selling their old DVDs. When the DVDs first came out, they sold for $19. They have now been marked down by 75%. What is the discounted price of a DVD?

_____

15. A manufacturer makes handwoven scarves for $10 and then ships them to retail boutiques around the country. The boutiques sell the scarves for $25. What percent markup do the boutiques charge their customers?

_____

16. (MP) **Model with Mathematics** Melissa makes apple pies and sells them with a markup of 78%.

A. Write an equation representing the retail price y of Melissa's apple pies in terms of the original cost x.

_____

B. If it costs Melissa $8.20 to make a pie, how much should she charge for a pie? Round your answer to the nearest cent if necessary.

_____

17. (MP) **Reason** A local jewelry store sells class rings, which it purchases for $60 each. The store engraves a name and date on the ring, and sells it using a markup rate of 340%.

   A. What is the markup rate in decimal form? _____

   B. The markup rate is the constant of proportionality in the equation $y = kx$. Write an equation that can be used to find the amount of markup on the cost x of a ring.

   _____

   C. Use the equation to find the markup amount by substituting the cost of a ring for x.

   _____

   D. Calculate the retail price of a ring. Show your work.

   _____

   During graduation week, the store is going to reduce the price to $184.80.

   E. Calculate what percent the sale price is of the retail price. Show your work.

   _____

   F. Think of the retail price of the ring as 100%. How does the sale price compare to the retail price? What does this tell you about the markdown rate?

   _____

   _____

   G. What is an equation in the form $y = kx$ that relates the sale price to the retail price x?

   _____

18. All of last year's car models were marked down 40%. Tracy wants to buy a car on sale for $18,000. What was the retail price of the car?

   _____

For Problems 19–22, find the new price after the markup, markdown, or discount given. Round to the nearest cent if necessary.

19. $100 marked down 65%

   _____

20. $78 discounted 12%

   _____

21. $145 marked up 175%

   _____

22. $34,589 discounted 8%

   _____

LESSON 2.2
**More Practice/
Homework**

ONLINE

Video Tutorials and
Interactive Examples

Markups and Discounts

1. A local nonprofit organization is selling popcorn to raise money for hurricane relief. The organization paid $4 per bag for the popcorn and sold it for $5 per bag. What was the percent markup on each bag of popcorn?

   _____

2. The high school decided to buy new uniforms for the girls' and boys' basketball teams. They plan to buy 35 uniforms with a total cost of $1,235. The store offers discounts based on the number of items the school buys, as shown. What will the discounted price be for the high school?

   _____

3. **Open Ended** Describe a real-life situation involving markup, markdown, or discount that the equation $y = x + 0.4x$ could represent.

   _____

   _____

   _____

**BASKETBALL UNIFORM
GROUP DISCOUNTS**

10% off Buy 10–24 items
Get 10% off
Use code: 10

15% off Buy 25–49 items
Get 15% off
Use code: 15

20% off Buy 50+ items
Get 20% off
Use code: 20

For Problems 4–8, find the new price for the markup, markdown, or discount given. Round to the nearest cent if necessary.

4. $6.25 marked up 25%

   _____

5. $13.50 discounted 75%

   _____

6. $112 marked down 40%

   _____

7. $220 marked up 60%

   _____

8. $5,250 marked down 15%

   _____

Test Prep

9. Nate just started working at a clothing store. He receives a 40% discount on any item once a month. This month Nate decided to buy a jacket that has a retail price of $74.99. How much did Nate pay for his jacket?

Ⓐ $29.99

Ⓑ $34.99

Ⓒ $44.99

Ⓓ $104.99

10. Cup o' Coffee buys its coffee for $1.25 a cup. The coffee shop then sells each cup for $3.75. What is the percent markup for a cup of coffee?

Ⓐ 300%

Ⓑ 200%

Ⓒ 66.6%

Ⓓ 33.3%

11. Write an equation that represents a discount of 18% on a retail price of $55. Let p represent the new price.

12. Brooke needs a new computer. On Friday, the computer was $200. On Saturday, the price of the computer was $149. Determine if there was a markup or markdown and by what percent.

Ⓐ markup; 25.5%

Ⓑ markup; 34.5%

Ⓒ markdown; 25.5%

Ⓓ markdown; 34.5%

Spiral Review

13. Determine whether the cost of grapes is proportional to the number of pounds. Explain.

Grapes (lb)	1	2	3	4
Cost ($)	3	6	9	12

14. Find the range of allowable values based on an expected mass of 250 grams for which values are allowed to vary by 5%.

Name _____

Taxes and Gratuities

(**I Can**) use equations to represent the total cost of items with taxes and gratuities.

Step It Out

1   Jeremy got a haircut and paid 15% as a tip.

A. What percent of the cost did Jeremy pay the barber, including the tip?

_____

B. What is the cost of the haircut?

_____

Haircuts $15

C. Calculate the total cost of the haircut, including the tip. Show your work.

_____

_____

D. If you only wanted to know the tip amount, how would you change the process you used in Part C to calculate the total cost?

_____

_____

Connect to Vocabulary

A **gratuity** is a percent that is given or paid in addition to the price of a service. It is also referred to as a **tip**.

Jeremy also bought a hair-care product priced at $13. The sales tax rate in his city is 7%.

E. Calculate the amount of tax. Show your work.

_____

_____

F. What is the total cost of the hair-care product plus tax?

_____

G. How else could you find the total cost, including the tax?

_____

_____

Connect to Vocabulary

Sales tax is a percent that is added to the price of goods or services.

 Turn and Talk How could you use fractions instead of decimals to calculate the amount of tax in Part E? Do you prefer to use fractions or decimals to compute taxes? Why?

     71

2▶ Kelsey and Jamal went to lunch on Saturday. Their lunch cost $17.60, they gave the waiter a 15% gratuity on the amount before tax, and they were charged a 5% tax rate on the amount before gratuity. What was the total cost of the lunch?

A. Write an equation in the form $y = kx$ to find the amount of the gratuity y in dollars on an amount of x dollars. Then find the gratuity on Kelsey and Jamal's bill.

$y = \boxed{}\ x$

$y = \boxed{} \cdot \boxed{} = \boxed{}$ The gratuity was $_____.

B. Write an equation in the form $y = kx$ to find the tax y in dollars on an amount of x dollars. Then find the tax on Kelsey and Jamal's bill.

$y = \boxed{}\ x$

$y = \boxed{} \cdot \boxed{} = \boxed{}$ The tax was $_____.

C. Find the total cost of the lunch.

$17.60 + \$_____ + \$_____ = \$_____.

 Turn and Talk Round up the cost and explain how to use mental math to calculate a tip. Round the tip to the nearest dollar.

3▶ Nolan buys office supplies for his home business. Nolan paid a total of $210, which included a sales tax rate of 5%. What was the cost of the supplies before tax was added?

A. Write an equation for the total cost of the supplies, $210, in terms of the original cost x of supplies before tax. Then simplify.

$\boxed{} = x + \boxed{}\ x$

$\boxed{} = \boxed{}\ x$

B. Solve the equation to find x, the original cost of the supplies before tax.

$\dfrac{\boxed{}}{\boxed{}} = \dfrac{\boxed{}\ x}{\boxed{}}$

$\boxed{} = x$

The total cost without the sales tax was $_____.

C. Does your answer seem reasonable? Explain.

_____

_____

4 Miriam buys the chair shown. The tax rate is 7.5%. How much was the tax on the chair?

$579

A. Write an equation in the form $y = kx$ to find the amount y in dollars of the tax on an amount of x dollars. Then find the amount of tax on Miriam's chair. Round to the nearest cent if necessary.

$y = \boxed{} x$

$y = \boxed{} \cdot \boxed{} = \boxed{}$

The tax was $_____.

B. How do you know your answer is reasonable?

_____

_____

_____

C. Miriam pays a service to deliver the chair to her house. Her bill is $24.75, and she tips the driver 20%. What is the total expense for the delivery?

$y = x + \boxed{} x$

$y = \boxed{} x$

$y = \boxed{} \cdot 24.75 = \boxed{}$

The total expense is $_____.

Check Understanding

1. Ella buys a computer for $785. Her local tax rate is 7%. How much does Ella pay for the computer, including tax?

_____

2. Kim works as a DJ and earns $1,250 to play music for 6 hours at a wedding reception. At the end of the night, she gets an 18% tip. How much in total did she earn?

_____

3. Adrian shops for school clothes and spends a total of $93.42. If the local tax rate is 8%, how much was the cost without tax?

_____

On Your Own

4. The amount that a charter boat captain charges a group to go deep-sea fishing is shown. If the group tips the captain 17%, what is the total amount that the captain receives for the fishing trip?

_____

DEEP-SEA FISHING

Full-Day Trips **$850**

5. The school secretary orders a new printer and pays $310.30 after tax. The tax rate is 7%. What was the original price of the printer?

_____

For Problems 6 and 7, find the total amount given the original price and tax rate. Round to the nearest cent if necessary.

6. $15.25, 7%   **7.** $31.69, 6%

_____   _____

8. Miguel buys a car for $14,999. The tax rate is 6%. What is the total purchase price of the car?

_____

9. The music boosters have their year-end banquet at a hotel that charges $750. The president of the boosters tips the banquet team 20%. What is the total amount spent?

_____

10. (MP) **Model with Mathematics** A family used a professional decorator to help furnish their new home. The decorator selected $1,580 worth of furnishings. The family paid for the furnishings, plus 4.5% tax on the purchases. The decorator's fee was 12% of the purchases, not including the tax.

A. Write an equation in the form of $y = kx$ to represent the decorator's fee. Then use the equation to calculate the amount of that fee.

_____

B. Write an equation in the form of $y = kx$ to represent the tax. Then use the equation to calculate the amount of tax.

_____

C. What is the total cost that the family paid? Show your work.

_____

For Problems 11 and 12, find the total amount given the original price and tip rate. Round to the nearest cent if necessary.

11. $22.22, 10%

12. $41.32, 15%

_____

_____

13. A group of friends receives a dinner bill of $287.50 at a restaurant. The bill includes a 15% tip for the server. How much was the bill before the tip was added? Explain how you found your answer.

_____

_____

For Problems 14 and 15, find the original price given the total amount and tip rate.

14. $51.84, 20%

15. $38.35, 18%

_____

_____

16. Jayme buys the painting shown for his apartment. The tax rate is 6.5%. How much did Jayme spend after tax? Round to the nearest cent if necessary.

_____

•$179.99

17. A business traveler buys a round-trip plane ticket for $629. The tax rate is 7.5%. How much was the cost after tax? Round to the nearest cent if necessary.

_____

For Problems 18 and 19, find the tax amount given the original price and tax rate. Round to the nearest cent if necessary.

18. $58.73, 6.5%

19. $73.81, 7.5%

_____

_____

20. Three coworkers buy a baby shower gift for $60. The local tax rate is 6%. How much was the tax?

_____

21. Devansh buys a house for $189,900. The tax rate is 7.5%. How much was the tax on the home?

_____

22. (MP) **Model with Mathematics** The cost x of the Sennet family's meal at a restaurant is $172.65, and they tip 20%. Write and use an equation to find the total cost y of the dinner.

_____

23. Mrs. Carissi purchased a new smartphone. The cost of the phone was $675 and the local tax rate is 6.2%.

A. Write an equation in the form $y = kx$ to represent the amount of tax. Use the equation to calculate the amount of the tax. Round to the hundredths place if necessary.

$$y = \boxed{}\, x$$

$$y = \boxed{} \cdot 675 = \boxed{}$$

The tax was _____.

B. 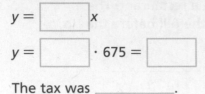 **Reason** How do you know your answer is reasonable?

_____

_____

_____

Mrs. Carissi hired a service to enter all her friends' numbers into her phone and to set up some apps. The service charged $22, and she added a tip of 15%.

C. Write an equation in the form $y = kx$, where k is the total rate in the form of a decimal. Use the equation to calculate the total expense of setting up the phone. Round to the hundredths place if necessary.

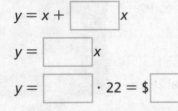

$$y = x + \boxed{}\, x$$

$$y = \boxed{}\, x$$

$$y = \boxed{} \cdot 22 = \$\boxed{}$$

D. How do you know your answer is reasonable?

_____

_____

_____

For Problems 24 and 25, write an equation for the total amount y after the given rate of increase is added to the original amount x.

24. 20%   **25.** 8.5%

_____   _____

For Problems 26 and 27, find the original price given each total amount and rate of increase. Round to the nearest cent if necessary.

26. $83.82, 10%   **27.** $93.72, 6%

_____   _____

Taxes and Gratuities

1. Beau buys a skateboard with a price tag of $82.50. The tax rate is 8%. How much does he pay, including tax?

   _____

2. Professor Burger orders flowers to be delivered to his mother. The flowers cost $59.95, not including tax. If there is a 6% sales tax, what is the total cost of the flowers to the nearest cent?

   _____

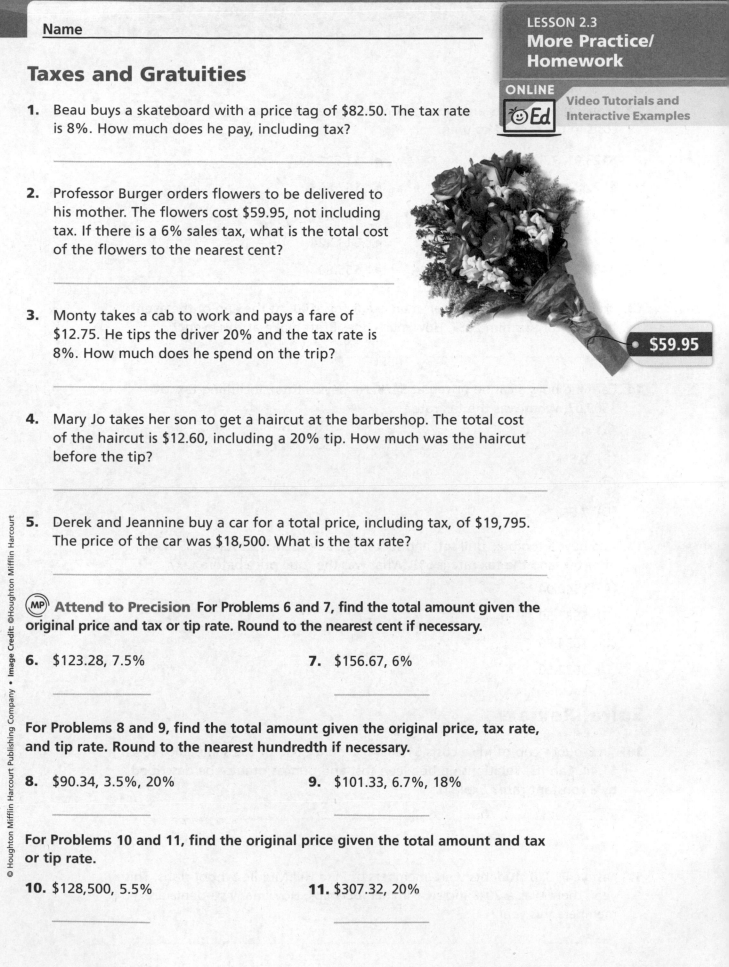

• $59.95

3. Monty takes a cab to work and pays a fare of $12.75. He tips the driver 20% and the tax rate is 8%. How much does he spend on the trip?

   _____

4. Mary Jo takes her son to get a haircut at the barbershop. The total cost of the haircut is $12.60, including a 20% tip. How much was the haircut before the tip?

   _____

5. Derek and Jeannine buy a car for a total price, including tax, of $19,795. The price of the car was $18,500. What is the tax rate?

   _____

(MP) Attend to Precision For Problems 6 and 7, find the total amount given the original price and tax or tip rate. Round to the nearest cent if necessary.

6. $123.28, 7.5%   7. $156.67, 6%

   _____   _____

For Problems 8 and 9, find the total amount given the original price, tax rate, and tip rate. Round to the nearest hundredth if necessary.

8. $90.34, 3.5%, 20%   9. $101.33, 6.7%, 18%

   _____   _____

For Problems 10 and 11, find the original price given the total amount and tax or tip rate.

10. $128,500, 5.5%   11. $307.32, 20%

   _____   _____

Test Prep

12. Match the amounts and tip or tax rates in the first column to the total costs in the second column.

$123.01, 7.5% ●   ● $1,336.66

$52.48, 6.5% ●   ● $57.86

$1,261, 6% ●   ● $258.19

$224.51, 15% ●   ● $132.24

$48.22, 20% ●   ● $55.89

13. Brett plays an acoustic guitar at an event for $500. At the end of the event, the sponsor tips him 20%. How much does Brett make at this event?

_____

14. Carmine buys a canoe priced at $478. He pays a total, including tax, of $509.07. What was the tax rate?

(A) 6%

(B) 6.5%

(C) 7%

(D) 7.5%

15. Ana buys a toolbox, drill set, and socket set. She spends a total of $564.45 after tax, and the tax rate is 6%. What was the total price before tax?

(A) $540.04

(B) $537.50

(C) $534.99

(D) $532.50

Spiral Review

16. An 8-ounce cup of juice costs $1.20. A 12-ounce cup of the same juice costs $1.44. Can the relationship between cost and ounces of juice be described by a constant rate? Explain.

_____

_____

17. Last year, 320 students were members of Pine Hill Middle School clubs. This year, there was a 20% increase in memberships. How many students are members this year?

_____

Name _____

Commissions and Fees

(I Can) **find the total earnings of a commission-based job.**

Step It Out

1 ▶ Harlan is a real estate agent whose total annual earnings are the sum of his annual salary and the commission shown. Last year, Harlan sold 10 homes that totaled $2,500,000 in sales. How much commission did Harlan earn?

1.75% commission

HOME SOLD SALE

A. The amount of Harlan's sales for the year is $_____.

Harlan will receive _____% of his sales as his

commission amount.

B. Calculate Harlan's commission.

2,500,000 × _____ = _____

Harlan earned a commission of $_____.

C. How do you know your answer is reasonable?

_____

_____

2 ▶ Linda sells furniture for a base monthly salary of $1,670 plus a commission of 4.5% of her total sales. Linda sold $607,500 of furniture in the last year. How much did Linda earn, including commission, last year?

A. Calculate Linda's commission for the year. Show your work.

_____

B. Calculate Linda's base salary for the year. Show your work.

_____

C. Calculate Linda's total earnings for the year by adding her commission to her salary for the year.

Linda earned $_____, including commission, last year.

> **Connect to Vocabulary**
>
> A **commission** is a fee a person earns for sales or services. The **commission rate** is a percent of an amount of sales. The person may or may not also earn a salary.

 Turn and Talk Describe the advantages and disadvantages of a commission-based pay system.

3 A **fee** can be either a fixed amount or a percent of an amount.

A. Yuan is an insurance salesman who makes a base monthly salary of $1,500 with a commission of 1% of the value of each policy he sells. In addition, each time his client makes an investment transaction, Yuan receives a $5.00 service fee.

This month, Yuan sells one policy valued at $50,000, and his client makes 4 investment transactions. How much does Yuan earn this month?

Total earnings

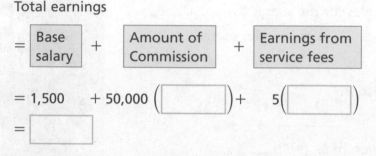

= Base salary + Amount of Commission + Earnings from service fees

= 1,500 + 50,000 (☐) + 5(☐)

= ☐

Yuan's total earnings this month are $_____.

B. Patrice is a financial adviser who makes a base monthly salary of $2,300 with a commission of 1.2% of the initial value that each client invests. In addition, each time the client makes an investment, Patrice receives a 0.5% service fee on the amount of the transaction. Assume Patrice recruits a new client whose initial investment is $100,000 and that client makes 3 investment transactions of $5,000 each this month. What does Patrice earn this month?

Total earnings

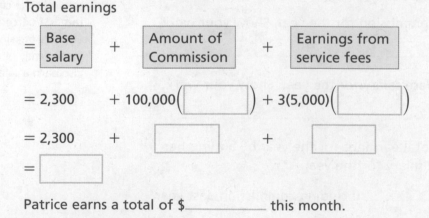

= Base salary + Amount of Commission + Earnings from service fees

= 2,300 + 100,000 (☐) + 3(5,000)(☐)

= 2,300 + ☐ + ☐

= ☐

Patrice earns a total of $_____ this month.

Turn and Talk How do the payments vary for the people described in this lesson so far?

© Houghton Mifflin Harcourt Publishing Company • Image Credit: ©PhotosIndia.com LLC/Getty Images

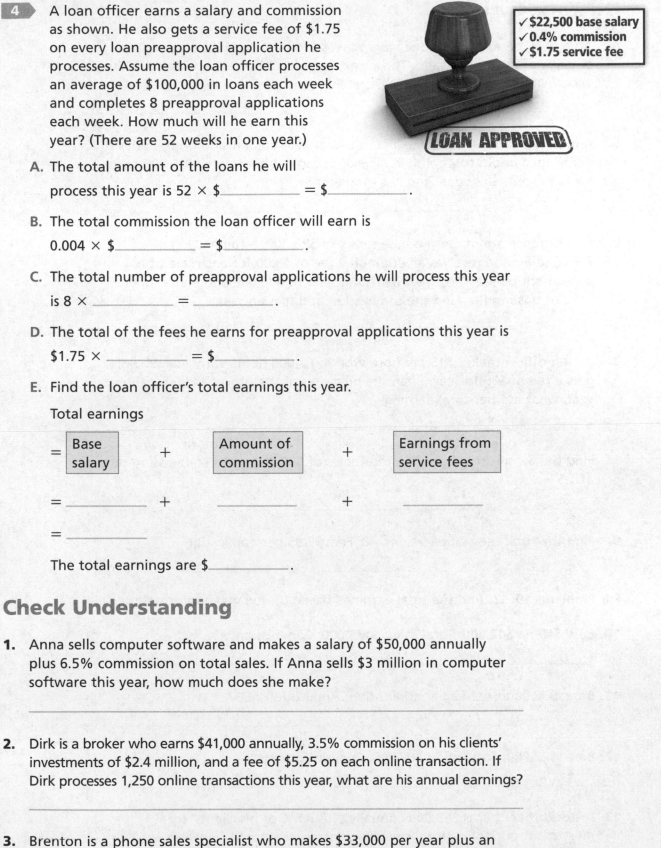

4 A loan officer earns a salary and commission as shown. He also gets a service fee of $1.75 on every loan preapproval application he processes. Assume the loan officer processes an average of $100,000 in loans each week and completes 8 preapproval applications each week. How much will he earn this year? (There are 52 weeks in one year.)

✓ $22,500 base salary
✓ 0.4% commission
✓ $1.75 service fee

LOAN APPROVED

A. The total amount of the loans he will

process this year is 52 × $_____ = $_____.

B. The total commission the loan officer will earn is

0.004 × $_____ = $_____.

C. The total number of preapproval applications he will process this year

is 8 × _____ = _____.

D. The total of the fees he earns for preapproval applications this year is

$1.75 × _____ = $_____.

E. Find the loan officer's total earnings this year.

Total earnings

= | Base salary | + | Amount of commission | + | Earnings from service fees |

= _____ + _____ + _____

= _____

The total earnings are $_____.

Check Understanding

1. Anna sells computer software and makes a salary of $50,000 annually plus 6.5% commission on total sales. If Anna sells $3 million in computer software this year, how much does she make?

_____

2. Dirk is a broker who earns $41,000 annually, 3.5% commission on his clients' investments of $2.4 million, and a fee of $5.25 on each online transaction. If Dirk processes 1,250 online transactions this year, what are his annual earnings?

_____

3. Brenton is a phone sales specialist who makes $33,000 per year plus an $8 fee for each sale he makes. If Brenton makes 15 sales per week, what are his annual earnings?

_____

81

On Your Own

4. An employee at a cell phone store makes $15 per hour plus a commission of 2.5% of her phone sales. This week she sold 40 phones averaging $450 each. What is her commission this week?

_____

5. A literary agent makes $30,000 a year plus 13% commission on the sales of her clients' books to publishers. The agent sold 4 books for $175,000 each for her clients this year. Find her total earnings.

_____

6. An insurance agent earns a base salary of $28,000, a commission of 2% of sales, and receives an additional fee of $9.00 for each sale of an investment policy. The agent had total sales of $75,000 and 6 investment policies this month. Find the commission and fees earned.

_____

7. A loan officer makes $15 per hour working 2,000 hours each year. She also gets a fee of $35 for each loan she processes. If she processes 900 loans a year, what are her total earnings?

_____

8. Find the commission based on total sales of $98,000 and a commission rate of 1.5%.

_____

9. Find the total fees: Applications: 48, Fee: $2.95 per application.

_____

For Problems 10–12, find the total earnings based on the given information.

10. Base Salary: $42,000; Total sales: $175,000; Commission: 4%

_____

11. Base: $38,000; Fee: $2 per application; Applications: 800

_____

12. Base: $22,000; Total sales: $99,000; Commission: 3%

_____

13. A stockbroker earns $53,000 annually plus 0.8% of his clients' total investment portfolios. If his clients' investments total $1.2 million, what is his commission this year?

_____

14. A golf equipment salesperson earns a base salary plus commission on golf equipment sold as shown. If the salesperson sells $78,000 worth of equipment in a year, what is the total annual salary earned?

$47,000 base salary

4% commission

_____

15. (MP) **Reason** A home sold for $286,000. The amount the homeowner received, before taxes and closing costs, was the selling price minus the commission to the real estate agent, which was 6%. How much commission did the real estate agent earn on the sale? How do you know your answer is reasonable?

_____

_____

_____

_____

16. (MP) **Reason** An oil painting was sold at an auction house for $6,550. The buyer agrees to pay that price plus a commission called the buyer's premium. For the painting, the rate for the buyer's commission was 25%. Calculate the amount of the commission. How do you know your answer is reasonable?

_____

_____

_____

_____

17. Takira is an appointment-setter for a sales organization. She makes $12 an hour plus a $3 fee for each appointment that is scheduled. This week Takira worked 40 hours and scheduled 31 appointments. What are her total earnings with fees this week?

_____

18. Beth is an inside sales agent. Her earnings include a salary plus $4.25 for each call she makes that results in an outside sales appointment. This month Beth made 60 outside sales appointments. What will her earnings from fees be this month?

_____

19. Find the commission earned on total sales of $164,000 at a commission rate of 3%.

_____

20. Tonio works for a website that sells theater tickets and receives a base salary of $18,200 per year. He earns a commission of 2.3% for all ticket sales, which average $15,500 per week. He also gets a "viewed" fee of 3 cents each time someone comes to the website, whether or not any tickets are purchased. The number of visitors to the website averages 12,400 per month.

A. What is the total commission Tonio will earn this year?

_____

B. What is the total amount Tonio earns from visits to the website?

_____

C. What are Tonio's total earnings for the year? Show your work.

_____

21. Irma works for a service that delivers groceries and pet supplies. She earns a base monthly salary of $1,900. In addition, she gets a commission of 1.8% of the cost of each grocery order, plus a fee of $11 for each delivery of pet supplies.

A. How is calculating Irma's total annual earnings different from calculating earnings based on salary and commission?

_____

B. Last month Irma's deliveries consisted of $33,600 in groceries, and she made 140 deliveries of pet supplies. How much does Irma earn in total for the month?

_____

Next year the delivery service is going to change the way it pays its delivery drivers. Irma will make a base monthly salary of $2,750. She will also earn a commission of 2.1% of the cost of groceries and a commission of 10.2% of the cost of pet supplies.

C. How will next year's pay structure differ from this year's pay structure?

_____

_____

_____

_____

D. Suppose Irma's deliveries during a month next year consist of $35,100 in groceries and $1,080 in pet supplies. How much will her earnings be that month?

_____

Name _____

LESSON 2.4
More Practice/ Homework

ONLINE

Video Tutorials and
Interactive Examples

Commissions and Fees

1. Maryanne sells cruise vacations. She makes a base salary of $2,500 per month plus 5% of the cost of each vacation. This month she sold $80,000 in cruises. What are her total monthly wages?

   _____

2. A realtor sells 3 houses this month for a total of $825,000, and each buyer uses her company to process their loan. She earns a base pay of $2,600 each month plus 1.5% of her total house sales. She also gets a fee of $12 for each loan she gets serviced through her company. What are her total earnings for the month?

   _____

3. A pharmaceutical sales representative gets paid $50,000 annually plus 3.5% commission on total sales. This year he sold $420,000 in pharmaceuticals. What are his annual total earnings?

   _____

4. A car salesman gets paid $3,750 each month plus 8.5% commission on his total sales. This month he sold 5 cars for a total of $138,000. What are his monthly total earnings?

   _____

For Problems 5–8, find the requested information based on the given facts.

5. The commission is 3.5% of the total sales of $55,000. Find the commission.

   _____

6. The fee is $2.75 per transaction for 175 transactions. Find the total fees.

   _____

7. The base salary is $54,300. The commission is 2.75% of the total sales of $950,000. Find the total earnings.

   _____

8. **(MP) Attend to Precision** The base salary is $48,000. The commission is 9% of the total sales of $256,000. The fee is $7.25 per transaction for 325 transactions. Find the total earnings.

   _____

Test Prep

For Problems 9 and 10, select all the true statements.

9. Marcus works for base pay: $25,000, commission: 2%, and fees: $3.75 per transaction.

   Ⓐ Commission on $50,000 is $1,000.

   Ⓑ Commission on $35,000 is $800.

   Ⓒ Fees for 25 transactions are $93.75.

   Ⓓ Total earnings for $75,000 in sales and 10 transactions are $1,537.50.

   Ⓔ Total earnings for $75,000 in sales and 10 transactions are $26,537.50.

10. Maddy works for base pay: $37,555 and commission: 5.5%.

    Ⓐ Commission on $155,000 is $852.50.

    Ⓑ Commission on $155,000 is $8,525.

    Ⓒ Total earnings for $85,000 in sales are $42,230.

    Ⓓ Total earnings for $45,000 in sales are $40,300.

    Ⓔ Total earnings for $115,000 in sales are $43,880.

11. Veronica sells Internet ads over the phone. She is paid $12 per hour plus $15 for every ad she sells. She works 4 hours a day 5 days a week and sells on average 13 ads per day. What are her average weekly earnings?

12. A trampoline salesman makes $25,000 annually plus 6% commission on his total sales. If he sold $40,000 worth of trampolines this year, what are his total earnings?

Spiral Review

13. Haley got a 93% on her first math test and an 86% on her second test. What is her percent decrease from Test 1 to Test 2 to the nearest tenth?

14. It takes Camden 45 minutes to complete $\frac{1}{5}$ of his art project. How many hours will it take him to complete the whole project if he works at the same rate?

15. Maggie eats at a restaurant and gets a bill for $23.50. She wants to leave a 20% gratuity. How much money should she leave altogether?

Name _____

Simple Interest

(I Can) calculate simple interest and the total value of an account after any period of time. I understand and can apply the equation *I = Prt*.

Step It Out

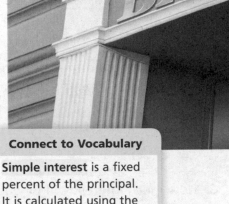

1 ▷ Big Money Bank loans $12,000 to Carlotta. This initial amount borrowed is called the **principal**.

Carlotta has to repay the loan to the bank at a rate of 5.5% simple interest per year over 8 years. What is the total amount of interest she will have to pay on her loan?

A. Find the amount of simple interest *I* that Carlotta must pay after one year.

Simple interest, *I*

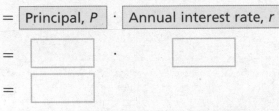

= | Principal, *P* | · | Annual interest rate, *r* |

= [   ] · [   ]

= [   ]

Carlotta must pay $ _____ in interest after one year.

> **Connect to Vocabulary**
>
> **Simple interest** is a fixed percent of the principal. It is calculated using the formula *I = Prt*, where *P* represents the principal, *r* the rate of interest, and *t* the time.

B. Calculate the total interest Carlotta must pay over the 8 years of the loan.

Interest paid over 8 years

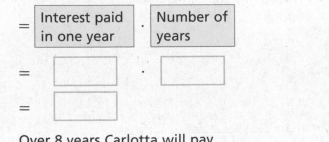

= | Interest paid in one year | · | Number of years |

= [   ] · [   ]

= [   ]

Over 8 years Carlotta will pay _____ in simple interest on her loan.

Turn and Talk Before she took out her loan, a different bank offered Carlotta a $12,000 loan at 5% interest to be paid back over 9 years. Would that loan cost Carlotta more interest than the loan she took, or less? How much is the difference?

2 Emilio opens a savings account at his local credit union with a $5,000 deposit. The account will pay 2.5% simple interest per year. How does Emilio's account grow over time?

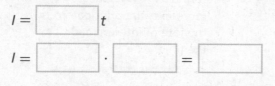

If you borrow money from a bank, you will have to pay interest. But if you open a savings account, the bank may pay you interest.

A. Find the amount Emilio's account earns in interest each year.

Simple interest for 1 year

$= \quad P \quad \cdot \quad r$

$= \boxed{} \cdot 0.025 = \boxed{}$

Emilio's account earns _____ per year in interest.

B. Write an equation for the amount of interest I Emilio's account earns in t years.

$I = P \cdot r \cdot \boxed{}$

$I = \boxed{} \, t$

C. How much interest will be added to Emilio's account after 12 years? Show your calculation.

$I = \boxed{} \, t$

$I = \boxed{} \cdot \boxed{} = \boxed{}$

---

3 Melanie deposits $8,200.00 in a bank account paying 4.4% simple interest. How much money will be in her account after 5 years and 6 months?

A. Find the amount Melanie's account earns in interest in 5.5 years.

$I = \quad P \quad \cdot \quad r \quad \cdot \quad t$

$I = 8{,}200 \cdot \boxed{} \cdot \boxed{}$

$I = \boxed{}$

The amount of interest in 5.5 years is $_____.

B. Find the total amount in Melanie's account after 5.5 years.

Total amount

$= \quad P \quad + \quad I$

$= \boxed{} + \boxed{} = \boxed{}$

Melanie's account will contain $_____ after 5 years and 6 months.

4 ▷ Gregory borrowed money as shown to buy a used car. It cost him $10,650 to repay the loan. How many years did Gregory spend repaying his loan?

$7,500 loan annual interest rate of 6%

USED CARS

A. Find the amount of simple interest *I* Gregory paid.

Total repaid = P + I

[ ] = 7,500 + [ ]

Gregory paid a total of _____ in interest.

B. Find the time *t* in years that it took Gregory to pay off his loan.

I = P · r · t

3,150 = [ ] · [ ] · t

3,150 = [ ] · t

[ ] = t

Gregory spent _____ years paying back his loan.

 Turn and Talk Describe the key steps that were taken to solve the problem.

Check Understanding

1. Arisia puts $500.00 into a savings account with an annual simple interest rate of 4.5%.

A. How much interest does she earn per year? _____

B. If the interest rate stayed the same, how much interest would Arisia's account earn after 15 years? _____

C. If the interest rate stayed the same, how much money would be in Arisia's account after 20 years? _____

On Your Own

2. (MP) **Model with Mathematics** Write an equation to find the amount of interest $450,000 earns in 1 year at a simple interest rate of 3.5%.

_____

3. Marcus borrows $3,000 from his local credit union, to be repaid with 3.5% simple interest over 4 years. What are the principal, interest rate, and time in this situation?

Principal	☐	
Simple Interest rate	$\dfrac{\boxed{}}{100} =$	☐
Time	☐ years	

4. Inez opens a savings account with $2,400. The account pays her 2.4% annual simple interest.

   A. Find the amount of simple interest that the account will earn per year.

   _____

   B. Calculate the total interest Inez would earn in 10 years.

   _____

5. Green Bank has the ad shown. Barry opens a savings account after seeing the ad. He deposits $1,300.

   Savings accounts over $1,000 earn 2.2% annual interest.

   A. Write an equation that relates the amount of time *t* in years that Barry holds his account to the amount of simple interest *I* that he earns.

   _____

   B. How much interest does Barry earn in 7 years?

   _____

   C. At the Blue Bank, Barry would earn $159.25 in simple interest in 7 years after depositing $1,300. What rate of simple interest is offered at the Blue Bank?

   _____

6. Avram borrows $14,500 at 5.4% simple interest to open a small business. His bank allows him 9 years to pay back the loan.

A. How much simple interest will Avram have to pay on the loan?

_____

B. How much money will Avram have to repay in all?

_____

7. Regina is buying a new car. She sees two advertisements in the paper for the same car at two different prices from two different dealerships. Both dealers are offering a simple-interest loan for the price of the car.

Ad A

$24,200
6.5% interest
XX years

Ad B

$XXXX
5.3% interest
9 years

A. Regina calculates that to buy the car in Ad A, the loan would ultimately cost her $41,503. Over how many years is the loan in Ad A to be paid back?

_____

B. Regina calculates that to buy the car in Ad B, the loan would ultimately cost her $38,402. What is the price of the car offered in Ad B?

_____

C. In either case, Regina would be paying back the dealer in equal monthly installments over the lifetime of the loan. What would her monthly payments be if she bought the car shown in Ad A?

_____

What would her monthly payments be if she bought the car shown in Ad B?

_____

D. Open Ended In your opinion, which ad is offering the better deal? Explain why you think so.

_____

_____

8. It costs $36,736 to repay a loan of $20,500 at 6.6% annual simple interest.

A. How much interest would you pay each year?

_____

B. How many years does it take to repay the loan?

_____

9. A savings account pays an annual simple interest rate of 1.5%.

A. How much interest would you earn in 1 year on $2,000?

_____

B. What would be the balance in your account after 5 years?

_____

C. How long would it take to earn $500 or more in interest?

_____

10. A loan of $9,000 has an annual simple interest rate of 3.5%.

A. If you repay the loan in 6 years, how much total interest will you pay?

_____

B. What is the total cost of the loan?

_____

C. What would be the simple interest rate if a loan of $9,000 that is repaid in 6 years has a total cost of $11,052?

_____

11. A loan of $25,000 has an annual simple interest rate of 5.5%. The total cost of the loan is $38,750.

A. How much total interest will you pay?

_____

B. How long does it take to repay the loan?

_____

© Houghton Mifflin Harcourt Publishing Company • **Image Credit:** ©ITTIGallery/Shutterstock

Name _____

LESSON 2.5
**More Practice/
Homework**

ONLINE

Video Tutorials and
Interactive Examples

Simple Interest

$?
4 years
3.25%
simple
interest
$3,500

1. Rena's grandfather opened a savings account as a college fund for her. His initial deposit and the yearly simple interest rate are shown. How much will Rena have in this account after 2 years and 6 months?

   _____

2. Big Money Bank has an offer for new customers: if you deposit $5,000 in a savings account, you will earn 6.5% simple interest over the first 10 years.

   A. How much interest will the account earn over this period?

   _____

   B. How much will be in the account after the 10-year period?

   _____

   C. At the Town Savings Bank, a new customer earns $2,950 in simple interest on a $5,000 deposit over the first 10 years. What rate of interest does that bank pay?

   _____

3. Dream Loan Bank offers loans. Carrie borrows $10,500 to help start a business. The loan must be repaid at 4.5% simple interest over 10 years. How much money will Carrie have to pay back?

   _____

4. **Financial Literacy** Kevin is going to open a savings account with $4,000. Two different banks offer him two different options:

   Bank A offers an account that will pay 6% simple interest for 6 years.

   Bank B offers a special account for new customers that will pay 7% simple interest for 3 years. After the 3 years, Kevin would have to transfer all his earnings to a regular account that will pay 5% simple interest on the *new* transferred principal.

   Which offer will leave Kevin with more money after 6 years? Explain.

   _____

   _____

   _____

Test Prep

5. Delilah deposits $8,255 in an account that pays 4.2% simple interest. How much money will be in her account after 8 years?

(A) $2,773.69

(B) $11,028.68

(C) $12,254.66

(D) $27,736.80

6. Edgar takes out a loan of $5,540, to be repaid over 7 years at 8.5% simple interest. How much interest will Edgar have to pay on the loan?

(A) $470.90

(B) $3,296.30

(C) $3,775.60

(D) $8,836.30

7. Gregoria borrowed $2,450, to be paid back at 3.5% simple interest. She spent $3,221.75 in all to repay the loan. How many years did Gregoria take to repay the loan?

_____

Spiral Review

Use the number line shown for Problems 8 and 9.

8. What number is 3 units to the right of 2 on the number line?

_____

9. What number is 3 units to the left of 2?

_____

10. Bianca had a weekly allowance of $8.50 two years ago. Last year, her weekly allowance was $9.75. This year, Bianca's weekly allowance is $12.00. Does it make sense to represent the relationship between the amount of her allowance and the year with a constant rate? Why or why not?

_____

_____

_____

Review

Vocabulary

Choose the correct term from the Vocabulary box.

Vocabulary
commission
gratuity
markdown
principal
sales tax

1. the amount by which a price is reduced so that an item will sell

   _____

2. an amount of money that is deposited or borrowed and that earns or is charged interest

   _____

3. an amount of money given as a tip to someone who has performed a service

   _____

4. an amount paid to an employee that represents a percent of the employee's sales

   _____

Concepts and Skills

5. (MP) **Use Tools** All sweaters at a store are on sale at a 20% discount. What would be the sale price of a sweater regularly priced $40? State what strategy and tool you will use to answer the question, explain your choice, and then find the answer.

   _____

   _____

6. The depth of water d in a swimming pool increases and decreases by 3% over a one-month period. Match each verbal description of the greatest and least water depths with all equivalent expressions.

	0.97d	1.03d	$d - 0.03$	$d + 0.03d$	$(1 - 0.03)d$
d increased by 3%	☐	☐	☐	☐	☐
d decreased by 3%	☐	☐	☐	☐	☐

7. Phillip wants to buy a baseball cap. Sales tax in his city is 8%. Select the prices of all caps Phillip could buy for less than or equal to $20 once sales tax is added.

(A) $18.18   (B) $18.50   (C) $18.68   (D) $19.00   (E) $19.90

8. Amy and two of her friends eat lunch at a restaurant. Their bill, including tax, comes to $27.63. They decide to split the bill equally. Amy wants to leave a 20% tip for her portion. What is the total amount Amy should pay, including tip? Round to the nearest cent.

$ _____

9. Mr. Bauer deposits $600 in an account that earns simple interest at an annual rate of 2%. Use numbers from the box at right to complete an expression that represents the amount, in dollars, that will be in Mr. Bauer's account after 3 years.

_____ (1 + _____ · _____)

| 0.02 |
| 0.2 |
| 2 |
| 3 |
| 100 |
| 600 |

10. A salesperson earns $8 per hour plus 6% commission on her sales. In a week when she worked 40 hours, her total earnings were $692. What was the total amount of her sales for the week? $ _____

11. The owner of an art supply store buys tubes of magenta oil paint for $10.80 and marks up the cost by 10% to determine the retail price. The tubes of paint do not sell well, so the owner marks down the retail price by 20%. To the nearest cent, what is the marked-down price of a tube of magenta oil paint?

(A) $9.50   (B) $11.88   (C) $18.14   (D) $22.68

12. A ticket company charges a service fee of 5% of the ticket price for each ticket to a concert. Use this information to complete the table.

Ticket price ($)	Service fee ($)	Total cost with service fee ($)
19.00		
	1.40	
		47.25

13. For a scale to pass inspection, the scale's reading can vary by at most 0.1% from the actual mass of an object on the scale. A test mass has an exact mass of 250.00 grams. In what range must the scale's reading be for the scale to pass inspection?

_____

14. This year, 17,884 people attended a basketball team's first game, and 17,150 people attended its second game. What is the percent decrease from the first game to the second game in the number of people who attended? Round to the nearest tenth of a percent.

_____ %

Rational Number Operations

Film Director

Michelle Dougherty and Daniel Hinerfeld are film directors. In 2016, they directed and produced *Sonic Sea*, a film about the negative impact of ocean noise on whales and other marine life. In 2017, *Sonic Sea* won two Emmy awards, including Outstanding Nature Documentary.

STEM Task:

Scientists use an underwater robot to collect specimens from five sea shelves located below the ocean's surface. The shelves are located at depths of 82.25 meters, 106 meters, 79.8 meters, 131.04 meters, and 90.7 meters. Order these depths from shallowest to deepest. What is the vertical distance from the shallowest shelf to the deepest shelf? Explain.

Learning Mindset

Strategic Help-Seeking Identifies Need for Help

Strategic help-seeking is more than just asking for help with a task. It means recognizing when you need help and knowing where to find it. Strategic help-seekers look for help that promotes their learning and understanding, not just for help that gives them the answer. Here are some ideas to think about when it comes to getting help.

- Do you need help? Avoid the habit of always asking for help right away—giving yourself a chance to struggle with a task is a great way to learn. On the other hand, if you've been struggling for some time and cannot move forward, that is a sign you may need some help.

- Where can you find help? Think about people, tools, references, and other resources.

- What help do you need? You have a better chance of getting the help you need if you can clearly communicate what you need assistance with. It may be useful to write down a question or sentence about what is challenging you or holding you back. Be as specific as you can.

Reflect

Q How do you know when you need help with a task?

Q What resources did you use to help you understand and complete the STEM Task?

Understand Addition and Subtraction of Rational Numbers

What's the Pattern?

Five explorers are each at different elevations in a cave. The rational numbers given show their elevations in kilometers. The signs of the numbers indicate the elevation above (+) or below (−) ground level.

Plot each rational number on the number line next to it.

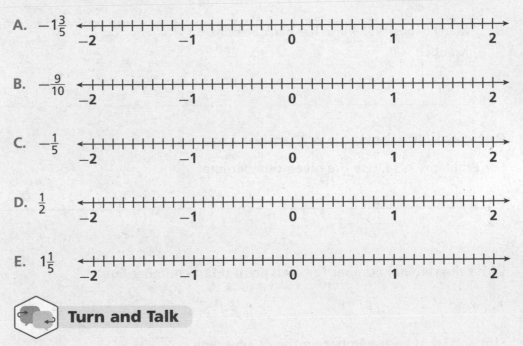

A. $-1\frac{3}{5}$

B. $-\frac{9}{10}$

C. $-\frac{1}{5}$

D. $\frac{1}{2}$

E. $1\frac{1}{5}$

Turn and Talk

What pattern is formed by the five elevations? Explain your reasoning.

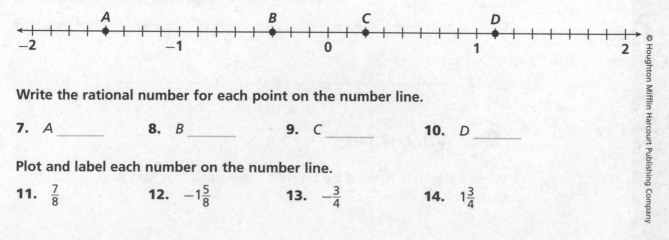

Are You Ready?

Complete these problems to review prior concepts and skills you will need for this module.

Add and Subtract Fractions and Decimals

Find the sum or difference.

1. $\frac{2}{5} + \frac{1}{2}$ _____   **2.** $\frac{5}{6} + \frac{1}{3}$ _____   **3.** $2\frac{3}{4} - 1\frac{5}{6}$ _____

Opposites and Absolute Value

Complete the table by describing the opposite of the given situation and representing it with a positive or negative number.

	Quantity	Opposite Quantity
4.	A football team gains 6 yards on a play. Number: +6	
5.	A penguin is $2\frac{1}{2}$ feet below sea level. Number: $-2\frac{1}{2}$	
6.	Marci deposits $38 into her bank account. Number: +38	

Rational Numbers on a Number Line

For Problems 7–14, use the given number line.

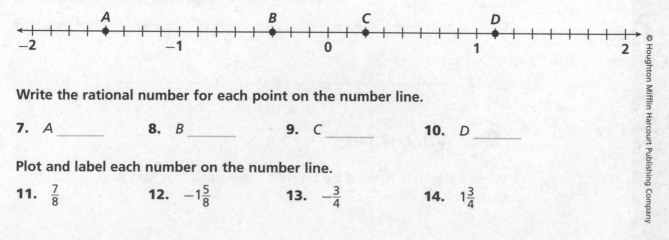

Write the rational number for each point on the number line.

7. A _____   **8.** B _____   **9.** C _____   **10.** D _____

Plot and label each number on the number line.

11. $\frac{7}{8}$ **12.** $-1\frac{5}{8}$ **13.** $-\frac{3}{4}$ **14.** $1\frac{3}{4}$

Name _____

Add or Subtract a Positive Integer on a Number Line

(I Can) add or subtract positive integers on a number line.

Spark Your Learning

John has an account balance of $20. He receives his weekly paycheck for work at his part-time job in the amount of $110. He can't find a bike he wants, so he buys some comic books for $40. Then John finds his dream bike priced as shown. If he buys the bike now, what will his account balance be?

Turn and Talk What happens when you subtract a greater positive number from a lesser positive number?

Build Understanding

1 ▶ Use the thermometer as a number line to answer the
following questions.

A. On Monday morning, it was 35 °F outside.
Plot this on the thermometer.

B. By afternoon, the temperature rose 20 degrees.

What distance will you move on the thermometer? _____

In which direction will you move? _____

C. Show the change in temperature on the thermometer. What was

the temperature Monday afternoon? _____

Monday

- 60 °F
- 50 °F
- 40 °F
- 30 °F
- 20 °F
- 10 °F
- 0 °F
- −10 °F
- −20 °F

D. Tuesday's high temperature was 25 °F.
The temperature dropped by 30 °F overnight.

What direction on the number line is this? _____

Show this on the number line.

What is the resulting temperature? _____

E. Explain why Tuesday's temperature drop resulted
in a negative temperature.

_____

_____

_____

Tuesday

- 60 °F
- 50 °F
- 40 °F
- 30 °F
- 20 °F
- 10 °F
- 0 °F
- −10 °F
- −20 °F

Turn and Talk Is it possible to start with a positive temperature and then
have a rise in temperature which leads to a negative temperature? Explain.

Name _____

2 Use a number line to answer the following questions. **Thursday**

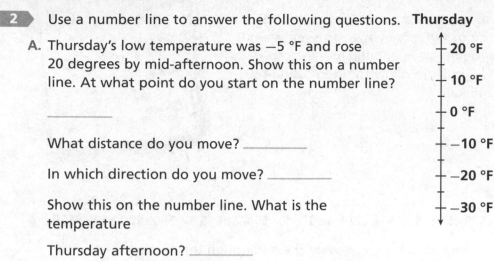

A. Thursday's low temperature was −5 °F and rose
20 degrees by mid-afternoon. Show this on a number
line. At what point do you start on the number line?

_____

What distance do you move? _____

In which direction do you move? _____

Show this on the number line. What is the
temperature

Thursday afternoon? _____

B. Friday's low temperature is −10 °F. During the day, the
temperature rises by 5 degrees. Show the movement on the

number line for Friday and give the result. _____

Friday

C. Sunday's high temperature is −10 °F. During the day, the
temperature drops 2 degrees. What is the temperature

Sunday afternoon? _____

Sunday

D. Explain why the temperatures on Friday and Sunday afternoons
are both negative, even though one is the result of an increase in
temperature and one is the result of a decrease in temperature.

_____

_____

_____

_____

Turn and Talk How can you predict whether the sum of a positive and a
negative number will be positive or negative by comparing the two numbers?

3 Jane wants to buy a new tablet that costs $100. She keeps a record of the money she earns and spends as shown. Will Jane have enough money to buy the tablet on Sunday? Follow the steps using the number line below.

Earning / Spending

Monday:
Starting balance $60

Tuesday:
Earned babysitting   + $25

Friday:
Weekly allowance   + $20

Saturday:
Food at football game – $10

```
←──┼───┼───┼───┼───┼───┼───┼───┼───┼───┼───┼───┼───┼───┼───┼───┼──→
  -$40 -$30 -$20 -$10  $0  $10 $20 $30 $40 $50 $60 $70 $80 $90 $100 $110
```

A. Jane's starting balance is _____. Plot the amount on the number line.

B. Jane earns _____ babysitting. Draw an arrow from the starting amount to represent the amount Jane earns by babysitting. How much money does Jane have now? _____

C. Jane received _____ for a weekly allowance. Draw another arrow from the end of the arrow from Step B to represent Jane's allowance.

How much money does Jane have now? _____

D. Jane spent _____ at the football game. Draw another arrow to represent the amount Jane spent at the football game. How much money does Jane have now? _____

E. The tablet costs _____. Draw an arrow to represent the amount Jane would spend on the tablet. Does she have enough money? Explain.

_____

_____

Check Understanding

1. A business has $10,000 in its bank account. In order to build an addition onto its office, it takes out a loan for $30,000. What is its new account balance once the loan is deposited?

```
←┼─────┼──────┼──────┼──────┼──────┼──────┼──────┼──────┼──→
 $0   $5,000 $10,000 $15,000 $20,000 $25,000 $30,000 $35,000 $40,000
```

_____

2. If the amount required to build the addition is actually $45,000, will the business in Problem 1 have enough to do it? Explain.

_____

On Your Own

Use the number line for Problems 3 and 4.

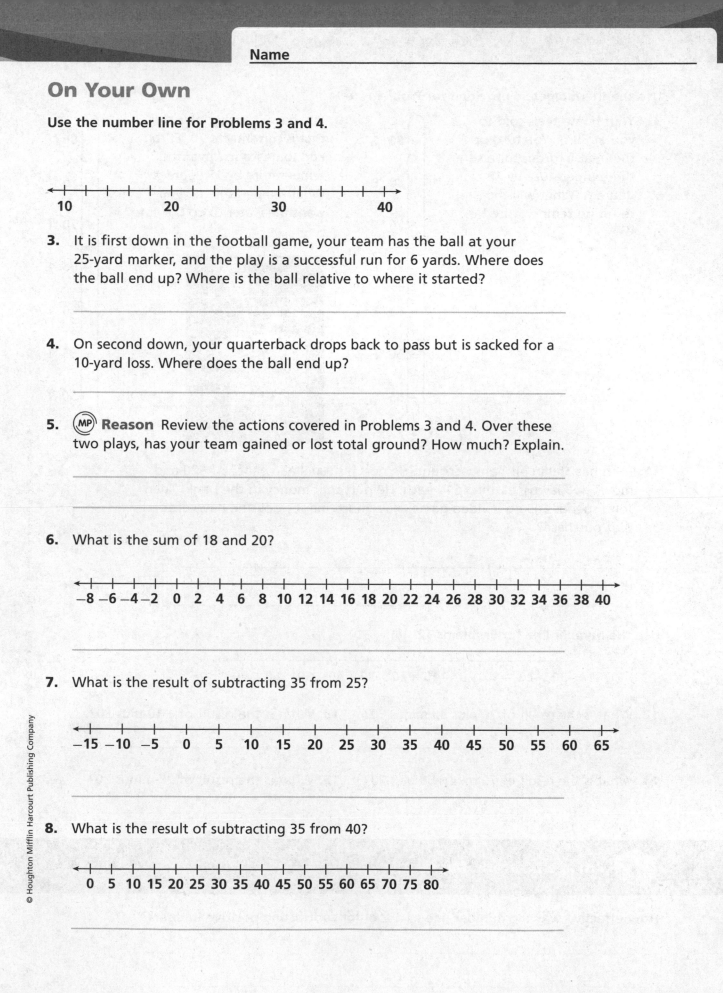

3. It is first down in the football game, your team has the ball at your 25-yard marker, and the play is a successful run for 6 yards. Where does the ball end up? Where is the ball relative to where it started?

_____

4. On second down, your quarterback drops back to pass but is sacked for a 10-yard loss. Where does the ball end up?

_____

5. **(MP) Reason** Review the actions covered in Problems 3 and 4. Over these two plays, has your team gained or lost total ground? How much? Explain.

_____

_____

6. What is the sum of 18 and 20?

_____

7. What is the result of subtracting 35 from 25?

_____

8. What is the result of subtracting 35 from 40?

_____

_____

_____

© Houghton Mifflin Harcourt Publishing Company

_____

Use the thermometers provided for Problems 9–11.

9. Your home feels cold to you at 60 °F. You turn up the heat in order to raise the temperature by 15 degrees. What will the resulting temperature be?

_____

10. You have a beaker of water that is currently at 70 °F. You add some ice to lower the temperature by 15 degrees. What temperature do you want the water to go down to?

_____

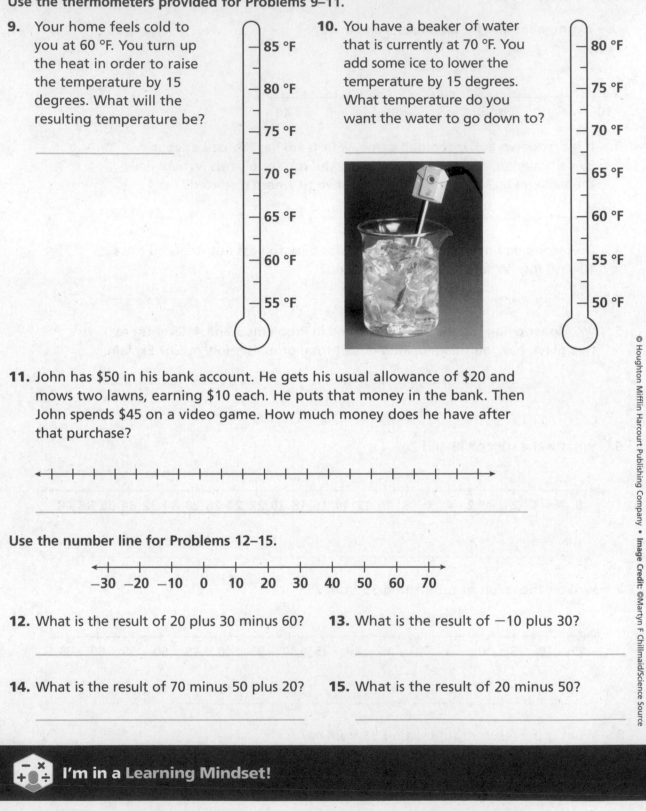

11. John has $50 in his bank account. He gets his usual allowance of $20 and mows two lawns, earning $10 each. He puts that money in the bank. Then John spends $45 on a video game. How much money does he have after that purchase?

_____

Use the number line for Problems 12–15.

12. What is the result of 20 plus 30 minus 60?

_____

13. What is the result of −10 plus 30?

_____

14. What is the result of 70 minus 50 plus 20?

_____

15. What is the result of 20 minus 50?

_____

I'm in a Learning Mindset!

How effective was the number line as a tool for subtracting positive integers?

_____

_____

LESSON 3.1
**More Practice/
Homework**

ONLINE
🙂Ed **Video Tutorials and
Interactive Examples**

Add or Subtract a Positive Integer on a Number Line

1. Ms. Howard buys a car for $500 and adds a music system that costs $200. Then she adds a pair of seat covers for the price shown. How much has Ms. Howard spent on the car so far?

_____

2. At the beginning of the week, Tideland Manufacturing had an inventory of 60,000 screws. This week they received a shipment of 30,000 more screws. Then they used 50,000 screws to make their Tideland mowers. How many screws do they have left in inventory?

_____

3. **STEM** A chemical reaction is _endothermic_ if it absorbs heat from its surroundings. It is _exothermic_ if it gives off heat to its surroundings. In her chemistry class, Lily is given a salt (ammonium nitrate) and a beaker of water at 60 °F. She dissolves the salt in the water and sees that the temperature of the solution is now 50 °F. Did the temperature of the solution increase or decrease? By how many degrees? What kind of reaction has occurred? Explain.

_____

_____

70 °F

60 °F

50 °F

40 °F

4. At the beginning of the month, Joe has $180 in his bank account. He wants to buy a new gaming system for $250 in two weeks. His parents have offered to loan him money if he needs it. He gets $20 a week for an allowance. Will he have enough money at the end of two weeks to make the purchase on his own? If not, how much will he have to borrow from his parents? Explain.

_____

$230

$220

$210

$200

$190

5. (MP) **Reason** Can you ever add two positive integers and get a negative integer? Explain.

$180

_____

_____

6. (MP) **Reason** Can you subtract a positive integer from a positive integer and get a negative result? Explain your answer.

_____

_____

© Houghton Mifflin Harcourt Publishing Company • Image Credit: ©Ukki Studio/Shutterstock

Test Prep

7. Marcus owes his mother $10. He babysits his little sister and earns $25. Then he cleans the garage and earns $32. After he pays his mother, how much money does Marcus have?

_____

8. The water in a lake is 4 feet above its usual level. Then the level of the lake drops 7 feet. If 0 represents its usual level, which number line shows the final level of the water in the lake?

Ⓐ
```
-8 -7 -6 -5 -4 -3 -2 -1  0  1  2  3  4  5  6  7  8  9 10 11 12
```

Ⓑ
```
-8 -7 -6 -5 -4 -3 -2 -1  0  1  2  3  4  5  6  7  8  9 10 11 12
```

Ⓒ
```
-8 -7 -6 -5 -4 -3 -2 -1  0  1  2  3  4  5  6  7  8  9 10 11 12
```

Ⓓ
```
-8 -7 -6 -5 -4 -3 -2 -1  0  1  2  3  4  5  6  7  8  9 10 11 12
```

Circle the word that best completes the sentence.

9. Donna subtracts a positive number from a greater positive number. The resulting difference will be | positive / negative |.

10. Devon subtracts a positive number from a lesser positive number. The resulting difference will be | positive / negative |.

Spiral Review

11. Elena draws a scale drawing for a garden. The scale drawing is 3 inches by 6 inches. The garden will be 12 feet by 24 feet. What is the scale of the drawing in inches to feet?

_____

12. Raoul makes shell necklaces to sell at a craft fair. The supplies for each necklace cost $3.75. Raoul sells the necklaces for $11.25. What is the percent markup for a shell necklace?

_____

13. Neveah goes out to dinner at a restaurant. The bill for dinner is $57.25, and Neveah gives the server a 20% tip. What is the total cost for dinner?

_____

Name _____

Add or Subtract a Negative Integer on a Number Line

(I Can) add or subtract negative integers on a number line.

Spark Your Learning

The scores of three contestants on a game show are shown. The final question is worth 50 points. A correct answer adds 50 points to a contestant's score. An incorrect answer deducts 50 points.

Show the possible final scores for each contestant. What circumstances are necessary for each contestant to win?

| 30 | 50 | -20 |
| MORGAN | CARLOS | KAYLEE |

⟵┼┼┼⟶

Turn and Talk How can you add a number to each score to show a loss?

Build Understanding

1 ▶ The table shows the scores of three contestants on a game show.

Game Show Scores		
Latrell	Mayumi	Scott
8	6	3

A. Latrell spins a wheel to find out how many points he adds to his score. The wheel stops on "−5 points." Use the number line to add −5 points to Latrell's score. Then complete the equation.

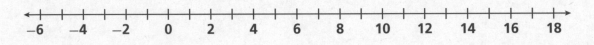

$8 + (-5) =$ _____

B. Mayumi spins the wheel next. The wheel stops on "−11 points." Use the number line to add −11 points to her score. Complete the equation.

$6 + (-11) =$ _____

C. How do Latrell's and Mayumi's final scores compare to their starting scores? Explain why this is reasonable.

_____

_____

_____

D. Because Scott started with the lowest score, he plays a penalty round. In the penalty round, the wheel determines the number of points that are *subtracted* from a player's score. The result of Scott's spin is shown. Use the number line to find Scott's score. Then complete the equation.

Penalty Round

Subtract:

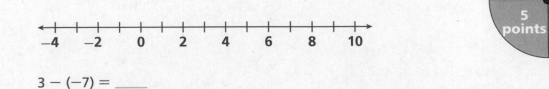

$3 - (-7) =$ _____

Turn and Talk Is it possible to subtract a loss from a positive number and result in a negative number? Why or why not?

2▶ The table shows the scores of three contestants on a game show.

Game Show Scores		
Natalie	Gina	Tyler
−2	−6	−6

A. Natalie spins a wheel to find out how many points she adds to her score. The wheel stops on "−6 points." Use the number line to add −6 points to Natalie's score. Then complete the equation.

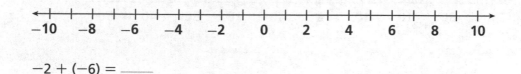

$-2 + (-6) =$ _____

B. Gina and Tyler both started with the lowest score, so they each play a penalty round. In the penalty round, the wheel determines the number of points that are *subtracted* from a player's score. The result of Gina's spin is shown. Use the number line to find Gina's score, and complete the equation.

Penalty Round

Subtract:

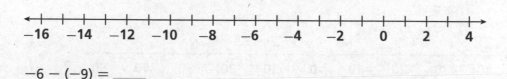

$-6 - (-9) =$ _____

C. Explain which direction to move on the number line when you subtract a negative integer.

_____

_____

_____

_____

_____

D. The result of Tyler's spin is shown. Use the number line to find Tyler's score, and complete the equation.

Penalty Round

Subtract:

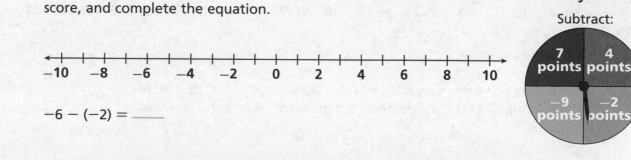

$-6 - (-2) =$ _____

Turn and Talk Is it possible to add a loss to a negative number and result in a positive number? Why or why not?

3 Jackson and Flora both have bank accounts, and they use credit cards. Use the number line to determine if they can pay off the credit card bill.

A. Jackson has $20 in his account. He uses a credit card to spend $30 on a coat and $10 on a movie. Jackson then deposits $50 into his account. How much will Jackson have left after he pays the credit card bill?

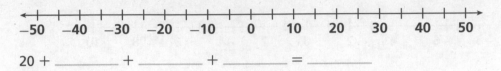

20 + _____ + _____ + _____ = _____

Can Jackson pay his credit card bill? Explain.

_____

B. Flora starts with $10 in her account. She uses a credit card to spend $20 on a gift and $40 on some shoes, and then she returns a $30 appliance for a refund to be applied to her card. Use the number line to show these transactions.

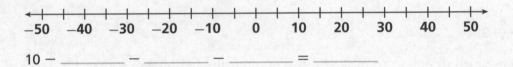

10 − _____ − _____ − _____ = _____

Can Flora pay her credit card bill? Explain.

_____

Check Understanding

1. Jessica starts at an elevation of 40 feet and descends 60 feet. Use the number line to find Jessica's current elevation. Then complete the equation.

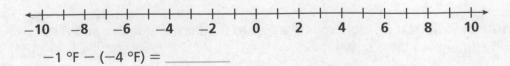

$40 + (-60) =$ _____

2. The temperature is −4 °F, and later the temperature is −1 °F. Use the number line to find the change in temperature. Then complete the equation.

number line from −10 to 10

$-1\,°F - (-4\,°F) =$ _____

On Your Own

3. Denny has a balance of $7 on his transit card. Each train ride debits $3, which is the same as adding −$3 to the card. Use the number line to add −$3 to Denny's balance, and complete the equation.

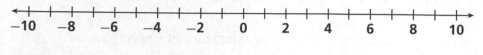

$7 + (−$3) = _____

Three friends are playing a board game. The table shows their current scores. Each player draws two cards. The first card says "add" or "subtract." The second card says a number of points. Use a number line and complete the equation to find each player's final score.

Player	Score
Andrew	−4
Saleema	−3
Cassie	−9

4. Andrew's cards say "add" and "−4 points."

−4 + (−4) = _____

5. Saleema's cards say "subtract" and "−7 points."

−3 − (−7) = _____

6. Cassie's cards say "subtract" and "−8 points."

−9 − (−8) = _____

7. Tomas and a friend are hiking in Death Valley National Park in California. They start at an elevation of −10 meters. During the hike, they ascend 30 meters, descend 40 meters, and then descend another 20 meters. Use the number line and complete the equation to find their final elevation.

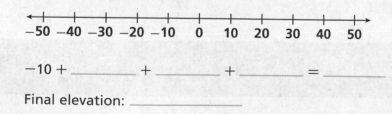

−10 + _____ + _____ + _____ = _____

Final elevation: _____

In the United States, the lowest point of elevation is found in Death Valley in California.

8. The temperature at midnight is −7 °F. Before noon, the temperature decreases by 2 °F, then increases by 5 °F, then increases by 4 °F. Use the number line and complete the equation to find the temperature at noon.

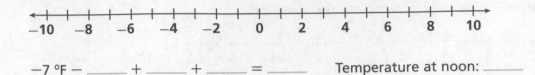

−7 °F − _____ + _____ + _____ = _____   Temperature at noon: _____

9. (MP) **Critique Reasoning** Leah said that when you add two negative integers the result must be negative. Do you agree or disagree? Use a number line to help explain your answer.

10. Open Ended Write a story problem for the number line shown. Provide the answer to the problem.

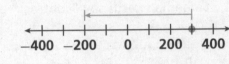

_____

_____

11. STEM The freezing point of seawater is −2 °C. The freezing point of nitric acid is −42 °C. How much greater is the freezing point of seawater than the freezing point of nitric acid?

_____

For Problems 12–17, use a number line to add or subtract.

12. $7 - (-3) =$ _____

13. $-20 + (-30) =$ _____

14. $-1 + (-6) =$ _____

15. $5 - (-4) =$ _____

16. $-8 - (-5) =$ _____

17. $5 + (-5) =$ _____

⬢ I'm in a Learning Mindset!

What is challenging about subtracting negative integers? Can I work through it on my own, or do I need help?

_____

_____

Name _____

Add or Subtract a Negative Integer on a Number Line

1. Brad has 8 points during a trivia game. He answers a question incorrectly and −12 points are added to his score. Use the number line to add −12 points to Brad's score, and complete the equation to show his final score.

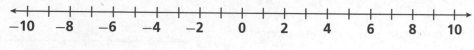

$8 + (−12) =$ _____

2. **Math on the Spot** A dolphin is swimming 3 feet below sea level. It dives down 9 feet to catch some fish. Then the dolphin swims 4 feet up toward the surface with its catch. What is the dolphin's final elevation relative to sea level?

_____

3. (MP) **Use Tools** Dario was scuba diving at an elevation of −20 feet, and then descended 20 feet more. After the descent, what was his elevation in relation to the other diver shown?

—30 ft

Dario

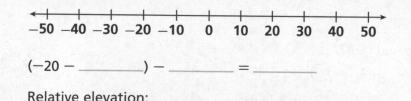

$(−20 −$ _____$) −$ _____ $=$ _____

Relative elevation: _____

4. Latisha has $40 in her checking account. She makes a withdrawal of $20 and then writes a check for $40. Then she deposits $30. Use the number line and complete the equation to find her final balance.

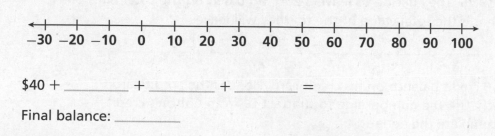

$40 +$ _____ $+$ _____ $+$ _____ $=$ _____

Final balance: _____

For Problems 5–10, use a number line to add or subtract.

5. $2 − (−4) =$ _____

6. $−2 + (−7) =$ _____

7. $−10 + (−60) =$ _____

8. $3 − (−1) =$ _____

9. $−7 − (−7) =$ _____

10. $2 + (−9) =$ _____

Test Prep

11. Elena wants to use a number line to find the difference $5 - (-7)$. Which is the best description of how she should do this?

  Ⓐ Start at -7 and move 5 units right.

  Ⓑ Start at -7 and move 5 units left.

  Ⓒ Start at 5 and move 7 units right.

  Ⓓ Start at 5 and move 7 units left.

12. Which sum or difference can you evaluate using the number line model shown?

  Ⓐ $-3 - (-2)$

  Ⓑ $-3 - 2$

  Ⓒ $-1 + 3$

  Ⓓ $-1 - (-3)$

13. Aaron is playing a board game and has a score of 20 points. He spins a spinner to see how many points will be added to his score. The spinner lands on "-50 points." Find Aaron's final score. Show your work.

14. Which sum or difference is equal to 0?

  Ⓐ $-7 - 7$

  Ⓑ $4 - (-4)$

  Ⓒ $-1 + (-1)$

  Ⓓ $6 + (-6)$

Spiral Review

15. At a restaurant, Brianna and Naomi each order an appetizer for $6.50 and an entree for $9.75. They decide to leave a 20% tip based on the total bill before tax. What is the total value of the tip they will leave?

_____

16. Colton has a $6 credit balance on his credit card. He uses the credit card to pay $9 for lunch. Use the number line to subtract $9 from Colton's credit balance, and complete the equation.

$\$6 - \$9 =$ _____

Name _____

Use a Number Line to Add and Subtract Rational Numbers

(I Can) use a number line to add or subtract rational numbers.

Spark Your Learning SMALL GROUPS

When a person owes money on a credit card, the credit card holder can think of it as a negative balance.

Devin has a balance of −$9.50 on a credit card. Which two items can he purchase without his balance going below −$15.00? Find all the pairs of items Devin can purchase.

Dinner rolls
$0.50

Pizza dough
$3.00

Cinnamon bread
$4.50

 Turn and Talk If the cinnamon bread was on sale for $2.00, could he purchase all three items? Explain.

Build Understanding

1 An underwater camera is dropped from a helicopter flying over the water as shown. The camera has an elevation change of −8 feet. Where is the camera now in relation to the surface of the water?

$4\frac{1}{2}$ feet

A. The number line represents distance from sea level.

What do positive numbers represent? _____

What do negative numbers represent? _____

What does 0 represent? _____

B. On the number line, draw an arrow representing the camera's change in elevation. Where is the camera after the change in elevation of −8 feet from the helicopter?

$4\frac{1}{2} + (-8) = $ _____

C. Later, the camera is at $-5\frac{1}{2}$ feet and has an elevation change of +3 feet. What is the camera's final elevation in relation to the surface?

On the number line a line would start at _____ and go

_____ 3 units. Draw an arrow representing the camera's change in elevation.

$-5\frac{1}{2} + 3 = $ _____

D. Now the camera is at $-5\frac{1}{2}$ feet again, and it sinks $2\frac{1}{2}$ feet. What is the camera's final elevation in relation to the surface? Use the number line to show your work.

$-5\frac{1}{2} + \left(-2\frac{1}{2}\right) = $ _____

> **Turn and Talk** If the camera is at −2.5 feet and undergoes a change of elevation of 0 feet, where will the camera be then? Will it be at the surface of the water?

Elevation (ft)

```
13
12
11
10
9
8
7
6
5
4
3
2
1
0
−1
−2
−3
−4
−5
−6
−7
−8
−9
−10
```

Step It Out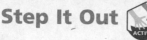

2 ▶ Carmela is playing with a ball.

A. The ball is on a platform 2.3 meters above the ground; then the ball falls to the ground. Use a number line to represent the change in height of the ball.

Begin at _____ to represent the height of the ball on the platform; then show the decrease in height.

B. Complete the equation to represent the situation in Part A.

$2.3 -$ _____ $=$ _____

C. The ball fell into a pit 1.5 feet below ground level. Carmela grabs the ball and puts it back on ground level.

Begin at _____ to represent the height of the ball in the pit; then show the increase in height.

D. Complete the equation to represent the situation in Part C.

$-1.5 +$ _____ $=$ _____

E. Carmela stands on the ground and kicks the ball 4.5 meters up into the air. It falls down and goes into another pit that is 3.5 meters deep.

Use the number line to show the changes in height of the ball.

Begin at _____ to represent the height of the ball on the ground, and show the increase followed by the decrease.

F. Complete the equation to represent the situation in Part E.

_____ $+ 4.5 -$ _____ $= -3.5$

G. Using the number line model in Parts C and D as an example, explain the **Addition Property of Opposites** which states that the sum of a number and its opposite equals zero. Another name for opposite is **additive inverse**.

_____

_____

_____

_____

Turn and Talk How can you interpret the model in Parts A and B as a sum to show that the sum of a number and its opposite is 0?

© Houghton Mifflin Harcourt Publishing Company

Module 3 • Lesson 3

119

3 Describe each situation in words.

A. Margarita has $50 in her bank account. What transaction would result in an account balance of $0?

_____

B. The temperature is 15 °F. What change in temperature would result in the temperature being 0 °F?

_____

C. A kite is 25 feet in the air. What needs to happen to the kite in order for it to be at ground level?

_____

D. Describe a situation in which opposite quantities combine to make 0.

_____

_____

Check Understanding

1. From an elevation of 2.5 feet above sea level, a bird dives 4 feet to catch a fish. How far below the surface is the fish?

A. Draw an arrow to represent this situation on the number line shown.

B. Complete the equation to represent the situation.

$2.5 - 4 =$ _____

2. Pietro used a number line to subtract $-\frac{1}{8} - (-\frac{1}{4})$. The figure shows the arrow he drew to represent the subtraction. Is he getting the right result? Explain.

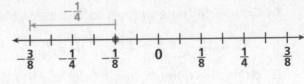

_____

_____

3. The overnight low temperature is −7 °F. By morning, the temperature increases by 15 degrees. Draw an arrow on the thermometer to represent this situation and find the morning temperature.

_____

4. Mr. Anderson has a credit card balance of −$80.23 at the end of the month. Use Mr. Anderson's credit card balance to describe a situation in which opposite quantities combine to make 0.

_____

_____

_____

On Your Own

(MP) Use Tools Use the thermometer to help solve Problems 5–8.

5. In the morning, the temperature is −5 °F. The temperature increases by 13 °F, then decreases by 5 °F. Write an equation to represent the situation.

_____

6. The high temperature for the day is 28 °F. The record high for the day was 54 °F. What is the difference in temperatures?

_____

7. The high temperature for the day is 28 °F. The record low for the day was −12 °F. What is the difference in temperatures?

_____

8. This morning the temperature was −5 °F. How much must the temperature change to reach 0 °F?

_____

9. **(MP) Reason** Evan added $\left(-2\frac{1}{2}\right) + 4$ and got $6\frac{1}{2}$. Draw arrows on the number line to represent the problem. Then explain Evan's error.

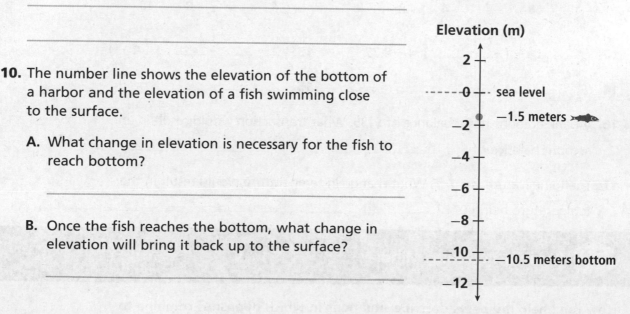

$$\begin{array}{ccccccc} -3 & -2 & -1 & 0 & 1 & 2 & 3 \end{array}$$

_____

_____

10. The number line shows the elevation of the bottom of a harbor and the elevation of a fish swimming close to the surface.

    A. What change in elevation is necessary for the fish to reach bottom?

    _____

    B. Once the fish reaches the bottom, what change in elevation will bring it back up to the surface?

    _____

Elevation (m)

2
0 -- sea level
−2 • −1.5 meters
−4
−6
−8
−10 --10.5 meters bottom
−12

60 °F
50 °F
40 °F
30 °F
20 °F
10 °F
0 °F
−10 °F
−20 °F

© Houghton Mifflin Harcourt Publishing Company

11. Financial Literacy Stock in Boomer Branding, Inc. started the week at $26.50 per share. During the week, the following changes in the share price were registered:

(+$2.75), (+$3.00), (−$9.25), (+$1.50), (−$5.25)

A. Show the changes on the number line.

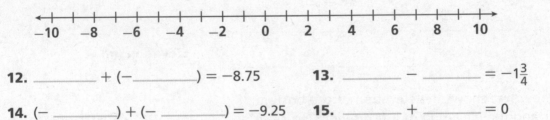

16   18   20   22   24   26   28   30   32   34

B. What was the price per share at the end of the week? _____

C. Open Ended Describe a situation using stocks in which opposite quantities combine to make 0.

_____

_____

_____

For Problems 12–15, find rational numbers to complete each equation. Use the number line to help.

−10   −8   −6   −4   −2   0   2   4   6   8   10

12. _____ + (−_____) = −8.75   **13.** _____ − _____ = −1$\frac{3}{4}$

14. (−_____) + (−_____) = −9.25   **15.** _____ + _____ = 0

16. A bank account has a balance of $135. What transaction would result in an account balance of $0? _____

17. The temperature is −7 °F. What change in temperature would result in the temperature being 0 °F? _____

I'm in a Learning Mindset!

How can I help my peers describe situations in which opposites combine to make 0?

_____

© Houghton Mifflin Harcourt Publishing Company • Image Credit: ©mdfiles/Fotolia

Name _____

LESSON 3.3
More Practice/ Homework

ONLINE

Video Tutorials and
Interactive Examples

Use a Number Line to Add and Subtract Rational Numbers

1. Caleb rode his bike for $3\frac{1}{2}$ miles in the morning. Then he rode his bike another $2\frac{1}{2}$ miles in the afternoon. How many miles did Caleb ride all together? Draw an arrow on the number line to show how to find the answer. Then write the answer below.

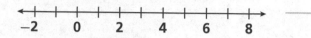

2. **(MP) Critique Reasoning** Jasmine evaluated the expression $10 - (-3)$ and says it is equal to 7. Is she right? If not, what was her mistake?

_____

3. On a number line, what other number is the same distance from -2.8 as -7.2 is?

_____

4. A number line is drawn left to right with integers spaced 1 centimeter apart. An ant crawls onto the number line at $+2$. It then crawls 3.5 centimeters left, 4.8 centimeters right, and 7.9 centimeters left.

   A. Where is the ant on the number line now? _____

   B. How far is it from its original position? _____

   C. What is the total distance the ant crawled along the number line?

   _____

   D. **Open Ended** Describe a situation in which the ant crawls in a way that results in opposite quantities combining to make 0.

   _____

   _____

   _____

(MP) Use Tools For Problems 5 and 6, draw arrows on the number line to show the operations indicated and fill in the answer.

5. $0.5 + (-1.5) - (-5.5) =$ _____

6. $-1\frac{1}{2} - \left(+3\frac{1}{2}\right) - \left(-\frac{5}{8}\right) =$ _____

Test Prep

7. If the temperature was 0 °C and then there was a temperature change of +5 °C, what temperature change would return the temperature to 0 °C?

(A) −10 °C

(B) −5 °C

(C) 0 °C

(D) 5 °C

8. Find the sum.

$-\frac{1}{8} + \frac{1}{8} + \frac{5}{8}$

(A) $\frac{1}{8}$

(B) $\frac{3}{8}$

(C) $\frac{5}{8}$

(D) $\frac{7}{8}$

9. Which set of operations corresponds to the arrows shown on the number line?

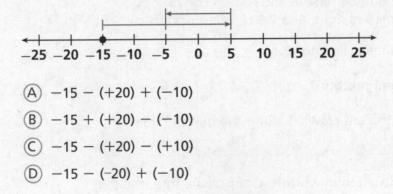

(A) $-15 - (+20) + (-10)$

(B) $-15 + (+20) - (-10)$

(C) $-15 - (+20) - (+10)$

(D) $-15 - (-20) + (-10)$

Spiral Review

10. A map is drawn using a scale of 1 centimeter to 25 kilometers. What actual distance is represented by a map length of 3.2 centimeters?

11. Find the percent change from 200 to 192.

12. You make an initial deposit of $2,500 in an account that offers 6% simple interest per year. How much will be in the account after 4 years?

Name _____

Review

Vocabulary

Select all terms that apply to each number.

		Positive Integer	Negative Integer	Rational Number
1.	23	☐	☐	☐
2.	$-\frac{3}{10}$	☐	☐	☐
3.	1.4	☐	☐	☐
4.	−7	☐	☐	☐

Concepts and Skills

5. **(MP) Use Tools** Name two numbers that are 7 units from 3. State what strategy and tool you will use to answer the question, explain your choice, and then find the answer.

_____

_____

6. A school, a bookstore, and a park are on the same straight street. The book store (B) is 2.25 miles from the school (S). The park (P) is 1.75 miles from the school. What is the distance from the park to the bookstore?

```
      B       S       P
←+—+•+—+—+—+—•+—+—+—•+—+→          _____ miles
 −3  −2  −1   0   1   2   3
```

7. Paolo is using number lines to find the value of the expression $\frac{1}{6} + \frac{2}{3} + \left(-1\frac{1}{3}\right)$. His first two steps are shown.

A. Draw an arrow on the number line provided to show the last step.

Step 1: Start at $\frac{1}{6}$.	←+—+—+—+—+—◆—+—+—+—+→ −1 0 1
Step 2: Add $\frac{2}{3}$.	←+—+—+—+—◆—+—+—+—+—+→ −1 0 1
Last step: Add $\left(-1\frac{1}{3}\right)$.	←+—+—+—+—+—+—+—+—+—+→ −1 0 1

B. What is the value of the expression $\frac{1}{6} + \frac{2}{3} + \left(-1\frac{1}{3}\right)$? _____

8. A number line is shown. Eric knows that n is the opposite of m. Which statement about m and n is true?

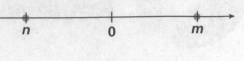

Ⓐ $m = n$ Ⓑ $m = -(-n)$ Ⓒ $m + n = 0$ Ⓓ $m - n = 0$

9. The difference $a - b$ is equal to c. The number line shows a and b. Select all statements about c that are true.

Ⓐ $c < 0$ Ⓓ c is closer to 0 on the number line than a.

Ⓑ $c = 0$ Ⓔ c is the same distance from 0 on the number line as a.

Ⓒ $c > 0$ Ⓕ c is farther from 0 on the number line than a.

10. On a quiz show, Anabel started with 0 points. She gained 10 points on her first turn and lost 10 points on her second turn. What is her combined score after her first two turns? Use addition of integers to explain your reasoning.

_____

_____

_____

11. An equation is shown, where $s > 0$ and $t < 0$.

$$r - s = t$$

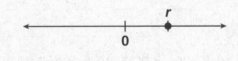

Plot and label two points on the number line to show possible locations of s and t.

12. Ivy's hair has grown $\frac{5}{8}$ inch since her last haircut. At this haircut, she has $1\frac{1}{2}$ inches of hair cut off.

A. Which expressions represent the total change, in inches, in the length of Ivy's hair between her two most recent haircuts?

Ⓐ $\frac{5}{8} - 1\frac{1}{2}$　　Ⓓ $-1\frac{1}{2} - \frac{5}{8}$

Ⓑ $\frac{5}{8} + \left(-1\frac{1}{2}\right)$　　Ⓔ $1\frac{1}{2} - \frac{5}{8}$

Ⓒ $\frac{5}{8} + 1\frac{1}{2}$

B. Plot a point on the number line to represent the total change, in inches, in the length of Ivy's hair after both haircuts.

$-1 \quad -\frac{1}{2} \quad 0 \quad \frac{1}{2} \quad 1$

Add and Subtract Rational Numbers

Which Sum Does Not Belong?

At Fun Times Pizza, customers can order a pizza in the shapes shown below.

Each diagram shows a sum of two rational numbers that represent combinations of pizza slices. Write an addition equation for the sum that is shown in the shaded part of each diagram.

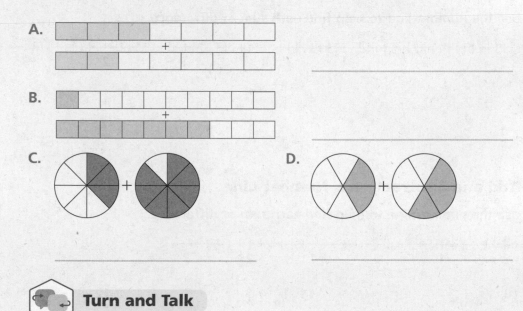

A.

_____

B.

_____

C.   D.

_____

Turn and Talk

Which of the sums do you think does not belong with the others? Justify your answer.

Are You Ready?

Complete these problems to review prior concepts and skills you will need for this module.

Add and Subtract Fractions and Decimals

Find the sum or difference.

1. $8.04 + 4.15$ **2.** $9.1 + 12.98$ **3.** $88.4 - 39.75$

_____   _____   _____

Opposites and Absolute Value

Find the absolute value.

4. $|-48|$ **5.** $|15|$ **6.** $|-150|$

_____   _____   _____

Add and Subtract on a Number Line

Use the number line to help find each sum or difference.

7. $-1.2 + 2.0$ **8.** $1.0 - 1.2$ **9.** $-0.3 - 1.7$

_____   _____   _____

Add and Subtract on a Number Line

Use the number line to help find each sum or difference.

10. $-\dfrac{5}{6} + \dfrac{2}{6}$ **11.** $1\dfrac{1}{6} - \dfrac{2}{3}$ **12.** $\dfrac{5}{3} - 3\dfrac{1}{6}$

_____   _____   _____

Name _____

Compute Sums of Integers

(I Can) identify integer addition problems. I feel confident that I can write and evaluate expressions to solve real-world integer addition problems.

Spark Your Learning

A submarine was stationed 700 feet below sea level. It ascends 250 feet every hour. If the submarine continues to ascend at the same rate, when will the submarine be at the surface?

 Turn and Talk How can you express the depth as an integer to show that the submarine is below water?

Build Understanding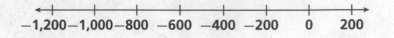

1 ▶ A submarine descends to 800 feet below sea level. Then it descends another 200 feet. What is the submarine's final elevation? First use a number line to find out. Then use **absolute value** to solve the same problem without a number line.

A. Write an addition expression, and use the number line to determine the final elevation of the submarine.

$$\xleftarrow{\quad\;\;|\qquad|\qquad|\qquad|\qquad|\qquad|\qquad|\qquad|\quad}\rightarrow$$
$$-1{,}200\;-1{,}000\;-800\;-600\;-400\;-200\qquad 0\qquad 200$$

_____

B. Recall that the **absolute value** of a number is the number's distance from 0 on the number line. For example, the absolute value of −4 is 4 because −4 is 4 units from 0.

Because the number line arrows both go the same direction, you can find the submarine's final distance from 0 by adding the absolute values of the numbers.

$|-800| + |-200| = \boxed{} + \boxed{} = \boxed{}$

C. How does the sum of the absolute values compare to the sum of −800 and −200?

_____

D. How can you use the sum of absolute values in Part B to find the final elevation—that is, to find the sum of −800 and −200?

_____

_____

E. Find −100 + (−300) by first adding the absolute values. Use the number line above to check your answer.

$|-100| + |-300| = \boxed{} + \boxed{} = \boxed{}$, so −100 + (−300) = $\boxed{}$

F. Complete the rule for adding integers with the same signs:

_____ the absolute values of the numbers and use the _____ of the **addends**.

 Turn and Talk Use a number line to explain why adding two integers with the same sign will always result in a sum that has the same sign as the addends.

2 ▶ The temperature in the morning in Sioux City, Iowa, is shown. By the afternoon, the temperature had risen 25 °F. What was the temperature in the afternoon? First use a number line to find out. Then use absolute value to solve the same problem without a number line.

Sioux City, IOWA

−5 °F

A. Write an addition expression and use the number line to determine the temperature in the afternoon.

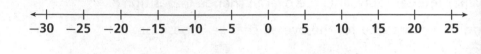

The temperature in the afternoon is _____ °F.

B. Use absolute value to find the distance of the final temperature from 0. Because the first number moves you left on the number line and the second number moves you right, subtract the lesser absolute value from the greater absolute value. How does the result compare to the sum in Part A?

_____

_____

C. On another day, the temperature was 30 °F but a severe ice storm caused a temperature drop of 35 °F. Write an addition expression and use the number line to determine the temperature after the ice storm.

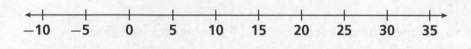

The temperature after the ice storm was _____ °F.

D. Consider the absolute values of the numbers. Use absolute value to find the distance of the final temperature from 0. Because the first number moves you right on the number line and the second number moves you left, subtract the lesser absolute value from the greater absolute value. How does the result compare to the sum in Part C?

_____

_____

E. Complete the rule for adding integers with different signs:

_____ the lesser absolute value from the greater absolute value and use the sign of the addend with the _____ absolute value.

Step It Out

Adding integers with the same signs: Add the absolute values of both numbers and use the sign of the addends.

Adding integers with different signs: Subtract the lesser absolute value from the greater absolute value and use the sign of the addend with the greater absolute value.

 The football team lost 10 yards on one play and gained 7 yards on the next play. What integer represents the overall change in position?

A. Write an addition expression for the overall change in position.

_____

B. Complete the sentence: The addends in Part A have the same / different signs, so the absolute values will be added / subtracted .

C. Subtract the lesser absolute value from the greater absolute value.

_____

D. Complete the sentences: The addend with the greater absolute value is positive / negative so the sign of the solution will be

positive / negative . The overall change in position is _____ yards.

E. Explain why your answer is reasonable.

_____

F. Later, the team lost 5 yards and then lost another 3 yards. Write an addition expression for the overall change in position.

_____

G. Explain how to evaluate the expression in Part F using absolute value. Then find this overall change in position.

_____

_____

_____

Check Understanding

1. The morning temperature is −15 °F. By the afternoon, the temperature rises by 20 °F. Write an addition expression for the afternoon temperature, and then find the temperature in the afternoon.

_____

2. During a game, Dennis lost 50 points in the first round and then lost 75 more points in the second round. Write an addition expression for the change in Dennis's score after two rounds, and then find the change.

_____

On Your Own

3. Belle's dad lends her $10. Then Belle borrows another $15 from him. Write and evaluate an expression that shows the change in the amount of money Belle's dad has.

4. The changes in the elevation of a plane while it was flying are shown below. Write and evaluate an expression that shows the plane's change in elevation compared to its altitude before the first descent.

Descends 1,500 ft

Ascends 900 ft

5. Phillip added 15 pencils to his collection. He then gave 30 pencils to a friend. Write and evaluate an expression that shows Phillip's net gain or loss.

6. The temperature started at −20 °F, then rose by 12 °F. Write and evaluate an expression for the current temperature.

7. **Financial Literacy** A customer withdrew $100 from a bank account. The customer then deposited $33 the next day. Write and evaluate an expression to show the net effect of these transactions.

For Problems 8–13, find each sum.

8. −7 + 10

9. −42 + (−6)

10. −5 + (−2)

11. −21 + (−5)

12. 18 + (−13)

13. −15 + 6

14. **(MP) Reason** Blake's journey through the elevators of his building is shown. Write and evaluate an expression that shows the change in Blake's location compared to his starting point.

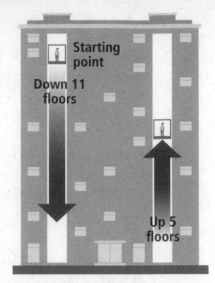

Starting point

Down 11 floors

Up 5 floors

_____

_____

15. Seth earned $76 and spent $42. Write and evaluate an addition expression that shows how much money Seth has left from the amount that he earned.

_____

_____

16. A scuba diver started at sea level and dove 100 feet. The diver then rose 25 feet. Write and evaluate an expression that shows the diver's current elevation relative to sea level.

_____

_____

17. The football team gained 10 yards but then lost 17. Write and evaluate an addition expression showing the team's net yardage.

_____

_____

For Problems 18–23, find each sum.

18. $-14 + 0$

_____

19. $4 + (-50)$

_____

20. $-12 + (-63)$

_____

21. $22 + (-7)$

_____

22. $36 + (-36)$

_____

23. $-28 + 14$

_____

24. **Financial Literacy** A bank account had a balance of $1,100. Then the customer withdrew $450. Write and evaluate an addition expression showing the new account balance.

_____

I'm in a Learning Mindset!

What questions can I ask my teacher or others to help me understand integer addition?

_____

Compute Sums of Integers

ONLINE

**Video Tutorials and
Interactive Examples**

1.  (MP) **Use Structure** Joni climbed 230 feet up a hill and then rappelled down 300 feet into a valley.

   A. Write an addition expression to represent the situation.

   _____

   B. Evaluate the expression to determine how far Joni was from where she started.

   _____

2. The temperature at 8:00 a.m. on a winter day was −2 °F. By noon, the temperature had increased by 28 °F. Should you add or subtract the absolute values to find the temperature at noon? Write and evaluate an absolute value expression to find the temperature at noon.

   _____

3. **Math on the Spot** Andrea's income from a lemonade stand was $28. Supply expenses were $9. Write and evaluate an addition expression to find Andrea's profit or loss.

   _____

   _____

For Problems 4–12, find each sum.

4. $14 + 8$

   _____

5. $20 + (-5)$

   _____

6. $-19 + 2$

   _____

7. $-10 + (-34)$

   _____

8. $46 + (-3)$

   _____

9. $-7 + (-24)$

   _____

10. $100 + (-26)$

    _____

11. $-57 + 90$

    _____

12. $75 + (-30)$

    _____

13. A car factory had an inventory of 327 car radios in stock. Then the company installed the radios in 243 cars and delivered those cars. Write and evaluate an addition expression for the remaining inventory of radios.

    _____

    _____

Test Prep

14. Melissa has $37 and spends $15. Which expression represents this situation?

Ⓐ 37 + 15

Ⓑ −37 + (−15)

Ⓒ −37 + 15

Ⓓ 37 + (−15)

15. A rock climber descends 22 feet into a small canyon. The climber then climbs up 7 feet. Which integer represents his final position relative to where he started?

Ⓐ 29 ft

Ⓑ 15 ft

Ⓒ −15 ft

Ⓓ −29 ft

16. Write and evaluate an expression for the following number line.

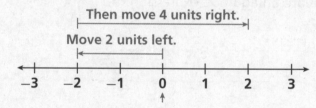

Spiral Review

17. A room is 15 feet long and 12 feet wide. A scale drawing of the room is 10 inches by 8 inches. What is the scale of inches in the drawing to inches in the actual room?

18. During a sale, cameras were discounted 30% from their original price of $295.99. How much was each camera during the sale to the nearest cent?

19. A bank pays 7% interest on 3-year certificates of deposit. What is the value of a $500 certificate after one year? Give your answer to the nearest cent.

Name _____

Compute Differences of Integers

(I Can) identify integer subtraction problems. I feel confident that I can write and evaluate expressions to solve real-world integer subtraction problems.

Spark Your Learning

Evan and Laura are playing a video game. Their scores are shown. By how many points is Laura winning the game? Show your thinking.

Scores	
Evan	−30
Laura	80

 Turn and Talk Write an addition expression that could be used to solve the problem. Does order matter in this problem? Why or why not?

Build Understanding

1 ▶ The temperature in the afternoon was 20 °F, and it went down by 30 °F by the evening.

A. Write a subtraction expression, and use the number line to determine what the temperature was by evening.

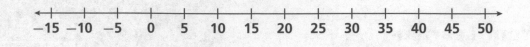

By evening the temperature was _____ °F.

B. What is the sign of the number you subtracted? What direction did

you move on the number line? _____

C. The thermometer shows the temperature on a Monday evening. The following evening it was expected to drop 10 °F. Write a subtraction expression, and use a number line to determine what the expected temperature was on Tuesday evening.

By Tuesday evening the expected temperature was _____ °F.

D. What is the sign of the number you subtracted? What direction did

you move on the number line? _____

E. Look at your number line movement for subtracting a positive number, and complete the equivalent addition expression for each subtraction expression.

$20 - 30 = 20 + \left(\boxed{} \right)$ $-5 - 10 = -5 + \left(\boxed{} \right)$

F. Complete the conjecture: To subtract a positive integer,

_____ its _____.

Turn and Talk Why do subtracting 30 and adding −30 give the same result? Is the same true for every integer? Explain.

2 Jenny borrows $20 from Bill. Jenny is now in debt to Bill. Her debt can be represented as −20 dollars. Bill tells Jenny to ignore $12 of that loan.

A. Write a subtraction expression that describes Jenny's debt as a negative number. Use the number line to determine the amount of money Jenny still owes Bill.

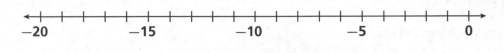

Write Jenny's debt to Bill as a negative number. _____ dollars

B. What is the sign of the number you subtracted? What direction did you

move on the number line? _____

C. Perry has $10. Perry also borrows $3 from Lily, and Lily tells him not to pay her back. This situation can be represented by the expression 10 − (−3). Use the number line to find to find the value of this expression and determine Perry's net amount of money.

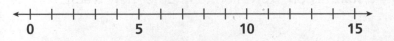

Perry's net amount of money is _____ dollars.

D. What is the sign of the number you subtracted? What direction did you

move on the number line? _____

E. Look at your number line movement for subtracting a negative number, and complete the equivalent addition expression for each subtraction expression.

$$-20 - (-12) = -20 + \boxed{} \qquad 10 - (-3) = 10 + \boxed{}$$

F. Complete the conjecture: To subtract a negative integer,

_____ its _____.

Turn and Talk In Part E, explain how the movements on the number line show that the expressions are equivalent.

Step It Out

To subtract an integer, add its opposite.

3 ▷ Complete the equivalent addition expression for each subtraction expression. Then evaluate.

A. $6 - 6 = 6 + \boxed{}$; $\boxed{}$

B. $5 - (-4) = 5 + \boxed{}$; $\boxed{}$

C. $-8 - 7 = -8 + \boxed{}$; $\boxed{}$

D. $-4 - (-9) = -4 + \boxed{}$; $\boxed{}$

E. Complete each statement.

After rewriting subtraction as addition, a statement that adds two negative numbers results in a _____ number.

After rewriting subtraction as addition, a statement that adds two positive numbers results in a _____ number.

After rewriting subtraction as addition, a statement that adds opposites results in _____ .

Check Understanding

1. Elise had a credit card balance of –$120. She made a payment of $70 this month. Write and evaluate a subtraction expression to find her new credit card balance.

_____

_____

2. The temperature on a Monday evening was 8 °F. Tuesday evening it was expected to drop 12 °F. Write and evaluate a subtraction expression to find the expected temperature on Tuesday evening.

_____

3. Complete the equivalent addition expression for each subtraction expression. Then evaluate.

A. $23 - 4 = 23 + \boxed{}$; $\boxed{}$

B. $7 - (-15) = 7 + \boxed{}$; $\boxed{}$

C. $-15 - 4 = -15 + \boxed{}$; $\boxed{}$

4. How do you subtract an integer from another integer without using a number line? Give an example.

_____

_____

On Your Own

5. The temperature is 2 °F and drops to −15 °F overnight. Write and evaluate a subtraction expression to determine the change in temperature.

_____

6. A submarine descended 500 feet below sea level. It then descended another 275 feet. Write and evaluate a subtraction expression to determine the new position of the submarine relative to sea level.

_____

7. Eddy has $45. He needs a new bike tire that costs $70. Write and evaluate a subtraction expression to determine how much more Eddie needs in order to get the bike tire.

_____

8. (MP) **Reason** An oil rig drill digs at a constant rate each day. The progress on Monday and Tuesday is shown. Write and evaluate a subtraction expression to determine the total change in depth of the dig by the end of Tuesday. Explain why your answer is reasonable.

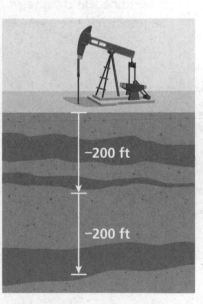

−200 ft

−200 ft

_____

_____

_____

For Problems 9–14, write each subtraction expression as an equivalent addition expression and evaluate it.

9. −12 − (−10)   **10.** 25 − 67

_____   _____

11. 0 − (−13)   **12.** −2 − (−10)

_____   _____

13. −15 − 12   **14.** 22 − 37

_____   _____

15. (MP) **Reason** Cheyenne is playing a board game. Her score was −175 at the start of her turn, and at the end of her turn her score was −325. What was the change in Cheyenne's score from the start of her turn to the end of her turn? How did you determine your answer?

_____

_____

_____

16. The West High football team gained 7 yards but then lost 15 yards. Write and evaluate a subtraction expression to determine the overall change in yardage.

_____

17. Financial Literacy Amy had a $10 monthly fee for music streaming due when she received her paycheck. After paying for the music streaming service, she had $65 remaining from her paycheck. Write and evaluate a subtraction expression to determine the original value of Amy's paycheck.

_____

18. At the beginning of the game, April had a score of −150 points. April played for another 20 minutes, and her final score was −355. Write and evaluate a subtraction expression to determine the change of her score from the beginning of the game to the end of the game.

_____

_____

For Problems 19–26, write each subtraction expression as an equivalent addition expression and evaluate it.

19. 41 − 41

_____

20. 36 − 48

_____

21. −13 − (−10)

_____

22. −9 − (−13)

_____

23. 21 − 6

_____

24. −33 − 7

_____

25. 0 − (−5)

_____

26. −19 − (−19)

_____

I'm in a Learning Mindset!

How effective was the number line for subtraction problems with integers?

_____

_____

Compute Differences of Integers

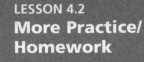
1. Sadie won her golf game with Brynn. What is the difference in their scores?

   A. Write a subtraction expression to represent the situation.

   _____

   B. What is the difference in the girls' scores?

   _____

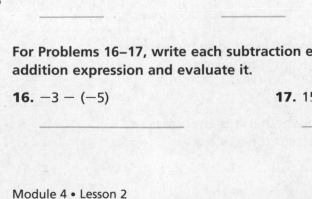

TOURNAMENT
GOLF
CHAMPIONSHIP

Sadie: −2   Brynn: 4

2. Wednesday morning, the temperature was −12 °F. By the afternoon, the temperature was 23 °F. Write and evaluate a subtraction expression to determine the number of degrees of change in temperature between the morning and the afternoon.

   _____

3. **Open Ended** Write a word problem that includes subtracting a negative number from a positive number.

   _____

   _____

Math on the Spot For Problems 4–6, find each difference.

4. $10 - 14$

5. $-7 - (-5)$

6. $-8 - 2$

_____   _____   _____

For Problems 7–15, find each difference.

7. $-14 - 5$

8. $23 - (-7)$

9. $-100 - 8$

_____   _____   _____

10. $24 - 57$

11. $65 - 65$

12. $-23 - (-5)$

_____   _____   _____

13. $-5 - (-11)$

14. $-16 - 9$

15. $24 - (-37)$

_____   _____   _____

For Problems 16–17, write each subtraction expression as an equivalent addition expression and evaluate it.

16. $-3 - (-5)$

17. $15 - 21$

_____   _____

Test Prep

18. Maya's bank account had $55. She wrote a check for $42. Which expression represents the situation?

(A) $55 + 42$

(B) $-42 - 55$

(C) $55 - 42$

(D) $42 - 55$

19. George had a score of 25 points in a game. During the rest of the game, he lost 59 points. What score did George have at the end?

(A) 34

(B) -34

(C) 84

(D) -84

20. The highest elevation in California is 14,505 feet, and the lowest elevation is -282 feet. Write and evaluate an expression to determine the distance between the lowest and highest elevations.

_____

21. Evaluate $-13 - (-17)$.

(A) -30

(B) -4

(C) 4

(D) 30

22. Evaluate $23 - (-9)$.

_____

Spiral Review

23. Kelsey jogs 60 feet in 6 seconds. What is this rate in miles per hour? Round to the nearest tenth.

_____

24. Find the percent change from 75 to 24. State whether it is an increase or decrease. Round to the nearest tenth of a percent if necessary.

_____

25. Find the percent change from 26 to 34. State whether it is an increase or decrease. Round to the nearest tenth of a percent if necessary.

_____

Name _____

Compute Sums and Differences of Rational Numbers

(I Can) identify and write expressions to represent rational number problems.

Spark Your Learning

SMALL GROUPS

Ryan wants to go camping. The list of all the locations he would like to visit is shown in the table with their corresponding elevations. What is the greatest difference between any two of the elevations? Explain.

Location	Elevation
Rocky Peak	$1\frac{2}{3}$ miles
Skyscraper	$4\frac{3}{4}$ miles
Daisy Valley	1.34 miles
Banjo Falls	$3\frac{3}{8}$ miles
Bluebird Creek	$-\frac{1}{10}$ miles
The Precipice	$4\frac{2}{5}$ miles
Butterfly Basin	$-\frac{1}{5}$ mile

Turn and Talk Does it matter which way you subtract the values when finding distance? Why or why not?

Build Understanding

1 A scuba diver jumps in the water and continues to descend until reaching −10.75 feet. How far did the diver descend?

The diver is 4.5 ft above the water's surface.

A. Use the number line to find the distance the diver traveled. Explain how you got your answer.

<----|||||||||||||||||||||||||||||||||||||||||||||||||||||||||||||||||||---->
−13 −12 −11 −10 −9 −8 −7 −6 −5 −4 −3 −2 −1　0　1　2　3　4　5　6　7

_____

_____

_____

_____

_____

B. Write and evaluate a subtraction expression to find the distance the diver traveled starting from the diver's elevation of 4.5 feet above sea level.

_____

C. Find the difference between the diver's ending point and starting point.

_____

D. How are your answers to Parts B and C alike, and how are they different? Are they equal or opposites?

_____

_____

E. Distance is always expressed as a positive number because it does not indicate direction. How can you use symbols to make sure that your result is always positive?

_____

_____

 Turn and Talk Do you think the Commutative Property is true for subtraction? Why or why not?

2 ▸ Evaluate $-2.5 + 5 - \left(-4\frac{1}{4}\right)$.

A. Complete the number line to evaluate the expression.

$$\overset{\longleftarrow -2.5}{\rule{2.5cm}{0pt}}$$

−10 −9 −8 −7 −6 −5 −4 −3 −2 −1 0 1 2 3 4 5 6 7 8 9 10

The answer is _____.

B. Complete the rule to add the first two numbers of the expression.

_____ the absolute values and take the sign of the one with the

_____ absolute value.

C. Explain how the number line supports the rule used in Part B.

_____

_____

_____

D. Write the rule to subtract $\left(-4\frac{1}{4}\right)$ from your answer to Part B. Show the work to use the rule to find the answer.

_____

_____

_____

E. Explain how the number line supports the rule used in Part D.

_____

_____

_____

F. In previous lessons, the rules were used with integers. Now they are being used with **mixed numbers** and decimals. Explain how the rules for adding and subtracting integers apply to rational numbers.

_____

_____

_____

Turn and Talk Describe a context that could be modeled by the expression in Task 2.

Step It Out

3 A scientist is studying the effect temperature has on a specific bacteria. The table shows some of the data collected from the study.

	Temperature (°C)	Bacteria
Monday	-9	6,000
Tuesday		3,500
Wednesday		6,125
Thursday		11,650
Friday		9,250

A. The scientist reduces the temperature by 3.5 °C on Tuesday. What is the new temperature? Show your work.

_____

B. On Wednesday, the temperature is increased by 20.7 °C. What is the new temperature? Show your work.

_____

C. Explain why your answer in Part B is reasonable.

_____

_____

_____

_____

D. On Thursday, the scientist increases the temperature by an additional 15.4 °C. What is the new temperature? Show your work.

_____

E. On the final day of the study, the temperature is decreased by $5\frac{1}{2}$ °C. What is the new temperature? Show your work.

_____

> **Turn and Talk** How would you explain to a friend why subtracting a negative number is the same as adding a positive number?

Check Understanding

1. An architect plans a courtyard with a width of 16.4 yards, then learns its width must change by −2.3 yards. What is the new width?

_____

2. Evaluate $-7\frac{1}{3} - \left(-\frac{2}{5}\right)$.

_____

On Your Own

3. **(MP) Reason** Ingvar is playing a video game that takes away points for losing treasures. His current score is shown, and then he loses a treasure worth 27.7 points.

Ingvar's current score is −56.2.

   A. Write and evaluate a subtraction expression to find Ingvar's current score.

   _____

   B. Is your answer reasonable? Why?

   _____

   _____

   _____

4. In the stock market, changes in value used to be indicated by fractions, which represented portions of $1. If a stock had a value of $11.50, write and evaluate an addition expression to find how much the stock is worth after an increase of $\frac{1}{4}$.

   _____

5. Jayvon has 33.6 points in a competition. He loses 5.5 points. Write and evaluate an addition expression to determine Jayvon's current points.

   _____

6. Malik earns an average of $4\frac{1}{2}$ points on his daily quizzes. Near the end of the quarter, his average decreases by $\frac{3}{4}$ point. Write and evaluate a subtraction expression to find his current quiz grade average.

   _____

7. **Financial Literacy** Miss Aliyah's checking account balance is $15.50. She withdraws $5.37. Write and evaluate a subtraction expression to find the new balance.

   _____

For Problems 8–11, evaluate the expression.

8. $\frac{5}{8} + \frac{1}{4}$

9. $18.7 - 12.3$

10. $-1\frac{1}{2} - \left(-\frac{1}{8}\right)$

11. $-5.75 + (-3.28)$

12. (MP) **Reason** The picture shows the approximate temperatures at which most seawater boils and freezes. How many degrees are there between the boiling point and freezing point?

A. Will your answer be positive or negative? Explain.

_____

_____

_____

_____

B. Write and evaluate an expression to solve the problem. Write an expression to represent the problem. Use absolute value if appropriate based on Part A. Then solve the problem.

_____

13. Brock rides a bike $22\frac{1}{8}$ miles to the nature preserve. On his way home, after $16\frac{1}{5}$ miles, he stops for lunch. How far is Brock from home? Write and evaluate an addition expression to solve the problem. Show your work.

_____

_____

120 °C

100 °C   100.7 °C   Seawater boils

80 °C

60 °C

40 °C

20 °C

0 °C   −2 °C

−20 °C   Seawater freezes

For Problems 14–19, evaluate the expression.

14. $\frac{3}{8} + \left(-\frac{1}{2}\right)$

15. $16.34 - (-7.67)$

_____

16. $-9.36 + 4.48$

17. $-2\frac{1}{2} - \frac{3}{4}$

_____

18. $\frac{5}{6} - \frac{1}{4}$

19. $13.97 + 8.16$

_____

I'm in a Learning Mindset!

How can I help others use a number line to depict subtraction?

_____

_____

LESSON 4.3
**More Practice/
Homework**

ONLINE
 **Video Tutorials and
Interactive Examples**

Compute Sums and Differences of Rational Numbers

1. Mr. Leander bought two shirts for a total of $46.72. He returned one of the shirts for a refund of $24.61. Write and evaluate an addition expression to show what Mr. Leander paid for the shirt he kept.

   _____

2. **STEM** Scientists are studying the effects of increased temperature, which causes bleaching on coral reefs. A scientist dives at two different reefs, one located $34\frac{1}{2}$ feet below sea level and one at $26\frac{1}{4}$ feet below sea level. Write and evaluate a subtraction expression to find the change in elevation needed in order for the diver to reach the deeper reef. Explain why you have chosen a positive or negative sign for your answer.

   _____

   _____

   _____

Coral reef that has been affected by bleaching

3. Savana walks $3\frac{1}{3}$ miles to the local park. On her way home, she stops at Randolph's house after $1\frac{2}{3}$ miles to pick up a book. Write and evaluate a subtraction expression to find how much farther Savana must walk to get home.

   _____

Coral reef that has not been affected by bleaching

4. Joseph removes $\frac{5}{8}$ gallon of white paint from a can. Then he adds $\frac{5}{8}$ gallon of blue paint to the can. Write and evaluate an addition expression to find the overall increase or decrease in the amount of paint in the can.

   _____

For Problems 5–8, evaluate the expression.

5. $\frac{1}{4} - \left(-\frac{1}{6}\right)$

6. $-233.2 - 25.8$

7. $-4\frac{1}{2} + 2\frac{3}{4}$

8. $27.81 + (-13.97)$

Test Prep

9. Marianna had an average of 84.6 in social studies before her final exam. After the final exam, her average changed to 82.9.

   A. Show how Marianna's average changed in social studies.

   _____

   _____

   B. Explain how you found your answer to Part A.

   _____

   _____

10. A rock climber ascends $18\frac{3}{4}$ feet to the top of a rock ledge. The climber descends $8\frac{1}{8}$ feet and takes a break on a rock outcrop. Write and evaluate an addition expression to show how much farther the rock climber must descend to reach the original level.

    _____

11. The total bill for a group's restaurant order is $56.27. One meal was not prepared properly and came to the table late, so the manager credited the bill $18.46. What was the resulting bill for the group's dinner?

    _____

12. Keith buys 3 yards of material to make a blanket. He trims off a total of $\frac{1}{6}$ yard before he begins sewing. How much material remains for the blanket?

    Ⓐ $\frac{1}{18}$ yard

    Ⓑ $\frac{2}{6}$ yard

    Ⓒ $2\frac{5}{6}$ yards

    Ⓓ $3\frac{1}{6}$ yards

Spiral Review

13. Gabe earns $10 per hour working for a landscaping business. He earned a raise to $10.75 per hour. What is the percent increase of Gabe's wages? If necessary, round your answer to the nearest tenth of a percent.

    _____

14. The temperature at 5 p.m. was −4 °F. The temperature rose 7 °F once the sun came up at 8 a.m. the next morning. What was the temperature at 8 a.m. that morning?

    _____

Name _____

Apply Properties to Multi-step Addition and Subtraction Problems

(I Can) identify and write expressions to represent multi-step addition and subtraction problems.

Step It Out

1 Andy usually skates for about 6 hours per week. On Monday, he spent $1\frac{1}{5}$ hours skating; on Wednesday, he spent $2\frac{3}{5}$ hours skating; and on Thursday, he spent $1\frac{5}{6}$ hours skating. Andy wrote the following expression to find the number of hours he spent skating. He grouped Wednesday and Thursday together at first because those were his best days, without thinking too much about what would be easiest to add.

$$1\frac{1}{5} + \left(2\frac{3}{5} + 1\frac{5}{6}\right)$$

A. Rewrite the expression to make it simpler to add.

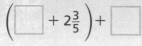
$$\left(\boxed{} + 2\frac{3}{5}\right) + \boxed{}$$

B. What property is demonstrated by rewriting the expression?

_____

C. Regrouping makes the problem simpler because it associates

two numbers with _____ .

D. To add the numbers in parentheses,

Add the whole numbers: $1 + \boxed{} = \boxed{}$

Add the like fractions: $\frac{1}{5} + \boxed{} = \boxed{}$

Combine the results: _____

E. Use your result from Part D to finish evaluating the expression.

$$3\frac{4}{5} + \boxed{} = \frac{\boxed{}}{5} + \frac{11}{6} = \frac{114}{\boxed{}} + \frac{55}{\boxed{}} = \frac{\boxed{}}{30} = \boxed{}$$

Turn and Talk Is there another way to solve this problem? Explain.

Rochelle dives into a lake from the water's surface. Her change in elevation in the lake is described. She:

- descends 15.5 feet and takes some pictures of fish;
- ascends $8\frac{1}{5}$ feet to explore another area;
- descends 1.6 feet to capture video while following a fish;
- descends 20.4 feet to find some feeding bass; and finally,
- ascends 15.5 feet to take more pictures.

How many feet does Rochelle have left to ascend before reaching the surface?

A. Write an addition expression to represent Rochelle's change in elevation from the water's surface.

_____

B. Rewrite the expression to make it simpler to find the sum by first adding opposites.

_____

C. What properties of operations did you use to rewrite your expression in Part B?

_____

_____

D. Add the opposites in your expression in Part B, and write the resulting expression.

_____

E. Evaluate your expression in Part D to determine Rochelle's elevation relative to the water's surface.

Identify the property used in the second line.

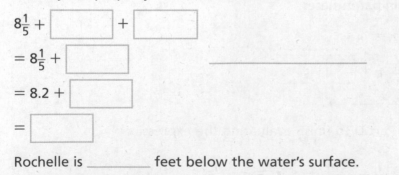

$8\frac{1}{5} + \boxed{} + \boxed{}$

$= 8\frac{1}{5} + \boxed{}$ _____

$= 8.2 + \boxed{}$

$= \boxed{}$

Rochelle is _____ feet below the water's surface.

Turn and Talk How are the properties of addition used to evaluate the expression in Task 2?

3 ▶ Terry is hiking in a valley at its lowest elevation. Abe is hiking on a different trail at an elevation of 23.5 meters above sea level. How much higher in elevation is Abe than Terry?

The lowest elevation of the trail is $19\frac{3}{4}$ meters below sea level.

A. How should elevation below sea level be written?

_____

B. Since one number is a decimal and one contains a fraction, you must either convert the decimal to a _____ or the fraction to a _____ before evaluating.

C. Complete the expression to show the difference between their elevations. Then evaluate the expression to solve the problem.

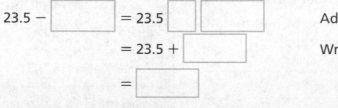

$23.5 - \boxed{} = 23.5 \,\boxed{}\,\boxed{}$ Add the opposite.

$= 23.5 + \boxed{}$ Write as a decimal.

$= \boxed{}$

Abe is _____ meters higher in elevation than Terry.

D. Is your answer reasonable? Explain.

_____

_____

_____

Turn and Talk If Abe's elevation was −23.5 meters instead of +23.5 meters, what would Terry and Abe's elevation difference be then? Explain.

Check Understanding

1. Soojin is adding some lengths of wood she used for a project. The lengths of wood are $1\frac{2}{3}$, $3\frac{3}{4}$, and $2\frac{1}{4}$ feet. How much wood did she use in all?

_____

2. Alfonzo started with $50.00 in his checking account. He recorded these transactions in his checkbook: −$12.75, −$5.43, $75.00, −$2.57, and −$22.25. How can you use the Commutative and Associative Properties of Addition to find his balance using mental math?

_____

_____

_____

On Your Own

3. **(MP) Use Structure** Dena cuts wood for a treehouse. She has five pieces of wood left over with the following lengths in centimeters: 12.7, $26\frac{3}{10}$, $15\frac{4}{5}$, $21\frac{1}{4}$, and 19.2.

   A. Write and evaluate an expression to find the total length of wood left over.

   _____

   B. Dena wants to make a birdhouse with the leftover wood. She needs $105\frac{3}{5}$ centimeters of wood for the birdhouse. Write and evaluate an expression to determine how much more wood will be needed.

   _____

4. **(MP) Use Repeated Reasoning** The table shows the highest and lowest elevations in four states.

   A. Write and evaluate an expression to find the difference in elevation in each state.

   _____

   _____

   _____

State	Highest elevation (ft)	Lowest elevation (ft)
Louisiana (LA)	535	−8
California (CA)	14,505	−282
Indiana (IN)	1,257	320
Florida (FL)	345	0

   B. Roger says the difference between the lowest elevation in California and the lowest elevation in Louisiana is −290 feet. Determine if his answer is reasonable. Explain.

   _____

   _____

5. The high temperatures (in °F) for a 4-day holiday weekend were:
   −2.6, 16.7, −3.4, 6.1
   Use properties of addition to help you find the sum. Then find the average high temperature over the four days.

   _____

   _____

For Problems 6–11, evaluate each expression.

6. $2.6 + (-3.7 - (-1.5))$

7. $-15 - 2\frac{3}{4} - 1.7 - \left(-2\frac{2}{5}\right)$

8. $-1\frac{1}{5} + 2.9 - \left(-3\frac{3}{8}\right)$

9. $2\frac{3}{4} + (-8.34) + \left(-7\frac{3}{10}\right)$

10. $-11.5 + 15\frac{2}{5} - 10.1$

11. $5\frac{1}{4} - (-3.55) + \left(-3\frac{2}{5}\right)$

12. (MP) **Use Repeated Reasoning** Ella dives three times into a lake. Her elevations relative to the water's surface are −6.9 feet, −8$\frac{2}{5}$ feet, and −7.5 feet. She dives three more times with each dive 0.75 feet deeper than each of the first three. Write and evaluate expressions to determine the elevations, in decimal form, of her fourth, fifth, and sixth dives.

13. Financial Literacy Chris wrote the following checks: $19.50, $25.75, $5.50, and $136.95. He began with $252.17 in his checking account. Write and evaluate an expression to determine his balance.

14. (MP) **Reason** Beylinn is driving on a road with an elevation of −245$\frac{5}{8}$ meters. Jay is driving on a different road at an elevation of −56.45 meters. Write and evaluate an expression to determine who is traveling at a higher elevation. How much higher? Explain.

15. Dino is learning to scuba dive. First, he descended 27.75 feet. After ten minutes, he descended another 9.45 feet. Write and evaluate an expression to determine his elevation relative to sea level.

16. Explain why you might want to use properties to change the order and grouping of the numbers in the following sum.
$-45.2 + (-7.9) + (-3.8)$

For Problems 17–24, evaluate each expression.

17. $-12\frac{2}{5} + 8\frac{9}{10}$

18. $45.16 - 72.5 + (-63.72) + 50$

19. $-27 - 6.5 + (-1.3) + 28\frac{7}{10}$

20. $-18 + 3.4 + (-2.5)$

21. $-\frac{5}{6} + 1\frac{1}{3} - 3.3$

22. $-\frac{2}{5} - 4\frac{1}{10} + (-10.53)$

23. $-2\frac{3}{5} - 3\frac{1}{2} + 1\frac{7}{10} + \left(-3\frac{3}{10}\right)$

24. $-15.35 + 83.5 + (-16.98) + 1.8$

25. Kasey had $98.17 in her account. Her receipts from the day are shown. Write and evaluate an expression to determine the balance in her account.

_____

26. Lupita rewrote an expression as follows.

$-5.5 + 10.63 + (-3.7) = -5.5 + (-3.7) + 10.63$

Did she use the Commutative or the Associative Property? What is the sum?

_____

Food Truck
taco meal #4   8.05
        tax   0.64
             $8.69

Abar Transportation
14.2 miles   10.65
      tax   0.85
            $11.50

Fun Stop
video game   11.31
        tax   0.90
             $12.21

27. (MP) **Construct Arguments** Terrance adds the lengths of fabric that he has left from a project. The lengths of fabric, in inches, are $15\frac{1}{6}$, $11\frac{1}{3}$, and $17\frac{1}{2}$. Terrance began with 100 inches. Write and evaluate an expression to determine how much fabric he used in all. How did you solve this problem?

_____

_____

_____

_____

28. Overnight, the temperature increased by $3\frac{1}{2}$ °F. The temperature began at -7.9 °F. Write and evaluate an expression to determine the current temperature.

_____

For Problems 29–36, evaluate each expression.

29. $(-5.8 + 9.1) - \left(-2\frac{1}{4}\right)$

30. $\left(15\frac{1}{2} + 2.6\right) - 18\frac{3}{5}$

31. $10.2 - (-2.14 - 4.9)$

32. $-13\frac{3}{4} + 5\frac{1}{3}$

33. $-5.5 - (12.36 - 8.3)$

34. $(-4.25 - 8.7) + \left(-1\frac{1}{2}\right) - 2.5$

35. $1\frac{9}{10} + \left(-4\frac{3}{4}\right) + (-7.93)$

36. $-5\frac{2}{5} - 3.16 - \left(-1\frac{1}{8}\right)$

37. Open Ended Write a word problem that includes using properties to add or subtract positive and negative numbers.

_____

_____

Name _____

LESSON 4.4
**More Practice/
Homework**

ONLINE

Video Tutorials and
Interactive Examples

Apply Properties to Multi-step Addition and Subtraction Problems

1. Brian is adding the lengths of wood posts that he has left from building a pen for his chickens. The lengths are $3\frac{2}{3}$, $2\frac{1}{4}$, and $2\frac{1}{3}$ feet. Brian began with 20 feet of wood. Write and evaluate an expression to determine how much wood he used for the pen.

_____

_____

2. At dinner time, the temperature outside was −13.9 °F. The temperature decreased by 12.8 °F overnight. Write and evaluate an expression to determine the temperature in the morning.

_____

3. Evaluate the expression. Identify the property used in each step.

$\frac{3}{4} + \left(-\frac{3}{8}\right) + \left(-\frac{1}{4}\right) = -\frac{3}{8} + \frac{3}{4} + \left(-\frac{1}{4}\right)$ _____

$= -\frac{3}{8} + \left[\frac{3}{4} + \left(-\frac{1}{4}\right)\right]$ _____

$= \boxed{}$

4. **Open Ended** Write a real-world problem that can be modeled by the equation $47\frac{1}{2} + \left(-47\frac{1}{2}\right) = 0$.

_____

For Problems 5–14, evaluate each expression.

5. $-12\frac{1}{2} - (-4.8)$

6. $-\frac{9}{10} + (-18.6)$

7. $89.2 + (-104.25) + (-17.9)$

8. $9\frac{9}{10} + 9\frac{1}{8} - 12.85$

9. $(-1.9 + (-2.5)) + 8.3$

10. $-10\frac{1}{2} - 19\frac{3}{4} - 15.2$

11. $(-2.8 + 4.98) + (-3.87)$

12. $-2\frac{2}{5} + \left(-7\frac{3}{10}\right) + 4.3$

13. $(-5.8 + 9.1) + \left(-2\frac{1}{4}\right)$

14. $12\frac{3}{4} - 6\frac{1}{10} - (-8.4)$

Test Prep

15. While Jackie was in Hawaii, she would dive for shells. One afternoon she dove 7.8 feet. Her next two dives were each $2\frac{1}{8}$ feet deeper than the dive before it. What were the elevations relative to sea level of her second and third dives?

_____

_____

16. On Friday, Ms. Patel told her reading group that if they read a combined total of 20 hours or more over the weekend, she would let them have a free period on Monday. The numbers of hours the students spent reading are in the table below. Do the students get a free period on Monday? Explain.

Hours Read Over the Weekend				
2	$1\frac{1}{6}$	4.125	0.75	$3\frac{1}{2}$
1.75	$\frac{5}{8}$	$2\frac{1}{2}$	$1\frac{5}{6}$	$2\frac{3}{8}$

_____

_____

17. This morning, the temperature was $13\frac{1}{2}$ °F. During the day, the temperature increased by 5.6 °F. At night, the temperature decreased by 23.8 °F. What was the temperature after it decreased?

(A) 19.1 °F

(B) 4.7 °F

(C) −4.7 °F

(D) −18.2 °F

18. Evaluate the expression: $-7\frac{7}{8} + 3.7 - (-15.9)$.

_____

Spiral Review

19. Overnight, the temperature decreased by $17\frac{1}{2}$ °F. If the temperature began at −3.6 °F, what is the current temperature?

_____

20. Pauline gets a 2% commission on her sales at her job. She sells $23,500 worth of products in May. How much commission does Pauline earn in May?

_____

Review

Vocabulary

For problems 1–3, choose the correct term from the box.

Vocabulary

absolute value

opposite

1. The number −4 is the _____ of 4.

2. The _____ of a number always represents the distance of that number from zero on a number line.

3. When subtracting two numbers, you add the _____ of the number being subtracted.

4. Which of the following statements is true?

   (A) The sum of two numbers is always positive.

   (B) The difference of two numbers is always negative.

   (C) The absolute value of a number is never negative.

   (D) The opposite of a number is always negative.

Concepts and Skills

5. (MP) **Use Tools** Is the value of $5 - (-4) - 3$ positive or negative? State what strategy and tool you will use to answer the question, explain your choice, and then find the answer.

   _____

   _____

6. The value of which expression is negative?

   (A) $1 + 2 - (-12)$

   (B) $2 + 5 - 17$

   (C) $4 - 5 - (-2)$

   (D) $7 - 6 - (-5)$

7. The temperature at 7:00 a.m. was 12 °C, and by 7:00 p.m. it had dropped to −10 °C. Which expression represents the change in temperature?

   (A) $12 + (-10)$

   (B) $12 - 10$

   (C) $-10 + 12$

   (D) $-10 - 12$

8. The temperature at 4:00 p.m. was −6 °C, and then it fell by 7 °C. Which expression represents the new temperature?

   (A) $-6 - 7$

   (B) $-7 - (-6)$

   (C) $6 - (-7)$

   (D) $-6 + 7$

For Problems 9–25, find the value of each expression.

9. $10 + (-6)$

10. $-3 + (-3)$

11. $-8 + 2$

12. $-1 + (-7)$

13. $7 - (-9)$

14. $-3 - 2$

15. $12 - (-9)$

16. $12 - 18$

17. $3 - 8\frac{2}{3}$

18. $-2.7 - 1.8$

19. $5\frac{1}{5} - \left(-2\frac{4}{15}\right)$

20. $46.33 - (-15.07)$

21. $-7\frac{3}{4} + 2\frac{1}{8}$

22. $-13\frac{4}{7} - \left(-6\frac{10}{21}\right) + \frac{1}{3}$

23. $15.47 - (-17.09) + 3.7$

24. $3\frac{1}{2} - 5.3 + \left(-5\frac{1}{10}\right)$

25. $-8.45 - 3\frac{1}{10} + 6.73$

26. Which is greater: $-999 + 1$ or $-999 + (-1)$? Explain.

_____

_____

_____

27. Samantha owes $25.50, and borrows another $20.00. She pays back $15.25 of her debt and then earns $45.00. Later, Samantha pays back $22.50 of her debt. How much does she still have to pay back? Show your work.

_____

_____

_____

Multiply and Divide Rational Numbers

The Price Is Not Right

A supermarket sells four different brands of granola. All of the brands are similar in quality, but one brand is much less popular with customers than the other three brands.

Find the cost per ounce.

A. Grandpa's Granola
16.4-oz bag — Now just $4.10

B. Healthy Day GRANOLA
8.25-oz box — On sale for $1.98!

C. CRUNCHO GRANOLA
8.4-oz bag — This week only $3.78

D. SUPER TASTE GRANOLA
13-oz box — New price: $3.38

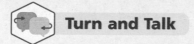 **Turn and Talk**

Based on the prices, which brand of granola do you think is the least popular? Explain.

Are You Ready?

Complete these problems to review prior concepts and skills you will need for this module.

Multiply with Decimals

Find each product.

1. 3.4×0.8 _____

2. 1.68×2.5 _____

3. 0.45×0.08 _____

4. Apples cost $1.47 per pound. Danielle buys an apple that weighs 0.62 pound. To the nearest cent, how much does Danielle's apple cost?

_____

Division Involving Decimals

Find each quotient.

5. $1.38 \div 0.3$ _____

6. $76.56 \div 2.4$ _____

7. $0.287 \div 0.35$ _____

8. A bicycle track forms a loop with a length of 3.2 miles. Trashcans are placed along the track every 0.2 mile. How many trashcans are placed along the track?

_____

Divide Fractions and Mixed Numbers

Find each quotient.

9. $3 \div \frac{1}{5}$ _____

10. $\frac{7}{8} \div \frac{1}{2}$ _____

11. $3\frac{2}{3} \div \frac{3}{5}$ _____

12. One serving of rice is equal to $\frac{3}{4}$ cup. Gerardo makes 4 cups of rice. How many servings of rice did Gerardo make?

_____

Name

Understand Multiplication and Division of Rational Numbers

(**I Can**) evaluate expressions and solve real-world problems involving rational number multiplication and division.

Spark Your Learning

Arnot wins a $50 gift card for a virtual reality arcade. If he does not use the card for a whole year, the balance on the card will be reduced by $5 each month that it continues to go unused. What will be the change in the value of the card if Arnot doesn't use it for 18 months?

Turn and Talk Did you use the same method? If not, explain your reasoning to make sure both methods are correct.

Build Understanding

1 ▶ Jordan is scuba diving and stops each time she descends 15 feet to take a photo. Starting at the surface, she does this 4 times until she reaches her final depth. What is her overall change in elevation?

A. What number represents each change in elevation?

_____

B. Use the number line to model Jordan's entire descent.

C. Write an addition expression to represent your model.

_____

D. Write a multiplication expression to represent your model.

The number line shows arrows moving ⬜ units ⬜ times. That

means the multiplication expression would be ⬜(⬜).

E. How should the value of the addition expression in Step C compare to the value of the multiplication expression in Step D? Explain your reasoning.

_____

F. Make a conjecture about the result of multiplying a negative number by a positive number. Explain your reasoning.

_____

_____

G. Use your conjecture in Step F to complete the last column in the table indicating the sign of the product pq.

H. Complete the rule for multiplication of rational numbers with different signs.

The product of two rational numbers with

different signs is a _____ number.

Products of Rational Numbers		
Sign of factor p	Sign of factor q	Sign of product pq
+	−	
−	+	

I. What is Jordan's overall change in elevation? _____

Turn and Talk Steps A–E support the first rule in the Products of Rational Numbers table. Which mathematical property supports the second rule? Explain your reasoning.

0
−10
−20
−30
−40
−50
−60
−70
−80
−90
−100

2 ▶ In order for operations like multiplication to work with negative numbers the same way they work with positive numbers, the operations have to satisfy the properties of operations.

A. Use the rule you wrote in the first task to complete the following.

$$3(6 + (-4)) = 3(6) + 3\left(\boxed{}\right)$$

$$3(2) = 18 + \left(\boxed{}\right)$$

$$6 = \boxed{}$$

B. What property is being applied in the first equation in Step A? Does applying the rule for multiplying numbers with different signs give the correct result? Why or why not?

_____

_____

C. Complete the following to make the statements true. Explain how you figured out the answer.

$$-3(6 + (-4)) = (-3)(6) + (-3)(-4)$$

$$-3(2) = -18 + \boxed{}$$

$$-6 = -6$$

This means that $-3(-4) = \boxed{}$.

_____

_____

D. Complete the table.

Products of Rational Numbers		
Sign of factor p	**Sign of factor q**	**Sign of product pq**
+	+	
−	−	

E. Write a rule for multiplication of rational numbers with the same sign. The product of two rational numbers with the same sign is

a _____ number.

 Turn and Talk Write another example like the example in Step C to show why the product $(-5)(-4)$ must be equal to 20.

3 You can use what you know about multiplying signed numbers to figure out the rules for dividing signed numbers. In multiplication, if one factor is 0, the product will be 0. In division, the divisor cannot be 0. Division by 0 is undefined.

A. Use the fact that division and multiplication are **inverse operations** to complete the number statements in the table.

Multiplication	Related division
$2 \cdot 4 = 8$	$8 \div \boxed{} = 4$ and $8 \div 4 = \boxed{}$
$-2 \cdot 4 = -8$	$-8 \div \boxed{} = 4$ and $-8 \div 4 = \boxed{}$
$2 \cdot (-4) = -8$	$-8 \div \boxed{} = -4$ and $-8 \div (-4) = \boxed{}$
$-2 \cdot (-4) = 8$	$8 \div \boxed{} = -4$ and $8 \div \boxed{} = -2$

B. Use your results from Step A to complete the table.

C. Complete the rules for division of rational numbers.

- The quotient of of two rational numbers with different signs is a _____ number.

- The quotient of of two rational numbers with the same sign is a _____ number.

Quotients of Rational Numbers		
Sign of dividend p	Sign of divisor q	Sign of quotient $\frac{p}{q}$
+	−	
−	+	
+	+	
−	−	

Check Understanding

1. Kaleb's football team lost 2 yards on each of 3 consecutive plays. Complete the statement to represent the change in position relative to the line of scrimmage after these three plays. How does this example show that the product of a positive number and a negative number is negative?

$3\left(\boxed{}\right) = -2 + (-2) + (-2) = \boxed{}$

_____

_____

2. How can you use the equation in Problem 1 to illustrate that the quotient of two negative numbers is positive?

_____

3. Compare the rules for finding the signs of products and quotients.

_____

_____

On Your Own

(MP) Model with Mathematics Model the situation with a multiplication and an addition expression involving negative numbers. Then evaluate.

All-Day Parking $5

4. Every day that Annabelle takes the train to work, she uses an app to charge the parking fee shown to her credit card. What will be her card balance for commuter parking if she parks and takes the train to work 10 times?

_____

_____

_____

5. Alejandro makes donations in the amount of $100 every December to 5 of his favorite charities. He pays for the donations by check. What is the change in his checking account balance after making these donations?

_____

_____

(MP) Use Repeated Reasoning Complete the statements. Explain how you figured out the answer.

6. $8(-5 + 7) = 8(-5) + 8(7)$

$8(2) = \boxed{} + 56$

$16 = 16$ This means that $8(-5) = \boxed{}$.

_____

_____

7. $-2(-5 + 9) = -2(-5) + (-2(9))$

$-2(4) = \boxed{} + (-18)$

$-8 = -8$ This means that $-2(-5) = \boxed{}$.

_____

_____

Identify the sign of the product or quotient. Do not evaluate.

8. $253 \times (-185)$

9. -59×819

10. $-1,200 \times (-490)$

11. $1,242 \div (-18)$

12. $-1,890 \div (-15)$

13. $-18,175 \div 125$

14. Complete each step to show that $(-1)(-1) = 1$.

$$(-1)(0) = \boxed{}$$ Multiplication Property of Zero

$$(-1)(-1 + 1) = 0$$ Addition Property of Opposites

$$(-1)(-1) + (-1)(1) = 0$$ _____

$$(-1)(-1) + \boxed{} = 0$$ Identity Property of Multiplication

$$(-1)(-1) + (-1) + \boxed{} = 0 + \boxed{}$$ _____

$$(-1)(-1) + (-1 + 1) = 0 + 1$$ _____

$$(-1)(-1) + \boxed{} = 0 + 1$$ Addition Property of Opposites

$$(-1)(-1) = \boxed{}$$ Identity Property of Addition

15. The value of a collectible baseball card decreased as shown.

Value decreased by $12 in 6 months.

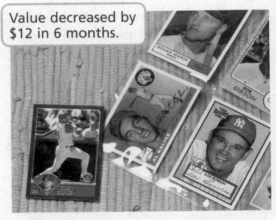

A. (MP) **Use Tools** To find the average monthly change in the value of the card, use the number line to find $-12 \div 6$.

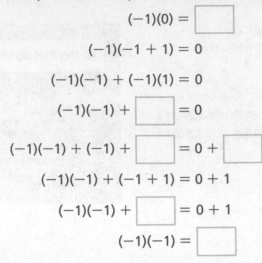

$$-12 \div 6 = \underline{\hspace{2cm}}$$

B. (MP) **Construct Arguments** What is the sign (positive or negative) of the quotient? Explain why this makes sense in the context of the problem.

_____

_____

16. Open Ended Write a different division problem involving negative numbers that can be solved using the number line given in Problem 15.

_____

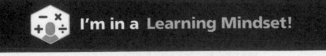 **I'm in a Learning Mindset!**

How can I use my understanding of rational number multiplication to help support my understanding of rational number division?

_____

_____

Understand Multiplication and Division of Rational Numbers

(MP) **Model with Mathematics** For Problems 1 and 2, model the situation with a multiplication and an addition expression involving negative numbers. Then evaluate.

1. After a gymnastics competition, the coaches reviewed all the gymnasts' scores to identify areas for improvement. A missed landing on an aerial cartwheel deducts 2 points from the score. The coaches found that aerial cartwheels were missed 5 times across the competition. How did these missed landings affect the scores overall?

   _____

   _____

   _____

2. The temperature fell by 3°F every hour during a 6-hour period. What was the overall change in temperature during the 6-hour period?

   _____

   _____

3. (MP) **Use Repeated Reasoning** Complete the statements. Explain.

   $-4(5 + (-2)) = \boxed{}(5) + \boxed{}(-2)$

   $-4\boxed{} = -20 + \boxed{}$ This means that $(-4)(-2) = \boxed{}$.

   $-12 = -12$

   _____

   _____

Identify the sign of the product (positive or negative). Do not evaluate.

4. $-819 \times (-324)$ 5. $-1,201 \times 54$ 6. $10,005 \times (-84)$

   _____   _____   _____

7. (MP) **Construct Arguments** Dario said that if the dividend and divisor have the same sign, then the quotient also has that same sign. Do you agree or disagree? Explain.

   _____

   _____

8. (MP) **Use Structure** Explain how you can use the fact that multiplication and division are inverse operations to help you determine whether the quotient $-10 \div (-5)$ is positive or negative.

   _____

   _____

Test Prep

9. Which quotients are negative? Select all that apply.

(A) $\frac{-52}{13}$

(B) $14 \div (-2)$

(C) $-36 \div (-9)$

(D) $\frac{-20}{-5}$

(E) $-27 \div 3$

(F) $\frac{7}{-1}$

10. Marley's bank charges a $3 service fee each time money is withdrawn from another bank's ATM. Marley is traveling and must withdraw money from another bank's ATM 4 times. Which expressions model the change in the balance of her account due to the service fees? Select all that apply.

(A) $-3 + (-3) + (-3) + (-3)$

(B) $-4 + (-4) + (-4) + (-4)$

(C) $4 \times (-3)$

(D) $-4 \times (-3)$

(E) 3×4

11. An equation is shown.

$a \cdot b = c$

Which statement is true?

(A) If $a > 0$ and $b > 0$, then $c < 0$.

(B) If $a > 0$ and $b < 0$, then $c < 0$.

(C) If $a < 0$ and $b > 0$, then $c > 0$.

(D) If $a < 0$ and $b < 0$, then $c < 0$.

Spiral Review

12. Miguel takes $50 to the mall. He buys a flannel shirt for $18.99 and a hat for $12.49. On his way home, he stops at the bank and withdraws $25. How much money does Miguel have now?

_____

13. A store marks up its inventory 45%. The wholesale price of an item was $130. What is the retail price of the item?

_____

14. Stephanie has a –$40 balance on her credit card. She makes two additional charges to pay $20 for gas and $25 for parking. Then she makes a credit card payment of $30. What is her remaining balance?

_____

Name _____

Multiply Rational Numbers

(I Can) compute the products of signed rational numbers using the properties of numbers to simplify calculations.

Spark Your Learning

Two submersibles, *Atlas* and *Pisces*, are exploring an ocean trench. Every hour, *Atlas* makes 5 descents of 10 meters each. Every hour, *Pisces* makes 2 descents of 50 meters each. What integer represents the total change in elevation for each submersible after 3 hours?

 Turn and Talk What mathematical operations could you use to solve the problem? Explain.

Build Understanding

1 The product 3(−8) represents the hourly change in elevation for the submersible *Argo,* as shown here. The total change in elevation after 4 hours is represented by the product 4(3)(−8).

Each hour: 3 descents of 8 meters each

A. First multiply the first two factors. What is the sign of the product of the first two factors, 4 and 3? Explain.

_____

_____

_____

B. Now multiply the result by the third factor, −8. What is the sign of the final product? Why is this reasonable?

_____

_____

C. Use the above method of multiplying pairs of factors to find each product and complete the table.

Product	Number of negative factors	Sign of product
(−3)(4)(7)		
(−5)(−5)(2)(6)		
(−1)(−3)(−10)		
(3)(−2)(−1)(−2)(−3)		
(−5)(−2)(3)(−1)(−1)(−4)		

D. What relationship do you see between the number of negative factors and the sign of the corresponding product?

_____

_____

E. How could you apply the **Associative Property of Multiplication** to the second expression to make it easier to simplify?

_____

 Turn and Talk How do the rules you learned previously for multiplying two numbers with the same sign and two numbers with different signs support your answer to Step D?

Step It Out

2 Find the product. Identify any properties that you used.

A. $(4)(-0.5)(-3) = \left(\boxed{}\right)(-3) = \boxed{}$

I used the order of operations and multiplied from _____ to _____.

The product is _____, because the number of negative factors is

| even / odd. |

B. $\left(-\frac{1}{3}\right)(-7)(-9) = \left(\boxed{}\right)\left(-\frac{1}{3}\right)(-9)$

$= \left(\boxed{}\right)\left[\left(-\frac{1}{\cancel{3}_1}\right)\left(-\cancel{9}^3\right)\right]$

$= \left(\boxed{}\right)\left[(-1)\left(\boxed{}\right)\right]$

$= \left(\boxed{}\right)(3)$

$= -21$

I used the _____ Property of Multiplication to switch

the order of the factors, and then I used the _____

Property of Multiplication to group factors to make the multiplication

easier. The product is _____, because the number of

negative factors is | even / odd |.

>
> **Turn and Talk** Why is it helpful to apply properties of operations when multiplying rational numbers?

Check Understanding

1. Jared writes a multiplication expression with eight rational factors. Half of the factors are positive and half are negative. Is the product positive or negative? Why? _____

2. The expression $(8)(2)(-1.5)$ represents the change in the scuba diver's elevation after 8 minutes. Find the change in elevation.

_____

Find each product.

3. $(-0.25)(-0.5)(4)(8)$ _____

4. $(10)(-3)\left(-\frac{4}{5}\right)\left(-\frac{5}{6}\right)$ _____

5. Name the property illustrated and the value of the expressions.

$[(3.95)(-0.2)](-5) = (3.95)[(-0.2)(-5)]$

_____

On Your Own

6. Every week, Estella has guitar lessons.

   A. Complete the expression to represent the change in Estella's account balance due to guitar lessons after 2 years.

$$\left(\boxed{} \right)(52)(-35)$$

   B. Find the product. Then explain what it represents.

   _____

   _____

   C. (MP) **Construct Arguments** Explain how you know your answer is reasonable.

   _____

   _____

7. DeMarcus multiplies all of the integers from -10 to -1, including -10 and -1. Should his answer be positive or negative? Explain your thinking.

_____

_____

Identify the property illustrated by the statement. Find the value of the equivalent expressions.

8. $(6)(-18)(5) = (-18)(6)(5)$

_____

9. $[(-0.7)(-2)](5) = (-0.7)[(-2)(5)]$

_____

Find each product.

10. $(-4)(-8)(-5)$

11. $(-4)(-2)(5)(3)$

12. $(-1)(9)(-2)(5)(-1)(-1)$

13. $(0.2)(50)(-0.9)$

14. $(0.1)(-0.2)(10)(-10)$

15. $(-28)(-0.5)(-0.5)(-0.1)(10)$

16. $\left(-\frac{1}{3}\right)\left(\frac{3}{5}\right)\left(-\frac{5}{7}\right)$

17. $\left(\frac{2}{7}\right)\left(\frac{14}{15}\right)\left(-\frac{1}{2}\right)$

18. $(-12)\left(\frac{5}{6}\right)\left(-\frac{3}{4}\right)\left(-\frac{4}{5}\right)$

(−×÷+) I'm in a Learning Mindset!

What is challenging about multiplying rational numbers? Do I need help, or can I work through it on my own?

_____

LESSON 5.2
**More Practice/
Homework**

ONLINE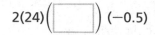
 **Video Tutorials and
Interactive Examples**

Multiply Rational Numbers

1. As part of an experiment, scientists decrease the temperature in a laboratory freezer as shown.

   A. Complete the expression to represent the change in the freezer's temperature at the end of 2 days.

      $2(24)\left(\boxed{}\right)(-0.5)$

   B. Find the product. Then explain what it represents.

      _____

      _____

**Experiment:
0.5 °F decrease
3 times per hour**

   C. Explain how you know your answer is reasonable.

      _____

      _____

      _____

2. **(MP) Use Structure** Complete the following to show how the expression can be simplified using the Commutative and Associative Properties of Multiplication.

$$(-0.5)(-7)(2) = \left(\boxed{}\right)\left(\boxed{}\right)(2)$$

$$= (-7)\left[\left(\boxed{}\right)\left(\boxed{}\right)\right]$$

$$= (-7)\left(\boxed{}\right)$$

$$= \boxed{}$$

Find each product.

3. $(3)(5)(-3)(-2)(10)(-1)$

   _____

4. $\left(-\frac{3}{4}\right)\left(\frac{1}{3}\right)\left(-\frac{4}{5}\right)$

   _____

5. $\left(\frac{2}{3}\right)\left(-\frac{9}{8}\right)\left(-\frac{4}{5}\right)(-1)$

   _____

6. $(-9)\left(\frac{7}{12}\right)\left(-\frac{4}{7}\right)\left(-\frac{1}{3}\right)$

   _____

7. $(0.5)(-0.5)(-4)(-4)(-1)$

   _____

8. $(-0.01)(-50)(-0.5)(-0.2)(-10)$

   _____

9. Which product has a negative value?

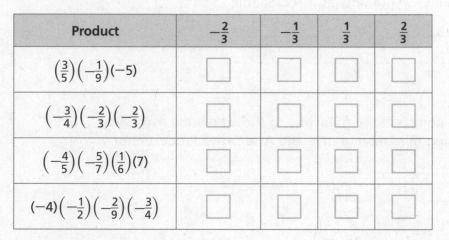

Ⓐ $\left(-\frac{1}{3}\right)\left(-\frac{3}{4}\right)\left(\frac{4}{5}\right)$

Ⓑ $\left(-\frac{1}{2}\right)\left(-\frac{2}{3}\right)\left(-\frac{3}{4}\right)$

Ⓒ $\left(-\frac{2}{3}\right)\left(-\frac{3}{4}\right)\left(-\frac{4}{7}\right)\left(-\frac{7}{8}\right)$

Ⓓ $\left(-\frac{1}{2}\right)\left(\frac{2}{5}\right)\left(\frac{5}{6}\right)\left(-\frac{6}{7}\right)$

10. Tyrell is exploring a cave. Every hour, he makes 4 vertical descents of 3.5 meters. The expression 3(4)(−3.5) represents his change in elevation in meters after 3 hours. What is his change in elevation?

Ⓐ −42 meters

Ⓑ −4.2 meters

Ⓒ 4.2 meters

Ⓓ 42 meters

11. Match the product to its value.

Product	$-\frac{2}{3}$	$-\frac{1}{3}$	$\frac{1}{3}$	$\frac{2}{3}$
$\left(\frac{3}{5}\right)\left(-\frac{1}{9}\right)(-5)$	☐	☐	☐	☐
$\left(-\frac{3}{4}\right)\left(-\frac{2}{3}\right)\left(-\frac{2}{3}\right)$	☐	☐	☐	☐
$\left(-\frac{4}{5}\right)\left(-\frac{5}{7}\right)\left(\frac{1}{6}\right)(7)$	☐	☐	☐	☐
$(-4)\left(-\frac{1}{2}\right)\left(-\frac{2}{9}\right)\left(-\frac{3}{4}\right)$	☐	☐	☐	☐

Spiral Review

12. Callie bought 4 pies from a bakery for a holiday dinner. The total cost was $75.80. If each pie cost the same, how much did one pie cost?

13. A graphic designer charges a fee of $1,600 to design a poster for a jazz festival. The designer also receives an 8% commission on sales of the poster at the festival. What is the designer's total income from this work, assuming that sales of the poster bring in $620 during the festival?

14. The temperature at 6:00 a.m. on a winter day is −6 °F. The temperature rises by 7 °F by noon. Use the number line to represent the situation. Then complete the equation.

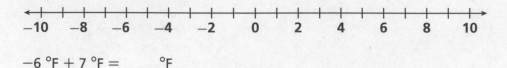

−6 °F + 7 °F = _____ °F

Name _____

Write Fractions as Decimals and Divide Integers

(I Can) express quotients in different forms.

Spark Your Learning

Hayley is buying herbs. She wants to buy $\frac{5}{6}$ ounce of basil. The scale she is using to weigh the basil displays the weight as a decimal. How will she know when the display on the scale is correct to the tenths place? Explain your reasoning.

Turn and Talk What do you think the digit in the hundredths place of the display will be? Explain your reasoning.

Build Understanding

1 ▶ Hayley wants to buy the amounts of herbs shown. How can you convert these fractions to decimals?

A. You can use equivalent fractions to convert a fraction to a decimal. Does that method work well for these fractions? Why or why not?

$\frac{3}{4}$ oz oregano, $\frac{2}{3}$ oz thyme

B. You can also use long division to convert a fraction to a decimal, because $\frac{a}{b} = a \div b$ for all fractions $\frac{a}{b}$.

Think about dividing 3 ounces into 4 equal parts as shown. How many tenths and hundredths will there be in each part?

$$\begin{array}{r} 0.75 \\ 4\overline{)3.00} \\ -\underline{28} \\ 20 \\ -\underline{20} \\ 0 \end{array}$$

C. How can you use the decimal form of $\frac{3}{4}$ ounce to find what Hayley will pay for basil that costs $5.80 per ounce?

D. Use long division to find the decimal equivalent of $\frac{2}{3}$ ounce to the thousandths place. Do not round.

E. Describe the pattern in the quotient. Will the pattern continue if you write a zero in the ten-thousandths place of the dividend and continue dividing? Why or why not?

$$3\overline{)2.}$$

Turn and Talk Can the number 20 be divided evenly by 3? What does your answer imply about the quotient in Step E? Explain.

Step It Out

2 Every quotient of integers is a **rational number** provided that the divisor is not zero. Every rational number can be written as a fraction in which the numerator and the denominator are integers. The fraction can be written as a decimal that either *terminates* (ends) or *repeats*.

Examples: terminating decimal: $\frac{3}{4} = 0.75$

repeating decimal: $\frac{2}{3} = 0.666...,$ or $0.\overline{6}$

The bar over the 6 means that it repeats forever.

$$
\begin{array}{r}
2.\square\square\square \\
6\,\overline{)\,1\ 7.\ 0\ \square\square} \\
-\ 1\ 2 \\
\hline
5\ 0 \\
-\ \square \\
\hline
2\ 0 \\
-\ \square \\
\hline
2\ 0 \\
-\ \square \\
\hline
2
\end{array}
$$

A. Suppose Hayley wants to buy $2\frac{5}{6}$ ounces of basil. Complete the statement to show that $2\frac{5}{6}$ is a rational number.

$2\frac{5}{6} = \dfrac{\square}{6}$, and _____ and _____ are integers.

B. Complete the long division shown to write $2\frac{5}{6}$ as a decimal. Then complete the statement.

$2\frac{5}{6} = $ _____, which is a terminating / repeating decimal.

3 Use the rules you've learned for dividing negative numbers.

A. Find each quotient. Then complete the statement.

$\dfrac{15}{-3} = $ _____ $\div$ _____ $=$ _____

$\dfrac{-15}{3} = $ _____ $\div$ _____ $=$ _____

$-\left(\dfrac{15}{3}\right) = $ _____

The rational numbers $\dfrac{15}{-3}$, $\dfrac{-15}{3}$, and $-\left(\dfrac{15}{3}\right)$ are / are not equivalent.

B. If p and q are integers and q is not zero, what can you conclude about $\dfrac{-p}{q}$, $\dfrac{p}{-q}$, and $-\left(\dfrac{p}{q}\right)$?

_____

C. Suppose that the value of a share of stock decreased by $15 in 3 days. Which expression in Part A best represents the average daily change in the stock's value? Explain.

_____

_____

 Turn and Talk Is the number $-2\frac{5}{6}$ a rational number? Why or why not?

4 What are some different ways that you can express the quotient $-100 \div 11$?

A. Express the quotient as a fraction in three different ways.

$$-100 \div 11 = \frac{\boxed{}}{11} = \frac{\boxed{}}{\boxed{}} = -\frac{\boxed{}}{\boxed{}}$$

B. Express the quotient as a mixed number.

$$-100 \div 11 = -\frac{\boxed{}}{11} = -9\frac{\boxed{}}{\boxed{}}$$

C. Express the quotient as a decimal.

$$-100 \div 11 = \underline{\hspace{3cm}}$$

$$
\begin{array}{r}
-9.\boxed{\ }\boxed{\ }\boxed{\ }\quad\boxed{\ }\boxed{\ }\boxed{\ } \\
11\overline{)-1\ 0\ 0\ .\ 0} \\
-\underline{9\ 9} \\
1\ 0 \\
-\underline{\ 0}
\end{array}
$$

© Houghton Mifflin Harcourt Publishing Company • **Image Credit:** ©Houghton Mifflin Harcourt

 Turn and Talk Predict the value of the quotient $-200 \div 11$. Explain your reasoning.

Check Understanding

1. Eloise needs $3\frac{5}{8}$ yards of fabric to make a costume.

A. Show that the amount of fabric is a rational number.

_____

B. Write the amount of fabric as a decimal.

_____

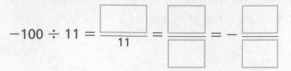

2. A. Write the mixed number $-5\frac{4}{9}$ as a fraction in three different ways. Then write the mixed number as a decimal.

_____

B. Explain why $-5\frac{4}{9}$ is a rational number.

_____

_____

3. The temperature outside dropped 27 degrees over a period of 3 hours. Find the quotient $-27 \div 3$ and explain what it means in this context.

_____

On Your Own

4. Rafael is buying $1\frac{3}{8}$ pounds of salad at a salad bar that charges the amount shown.

Salad bar: **$6.80/lb**

   A. Show that the amount of salad is a rational number.

   _____

   B. Write the amount of salad as a decimal.

   _____

   C. What will Rafael pay for the salad?

   _____

5. The temperature dropped steadily by 40 °F over a 20-hour period. Find the quotient −40 ÷ 20 and explain what it means in this context.

_____

6. The balance on Mr. Finch's credit card is −$210. It is 3 times the balance on Mr. Nguyen's credit card. Find the quotient −210 ÷ 3 and explain what it means in this context.

_____

7. (MP) **Use Repeated Reasoning** Use the table shown.

   A. Convert each fraction in the table to a decimal. Describe a pattern in the results.

   _____

   _____

Fraction	Decimal
$\frac{1}{8}$	
$\frac{2}{8}$	
$\frac{3}{8}$	

   B. Does this pattern continue? Why or why not?

   _____

   _____

   _____

8. Michelle has to find the decimal equivalent of $15\frac{1}{8}$ yards. How can she do this without first writing the mixed number as a fraction?

_____

_____

9. The value of a gift card to a rock climbing gym decreased by $34 after 4 equal charges to the card. Find the quotient $-34 \div 4$ and explain what it means in this context.

_____

_____

10. (MP) **Reason** Are all integers rational numbers? Explain.

_____

_____

_____

Convert each number to a decimal.

11. $\frac{5}{8}$ _____

12. $\frac{5}{16}$ _____

13. $\frac{7}{9}$ _____

14. $1\frac{1}{6}$ _____

15. $10\frac{4}{11}$ _____

16. $7\frac{3}{11}$ _____

Write two fractions equivalent to the given fraction.

17. $\frac{-3}{5}$ _____

18. $-\left(\frac{7}{10}\right)$ _____

19. Explain why $-7\frac{3}{5}$ is a rational number.

_____

Find each quotient.

20. $-84 \div 7$ _____

21. $-52 \div (-4)$ _____

22. $\frac{-69}{-11}$ _____

23. $\frac{60}{-8}$ _____

24. **Open Ended** Write two quotients of integers that can be converted to terminating decimals and two that can be converted to repeating decimals.

_____

I'm in a Learning Mindset!

How effective was using long division to write a fraction as a decimal? Do I still have questions?

_____

_____

Write Fractions as Decimals and Divide Integers

1. Sean is buying $\frac{9}{16}$ pound of tea at a tea shop. The cost of the tea is shown.

   A. Write the amount of tea as a decimal.

   _____

   B. What will Sean pay for the tea?

   _____

$24 per lb

Convert each number to a decimal.

2. $\frac{1}{3}$

3. $4\frac{7}{8}$

_____ _____

4. Write three fractions equivalent to the quotient $50 \div (-17)$ using only the numbers -50, -17, 17, or 50. Then explain why the quotient is a rational number.

_____

_____

_____

Find each quotient.

5. $42 \div (-7)$ _____

6. $-56 \div 8$ _____

7. $\frac{-27}{5}$ _____

8. $\frac{35}{-3}$ _____

9. **(MP) Use Repeated Reasoning** Use the table shown.

   A. Convert each fraction in the table to a decimal. Describe a pattern in the results.

   _____

   _____

Fraction	Decimal
$\frac{1}{9}$	
$\frac{2}{9}$	
$\frac{3}{9}$	

   B. Does this pattern continue? Why or why not?

   _____

   _____

   _____

Test Prep

10. Which of the following are equivalent to $-\left(\dfrac{a}{b}\right)$? Select all that apply.

(A) $\dfrac{a}{b}$

(B) $\dfrac{-a}{-b}$

(C) $\dfrac{-a}{b}$

(D) $\dfrac{a}{-b}$

(E) $-\left(\dfrac{a}{-b}\right)$

11. Draw a line to match each quotient to its value.

$-64 \div 8$ •   • -8

$\dfrac{-48}{-6}$ •   • -6

$-36 \div (-6)$ •   • 6

$\dfrac{24}{-4}$ •   • 8

Spiral Review

12. Use the number line to show how to find the given difference. Then write an equivalent addition expression.

$1 - 6 = $ _____

13. In 2016, the price of a stock decreased by $11. In 2017, the price decreased by $13. Write a sum of two integers that represents the overall change in the price of the stock for the two years. Then find the sum and explain what it tells you about the price of the stock.

_____

_____

14. Audra has a subscription to a news site. To pay for the subscription, $8 is automatically deducted from her checking account once per month.

A. Write a product of three or more integers that represents the change in Audra's account after three years.

_____

B. What integer represents the change in Audra's account after three years?

_____

Name _____

Multiply and Divide Rational Numbers in Context

(I Can) multiply and divide rational numbers in context.

Step It Out

1 ▸ A hot air balloon is flying at an altitude of 570 meters. Air is released from the balloon in order to change the altitude by −2.5 meters every second for 4 seconds. What is the new altitude of the balloon?

A. Write and use a model to find the change in altitude.

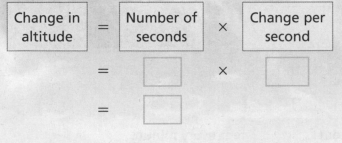

Change in altitude	=	Number of seconds	×	Change per second

$$= \boxed{} \times \boxed{}$$

$$= \boxed{}$$

The altitude changes by _____ meters.

B. Write and use a model to find the new altitude.

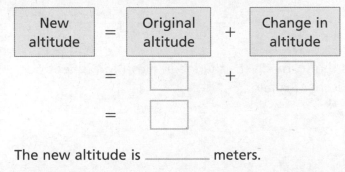

New altitude	=	Original altitude	+	Change in altitude

$$= \boxed{} + \boxed{}$$

$$= \boxed{}$$

The new altitude is _____ meters.

C. Use a number line to show that your answer is reasonable.

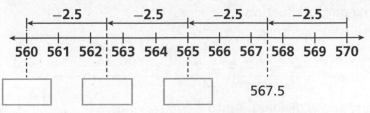

567.5

> **Turn and Talk** Write and solve your own multiplication problem based on this situation.

2 In $4\frac{1}{2}$ minutes, a scuba diver swims from the surface to an elevation of −85 feet, swimming at a constant speed. Later, the diver swims upward 5 feet following a fish. Finally, the diver takes $10\frac{2}{3}$ minutes to ascend to the surface, swimming at a constant speed.

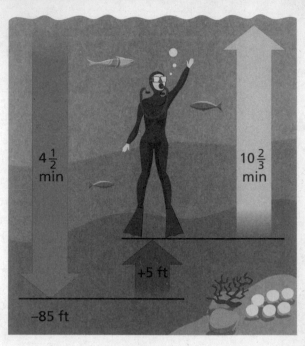

4$\frac{1}{2}$ min

10$\frac{2}{3}$ min

+5 ft

−85 ft

A. Write and use a model to find how many feet the elevation changes every minute during the descent.

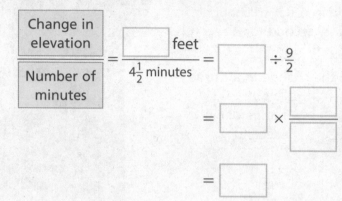

$$\frac{\text{Change in elevation}}{\text{Number of minutes}} = \frac{\boxed{} \text{ feet}}{4\frac{1}{2} \text{ minutes}} = \boxed{} \div \frac{9}{2}$$

$$= \boxed{} \times \frac{\boxed{}}{\boxed{}}$$

$$= \boxed{}$$

The elevation changes by about _____ feet every minute.

B. How do you know that your answer is reasonable?

_____

_____

 Turn and Talk What is the scuba diver's change in elevation in feet per minute during the final ascent? Explain.

Check Understanding

1. If the scuba diver in Task 2 originally swam $-12\frac{1}{2}$ feet per minute, for $4\frac{1}{2}$ minutes, how would this change the situation?

_____

_____

2. Susan has $\frac{3}{4}$ cup of raisins and she is dividing it into $\frac{3}{8}$ cup servings. Complete the following. What does the answer represent?

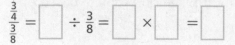

$$\frac{\frac{3}{4}}{\frac{3}{8}} = \boxed{} \div \frac{3}{8} = \boxed{} \times \boxed{} = \boxed{}$$

_____

On Your Own

3. **STEM** Air temperature changes as you move away from Earth's surface. Under certain conditions in Earth's lower atmosphere, the temperature changes with increase in elevation as shown. Use this relationship to solve each problem.

Temperature change: about −18.8 °F per mile increase in elevation

    A. Find and interpret the change in temperature for an increase in elevation of 0.2 mile.

    _____

    _____

    B. Find and interpret the change in temperature for a decrease in elevation of 0.2 mile.

    _____

    _____

    C. How are your answers to Parts A and B related?

    _____

4. A butterfly is flying $8\frac{3}{4}$ feet above the ground. It descends at a steady rate to a spot $6\frac{1}{4}$ feet above the ground in $1\frac{2}{3}$ minutes. What is the butterfly's change in elevation in feet per minute?

    _____

5. One scuba diver's elevation changed by $-15\frac{5}{8}$ feet every minute. This was $1\frac{1}{4}$ times the rate of change for a second scuba diver. What was the rate of change in elevation of the second scuba diver in feet per minute? Show your work.

    _____

    _____

6. **Open Ended** Write a real-world problem based on one of the contexts in the lesson that can be solved using multiplication or division of negative fractions or decimals.

    _____

    _____

    _____

7. Carl has $3\frac{1}{2}$ cups of blueberries. He is storing them in containers that each hold $\frac{2}{3}$ cup. How many containers can he fill? Find the answer and interpret the result.

_____

_____

_____

8. Mrs. Anderson writes a check for $10.50 to each of her four nieces. What will be the total change in Mrs. Anderson's checking account balance after all four checks are cashed? _____

9. The denominator of a fraction is $\frac{-3}{4}$. The numerator is $\frac{1}{4}$ more than the denominator. Identify the fraction. Then show that it is a rational number.

Find each quotient.

10. $\dfrac{\frac{7}{10}}{\frac{-1}{5}}$ _____

11. $\dfrac{\frac{5}{6}}{\frac{-6}{7}}$ _____

12. $\dfrac{\frac{252}{4}}{\frac{3}{-8}}$ _____

13. $\dfrac{2.8}{-4}$ _____

14. $-\dfrac{5.5}{0.5}$ _____

15. $\dfrac{0.72}{-0.9}$ _____

© Houghton Mifflin Harcourt Publishing Company

⊟ ×
+ ● ÷   **I'm in a Learning Mindset!**

What questions can I ask my teacher to help me understand how to set up a problem that involves division?

_____

_____

Name _____

LESSON 5.4
**More Practice/
Homework**

ONLINE

Video Tutorials and
Interactive Examples

Multiply and Divide Rational Numbers in Context

1. **Math on the Spot** Sarah drove her police car at a constant speed down a mountain. Her elevation decreased by 200 feet over a 10-minute period. What was the change in elevation during the first minute?

   _____

2. A submarine descends $\frac{1}{120}$ mile every minute. Write a product of three or more rational numbers to represent the change in the submarine's elevation after 3 hours. Then find the value of the product, and explain what it represents.

   _____

   _____

3. **Financial Literacy** Tanisha takes a dance class that is priced as shown. The charge appears as negative on her account balance until she makes her monthly payment.

   A. Show how to find the balance of Tanisha's account for dance classes during a 4-week period in which she attends 3 classes per week.

   _____

   B. (MP) **Reason** Suppose the balance on Tanisha's account for a 2-week period is −$100. If Tanisha attended at least 1 dance class per week, how many classes could she have attended each week? Explain your reasoning.

   $12.50 per class

   _____

   _____

   _____

   C. Evaluate the expression −112.50 ÷ (−12.50) and interpret what it could mean in this context.

   _____

   _____

Find each quotient.

4. $\dfrac{\frac{-5}{8}}{\frac{15}{16}}$ _____

5. $\dfrac{\frac{-2}{3}}{\frac{4}{-9}}$ _____

6. $\dfrac{\frac{24}{7}}{\frac{-6}{35}}$ _____

Test Prep

7. Salton Sea Beach in California has an elevation of about −230 feet. This is about 11.5 times the elevation of Indio, California. What is the elevation of Indio, California?

about _____ feet

8. During a winter cold spell, the temperature change was −1.2 °F per hour for a period of 4.5 hours. Which expressions can be used to find the overall change in temperature during that time period?

Ⓐ 4.5 ÷ (−1.2) degrees Fahrenheit

Ⓑ 4.5 × (−1.2) degrees Fahrenheit

Ⓒ 4.5 − (−1.2) degrees Fahrenheit

Ⓓ (−1.2) + (−1.2) + (−1.2) + (−1.2) degrees Fahrenheit

Ⓔ 4(−1.2) + (0.5)(−1.2) degrees Fahrenheit

9. Which expression is equivalent to $\dfrac{-\frac{5}{6}}{\frac{10}{3}}$?

Ⓐ $-\dfrac{5}{6} \div \dfrac{3}{10}$

Ⓑ $-\dfrac{5}{6} \div \dfrac{10}{3}$

Ⓒ $-\dfrac{5}{6} \times \dfrac{10}{3}$

Ⓓ $-\dfrac{6}{5} \times \dfrac{3}{10}$

Spiral Review

10. What is the difference when −2 is subtracted from 2?

_____

11. Complete the number line diagram. What addition problem does the diagram represent?

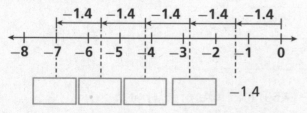

_____

_____

Review

Vocabulary

For Problems 1–5, choose the correct term or terms from the Vocabulary box to label each boxed number.

Vocabulary

dividend
divisor
factor
product
quotient
rational number

1.

2.

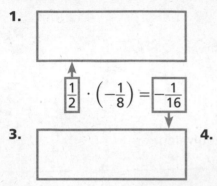

$$\frac{1}{2} \cdot \left(-\frac{1}{8}\right) = -\frac{1}{16}$$

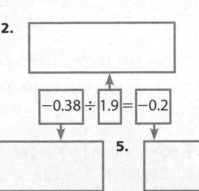

$$-0.38 \div 1.9 = -0.2$$

3.

4.

5.

Concepts and Skills

6. Complete the table to show the total changes and the average (mean) daily changes in the prices of four stocks over a 5-day period.

Stock	Total change in price ($)	Average daily change in price ($)
A	−1.30	
B		−0.14
C	3.25	
D		−0.32

7. An equation is shown, where $a < 0$, $c > 0$, and $|a| > |c|$.

$$a \cdot b = c$$

Which statements about the value of b are true?

Ⓐ $b < 0$

Ⓑ $b > 0$

Ⓒ $b > 1$

Ⓓ $|b| < 1$

Ⓔ $|b| < 0$

Ⓕ $|b| > 1$

8. (MP) **Use Tools** A horse's weight decreases by $\frac{1}{2}$ pound per week. At this rate, how many weeks will it take for the horse to lose a total of $5\frac{1}{2}$ pounds? Write an expression that could be used to model the situation. State what strategy and tool you will use to answer the question, explain your choice, and then find the answer.

_____

_____

9. An equation is shown, where $p < 0$.

$$p \cdot q = r$$

A. Assume $r > 0$. Plot a point on the number line to identify a possible location for q.

$$\xleftarrow{\hspace{2cm}}\underset{0}{|}\xrightarrow{\hspace{2cm}}$$

B. Assume $r < 0$. Plot a point on the number line to identify a possible location for q.

$$\xleftarrow{\hspace{2cm}}\underset{0}{|}\xrightarrow{\hspace{2cm}}$$

10. The total change in the outdoor temperature over 6 hours was $-21\ °$F.

What was the mean change in temperature per hour?

_____ °F per hour

11. Which expressions are equivalent to $\left(-\frac{1}{3}\right)(-2)(6)$? Select Equivalent or Not Equivalent for each expression.

	Equivalent	Not Equivalent
$-\frac{1}{3}(-2 \cdot 6)$	☐	☐
$(-2)\left(-\frac{1}{3}\right)(6)$	☐	☐
$-\left(\frac{1}{3} \cdot 2 \cdot 6\right)$	☐	☐
$-\left(\frac{1}{3} \cdot 6\right) - 2$	☐	☐
$\dfrac{\left(-\frac{1}{3}\right)(-2)}{\frac{1}{6}}$	☐	☐

12. The depth of water in a swimming pool decreases by $\frac{1}{8}$ inch per day due to evaporation. No water is added to the pool for a 2-week period. What is the total change in the depth of the water during this time period?

Ⓐ $-1\frac{3}{4}$ inches   Ⓒ $1\frac{7}{8}$ inches

Ⓑ $-\frac{1}{4}$ inch   Ⓓ 16 inches

13. Which expression is equivalent to $-\left(\frac{2}{5}\right)$?

Ⓐ $-\frac{(-2)}{5}$ Ⓑ $-\frac{2}{(-5)}$ Ⓒ $\frac{-2}{-5}$ Ⓓ $\frac{2}{-5}$

14. Which decimal is equivalent to $\frac{5}{9}$?

Ⓐ $0.\overline{5}$ Ⓑ 0.55 Ⓒ 1.8 Ⓓ 5.9

Solve Multi-step Problems Using Rational Numbers

Can **You** Find the **Mystery** Number?

Missing a Number?
Can't find x?
Call the **Math Detective Agency!**

You are the new investigator for the Math Detective Agency. Your first case depends on finding a mystery number. Follow these steps.

A. Find each sum or difference.

$-7 + 9 =$ _____ $-5 - (-4) =$ _____

$-\frac{4}{5} - \frac{4}{5} =$ _____ $-\frac{1}{10} + \frac{3}{5} =$ _____

$-1 + 1\frac{1}{10} =$ _____ $-\frac{1}{5} - \frac{1}{2} =$ _____

B. Plot and label each sum or difference from Part A on the number line.

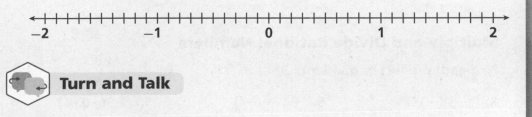

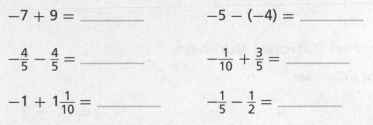 **Turn and Talk**

The mystery number is the distance between the two closest points that you plotted. What is the mystery number? Explain how you found it.

Are You Ready?

Complete these problems to review prior concepts and skills you will need for this module.

Write and Interpret Numerical Expressions

Write a numerical expression to express the calculation. Do not simplify the expression.

1. The comic books in Cora's favorite series regularly cost $2.99. Today, they are on sale for $0.50 off the regular price. Cora subtracts $0.50 from $2.99 and multiplies the result by 4 to find the cost of 4 comic books at the sale price.

_____

2. Kendal has a 5-pound bag of flour that holds $18\frac{1}{2}$ cups. His bread recipe calls for $3\frac{1}{4}$ cups of flour per loaf. Kendal starts with $18\frac{1}{2}$ and subtracts 5 times $3\frac{1}{4}$ to find how much flour he will have left after making 5 loaves of bread.

_____

Add and Subtract Rational Numbers

Find each sum or difference.

3. $-5 + 12$

4. $15 - (-7)$

5. $2.8 + (-8.7)$

6. $-\frac{3}{5} + \left(-1\frac{4}{5}\right)$

7. $-\frac{1}{3} - \frac{5}{6}$

Multiply and Divide Rational Numbers

Find each product or quotient.

8. $(-3)(-15)$

9. $84 \div (-4)$

10. $1.9(-0.04)$

11. $-\frac{1}{8} \cdot \frac{2}{3}$

12. $-2\frac{1}{2} \div \frac{3}{4}$

Name _____

Apply Properties and Strategies to Operate with Rational Numbers

(I Can) write and evaluate expressions involving rational numbers and name the properties used.

Step It Out

1 Remember that the properties of operations you used for integers, such as the Commutative and Associative Properties, the Inverse and Identity Properties, and the Distributive Property, can all be used for any rational numbers.

Stefan has 5 ounces of chlorine, and he needs to find out whether that is enough chlorine for two swimming pools. The amount of chlorine per gallon that Stefan will add is shown. One pool has volume 1,721.25 cubic feet, and the other has volume 1,998.75 cubic feet. There are about 7.5 gallons per cubic foot.

> **Add chlorine to water: 0.00013 oz per gal**

A. Write and evaluate an expression for the number of gallons in both pools.

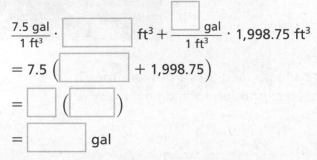

$$\frac{7.5 \text{ gal}}{1 \text{ ft}^3} \cdot \boxed{} \text{ ft}^3 + \frac{\boxed{} \text{ gal}}{1 \text{ ft}^3} \cdot 1{,}998.75 \text{ ft}^3$$

$$= 7.5 \left(\boxed{} + 1{,}998.75 \right)$$

$$= \boxed{} \left(\boxed{} \right)$$

$$= \boxed{} \text{ gal}$$

B. Write and evaluate an expression for the number of ounces of chlorine needed in both pools.

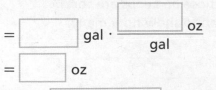

$$= \boxed{} \text{ gal} \cdot \frac{\boxed{} \text{ oz}}{\text{gal}}$$

$$= \boxed{} \text{ oz}$$

C. Stefan | does / does not | have enough chlorine for both pools.

> **Turn and Talk** Which property of operations did you use in Part A above? Explain.

2 Use properties to evaluate $\frac{4}{7}\left(-\frac{3}{5}\right) \cdot \frac{5}{3}\left(-\frac{9}{10} - \frac{3}{10}\right)$.

$\frac{4}{7}\left[\left(-\dfrac{\boxed{}}{\boxed{}}\right) \cdot \dfrac{\boxed{}}{\boxed{}}\right]\left(-\frac{9}{10} - \frac{3}{10}\right)$ _____ Property of Multiplication

$= \frac{4}{7} \cdot \left(\boxed{}\right)\left(-\frac{9}{10} - \frac{3}{10}\right)$ **Inverse Property of Multiplication**

$= \boxed{}\left(-\frac{9}{10} - \frac{3}{10}\right)$ **Identity Property of Multiplication**

$= \boxed{}\left(\boxed{}\right)$ Subtraction

$= \dfrac{\boxed{}}{\boxed{}}$ Multiplication

3 A model car club has 6 ounces of white paint. They give $\frac{1}{3}$ of the paint to a craft club. The amount of paint to use on each car is shown. Write and evaluate an expression to find the number of cars they can paint. Use the **order of operations**.

$\left[6 - \left(\boxed{}\right) \cdot 6\right]$ oz paint $\cdot \dfrac{1 \text{ car}}{\boxed{} \text{ oz paint}}$

Paint Required: 0.02 oz / car

$= \dfrac{6 - \boxed{}}{\boxed{}} = \dfrac{\boxed{}}{\boxed{}} = \boxed{}$ cars

Check Understanding

1. Sarah buys 8 packages, each with 20 balloons, and uses $\frac{1}{4}$ of them to decorate the hall. Write and evaluate an expression to find how many balloons Sarah has left.

_____

2. Suresh has 4 coupon books, each with 6 coupons. He keeps $\frac{1}{3}$ of the coupons and gives the rest away. Fifty percent of those he keeps are for the movie theater. Write and evaluate an expression to show how many movie theater coupons he has.

_____

3. Explain how to use the properties to evaluate the expression mentally.
$-\frac{3}{21} \cdot \frac{3}{5} \cdot 7 \cdot 15$

_____

_____

On Your Own

4. **(MP)** **Model with Mathematics** Liu Tse is 6 years older than four times the age of her daughter, Lan. Lan will be 9 years old in 3 years.

A. Write and evaluate an expression that shows Lan's age.

_____

B. Use Lan's age to write and evaluate the expression for Liu Tse's age.

_____

5. **(MP)** **Reason** Ella has $\frac{1}{3}$ as many trading cards as Kip. Adira has 3 more than 50% of the number of cards that Kip has. Kip has 18 cards.

A. Write an expression for the total number of cards the group has.

_____

B. Evaluate the expression.

_____

6. **(MP)** **Use Tools** Tamir bought $2\frac{1}{2}$ pounds of fish at $5.50 per pound, and two bananas at the price shown.

Bananas: $0.45 each

A. Write an expression to show how much change he received from a $20 bill.

_____

B. Evaluate the expression to show his change.

_____

7. Tre is shown earning an hourly wage. An expression for the amount of money earned in one week is $16\left(3\frac{1}{2}\right) + 16\left(2\frac{1}{4}\right) + 16\left(5\frac{3}{4}\right) + 16\left(4\frac{1}{2}\right)$. Rewrite the expression so that it only has one multiplication operation, and then evaluate the expression.

_____

8. (MP) **Attend to Precision** Erin has 10 bags of apples. The following are the weights of the bags in pounds: $2\frac{1}{2}$, $2\frac{3}{4}$, $2\frac{1}{2}$, $2\frac{1}{4}$, $1\frac{1}{4}$, $2\frac{1}{2}$, $2\frac{1}{2}$, $1\frac{1}{4}$, $2\frac{1}{4}$, $2\frac{1}{4}$. Write an expression that shows the average weight of a bag. Evaluate the expression.

9. Rewrite the expression $6 \cdot \left(-\frac{1}{3}\right) + 2\left(\frac{1}{2}\right) - 2\left(\frac{3}{4}\right)$ using the Distributive Property. Then evaluate the expression.

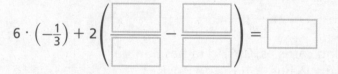

10. Evaluate the expression $[0.75 \cdot (-12)] - \left(-6 \div \frac{2}{3}\right)$.

_____

11. Rewrite the expression $-\frac{1}{4} \cdot 3\frac{1}{3} \cdot 8 \cdot \left(-1\frac{1}{5}\right)$ using the Commutative Property of Multiplication. Then evaluate the expression.

12. Rewrite the expression $\frac{1}{2} \cdot 33 \cdot \frac{1}{11}$ using the Associative Property of Multiplication. Evaluate the expression.

_____

LESSON 6.1
**More Practice/
Homework**

ONLINE

Video Tutorials and
Interactive Examples

Apply Properties and Strategies to Operate with Rational Numbers

1. (MP) **Model with Mathematics** Mr. Chung teaches a 1-hour math class. Six minutes are used for attendance and turning in homework. Then he teaches for 18 minutes. For the rest of the class, the students work on problems. For each problem, the students spend 3 minutes working on it, then Mr. Chung takes 6 minutes to explain it. After the class completes 4 problems, all of the class time is used up. Write and evaluate an expression to show this.

   _____

2. (MP) **Use Tools** An online pet store ships 2 cases of dog food and 4 bags of treats. The dog food weighs $13\frac{1}{2}$ ounces per can, and there are 12 cans in a case. The dog treats are shown. Write and evaluate an expression to show the total weight of the items.

   2.375 lb/bag

   _____

   _____

3. Evaluate $5 - 44 \cdot (-0.75) - 18 \div \frac{2}{3} \cdot 0.8 + \left(-\frac{4}{5}\right)$.

   _____

4. The sum of 7 and 2.6 is multiplied by 9. Then this product is divided by the result of $4 - 2.8$. Add parentheses to the expression, $9 \cdot 7 + 2.6 \div 4 - 2.8$, to show the correct order for the calculations described.

   _____

5. (MP) **Use Structure** This expression can be evaluated quickly by doing the computation in only one of the parentheses. Which set of parentheses is it, and what is the value of the expression? Explain.

   $-3\left(\frac{6}{11} + \frac{7}{19}\right) \cdot \left(\frac{3}{8} + \frac{7}{15}\right) \cdot \left(-\frac{3}{2} + 2\frac{1}{8} - \frac{5}{8}\right)$

   _____

   _____

6. A teacher gave a test with 50 questions, each worth the same number of points. Donovan got 39 out of 50 questions right. Marci's score was 10 percentage points higher than Donovan's. What was Marci's score? Explain.

   _____

   _____

Test Prep

7. Which expression has a value of 7?

   Ⓐ $4 + 0.5 \times 8 - 2$

   Ⓑ $(4 + 0.5) \times 8 - 2$

   Ⓒ $4 + 0.5 \times (8 - 2)$

   Ⓓ $(4 + 0.5) \times (8 - 2)$

8. Chandra bought twice as many plants as Marvin. Kira bought $\frac{1}{3}$ as many plants as Chandra. Marvin bought 6 plants. Write an expression that shows the total number of plants purchased. Who bought the most plants?

9. The art class lasts 90 minutes. The teacher explains the project for 25 minutes and allows 15 minutes for questions and discussion. He talks to each student about their project for 5 minutes and then all of the class time is used up. Write and evaluate the expression that shows how many students are in the class.

Spiral Review

10. Evaluate $-3 - (-3 - 7)$.

11. Evaluate $\dfrac{\frac{5}{3} \times 1\frac{1}{5}}{\frac{1}{4}}$.

12. An account that yields 6% simple interest annually has $2,000. How much will be in the account after 3 years if no other deposits or withdrawals are made?

13. At the beginning of the month, Sammi has saved $120 in her bank account. She wants to buy a new gaming system for $200 in three weeks. She earns $20 a week. Will she have enough money at the end of three weeks to make the purchase? If not, how much more will she have to earn?

© Houghton Mifflin Harcourt Publishing Company

Name _____

Estimate to Check Reasonableness

(I Can) use underestimates and overestimates to check
the reasonableness of answers.

Step It Out

1 ▶ Sandi says that her family of 4 will go to the park 3 times this year.
She says they will save about $200 if they buy the season pass. Use
estimation to determine whether her statement is reasonable.

A. Estimate the cost of 4 season passes.

$ ☐ · 4 = $ ☐

Season pass:	$249.99
Day pass:	$82.99

B. Overestimate the cost of 4 day passes for 3 days. Use the
Distributive Property to make calculations easier.

4 day passes:

$ ☐ · 4 = (☐ + ☐)4 = ☐ + ☐ = $ ☐

4 day passes for 3 days:

$ ☐ · 3 = (☐ + ☐)3 = ☐ + ☐ = $ ☐

C. Sandi's estimation of saving about $200 [is / is not]
reasonable. Explain.

_____

_____

_____

Turn and Talk If the family of 4 visited the park 4 times, would season passes
save them money? Explain.

2 ▶ Estimate $-3.8 \cdot 3 - \frac{117}{20}$ using integers. Tell whether your estimate is an
underestimate or an overestimate. Explain.

$-3.8 \cdot 3 - \frac{117}{20} \approx$ ☐ · ☐ − ☐ ≈ ☐

_____

_____

_____

_____

3 Tasha and Lydia have a yard-service company. Their last three jobs brought in $287.50, $184.25, and $95. Lydia worked about 65% of the hours on those jobs. Use **compatible numbers** to estimate Lydia's share of the earnings.

Money earned from jobs:

$287.50 + $184.25 + $95

Estimated money earned:

$ [ ] + $ [ ] + $ [ ] = $ [ ]

Lydia's estimated share:

65% of $ [ ] ≈ [ ]/[ ] · [ ] = $ [ ]

Turn and Talk What are two different ways to estimate 65%?

Check Understanding

1. The soccer club held a spaghetti dinner. They sold 39 child tickets for $3.75 each and 27 adult tickets for $5.95 each. The amount for 11 child tickets was refunded.

   A. Estimate the amount of income received by the soccer club. Show your work.

   _____

   _____

   B. Was the estimate for the amount of income in Problem 1 an overestimate or underestimate? Explain.

   _____

   _____

   _____

2. Mrs. Gomez earns $19.50 per hour and gets a 5% raise. Use compatible numbers to estimate her new hourly rate. Explain.

   _____

   _____

On Your Own

3. A desert tour includes 305 people traveling by van. Each van can transport 18 people.

A. Estimate the number of vans needed.

_____

B. (MP) **Construct Arguments** Is it an overestimate or underestimate? In this situation, would it be better to overestimate or underestimate? Explain your choice.

_____

_____

_____

4. (MP) **Critique Reasoning** A bag of dry pet food costs the pet store $18.66. A case of canned food costs $11.43. The owner puts in an order for 27 bags of dry food and 34 cases of canned food. The owner thinks he owes $1,835.49.

A. Estimate the total amount of the order.

_____

_____

B. Is the owner's total reasonable? Explain your answer.

_____

5. **STEM** Sound travels about 1,125.33 feet in a second. An engineer detects the sound of an explosion from a test site 8 seconds after the blast.

A. Use the equation $d = rt$ to estimate how far away the engineer was in feet and in miles from the blast.

_____

_____

You can use the speed of sound to calculate the distance away from a visible loud object.

B. If the engineer wants to find the exact spot of the blast should she use the estimate or an exact answer? Explain your choice.

_____

_____

6. **(MP) Use Structure** The school basketball team had the following scores for its games this year: 47, 36, 42, 29, 39, 49, 44, and 32. Estimate how many points they scored this year. Explain your estimate.

_____

_____

_____

7. Sam buys a drink for $2.05 and a sandwich for $4.20 each day Monday through Friday for lunch. He also leaves a $1.25 tip each day. Estimate what he pays for lunch for the week. Is this an underestimate or overestimate?

_____

_____

_____

8. Use compatible numbers to estimate $\frac{-594}{-27} \cdot \left(\frac{-924}{21}\right)$. Is -482 a reasonable answer? Explain your answer.

_____

_____

9. **Open Ended** Two 3-digit numbers are added. Give an example where you would not want to round both 3-digit numbers to the nearest hundred to get the best estimate.

_____

_____

_____

10. Marin evaluated $-0.238 \cdot \frac{2}{10} - (1{,}003 \cdot 0.0062)$ and got -6.65 rounded to the nearest hundredth.

   A. Estimate the value of the expression.

   _____

   B. **(MP) Construct Arguments** Is the estimate an overestimate or underestimate? Explain.

   _____

   _____

   _____

   _____

Estimate to Check Reasonableness

1. Students sold 342 tickets to the school carnival at $11.75 each.
Nine tickets were refunded. Estimate the amount of money that
the school took in. Is your estimate an overestimate or underestimate?

_____

2. (MP) **Construct Arguments** The dimensions of a room with one window
and one door at a community center are shown. Ivan wants to have
the four walls painted. The painter says the area is 542.2 square feet.
Estimate the total area that needs to be painted. Was the painter's answer
reasonable? Explain.

_____

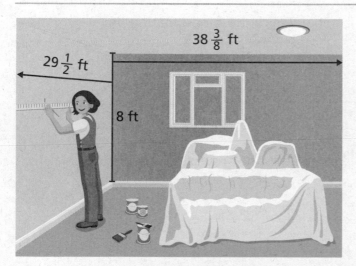

3. Estimate $20 \cdot 37 \cdot \frac{21}{5} \div 98$. Is it an overestimate or underestimate? Explain.

_____

_____

_____

4. Carol says that $-\frac{520}{105} \cdot \frac{16}{15} \cdot \left(-\frac{1}{2}\right)$ is less than 2.5. Do you agree? Explain.

_____

_____

5. Estimate $210 \div 5.2 \cdot 9\frac{3}{4} + (-205)$. Is 188.75 a reasonable answer? Explain
your answer.

_____

_____

Test Prep

6. Which is the best estimate for the area of a piece of property that is 52 yards by 77 yards?

 Ⓐ $50 \times 70 = 3{,}500 \text{ yd}^2$ Ⓒ $60 \times 70 = 4{,}200 \text{ yd}^2$

 Ⓑ $50 \times 80 = 4{,}000 \text{ yd}^2$ Ⓓ $60 \times 80 = 4{,}800 \text{ yd}^2$

7. A car can travel 32 miles using 1 gallon of gas. The car has 12 gallons of gas.

 A. Can the car travel 370 miles without needing more gas? Estimate and explain.

 _____

 _____

 _____

 B. Explain why an underestimate is not a wise choice for estimating the gasoline needed for a roadtrip.

 _____

 _____

 _____

8. Zana calculates $-\frac{15}{49}\left[19 + (-3)\right] \cdot \frac{19}{11} = -8\frac{248}{539}$. Is the answer reasonable? Explain.

_____

Spiral Review

9. A bottle contains 0.78 liter of medicine. Each dose is supposed to be 0.02 liter. How many doses are in the bottle?

_____

10. Which costs less per banana, 8 bananas for $1.95 or 12 bananas for $2.29? Explain.

_____

_____

_____

11. Which property is demonstrated by $1{,}326 \cdot 367 = 367 \cdot 1{,}326$?

_____

12. James is building a rectangular fire pit. He dug a hole 20 inches by 20 inches. He decides to make each side of the fire pit 4 inches longer instead. What is the percent increase in the area of the fire pit?

_____

Name _____

Solve Multi-step Problems with Rational Numbers in Context

(**I Can**) solve multi-step problems that involve rational numbers in different forms and multiple operations.

Step It Out

1 Jordan uses the recipe shown to make yogurt putty. He buys a bag of cornstarch for $3.89 that contains 128 servings that are each $\frac{1}{8}$ cup.

What is the maximum number of batches of putty Jordan can make with the cornstarch? How much does the cornstarch for each batch cost?

Yogurt Putty
$2\frac{1}{4}$ cups cornstarch
3 cups yogurt
1 drop food coloring
Yield: 1 batch

A. How many cups of cornstarch are in the bag?

_____ servings × _____ cup per serving = _____ cups

B. How many batches of putty can Jordan make? Use decimals for the cups of cornstarch per batch. Round your answer to the nearest tenth.

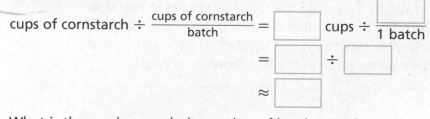

C. What is the maximum whole number of batches Jordan can make with the cornstarch? Explain.

_____

_____

_____

D. How much does the cornstarch for each batch cost?

$ _____ ÷ _____ ≈ _____ , which is approximately

$ _____ per batch.

Turn and Talk How can you use estimation to check that your answer for the cost per batch is reasonable?

2 Charise collects antique salt and pepper shakers. The value of her cactus salt and pepper shakers is shown. The value of these salt and pepper shakers is expected to change by an average of $-2\frac{2}{5}\%$ per year. What is the value of the salt and pepper shakers projected to be in two years?

$56.28

A. Explain why it is useful to convert the percent to a decimal.

_____

_____

B. Convert the mixed-number percent to a decimal percent. Then divide the resulting value in the percent by 100.

$-2\frac{2}{5}\% =$ _____ $\% =$ _____

C. Find the value of the salt and pepper shakers after the first year.

$56.28 \times ($ _____ $) =$ _____

$56.28 + ($ _____ $) =$ _____

To the nearest cent, the value after the first year is $ _____

D. You can use substitution to rewrite the two expressions in Part C as a single expression: $56.28 + [56.28 \times (-0.024)]$. Use properties of operations to write this expression as a product of two factors, and show that it has the same value as the final answer to Part C.

E. Find the value of the salt and pepper shakers after the second year. Round your answer to the nearest cent. Show your work.

Turn and Talk A student said that you can solve this problem by finding $2\frac{2}{5}\%$ of $56.28 and then subtracting this amount twice from $56.28. Does this method work? Why or why not?

© Houghton Mifflin Harcourt Publishing Company • Image Credit: ©Mark R. Coons/Shutterstock

3 Suppose the aquarium shown developed a leak at the bottom corner and lost water at an average rate of $6\frac{3}{4}$ fluid ounces per minute. How many hours, to the nearest tenth, would it take for the aquarium to be empty?

20-gallon tank

A. Multiply by equivalent forms of 1 to convert gallons to fluid ounces.

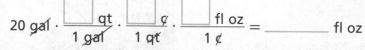

$20 \text{ gal} \cdot \dfrac{\boxed{} \text{ qt}}{1 \text{ gal}} \cdot \dfrac{\boxed{} \text{ c}}{1 \text{ qt}} \cdot \dfrac{\boxed{} \text{ fl oz}}{1 \text{ c}} = \underline{\hspace{1cm}} \text{ fl oz}$

B. Find the number of minutes, to the nearest tenth, that it takes for the aquarium to empty.

$\underline{\hspace{2cm}} \div 6\frac{3}{4} = 2{,}560 \div \underline{\hspace{1.5cm}} \approx \underline{\hspace{1.5cm}} \text{ minutes}$

C. What remaining work do you need to do to solve the problem? Solve the problem and show your work.

_____

_____

_____

D. Explain how you can check your answer for reasonableness.

_____

_____

_____

_____

_____

Check Understanding

1. A block of clay contains twenty 4-ounce portions of clay. A ceramics teacher wants to use the block to make as many spheres of clay as possible, each weighing $\frac{2}{5}$ pound. How many spheres can the class make?

_____

2. A laptop computer costs $356.75 when it is new. The value of the computer is expected to change by $-11\frac{3}{4}\%$ per year. What is the expected value, to the nearest cent, of the computer after 3 years? Is the answer reasonable? Explain.

_____

_____

On Your Own

3. Luis is hiking at a park. He sees the sign shown and decides to hike to Wandering Twin Lake. Luis knows that he can hike at an average rate of $\frac{1}{3}$ mile in 6 minutes.

   A. How many hours will it take Luis to reach Wandering Twin Lake?

   _____

   B. Explain how you know your answer is reasonable.

   _____

   _____

   _____

   _____

4. **Financial Literacy** Mr. Liling bought 10 shares of stock in QJZ Software at the beginning of 2016 for $198.58 per share. The table shows how the value of the stock changed during 2016 and during 2017.

   A. What was the total value of Mr. Liling's shares, rounded to the nearest cent, at the end of 2016?

   _____

QJZ Software	
Year	Change in stock price
2016	$-4\frac{9}{10}\%$
2017	$+10\frac{1}{4}\%$

   B. What was the total value of Mr. Liling's shares, rounded to the nearest cent, at the end of 2017?

   _____

   C. Explain how you know your answers are reasonable.

   _____

   _____

   _____

   _____

   _____

   _____

5. According to Denise's recipe, each batch of granola requires 1.75 cups of shelled sunflower seeds. She has 3 bags of shelled sunflower seeds that each contain eleven $\frac{1}{4}$-cup servings. What is the maximum number of batches of granola that Denise can make with the sunflower seeds?

   _____

6. In 2016, a maglev train in Japan traveled 1.1 miles in $10\frac{4}{5}$ seconds.

   A. Find the speed of the train in miles per hour.

Maglev trains use magnets to hover above the tracks. This helps them reach extraordinary speeds.

   B. How can you use estimation to show that your answer is reasonable?

   _____

   _____

   _____

   _____

7. Brad is using the recipe shown to make trail mix for his hiking club. He buys two 20-ounce canisters of raisins for $4.31 each. A canister holds 17 servings of raisins. Each serving is $\frac{1}{4}$ cup.

Trail Mix

$1\frac{1}{4}$ cups raisins

$1\frac{1}{2}$ cups mixed nuts

$\frac{3}{4}$ cup pumpkin seeds

Mix ingredients in a large bowl.

Yield: 1 batch

   A. If Brad only wants to make whole batches of trail mix, what is the maximum number of batches he can make using the raisins?

   _____

   B. Use your answer from Part A to find the cost of the raisins per batch of trail mix. Round your answer to the nearest cent.

   _____

8. The *percent error* of a measurement tells how close the measurement is to the actual value. Dani ran four times around the track, a total distance of 1,600 meters. Her GPS watch recorded the distance as 1,592 meters.

   A. To find the percent error, first find the absolute value of the difference between the distance recorded on Dani's watch and the actual distance.

   _____

   B. Now express the difference from Part A as a percent of the actual value. This is the percent error.

   _____

9. A student identified the volume of a solution to be 13 milliliters. The true volume was 12.5 milliliters. What is the percent error of the measurement? Use the definition of *percent error* in Problem 8.

_____

10. Gianna is taking a walking tour in her city. The entire tour is $10\frac{1}{10}$ kilometers long. According to an app on her phone, Gianna's average walking rate is 1.6 meters per second.

   A. What is Gianna's average walking rate in kilometers per hour?

   _____

   B. About how long will it take Gianna to complete the walking tour? Express your answer in hours and minutes.

   _____

   C. (MP) **Construct Arguments** Explain how you know your answer is reasonable.

   _____

   _____

   _____

   _____

11. **Open Ended** A container of oatmeal costs $3.79 and contains about 17 servings of the size shown. Write a word problem involving the serving size, the number of servings per container, and the price of the oatmeal.

Serving size: $\frac{1}{4}$ cup uncooked

   _____

   _____

   _____

   _____

   _____

12. (MP) **Attend to Precision** A snail is moving along a path that is 4 meters long. The snail moves at an average rate of $3\frac{3}{10}$ inches per minute.

   A. Find the length of the path to the nearest inch. (*Hint:* 1 in. ≈ 2.54 cm)

   _____

   B. To the nearest minute, how long does it take the snail to reach the end of the path?

   _____

Solve Multi-step Problems with Rational Numbers in Context

1. **Math on the Spot** Sophia uses $3\frac{3}{4}$ cups of flour for each cake she makes. She has a 10-pound bag of flour that cost $8.79 and contains 152 quarter-cup servings.

   A. How many cakes can Sophia make with this flour? _____

   B. Use your answer from Part A to find the cost of the flour for each cake. Round your answer to the nearest cent. _____

2. (MP) **Use Tools** A bobsled team is practicing runs on a track. Their first run takes 4.85 minutes. On each of the next two runs, the team's time changes by $-5\frac{1}{2}\%$ compared to the previous time.

   A. What was the team's time, rounded to the nearest hundredth of a minute on their final run?

   _____

   B. Explain how you can check your answer for reasonableness.

   _____
   _____
   _____
   _____

3. (MP) **Use Tools** Calvin maintains a 55-gallon artificial pond. He fills the pond with a hose at an average rate of $9\frac{3}{16}$ quarts per minute.

   A. How long, to the nearest tenth of a minute, does it take to fill the pond?

   _____

   B. Explain how you can check your answer for reasonableness.

   _____
   _____
   _____

4. (MP) **Use Tools** Kayla bikes for 2.25 hours at an average rate of $10\frac{1}{2}$ miles per hour. Talisha bikes the same distance at an average rate of $12\frac{2}{5}$ miles per hour. How long does Talisha take to complete the ride?

   _____

Test Prep

5. A new mobile device has a value of $256.25. Its value changes by $-22\frac{1}{2}\%$ each year. What is the value of the phone after two years?

Ⓐ $140.93

Ⓒ $153.91

Ⓑ $198.59

Ⓓ $57.66

6. Khalid has 2 bags of cornmeal that each contain 25 servings. One serving is $\frac{3}{4}$ cup. Khalid is making muffins that require 2.5 cups of cornmeal per batch. What is the maximum number of batches of muffins that Khalid can make using the cornmeal?

Ⓐ 7   Ⓑ 15   Ⓒ 18   Ⓓ 37

7. A $2\frac{1}{2}$-quart container of juice develops a leak and loses juice at an average rate of 3.3 fluid ounces per minute. Which is the best estimate of the time it takes until the container is empty?

Ⓐ 0.75 minute

Ⓒ 24 minutes

Ⓑ 8 minutes

Ⓓ 80 minutes

8. Laura jogs at an average rate of 5.6 miles per hour for $2\frac{1}{10}$ hours. Priya jogs the same distance but takes $1\frac{3}{5}$ hours. Write an expression you can use to find Priya's average rate, using a decimal value or an operation symbol $(+, -, \times, \div)$ to fill in each box.

$5.6 \times \boxed{}\boxed{}\boxed{}$

Spiral Review

9. Nicolas and Jerome are scuba diving. Nicolas is at an elevation of -25 feet compared to the surface of the water. Jerome is at an elevation of -32 feet. Which diver is closer to the surface of the water? How much closer is he compared to the other diver?

_____

10. The temperature at noon on a winter day was 2 °F. By 6 p.m., the temperature had dropped to -9 °F. Write a subtraction expression you can use to find the number of degrees the temperature dropped. Then evaluate the expression.

_____

11. Write an equation to represent the situation in the table.

_____

Time (min), x	Distance (ft), y
4	92
6	138
8	184

Review

Vocabulary

Choose the correct term from the Vocabulary box.

1. Choose the correct term from the Vocabulary box.

   To find the value of $7 + \frac{1}{3} \cdot 6$, you first find the product

   of $\frac{1}{3}$ and 6. This is justified by the

   _____ .

Concepts and Skills

2. A group of hikers starts at an elevation of 2.53 kilometers. When they stop for lunch, their elevation has increased by 1.24 kilometers. When they stop to camp, their elevation has decreased by 0.53 kilometer compared to their lunch stop. Which expressions represent the elevation, in kilometers, of the group's campsite? Select all that apply.

   (A) $2.53 - (1.24 - 0.53)$ (D) $2.53 + (1.24 - 0.53)$

   (B) $2.53 - (1.24 + 0.53)$ (E) $2.53 + 1.24 - (-0.53)$

   (C) $(2.53 - 0.53) + 1.24$ (F) $1.24 + [2.53 + (-0.53)]$

3. The total change in the water level in a lake over a period of 5 weeks was $-5\frac{1}{4}$ inches. Complete the table to show possible changes in the water level in week 2 and week 5.

4. (MP) **Use Tools** Tessa and Marisol run in a 100-meter race. Tessa runs at an average speed of 8.1 meters per second. Five seconds after the race begins, she is 3.5 meters ahead of Marisol. To the nearest hundredth of a second, how long will it take Marisol to run the entire race if she does not speed up or slow down? State what strategy and tool you will use to answer the question, explain your choice, and then find the answer.

   _____

   _____

Week	Change in Water Level (in.)
1	$-2\frac{3}{4}$
2	
3	$2\frac{1}{4}$
4	$-3\frac{1}{4}$
5	
Total	$-5\frac{1}{4}$

5. When the air conditioner in a building is running, the temperature in the building changes at a rate of -1 °F every 18 minutes. At this rate, how many hours should it take to cool the building from a temperature of 85.5 °F to a temperature of 78 °F?

   _____ hours

6. Kyle plans to make 15 hamburger patties, each weighing $\frac{1}{4}$ pound, for a cookout. At the store, hamburger meat is priced at $3.66 per pound. If Kyle orders the exact amount of meat he needs, how much will it cost, rounded to the nearest cent?

$ _____

7. The percent error of a measurement tells how close the measurement is to the actual value. The label on a mineral sample in a kit gave the weight of the sample as 60.5 ounces. The true weight was found to be 62.5 ounces.

A. To find the percent error, first find the absolute value of the difference between the weight on the label and the true weight.

_____

B. Now express the difference from Part A as a percent of the actual value. This is the percent error.

_____

8. A rectangular backyard has a length of 68 feet and a width of $40\frac{1}{2}$ feet. The owner wants to plant 75% of the yard with grass seed. The planting rate for the seed is 1.5 pounds per 1,000 square feet of area. To the nearest tenth of a pound, how much grass seed will the owner need to plant?

_____ pounds

9. Which expressions are equivalent to $-\frac{3}{4}(10 \cdot 8)$? Select Equivalent or Not Equivalent for each expression.

	Equivalent	Not Equivalent
$-3 \cdot \frac{10}{4} \cdot \frac{8}{4}$	☐	☐
$\left(-\frac{3}{4} \cdot 8\right)(10)$	☐	☐
$-\frac{1}{4}(3 \cdot 10 \cdot 8)$	☐	☐
$-\frac{3}{4}(10) - \frac{3}{4}(8)$	☐	☐

10. Joanna has $25.00 to spend at the zoo. Admission costs $12.25, and she plans to buy a combo meal for $8.92 at the snack bar for lunch. It costs $2.00 to buy a food pellet to feed the giraffes. Which expressions could Joanna use to estimate the number of pellets she can afford if she wants to be certain not to run out of money? Select all that apply.

Ⓐ $(25 - 10 - 8) \div 2$ Ⓓ $(25 - 13 - 10) \div 2$

Ⓑ $(25 - 12 - 8) \div 2$ Ⓔ $(30 - 10 - 8) \div 2$

Ⓒ $(25 - 13 - 9) \div 2$ Ⓕ $(30 - 12 - 8) \div 2$

Model with Expressions, Equations, and Inequalities

Archaeologist

STEM
POWERING INGENUITY

An archaeologist collects and analyzes data about past civilizations in order to learn about human life and cultures. Sarah Parcak is a space archaeologist who uses satellite images to identify ancient sites. Her wish is "for us to discover the millions of unknown archaeological sites across the globe" and to "find and protect the world's heritage."

STEM Task:

Volunteers often help archaeologists at excavation sites. At one excavation site, there can be no more than 8 volunteers for every field guide. If a total of 50 people are working at the site, what is the greatest possible number of volunteers? Explain your thinking.

Learning Mindset
Resilience Identifies Obstacles

Resilience is the ability to recover from a setback. Everyone encounters challenges or obstacles at some point. Resilience allows you to overcome them and continue moving forward. Next time you run into some difficulty completing a task or reaching a goal, try following these steps.

- Identify the problem or obstacle. What is holding you back from moving ahead?

- Develop a list of ideas for overcoming the obstacle. Visualize strategies you can apply to the problem and ways you can break the problem down into smaller steps. If you're still not sure what to do, think about where you can look for help.

- Choose an idea from your list and give it a try.

- Did you successfully overcome the obstacle? If not, try a different approach. And if that one does not work, try another one. Ask for help if you need it, but don't give up.

Reflect

Q What challenges or problems did you encounter as you worked on the STEM Task? How did you address them?

Q Have you given up in the past when you encountered an obstacle or difficulty? What can you do to improve your resilience?

Solve Problems Using Expressions and Equations

BALANCE Mystery

Jada has set up several balance mysteries for her friends. She has made stacks of 1, 2, or 3 blocks and hidden some blocks in cups. She is challenging her friends to figure out how many blocks are in each cup. If more than one cup is on a balance, there is an equal number of blocks in each cup. The cups are light enough that their mass does not impact the balance.

Write and solve an equation for each balance.

A.

B.

C.

D.

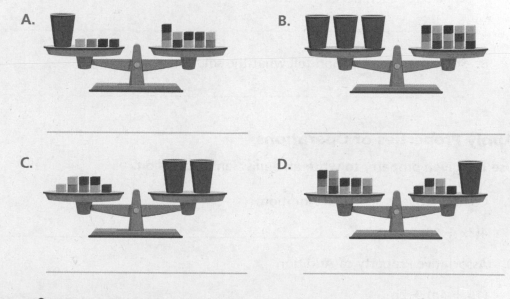

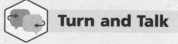

Turn and Talk

Darius says, "Balances A and D are both solved with the same operation." What pattern did Darius notice? Explain.

Are You Ready?

Complete these problems to review prior concepts and skills you will need for this module.

Solve One-Step Equations

Solve the equation.

1. $c + 27 = 68$ _____

2. $t - 1.5 = 7.9$ _____

3. $\frac{a}{3} = 21$ _____

4. $r + \frac{3}{4} = \frac{7}{8}$ _____

5. $4.2x = 25.2$ _____

6. $15b = 75$ _____

7. All tickets to a play have the same cost. A group bought 6 tickets and paid a total of $99.

   A. Write a multiplication equation that can be used to determine cost c in dollars for each ticket.

   _____

   B. Solve the equation and tell what the solution represents.

   _____

Apply Properties of Operations

Use the given property to write an equivalent expression.

8. Commutative Property of Addition

   $4(3x + 10)$ _____

9. Associative Property of Addition

   $(16 + 4n) + 2n$ _____

10. Distributive Property

   $2(a - b)$ _____

11. Associative Property of Multiplication

   $\frac{1}{4}(12p)$ _____

Name

Write Linear Expressions in Different Forms for Situations

(I Can) write different forms of linear expressions to represent the same real-world situation.

Spark Your Learning

A bus driver has students going on a field trip enter the bus in pairs. He fills one row of the bus at a time, front to back. Write a rule that shows the total number of people on the bus after any number of rows is filled. Let the bus driver's seat count as Row 1.

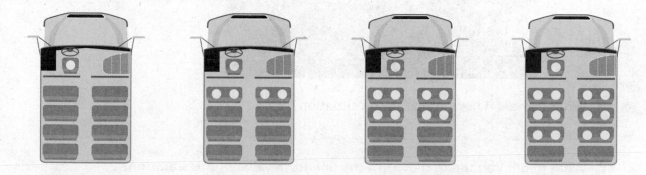

x	y

Turn and Talk How would your rule change if the second row of each bus only sat 2 students to make room for a wheel chair?

© Houghton Mifflin Harcourt Publishing Company

Build Understanding

1 Henry is remodeling a kitchen and needs some wiring installed for additional outlets and lighting. An electrician provides him an estimate which includes a one-time service fee plus an hourly rate, as shown, to complete the wiring.

service fee of $89.95 plus $54.50 per hour

A. What is the unknown value in this situation?

_____

B. What might you use to represent the unknown value in this situation?

_____

C. Write an expression that would represent the total charges.

_____

D. Electricians who work on Saturday earn time and a half. That means the pay is 1.5 times the normal hourly rate for each hour. Write expressions to represent pay earned on a Saturday in two different ways.

_____

E. The electrician decides to bring an apprentice on the job, so they split the hourly rate paid by the customer. The electrician takes a reduced hourly wage of $40, and pays the apprentice the remaining $14.50 per hour. Write an expression that models how the total charges are shared.

_____

F. Are the expressions in Parts C and E equivalent? Why?

_____

_____

 Turn and Talk Why is it useful to represent an amount with a variable in real-world models?

2 ▶ A department store is offering a promotion on candles as shown. Rhonda is buying three candles at the same original price for a birthday present.

Buy 2 candles, **get 40% off** 3rd candle.

A. What is the unknown value in this situation, and what could you use to represent the unknown?

_____

_____

B. The third candle is discounted. Find the percent of the original price of the candle Rhonda would be paying, and explain your reasoning.

_____

_____

C. Write an expression for the total cost before tax in relation to the cost of the first two candles and the cost of the discounted candle.

_____

D. Is there another way to write the total cost expression? If so, write the expression and explain why the expressions are equivalent.

_____

_____

_____

 Turn and Talk What other equivalent expressions could you write to represent the total cost of the candles?

Check Understanding

1. Abigail's parents pay her $5 an hour for weeding the yard and pay her little sister $3 an hour for raking leaves. Write an expression in two different ways to represent the amount her parents will pay Abigail and her sister for working the same number of hours.

_____

2. Juice is on sale with the rule "buy one, get one half-off." Write an expression in two different ways to represent the cost of buying two containers of juice on sale.

_____

On Your Own

3. (MP) **Use Structure** A wedding photographer and an assistant work together to photograph weddings. The rates are shown in the advertisement. Write an expression to represent the total cost for photography at a wedding in two different ways.

Wedding Photographer

$50 sitting fee
- plus $40 per hour for photographer's time
- plus $15 per hour for assistant's time

_____

_____

4. (MP) **Use Structure** Benita buys 2 shirts for the same price. The sales tax rate is 6.5%. Write an expression to represent the total cost for the shirts in two different ways.

_____

5. (MP) **Use Structure** A hobby store is having a promotion on picture frames: buy 3 get the 4th frame at 75% off. Write an expression to represent the total cost for 4 frames in two different ways.

_____

For Problems 6–7, decide whether the expressions are equivalent and write yes or no. If no, write an expression that is equivalent to the first one.

6. $k + 0.10k$ and $1.1k$

_____

7. $2m - 0.2m$ and $2.2m$

_____

8. **Open Ended** Write an expression equivalent to $0.65b$.

_____

9. **Open Ended** Write an expression equivalent to $22 - 0.58y$.

_____

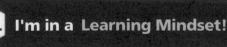
I'm in a Learning Mindset!

What about writing linear expressions causes a fixed-mindset voice in my head? What can I do about it?

_____

_____

Write Linear Expressions in Different Forms for Situations

ONLINE

Video Tutorials and
Interactive Examples

1. (MP) **Use Structure** A plumber charges a customer a one-time service fee of $79, $62 per hour for labor, and a surcharge of $15 per hour due to the call being an emergency. Write an expression to represent the total charges for the plumber in two different ways.

_____

2. (MP) **Use Structure** Mia buys ink at the office supply store for a business. She buys 3 printer cartridges, and the sales tax is 7%. Write an expression to represent the total cost of ink supplies in two different ways.

_____

3. (MP) **Use Structure** Emilio buys liter bottles of shampoo when the store has the promotion shown. Write an expression in two different ways to represent the total cost of 3 liters of shampoo.

_____

Buy 2 liters, get 30% off 3rd liter.

4. (MP) **Reason** Maribelle uses x yards of material to make a quilt. A customer requests 5 quilts that are 20% larger than the normal pattern. Write an expression to represent the total yards of material needed for the requested quilts in two different ways.

_____

5. (MP) **Use Structure** Gavin works two part-time jobs to pay for college. He works 8 hours each week tutoring and 10 hours each week in the dining hall. He gets paid the same hourly wage at each job. His parents also provide Gavin $50 per week for expenses. Gavin writes this expression, $18w + 50$, where w represents his hourly wage, to represent his total weekly income. Write another expression equivalent to Gavin's.

_____

For Problems 6–9, decide whether the expressions are equivalent and write *yes* or *no*.

6. $3n + 4n + 1 + 2n - 3$ and $9n - 2$

_____

7. $3.1b - 0.22b$ and $2.88b$

_____

8. $13x - 7x + 4$ and $20x + 4$

_____

9. $18 + 3.1m + 4.21m - 2$ and $16 + 7.31m$

_____

Test Prep

10. Students running a food drive have collected their goal amount of canned goods. Over the weekend, volunteers collect an additional 18% of the goal. Write an expression to represent the total percent of their goal collected in two different ways.

_____

11. A bookstore has a bargain table where every book is the same price. In addition, the bookstore gives 20% off every 5th book purchased from the bargain table. Write an expression to represent the total cost of purchasing 5 books in two different ways.

_____

12. A restaurant offers a dinner special for $25 per person plus a $5-per-person tip. Select all the expressions that represent the total cost of the special for m people.

Ⓐ $25m + 5m$

Ⓑ $25m - 5m$

Ⓒ $30m$

Ⓓ $25 + 5m$

Ⓔ $25m + 5$

13. Leon orders sheets of metal for an art class he teaches. He needs 12 sheets for his Tuesday night class and 8 sheets for his Thursday night class. There is also a $7.95 delivery fee. Select all the expressions that represent the total cost of Leon's order, if x is the cost of one sheet.

Ⓐ $12x + 8x$

Ⓑ $12x + 8x + 7.95$

Ⓒ $20x + 7.95$

Ⓓ $12x + 8x - 7.95$

Ⓔ $12x + 8x + 7.95x$

Spiral Review

14. Henri paid $10.75 for a calculator, $4.98 for copier paper, and $3.21 for folders. He paid with a $20 bill and got $1.06 in change. Show by using estimation that Henri's change is reasonable.

_____

_____

15. What are the common factors of 6, 9, and 18? _____

Name

Add, Subtract, and Factor Linear Expressions with Rational Coefficients

(I Can) identify problems that require me to add, subtract, factor, and expand linear expressions with rational coefficients.

Spark Your Learning SMALL GROUPS

Wallace made a quilt with the regular hexagon pattern shown. On each hexagon piece, he will sew a trim along each side. What expression represents the total length of trim on a hexagon?

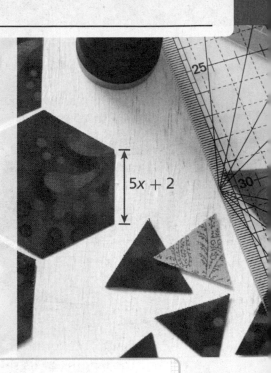

$5x + 2$

Turn and Talk Which is a like term with 5x: 10x, 5y, or 5? Explain.

Build Understanding

 1 A yard is shaped like an irregular quadrilateral with the side lengths shown.

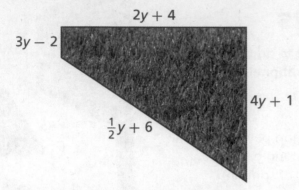

$2y + 4$

$3y - 2$

$4y + 1$

$\frac{1}{2}y + 6$

A. Write an expression that shows the perimeter of the yard as the sum of the lengths of its sides.

_____

B. Rewrite the expression as addition of **terms**.

_____

C. Use the **Commutative Property of Addition** and the **Associative Property of Addition** to rearrange the terms so that all of the *y*-terms are together and all of the integer terms are together.

_____

D. How can you identify **like terms** in an expression?

_____

E. Simplify the expression by combining like terms.

_____

F. Show how you used the Distributive Property to combine the *y*-terms.

_____

 Turn and Talk Explain why you might want to combine like terms before evaluating an expression. Discuss why the expressions in Part A and Part E look so different.

2 ▸ A path in a park forms the shape of an **equilateral triangle** with the side lengths shown.

(7.2d – 4)

A. Write an expression that represents the length of the path as a sum of the lengths of the three sides.

_____

B. Use the Commutative and Associative Properties of Addition to reorder and group like terms in your expression from Part A. Then combine like terms to simplify the expression.

_____

_____

C. Write an equivalent expression for the length of the path using the factor 3 and the length of one side.

$3\left(\boxed{}\right)$

D. Use the Distributive Property to *expand* the expression from Part C, and then simplify it.

$3\left(\boxed{}\right) = 3\left(\boxed{}\right) + 3\left(\boxed{}\right) = \boxed{}$

Turn and Talk What do you notice about your expressions in Part B and Part D? Discuss your observations.

3 ▸ Another path in the park goes around a square playground. The length of the entire path can be represented by the expression $20x + 8$.

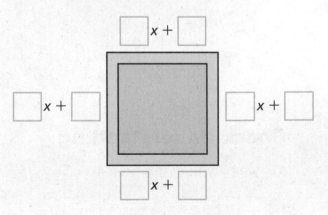

A. Find an expression that represents the length of each side of the square. Complete the expressions on the diagram.

B. Complete the equivalent expression for the length of the path, $20x + 8$.

$20x + 8 = 4\left(\boxed{}\right)$

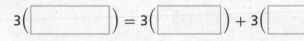

Turn and Talk In Part B, you *factored* the expression $20x + 8$ by writing it as a product. Explain how you used division and the Distributive Property to do this.

© Houghton Mifflin Harcourt Publishing Company

Step It Out

4 ▶ Apply what you have learned about adding, subtracting, factoring, and expanding linear expressions to simplify the expressions.

A. Simplify $(-t - 5) + (-2t + 3)$.

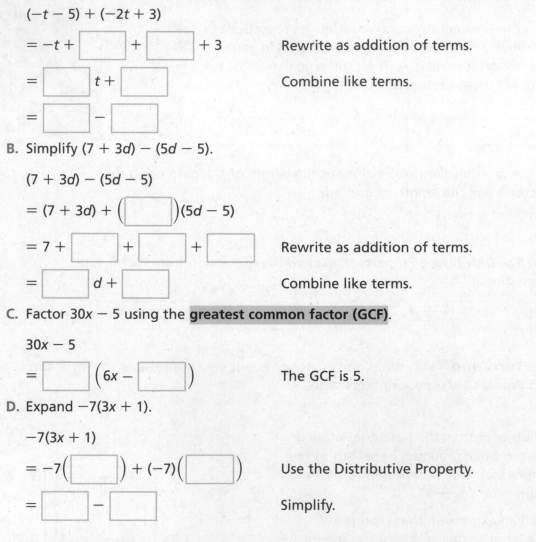

$(-t - 5) + (-2t + 3)$

$= -t + \boxed{} + \boxed{} + 3$ Rewrite as addition of terms.

$= \boxed{} \, t + \boxed{}$ Combine like terms.

$= \boxed{} - \boxed{}$

B. Simplify $(7 + 3d) - (5d - 5)$.

$(7 + 3d) - (5d - 5)$

$= (7 + 3d) + \left(\boxed{} \right)(5d - 5)$

$= 7 + \boxed{} + \boxed{} + \boxed{}$ Rewrite as addition of terms.

$= \boxed{} \, d + \boxed{}$ Combine like terms.

C. Factor $30x - 5$ using the **greatest common factor (GCF)**.

$30x - 5$

$= \boxed{} \left(6x - \boxed{} \right)$ The GCF is 5.

D. Expand $-7(3x + 1)$.

$-7(3x + 1)$

$= -7 \left(\boxed{} \right) + (-7) \left(\boxed{} \right)$ Use the Distributive Property.

$= \boxed{} - \boxed{}$ Simplify.

Check Understanding

1. Simplify the expression $4x - 6x + 15 - x - 4$.

_____

2. Use the Distributive Property to expand the expression $3(3x + 6)$. Then simplify the expression.

_____

3. Factor $24x - 20$ using the GCF.

_____

4. Simplify the expression $4\left(\frac{3}{2}f + 1\right) - 7(f + 5)$.

_____

On Your Own

5. A regular polygon has sides that are all equal in length and angles that all have the same measure. A regular decagon has the side lengths as shown.

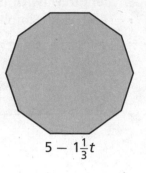

$5 - 1\frac{1}{3}t$

   A. (MP) **Model with Mathematics** Write an expression for the perimeter of the regular decagon as a product of one side length. Explain.

   _____

   _____

   _____

   B. Use the Distributive Property to expand the expression from Part A. Then simplify.

   _____

6. Factor $14f + 21$ using the GCF.

   _____

7. (MP) **Model with Mathematics** A pentagon has side lengths: $(12 + 4x)$, $(10 + 8x)$, $(15 + 3x)$, $(9 + 2x)$, and $(14 + 3x)$.

   Write a simplified expression that represents the perimeter of the pentagon. Explain.

   _____

   _____

   _____

For Problems 8–9, factor the expressions using 3 as one factor.

8. $3x - 30$

9. $3x + 15$

For Problems 10–11, simplify the expressions using properties of operations.

10. $(4x - 7.2) + (-5.3x - 8)$

11. $(t - 1) - (-7t + 2)$

For Problems 12–13, expand the expressions using the Distributive Property. Then simplify the expressions.

12. $4(7x + 3)$

13. $9(3y - 5)$

14. (MP) **Model with Mathematics** The width of a rectangle is shown. The length is twice the width. Write an expression for the perimeter listing each side. Simplify the expression.

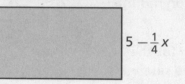 $5 - \frac{1}{4}x$

_____

15. Katelyn drew a pentagon. The side lengths are $(6.7t + 4.3)$, $(-t + 11)$, $(4.8t + 3)$, $(9.7t - 0.4)$, and $(8.6t - 0.2)$.

A. (MP) **Model with Mathematics** Write an expression for the perimeter. Group the like terms. Then combine like terms to simplify.

_____

_____

B. What two properties allowed you to reorder and regroup the terms?

_____

For Problems 16–17, simplify the expressions using properties of operations.

16. $\left(-6s - 7\frac{2}{5}\right) + (-6s + 6)$

17. $5(y - 7) - (2y + 9)$

_____   _____

For Problems 18–19, expand and simplify the expressions using properties of operations.

18. $8(3x - 7)$

19. $14(3b + 2)$

_____   _____

In Problems 20–21, simplify using properties of operations and then factor the expressions using the GCF.

20. $(10p + 10) + (8p - 1)$

21. $(2g + 2) - (-4g - 7)$

_____   _____

I'm in a Learning Mindset!

How can I apply my prior knowledge of the Distributive Property to factoring algebraic expressions?

_____

Name _____

LESSON 7.2
**More Practice/
Homework**

ONLINE

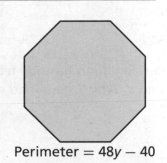 Ed

Video Tutorials and
Interactive Examples

Add, Subtract, and Factor Linear Expressions with Rational Coefficients

1. (MP) **Model with Mathematics** Write a simplified expression that represents the perimeter of an irregular quadrilateral with side lengths $\left(2\frac{1}{4}t - 5\right)$, $(4t + 3)$, $\left(\frac{1}{2}t - 1\right)$, and $(3t + 2)$.

_____

2. (MP) **Reason** The length of a rectangle is represented by $4 + 6x$. The width is half the length. What expression represents the perimeter of the rectangle? Explain your reasoning.

_____

_____

_____

3. (MP) **Model with Mathematics** The regular octagon has a perimeter represented by the expression shown. Write an expression to represent the length of one side of the octagon.

_____

Perimeter $= 48y - 40$

For Problems 4–9, simplify the expressions using properties of operations.

4. **Math on the Spot** $5(x - 4) + 2x$

_____

5. $18t - 3 - 5t + 8$

_____

6. $7.5 + 5f + 16.2 + 2f$

_____

7. $-8(1 + x) + 7x$

_____

8. $7\frac{1}{3}t - \left(10\frac{2}{3}t - 6\right)$

_____

9. $(-r - 5) - (-2r - 4)$

_____

For Problems 10–11, expand and simplify the expressions using properties of operations.

10. $7(11c + 3)$

_____

11. $6(7y - 8)$

_____

Test Prep

12. A square has a perimeter represented by the expression $8.8s - 20$. Write an expression to represent the length of one side of the square.

_____

_____

13. Simplify $-5(7 + x) + 2\frac{5}{6}x$.

_____

_____

14. Which expression is equivalent to $9y + 2(1 - 5y)$?

Ⓐ $4y + 2$

Ⓑ $19y + 2$

Ⓒ $y + 2$

Ⓓ $-y + 2$

15. An irregular pentagon has side lengths of $(x + 3)$, $(2x - 4)$, $(4x + 5)$, $(3x - 1)$, and x. Which simplified expression represents the pentagon's perimeter?

Ⓐ $11x - 3$

Ⓑ $24x + 60$

Ⓒ $11x + 3$

Ⓓ $-9x + 3$

Spiral Review

16. Jovan is 15 years old. His sister is 6 years older than $\frac{1}{3}$ his age. How old is Jovan's sister?

_____

17. Steven multiplies all the integers from -99 to -90, including -99 and -90. Should his answer be positive or negative? Explain your thinking.

_____

_____

_____

_____

© Houghton Mifflin Harcourt Publishing Company

Name _____

Write Two-Step Equations for Situations

(I Can) write two-step equations for various situations.

Spark Your Learning

Write an equation to represent each scenario.

Scenario 1: The cook at Sam's Diner made 19 quiches today. This is 1 more than 3 times the number of quiches he made yesterday. How many quiches did he make yesterday?

Scenario 2: Javier buys four dozen eggs. He saves $1.50 by using a coupon. The total he pays is $8.50. What was the cost of a dozen eggs without the coupon?

Scenario 3: Lina ate $\frac{1}{4}$ of a quiche for lunch. Each of her two sisters split another piece equally. The three ate a total of $\frac{7}{12}$ of the quiche. What fraction of the quiche did each of Lina's sisters eat?

> A quiche is a pastry crust, like a pie crust, filled with a mixture of eggs and milk or cream with any variety of other ingredients, as desired.

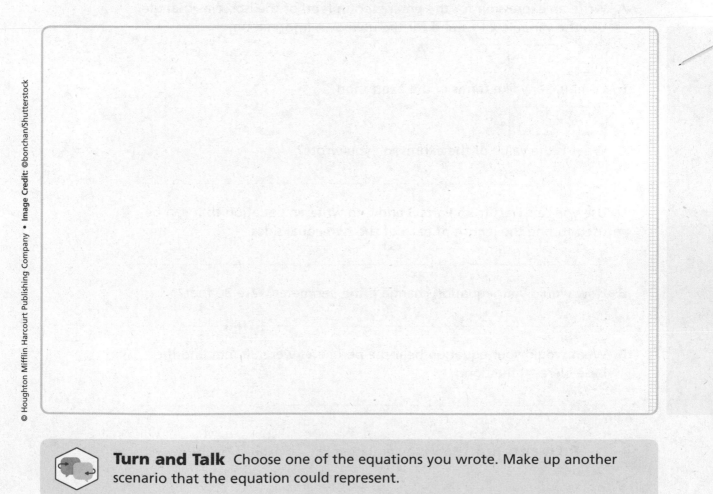

Turn and Talk Choose one of the equations you wrote. Make up another scenario that the equation could represent.

Build Understanding

 The perimeter of an **isosceles triangle** is 60 feet. The base is 12 feet long. Write an equation that could be used to find the lengths of the congruent sides.

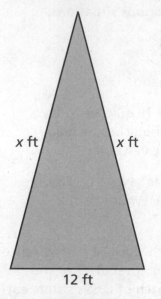

x ft   *x* ft

12 ft

A. Write an expression for the **perimeter** (in feet) of the isosceles triangle. Use the variable *x* to stand for the unknown information.

$\boxed{} + \boxed{} + \boxed{}$

B. Combine any like terms in the expression.

$\boxed{} + \boxed{}$

C. What is the value of the expression you wrote?

_____

D. Use your answers from Parts B and C to write an equation that can be used to find the length of each of the two equal sides.

_____

E. How would your equation change if the perimeter were 80 feet?

_____

F. What would your equation be if the perimeter were 80 feet and the base were 10 feet long?

_____

 Turn and Talk How is an equation like an expression? How is it different?

Step It Out

2 Chelsea buys a shirt and shoes at the store with the coupon at the right. The price of the shirt before the discount is $22, and her total discount is $18.55. Write an equation to find the price of the shoes before the discount.

50% off
entire purchase

A. What information are you trying to find? How can a variable help determine that information?

_____

_____

_____

B. Write an equation that can be used to find the unknown information. Use *x* as the variable.

_____

C. What does each side of the equation represent?

_____

_____

_____

_____

D. What does the variable *x* represent?

_____

Check Understanding

1. Each time Cheryl runs, she runs 3 miles. She rides her bike only on Saturdays and always for 10 miles. She exercises the same amount each week. She rides and runs for a total of 22 miles in a week. Write an equation that can be used to find out how many times Cheryl goes running each week.

_____

2. Mrs. Wu uses a 25% off coupon to buy 1 adult ticket and 1 child ticket to a movie. She pays a total amount of $9.00. A child ticket without the coupon costs $4.00. Write an equation that can be used to find the cost of an adult ticket without the coupon.

_____

On Your Own

(MP) Model with Mathematics For Problems 3–8, write an equation to represent the situation.

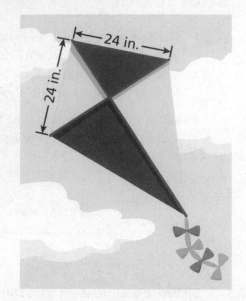

3. Carl is making the kite shown. It has a perimeter of 120 inches. The two longer sides of the kite are the same length. Write an equation that could be used to find the length of each of the longer sides.

_____

4. Ms. Malia bought a laptop with a 10% discount. She also bought a mouse for $13.99 and spent a total of $621.49 before taxes. Write an equation to find the original cost of the laptop.

_____

5. Paolo is using his grandmother's cookie recipe. He always doubles the amount of chocolate chips and oats. The recipe calls for $2\frac{1}{2}$ cups of chocolate chips. The total amount of chips and oats after doubling is $6\frac{1}{3}$ cups. Write an equation to find the original amount of oats in the recipe.

_____

6. A square has side lengths as shown in the picture and a perimeter of 54.8 centimeters. Write an equation to find the value of x.

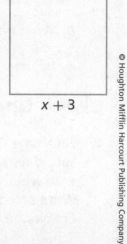

$x + 3$

_____

7. Ms. Emily buys a hat and gloves with a coupon for 30% off her entire purchase. The gloves cost $35 before the discount. Her bill before tax is $44.80. Write an equation to find the original cost of the hat.

_____

8. Bo's sister Anna is $\frac{3}{4}$ his age minus 1 year. She is 11 years old. Write an equation to find Bo's age.

_____

➖✖➕➗ I'm in a **Learning Mindset!**

What barriers do I perceive to writing two-step equations for situations?

_____

_____

LESSON 7.3
**More Practice/
Homework**

ONLINE

Video Tutorials and
Interactive Examples

Write Two-Step Equations for Situations

(MP) **Model with Mathematics** For Problems 1–4, write an
equation to represent the situation.

1. Pierce is making a rectangular frame for a photo collage that has a
   perimeter of 72.2 inches. The length of the frame is 20.3 inches.
   Write an equation to find the width of the frame.

   _____

2. Kendra is 3 times her daughter's age plus 7 years. Kendra is 49 years old.
   Write an equation to find her daughter's age.

   _____

3. Mitchell orders a plain turkey sandwich and a drink for lunch. The drink
   is $2.95. Instead he is served the super sandwich with lettuce, tomato,
   and mayonnaise. The restaurant manager takes 15% off the price of the
   sandwich. Write an equation to determine the original price of Mitchell's
   sandwich if his new bill is $8.05.

   _____

4. Bianca and Meredith are sisters. Meredith's height is $\frac{2}{3}$ of
   Bianca's height plus 32 inches. Meredith is 60 inches tall.
   Write an equation to find Bianca's height in inches.

   _____

5. **Health and Fitness** Tyler does squats and pushups. He
   wants to increase the number of each type of exercise by
   20% by the end of the month. He currently does 25 pushups.
   If Tyler meets his goal, he will do a total of 13 more squats
   and pushups than he does now. Write an equation to find
   how many squats Tyler does now.

   _____

6. (MP) **Model with Mathematics** An equilateral triangle has
   side lengths that measure $x + 4$ inches. The perimeter of the
   triangle is 18.6 inches. Write an equation to find the value of x.

   _____

60 in.

7. (MP) **Model with Mathematics** Ms. Lynette earns $19.50
   an hour when she works overtime. She worked overtime
   twice this week. One day she worked 3 hours of overtime.
   Her total overtime pay for the week is $146.25. Write an
   equation to find the number of overtime hours worked
   on the second day.

   _____

Test Prep

8. A parallelogram has a perimeter of $50\frac{1}{2}$ inches. The two longer sides of the parallelogram are each $16\frac{1}{4}$ inches. Write an equation to find the length of each of the shorter sides.

_____

9. A baby usually gains 10% of its birth weight plus 2 pounds in the first six weeks after birth. A baby gained 2.8 pounds. Write an equation to find the baby's birth weight.

_____

10. A rhombus has sides of length $x + 6$ inches and a perimeter of 49 inches. Which equation represents this situation?

   Ⓐ $4x + 6 = 49$

   Ⓑ $4(x + 6) = 49$

   Ⓒ $x + 6 = 49$

   Ⓓ $x + 24 = 49$

11. Mrs. Owens has a coupon for 40% off a pair of shoes. She pays $111.79 for a pair of shoes and a dress after using the coupon. The dress costs $64.99. Which equation can be solved for x, the retail price of the shoes?

   Ⓐ $0.6x + 64.99 = 111.79$

   Ⓑ $0.4x + 64.99 = 111.79$

   Ⓒ $0.6(x + 64.99) = 111.79$

   Ⓓ $0.4(x + 64.99) = 111.79$

Spiral Review

12. Sarah began the school week with $2.60 in her lunch account. She deposited $20 on Monday, and then spent $4.75 each day that week for lunch. What was the balance in her lunch account at the end of the day on Friday?

_____

13. Mr. Alvarado goes shopping at the mall with $70. He buys a pair of pants for $33.76 and a shirt for $29.52. He also returns a hat he bought the previous week for $19.67. How much money does Mr. Alvarado have after he buys the pants and shirt and returns the hat?

_____

Name _____

Apply Two-Step Equations to Solve Real-World Problems

(I Can) use two-step equations to solve a variety of problems.

Spark Your Learning

A diagram of the rectangular sitting area in a botanical garden is shown. What is the length of the sitting area in the garden?

Perimeter = 60 ft   10 ft

Turn and Talk How else could you have represented the situation with the garden?

Build Understanding

1 ▸ Lucy scored 20 points in her basketball game. She made 4 of her free throws, worth 1 point each, and made no 3-point field goals. How many 2-point field goals did she make?

Connect to Vocabulary

A **solution of an equation** is the value we can put in place of a variable (such as *x*) that makes the equation true.

A. Write an equation to represent this situation. _____

B. Model the equation with algebra tiles.

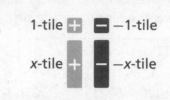

1-tile ⊞   ⊟ —1-tile

x-tile ⊞   ⊟ —*x*-tile

C. How can you work with the algebra tiles on the equation mat so that one side of the mat has only variables?

_____

D. How can you now use the tiles to find the value of the variable?

_____
_____

E. What is the solution of the equation and the solution to the problem?

_____

F. What was the sequence of math operations used in this model?

_____

G. Jerry solved the equation $2x - 4 = 20$ by adding four 1-tiles to each side. Explain why Jerry's method works.

_____
_____
_____
_____
_____

Turn and Talk How are solving $2x + 4 = 20$ and $2x - 4 = 20$ alike? How are they different?

Step It Out

 Mr. Maxwell bought new basketball shoes with the discount shown. He has a $10-off coupon he can use after the percentage discount. If Mr. Maxwell bought the shoes for $61.25, what was the original price?

A. If the shoes are discounted 25%, what percent of the original price is the discounted price?

25% discount is the same as ☐ % of the original price.

B. Fill in the boxes to set up the equation to find the original price of the shoes.

☐ % · Original Price − ☐ = 61.25

C. What would be the price without a $10-off coupon?

61.25 + ☐ = ☐ $ _____

D. Complete the equation that can be solved to find the price of the shoes before the 25% off discount.

☐ · Original Price = ☐

E. Find the original price of the shoes.

Original Price = 71.25 ÷ ☐

The original price was $ _____ .

F. Solve the equation from Step B algebraically. Then solve the problem. Let x represent the original price of the shoes.

$0.75x - 10.00 = 61.25$

+ ☐   + ☐   Addition Property of Equality
_____

$0.75x$ = ☐

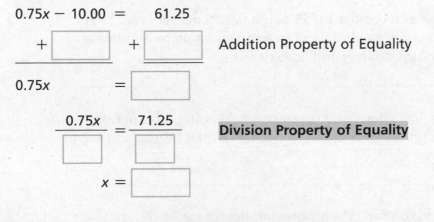

$\dfrac{0.75x}{☐} = \dfrac{71.25}{☐}$ **Division Property of Equality**

$x =$ ☐

The original price of the shoes was $ _____ .

Turn and Talk Compare the arithmetic solution from Parts C, D, and E to the algebraic solution in Part F.

3 Tracy's fitness goal for this week is shown on her planner. To meet her goal, she will need a total of 8 pushups more than her current daily total of morning and evening pushups. Tracy has been doing 25 pushups in the evening. How many pushups has she been doing in the morning?

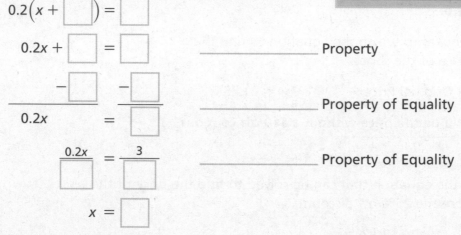

Weekly Planner GOAL: 20% improvement on pushups

	Mon.	Tues.	Wed.	Thurs.	Fri.
AM	Pushups ✓		Pushups ✓		Pushups ✓
PM	Pushups ✓		Pushups ✓		Pushups ✓

A. Write and solve an equation to find her current number of morning pushups.

$0.2\left(x + \boxed{}\right) = \boxed{}$

$0.2x + \boxed{} = \boxed{}$ _____ Property

$$\frac{-\boxed{} \quad -\boxed{}}{0.2x \quad = \boxed{}}$$ _____ Property of Equality

$\dfrac{0.2x}{\boxed{}} = \dfrac{3}{\boxed{}}$ _____ Property of Equality

$x = \boxed{}$

B. Check your solution.

$0.2(x + 25) = 8$

$0.2\left(\boxed{} + 25\right) = \boxed{}$ ✓

$8 = 8$

Check Understanding

1. Cookie Castle sells 8-inch cookies for $3 plus a flat $5 delivery fee. Zach has $14 to spend on cookies. Write and solve an equation to determine how many cookies Zach can buy and have delivered.

   _____

2. A kitten is born having a mass of 90 grams and gains 10 grams per day. How many days will it take the kitten to double its mass? Write and solve the equation.

   _____

3. Mr. Muñoz has a coupon for 15% off his entire purchase. He buys binoculars for $105 and hiking boots. He spends a total of $170 before tax. Write and solve an equation to find how much the hiking boots cost before the discount.

   _____

On Your Own

4. The formula $F = 1.8C + 32$ can be used to convert temperature units. F is degrees Fahrenheit, and C is degrees Celsius. Convert the December record low temperature to Celsius. Round to the nearest tenth.

Record Low Temperatures	
December	−5 °F
January	−10 °F
February	−7 °F

_____

5. Dirk sold 7 more than 2 times as many gym memberships this month than last month. This month he sold 43 memberships.

A. Use arithmetic to find the number of memberships Dirk sold last month.

_____

B. Use algebra to find the number of memberships Dirk sold last month.

_____

C. Compare the sequence of math operations in Part A and Part B.

_____

6. (MP) **Model with Mathematics** Arlene buys a phone case and charging cord for 15% off. The original cost of the phone case is $18. Her total discount is $4.20. Write and solve an equation to find the original price of the charging cord.

_____

7. (MP) **Model with Mathematics** Taka is playing a game of darts. She scores 52 points. In the game she is playing, she gets a −3 score each time she misses the board. Her final point total is 37. Write and solve an equation to find out how many times she missed the board.

_____

For Problems 8–15, solve each equation. Check your solution.

8. $-9d - 1 = 17$

9. $2 + \frac{1}{6}a = -4$

10. $24 = 3(w + 5)$

11. $-\frac{4}{5}(f + 5) = -12$

12. $\frac{g}{3} - 7 = 15$

13. $-3 + \frac{p}{7} = -5$

14. $-17 + \frac{b}{8} = 13$

15. $\frac{k}{2} + 9 = 30$

16. **(MP) Model with Mathematics** Mr. Burns takes a one-day trip and rents a car using the rates shown. The car rental cost is $68.25. Write and solve an equation to find how many miles he traveled.

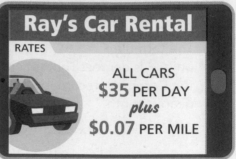

Ray's Car Rental
RATES
ALL CARS
$35 PER DAY
plus
$0.07 PER MILE

_____

17. **(MP) Model with Mathematics** Geoff works at a warehouse, earning $17.50 per hour plus a $200 one-time hiring bonus. In Geoff's first week, his pay including the bonus was $637.50. Write and solve an equation to find how many hours Geoff worked his first week.

_____

18. **(MP) Attend to Precision** A regular hexagon has sides of length $x + 5$ and a perimeter of 72 inches. Write and solve an equation to find x. How long is a side?

_____

For Problems 19–26, solve each equation. Check your solution.

19. $-3(n + 5) = 12$

_____

20. $7(c - 12) = -21$

_____

21. $-9h - 15 = 93$

_____

22. $\frac{z}{5} + 3 = -35$

_____

23. $\frac{3}{8}n + 1 = -25$

_____

24. $2x - 5 = 15$

_____

25. $3\left(y + \frac{2}{5}\right) = -\frac{1}{5}$

_____

26. $2(p + 14) = 0$

_____

27. **Open Ended** Write a word problem that is represented by the equation $3x + 15 = 42$.

_____

_____

_____

© Houghton Mifflin Harcourt Publishing Company

⊹ I'm in a Learning Mindset!

How do I keep myself motivated to solve problems with two-step equations?

_____

Apply Two-Step Equations to Solve Real-World Problems

1. (MP) **Model with Mathematics** Julie wants to buy tulip bulbs to plant. Each bulb costs $0.50 plus a one-time $4.50 shipping cost. She has $22 to spend. Write and solve an equation to determine how many bulbs Julie can buy and have shipped.

   _____

2. **Math on the Spot** The total charge for a yearly Internet movie rental membership is $231. A registration fee of $15 is paid up front, and the rest is paid monthly. How much do new members pay each month?

   _____

3. (MP) **Attend to Precision** Beverly is making peanut butter–banana bread. She always doubles the amount of nuts and peanut butter chips. The total amount of chips and nuts after doubling is $4\frac{1}{2}$ cups. Write and solve an equation to find the original amount of nuts in the recipe.

   _____

$1\frac{1}{2}c$ peanut butter chips
? c nuts
3 very ripe bananas

For Problems 4–7, solve each equation. Check your solution.

4. $3 = 0.2m - 7$

5. $1.3z + 1.5 = 5.4$

6. $-3(t + 6) = 0$

7. $-8(1 - g) = 56$

8. **Open Ended** Write a two-step equation that involves multiplication and subtraction, includes a negative coefficient, and has a solution of $x = 7$.

   _____

9. **Open Ended** Write a two-step equation that involves division and addition and has a solution of $x = -25$.

   _____

Test Prep

10. Leo started working for a new company that paid him $25 per hour with a hiring bonus of $100. During the first two weeks he was paid $1,200, which included the bonus. How many hours did he work during the first two weeks?

- (A) 40
- (B) 44
- (C) 48
- (D) 52

11. To convert to degrees Fahrenheit, use the formula $F = \frac{9}{5}C + 32$, where C is the degrees in Celsius. From the choices below, which is the first step to solve for Celsius if the temperature is 70 °F?

- (A) Add 32 to both sides.
- (B) Subtract 32 from both sides.
- (C) Divide both sides by $\frac{5}{9}$.
- (D) Multiply both sides by $\frac{9}{5}$.

12. Fred earns $16.50 an hour for overtime. He worked overtime on Monday and Thursday this week. On Monday, he worked 4 hours of overtime. His total overtime pay for the week was $123.75. Write and solve an equation to find the number of overtime hours Fred worked on Thursday.

_____

13. Solve $\frac{1}{2}m - 5 = 23$.

- (A) 13.5
- (B) 27
- (C) 33
- (D) 56

Spiral Review

14. Apples at the farmers' market cost $2.50 for 5 apples or $0.70 for 1 apple. Which is the better buy if you want 5 apples? Explain.

_____

15. Mr. Spencer drives 200 miles in 5 hours. What is his unit rate?

_____

Apply Two-Step Equations to Find Angle Measures

(**I Can**) identify angle relationships, and use them to write and solve equations.

Step It Out

You previously learned that a **right angle** measures 90°. In this lesson, you will also work with pairs of angles called complementary angles and supplementary angles.

1. Use the diagram for Parts A–H.

    A. Name the right angles. ∠ _____ and ∠ _____

    B. Name a pair of complementary angles. ∠ _____ and ∠ _____

    C. What is the measure of ∠ABE? _____

    D. Name a pair of supplementary angles.

    ∠ _____ and ∠ _____

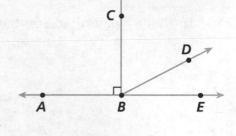

    E. If the measure of ∠CBD is equal to (5x)° and the measure of ∠DBE is 40°, use what you know about complementary angles to write an equation to solve for x. Then solve it.

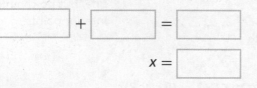

    $$x = \boxed{}$$

    F. If the measure of ∠ABD is (5y + 15)° and the measure of ∠DBE is 40°, write an equation and solve for y.

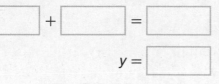

    $$y = \boxed{}$$

Turn and Talk If ∠ABD were the only known angle measure, how could you determine the measures of the other angles in the diagram?

Use Figure 1 for Parts A–C and Figure 2 for Parts D–F.

A. Name two pairs of vertical angles.

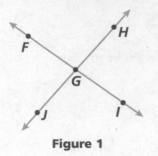

Figure 1

∠ _____ and ∠ _____

∠ _____ and ∠ _____

B. Vertical angles [are / are not] congruent.

C. Given ∠FGH measures $(6x - 24)°$ and ∠JGI measures 96°, write an equation that can be used to determine the value of x. Solve for x.

⬚ = ⬚ and $x =$ ⬚

D. Name a pair of adjacent angles in Figure 2.

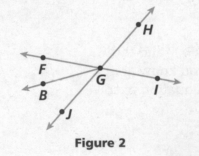

Figure 2

∠ _____ and ∠ _____

E. Given m∠FGJ = 84°, m∠FGB = $(4x)°$, and m∠JGB = $(5x + 3)°$, write an equation that can be used to determine the value of x. Solve for x.

⬚ + ⬚ = ⬚ and $x =$ ⬚

F. Explain why ∠FGJ and ∠FGB are not adjacent.

_____

_____

Turn and Talk Explain why ∠FGB does not have a vertical angle in Figure 2.

3 In Figure 3, ∠AOD measures $(3x + 15)°$.

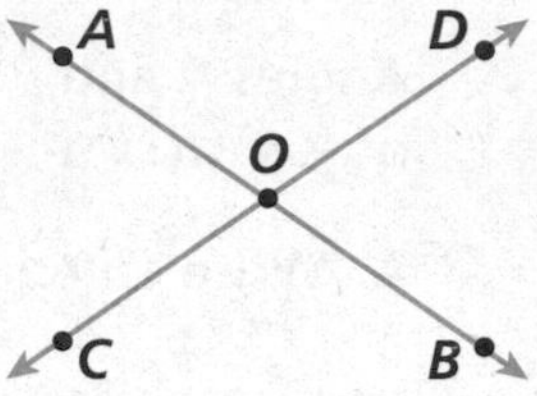

A. What is the sum of the measures of ∠AOD and ∠DOB?

_____

B. If the measure of ∠DOB is $(2x + 15)°$, write an equation to determine the value of x.

$$\boxed{} + \boxed{} = \boxed{}$$

C. Solve for x.

$x =$ _____

D. What is the measure of ∠AOD?

_____

E. What angle makes vertical angles with ∠AOD? What is its measure?

m _____ = _____

F. What two angles are adjacent to ∠AOD? What are their angle measures?

m _____ = _____

m _____ = _____

Figure 3

Check Understanding

1. Two angles are complementary. The first angle measures $(2x + 15)°$, and the second measures $(4x + 9)°$. Write an equation to determine the value of x. Then solve your equation and find the measures of both angles.

_____

_____

_____

2. ∠A and ∠B are adjacent. The sum of their measures is 92°. ∠A measures $(2x + 5)°$. ∠B is three times the size of ∠A. Write an equation to determine the value of x. Then solve your equation and find the measures of both angles.

_____

On Your Own

3. Angles A and B are adjacent angles and are supplementary. The measure of $\angle A$ is $(3x + 10)°$, and the measure of $\angle B$ is $(12x + 35)°$.

A. Write an equation that can be used to determine the value of x.

_____

B. What is the value of x?

_____

C. What is the measure of $\angle A$?

_____

4. Describe $\angle COA$ in relation to $\angle DOB$.

_____

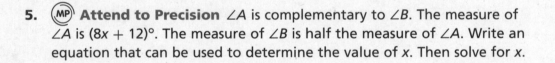

5. (MP) **Attend to Precision** $\angle A$ is complementary to $\angle B$. The measure of $\angle A$ is $(8x + 12)°$. The measure of $\angle B$ is half the measure of $\angle A$. Write an equation that can be used to determine the value of x. Then solve for x.

_____

_____

For Problems 6–7, use Figure 4.

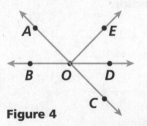

Figure 4

6. Describe the relationship between $\angle BOC$ and $\angle COD$. What is the sum of their angle measures?

_____

_____

7. Describe the relationship between $\angle AOB$ and $\angle COD$. Are their measures equal?

_____

8. **STEM** A rocket blasts off at a 90° angle from Earth. A second rocket launches at a different angle as shown in the diagram.

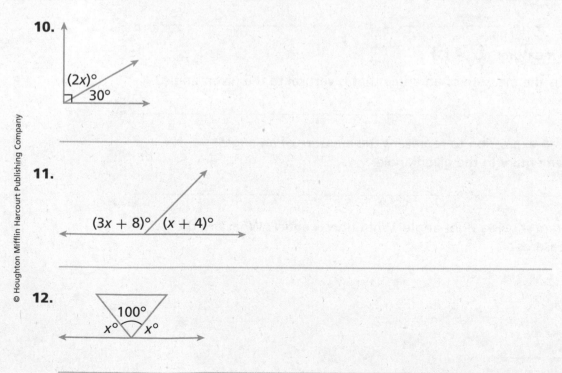

Rocket 1   Rocket 2

$(3x + 7)°$

$(5x + 3)°$

Earth

   A. Write an equation that can be used to determine the value of x.

   _____

   B. What is the value of x?

   _____

   C. What is the measure of the angle of the second rocket launch in relation to Earth?

   _____

9. Two lines intersect to form an X. The measure of one angle is 58°.

   A. What is the measure of one of the angles sharing a side with the 58° angle? Explain.

   _____

   B. Since the angles are sharing a side, what are they called?

   _____

(MP) **Model with Mathematics** For Problems 10–12, write an equation that can be used to determine the value of x.

10.

$(2x)°$ $30°$

_____

11.

$(3x + 8)°$ $(x + 4)°$

_____

12.

$100°$

$x°$ $x°$

_____

13. (MP) **Look for Repeated Reasoning** Based on the diagram, if one angle measure is given, how can you determine all of the other angle measures?

_____

_____

_____

_____

For Problems 14–15, use the expressions given for the measures of complementary angles to solve for x. Then find the angle measures.

14. $(5x + 14)°$ and $(3x + 20)°$

15. $(4x + 3)°$ and $(4x + 7)°$

_____   _____

_____   _____

For Problems 16–17, use the expressions given for the measures of supplementary angles to solve for x. Then find the angle measures.

16. $(9x + 17)°$ and $(6x + 13)°$

17. $(6x + 7)°$ and $(5x + 8)°$

_____   _____

_____   _____

18. An angle measures $(2x + 11)°$.

A. What is the measure of an angle that is vertical to the given angle?

_____

B. Write an expression to represent the measure of an angle supplementary to the given angle.

_____

19. The diagram shows a right angle. What does x equal? What are the angle measures?

$(3x + 5)°$

$(2x + 5)°$

Apply Two-Step Equations to Find Angle Measures

1. Libby is putting together a piece of furniture. She notices that two of the pieces form a right angle. If these right angles are cut in half, or *bisected*, by another bar, what would each angle measure within that right angle?

2. The diagram shows a right angle. Write an equation to determine the value of x. Solve for x.

$(8x)°$

$(6x + 6)°$

3. A given angle measures 30°, and the measure of its vertical angle is expressed as $(5x + 5)°$.

A. Write an equation to determine the value of x. Solve for x.

B. If the measure of an angle adjacent to the given angle is represented by the expression $(24x + 30)°$ using the same value for x, what is the measure of the adjacent angle?

4. (MP) **Attend to Precision** Ms. Baumgartner draws a pair of supplementary angles and tells the class that the angle measures are $(4x + 30)°$ and $(2x + 6)°$.

A. Write an equation to determine the value of x. Solve for x.

B. What does the larger angle measure? What does the smaller angle measure?

5. **Math on the Spot** Use the diagram to find $m∠2$ if $m∠1 = 105°$.

4 3
1 2
105°
?

Test Prep

6. Consider adjacent angles that measure $(2x + 45)°$ and $(3x + 55)°$. The sum of the measures of these two angles is $135°$.

    A. Write and solve an equation to find the value of x.

    _____

    B. Using the value of x, what is the angle measure represented by the expression $(2x + 45)°$?

    _____

7. An angle has a measure of $(3x + 5)°$, and its complementary angle has a measure of $(2x + 5)°$. Which is the correct equation to find x?

    Ⓐ $5x + 10 = 180$

    Ⓑ $5x = 180 + 10$

    Ⓒ $5x + 10 = 90$

    Ⓓ $5x = 90 + 10$

8. Vertical angles have the same measure. True or False?

_____

9. The sum of the measures of adjacent angles is always $90°$. True or False?

_____

10. Draw lines to match.

    $\angle AOB$ and $\angle COD$ •   • complementary, adjacent

    $\angle DOE$ and $\angle COD$ •   • supplementary, adjacent

    $\angle AOB$ and $\angle AOD$ •   • vertical

Spiral Review

11. Frankie and Marcel are picking apples. Frankie has 18 apples, which is 4 times plus 2 more apples than Marcel has. How many apples does Marcel have?

_____

12. Is 10 a solution of the inequality $x \geq 12$?

_____

Review

Vocabulary

Choose the correct term from the Vocabulary box.

1. a pair of angles with measures that add to 90°

_____

2. a pair of angles with measures that add to 180°

_____

3. a pair of opposite angles formed by two intersecting lines

_____

4. a pair of angles that share a vertex and a ray but have no

interior points in common _____

> **Vocabulary**
>
> adjacent angles
> complementary angles
> supplementary angles
> vertical angles

Concepts and Skills

5. To fence a rectangular cornfield, a farmer uses 2,600 meters of fencing. The length of the field is 800 meters. Complete the equation that can be used to determine the width w of the field in meters. Use values from the box to complete the equation.

| 2 | 4 | 1,000 | 1,600 | 2,600 | w |

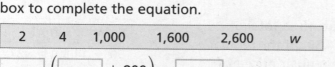

6. **(MP) Use Tools** The regular price r of a sweater was marked down by $5. Then the marked-down price was reduced by 20%. Write two expressions that represents the final reduced price of the sweater. State what strategy and tool you will use to answer the question, explain your choice, and then find the answer.

_____

_____

7. The McCray family ate at a restaurant. The expression shown represents the amount of tip they left, where b is the amount of the bill.

0.15b

Write two different expressions in terms of b to represent the total amount that the family spent for the meal, including the tip.

Expression 1: _____   Expression 2: _____

Determine the measure in degrees of the angle indicated with an arc.

8.

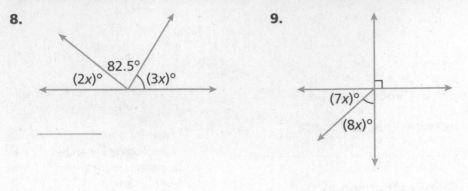

82.5°
$(2x)°$ $(3x)°$

_____

9.

$(7x)°$

$(8x)°$

_____

10. Simplify the expression.

$\left(\frac{7}{8}x - 4\right) - 3\left(\frac{1}{4}x + 6\right)$ _____

11. A website designer charges $200 plus $49 per hour to make a website. The designer charges a bakery a total of $1,204.50 to make its website.

  A. Write an equation that models this situation, where h represents the number of hours the designer worked on the bakery's website.

  _____

  B. How many hours did it take the designer to make the bakery's website?

  _____ hours

12. A coach buys 5 identical baseball bats for a total of $327.45. The bats are on sale for $14.50 off the regular price. Darius tried to determine the regular price r of each bat, but his work contains an error.

  A. Describe the error that Darius made.

  _____

  _____

  _____

Darius's Work
$5(r - 14.50) = 327.45$
$5r - 72.50 = 327.45$
$5r = 254.95$
$r = 50.99$
The regular price is $50.99.

  B. What is the correct regular price of each bat? $ _____

13. Which expression is equivalent to $(8x + 6) + (10x - 30)$?

  Ⓐ $6(3x - 4)$ Ⓒ $18(x - 24)$

  Ⓑ $9(2x - 24)$ Ⓓ $18x - 36$

Solve Problems Using Inequalities

The Suspect is Over There!

> I believe the suspect is greater than or equal to four-fifths.

In your work with the Math Detective Agency, you have been asked to locate an integer suspect using witness reports given as inequalities. For example, the report $x \geq \frac{4}{5}$ means that the witness believes the suspect is greater than or equal to four-fifths.

Summarize each report by graphing the inequality on the number line.

A. $x \geq \frac{4}{5}$ 0 1 2 3 4 5 6 7 8

B. $y < 6$ 0 1 2 3 4 5 6 7 8

C. $n \leq 2.8$ 0 1 2 3 4 5 6 7 8

D. $p > \frac{8}{5}$ 0 1 2 3 4 5 6 7 8

Turn and Talk

If all the witness reports are correct, do you have enough information to determine which integer is the suspect? Explain.

Are You Ready?

Complete these problems to review prior concepts and skills you will need for this module.

Compare Rational Numbers

Compare. Write $<$ or $>$.

1. $-7 \;\square\; -3$

2. $0 \;\square\; -1$

3. $\frac{1}{3} \;\square\; -\frac{3}{4}$

4. $-2.10 \;\square\; -2.19$

5. $-7\frac{2}{5} \;\square\; 5\frac{1}{2}$

6. $-\frac{2}{5} \;\square\; -0.35$

Interpret, Write, and Graph Inequalities

For each inequality, circle the values in the box that can be substituted for the variable to make the inequality true.

7. $x + 2.4 < 8.6$

| 0 | 2.4 | 5.7 | 8.5 | 9.1 |

8. $\frac{1}{3}n > \frac{2}{5}$

| $\frac{3}{4}$ | 1 | $\frac{6}{5}$ | $\frac{4}{3}$ | 2 |

Write an inequality to represent each situation.

9. The temperature t in a freezer must be at most -10 °F.

_____

10. A person's weight w must be more than 110 pounds for the person to donate blood to a blood bank.

_____

Graph each inequality.

11. $x < 16$

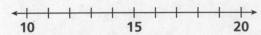

12. $n > 5.2$

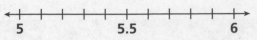

Name _____

Understand and Apply Properties to Solve One-Step Inequalities

(I Can) solve one-step inequalities by applying properties and graph the solutions on a number line.

Spark Your Learning

Suppose the lowest elevation to which the submarine shown has been tested is −490 meters. If it is currently at an elevation of −125 meters, how many meters more can it dive without going below the lowest elevation tested?

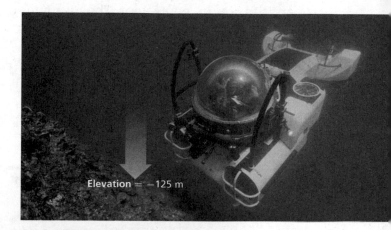

Elevation = −125 m

Turn and Talk Can the submarine dive 200 meters more without going below the lowest elevation tested? 400 meters more? How do you know?

Build Understanding

Connect to Vocabulary

The **solution of an inequality** is a value or values that makes an inequality true.

Recall that an equation is a mathematical sentence showing that two quantities are equal, or **equivalent**. Likewise, an **inequality** is a mathematical sentence showing that two quantities are not equivalent. The meanings of inequality symbols are shown in the table.

Greater than	>	Greater than or equal to	$\geq$
Less than	<	Less than or equal to	$\leq$

The number line shows $x \leq 365$. Note the closed circle represents "or equal to" in the inequality to indicate the inclusion of 365.

```
  +--+--+--+--+--+--+--+--+--●--+--+--+--+--+--+--+--+--+--+--+-->
 300  310  320  330  340  350  360  370  380  390  400
```

1 ▶ A submarine is at sea level, and it descends with a rate of change of −10 feet per second.

A. Write an inequality to represent the time t it takes the submarine to reach an elevation of −140 feet or deeper.

_____

B. Write three values for t that will make the inequality from Part A true. Substitute each value in the inequality to check. Then describe the set of numbers that can make the inequality true.

_____

_____

C. Solve the inequality from Part A by writing a simple inequality that describes all of the numbers that will make the inequality true. Write an inequality symbol in the first box and a number in the second box.

t ☐ ☐

D. Graph the inequality from Part C. Can the submarine reach an elevation of −140 feet or deeper in less than 14 seconds?

```
  +--+--+--+--+--+--+--+--+--+--+--+--+--+--+--+--+--+--+--+--+-->
  0   2   4   6   8   10  12  14  16  18  20
                    Time (seconds)
```

_____

E. How are solving $-10t = -140$ and $-10t \leq -140$ alike? How are they different?

_____

_____

Step It Out

2 ▶ During the spring rains, the water level in a lake rises. Although the lake has a dam, when the water reaches the top of the dam, water will begin flowing over the top.

Top of dam = 152 ft

Lake water level = 127 ft

A. Write an inequality that expresses how much more the lake can rise *r* so that the water does not flow over the top of the dam.

_____

B. Write three values for *r* that will make the inequality from Part A true. Then write and graph a simple inequality that describes all of the numbers that will make the inequality true.

_____

r [ ] [ ]

0 5 10 15 20 25 30 35 40 45 50

 Turn and Talk How are solving $127 + r \leq 152$ and solving $127 + r = 152$ alike, and how are they different?

The properties of equality you used when solving equations hold true for inequalities, with one exception. When you multiply or divide by a negative number, you must reverse the inequality symbol.

3 ▶ Apply properties of inequalities to solve each inequality.

A.

$m - 0.3 > 1.45$

$+ \boxed{} \quad + \boxed{}$

$m > \boxed{}$

B.

$3.5n \leq 7$

$\dfrac{3.5n}{\boxed{}} \leq \dfrac{7}{\boxed{}}$

$n \leq \boxed{}$

C.

$-2 \geq b + \frac{1}{8}$

$- \boxed{} \qquad - \boxed{}$

$\boxed{} \geq b$

$b \leq \boxed{}$

D.

$-\frac{1}{2}y < 6$

$\boxed{} \cdot -\frac{1}{2}y > \boxed{} \cdot 6$

$y > \boxed{}$

E.

$-x < -4$

$\boxed{} \cdot -x > \boxed{} \cdot -4$

$x > \boxed{}$

F.

$\dfrac{-2a}{3} > 6$

$-\frac{2}{3}a > \boxed{}$

$\boxed{} \cdot -\frac{2}{3}a < \boxed{} \cdot \boxed{}$

$a < \boxed{}$

Leila is designing a rectangular table. What is the range of values for x if the area of the table shown is to be 12 square feet or less?

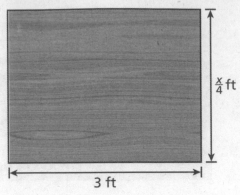

$\frac{x}{4}$ ft

3 ft

A. What is the inequality using the formula for the area of a rectangle?

_____

B. Solve the inequality for x.

_____

C. Give the range of values for x that are reasonable in the context of this problem. Graph the solution.

_____

_____

```
<-+--+--+--+--+--+--+--+--+--+--+--+--+--+--+--+--+--+--+--+->
  -6 -4 -2  0  2  4  6  8 10 12 14 16 18 20 22 24 26 28 30 32 34
```

 Turn and Talk What is the longest the unknown side of the table can be? Explain.

Check Understanding

1. The veterinarian told Hector that his 8-inch puppy would get no taller than 24 inches. Write and solve an inequality to find how much more his puppy, shown here, may grow.

_____

_____

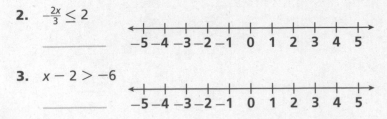

For Problems 2–3, solve the inequality. Graph the solution.

2. $-\frac{2x}{3} \leq 2$

_____

```
<-+--+--+--+--+--+--+--+--+--+->
 -5 -4 -3 -2 -1  0  1  2  3  4  5
```

3. $x - 2 > -6$

_____

```
<-+--+--+--+--+--+--+--+--+--+->
 -5 -4 -3 -2 -1  0  1  2  3  4  5
```

On Your Own

For Problems 4–5, use the given information:

Harun is designing a room addition for a home and wants a rectangular window with area that is more than 12 square feet but not more than 24 square feet. Harun knows he wants the window to be 4 feet wide.

4. **(MP) Model with Mathematics** Write and solve an inequality to find the length x that will guarantee that the window is not too small. Explain.

_____

_____

_____

5. **(MP) Model with Mathematics** Write and solve an inequality to find the length x that will guarantee that the window is not too large. Explain.

_____

_____

_____

6. **(MP) Use Structure** Emir is solving the inequality $-\frac{2}{3}x < 18$. What steps should he follow to find the solution?

_____

_____

For Problems 7–10, solve the inequality. Graph the solution.

7. $10 \le x + 7$ _____

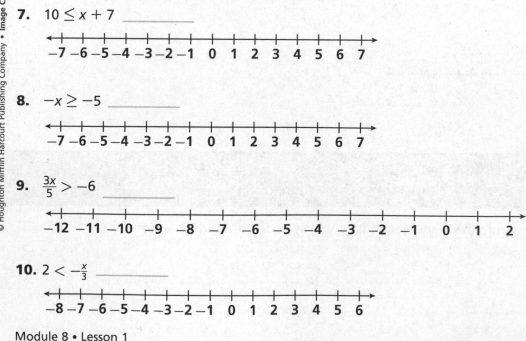

8. $-x \ge -5$ _____

9. $\frac{3x}{5} > -6$ _____

10. $2 < -\frac{x}{3}$ _____

For Problems 11–13, use the given information:

Three friends are shopping at the garage sale shown.

11. (MP) **Attend to Precision** Ming has $24. Write and solve an inequality for the number of shorts she can buy. Interpret the solution in the context of the problem.

Garage Sale	
Pants	$8
Shirts	$6
Shorts	$4
Belts	$3

_____

_____

12. (MP) **Attend to Precision** Camille can buy up to 5 shirts. How much money could she have?

_____

13. (MP) **Construct Arguments** Juanita has $24. Can she buy 5 shirts? Explain your answer.

_____

14. (MP) **Model with Mathematics** Rudo has a target of at least $150 in pledges for a walkathon. He currently has $65 in pledges. Write and solve an inequality for the amount p Rudo has left to raise.

_____

For Problems 15–17, solve the inequality. Graph the solution.

15. $x - 2.5 > 8.7$ _____

<---+++++++++++++++++++++++++++++++---->
　　6　7　8　9　10　11　12

16. $1.8x \leq 13.5$ _____

<---+++++++++++++++++++++++++++++++---->
　　4　5　6　7　8　9　10

17. $x + 1\frac{3}{5} < -2$ _____

<---+++++++++++++++++++++++++++++++---->
　−5　−4　−3　−2　−1　0　1

I'm in a Learning Mindset!

What part of solving one-step inequalities elicits a fixed-mindset voice in my head?

_____

_____

Understand and Apply Properties to Solve One-Step Inequalities

1. **(MP) Model with Mathematics** Cara is designing the rectangular patio shown. She wants the area of the patio to be larger than 72 square feet but no greater than 156 square feet.

   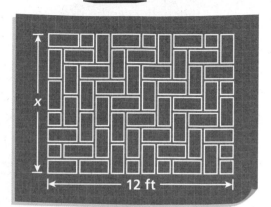

   A. Write and solve an inequality representing a length that meets the requirement for the minimum area.

   _____

   B. Write and solve an inequality representing a length that meets the requirement for the maximum area.

   _____

   C. Describe the possible lengths for the unknown side.

   _____

2. **Math on the Spot** Solve the inequality. Graph the solution.

   A. $-4x < 12$ _____

   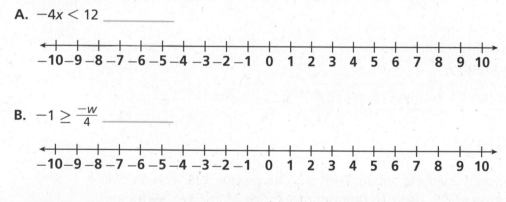

   B. $-1 \geq \frac{-w}{4}$ _____

   -10 -9 -8 -7 -6 -5 -4 -3 -2 -1 0 1 2 3 4 5 6 7 8 9 10

3. **STEM** In the science lab, Will is testing the freezing point of a substance, which should be −24 °C. He is changing the temperature at a rate of −3 °C per minute, starting at 0 °C. Write and solve an inequality for the time t before the temperature reaches the freezing point.

   _____

4. **(MP) Model with Mathematics** Tania has already saved $25.75. She needs at least $53.88 to buy a set of headphones. Write and solve an inequality that shows how much more she needs to earn to buy headphones.

   _____

Test Prep

5. Chan is in a running club and needs to run at least 500 miles in a year to earn the gold level of achievement. He is presently at 220 miles. Which inequality can be used to determine the additional number of miles he can run and earn gold?

(A) $x + 220 < 500$

(B) $x + 220 \geq 500$

(C) $x + 500 > 220$

(D) $x + 500 \leq 220$

6. Select the number line that represents the solution of the inequality $7 - x \geq 4$.

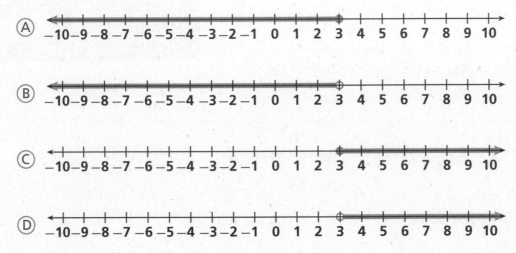

7. Shawna earns $12.75 per hour. How many hours does she need to work to earn $102 or more?

at least / at most / less than / more than _____ hours

Spiral Review

8. Francisco bought 2 tickets online. The total charge was $35 with an online booking charge of $5. Use x to represent the price of a ticket. Write an equation that could be used to find the price of a ticket. _____

9. Solve for x.

_____

$2x$ / $50°$

10. The perimeter of the table shown is 16 feet. Write an equation in the form $px + q = r$ to solve for x.

_____

x

3

© Houghton Mifflin Harcourt Publishing Company

Name _____

Write Two-Step Inequalities for Situations

(I Can) write two-step inequalities for real–world scenarios and determine whether given values are solutions.

Spark Your Learning

A small business owner is planning to upgrade the computer system. A new system will cost $1,200, but the total cost can be more with installation. The owner has saved $300 and will continue to save $30 from profits each day for the new system. How many days will it take the business owner to save enough money to purchase the new computer system?

Select the inequality that represents this situation. Describe what each part of the inequality represents.

$300 + 30x \geq 1,200$ $300 + 30x \leq 1,200$

$300 + 30x < 1,200$ $300 + 30x > 1,200$

 Turn and Talk Describe a situation that could be represented by changing the direction of the inequality symbol in the inequality above. Explain.

Build Understanding

As you have learned, a one-step inequality involves one operation. For example, $x + 1 > 3$ is a one-step inequality. In this example, 4, 40, and 4,000,000 are all *solutions* because they make the inequality true when substituted for x, but 1 is not a solution because it does not make the inequality true when substituted for x.

A two-step inequality involves two operations.

1 Caitlyn wants to buy sheets of trumpet music at the price shown. She has only $25, and she first needs to pay back $5 to her friend. How many sheets can Caitlyn buy?

Trumpet Music
$3 per sheet

A. Describe how this problem represents an inequality situation.

_____

_____

B. Describe the part of this situation that is variable.

_____

C. What are all the costs that Caitlyn's money will cover?

_____

D. Write an expression to represent all the costs that Caitlyn's money will cover.

_____

E. Write an inequality for this situation.

_____

F. State a possible solution for this inequality.

_____

G. State a value for the variable that would NOT be a possible solution for this inequality.

_____

 Turn and Talk If Caitlyn wanted more than $4 left over, how would you change the inequality? Explain.

Step It Out

2 ▸ Kyle is renting a boat with his family at a lake. The rental company initially charges $50 for the boat plus the hourly fee shown. The family plans to spend no more than $250 on the boat rental.

$25 PER HOUR

A. Describe how this problem represents an inequality situation.

_____

_____

B. What are the values in the problem that cannot change?

_____

_____

C. What value in the problem can vary? How can this be represented?

_____

_____

D. Write an inequality for how many hours the family can rent the boat.

_____

3 ▸ A manager wants to buy headsets for the customer service team members to use. The headsets cost $12 each. The budget allows $155 to be used for customer service equipment, but the manager wants to save more than $20 for later in case it is needed for something else. How many headsets can the manager buy?

A. Will the inequality for this situation involve addition or subtraction? Explain.

_____

_____

B. Write an inequality for how many headsets the manager can buy while staying within the limits.

_____

C. Explain why the inequality does or does not include *equal to* as part of the inequality symbol.

_____

_____

_____

4 Ms. Alomry drives to school every day. Today she has 5 gallons of gas in her car. The fuel warning light comes on if the amount of gas in the tank drops below 2 gallons. She uses about $\frac{1}{2}$ gallon of gas per round trip. How many round trips can Ms. Alomry take before her warning light turns on?

A. In this situation, is Ms. Alomry adding gas or using gas as she drives?

_____

B. Would the inequality have an addition or a subtraction sign in it?

_____

C. What is the variable or the unknown in the situation?

_____

D. Ms. Alomry has to keep the gas level in her car *at* 2 gallons or *above*. Therefore, what inequality symbol should be used when referencing 2 gallons?

_____

E. Write the inequality.

_____

Check Understanding

1. Gloria is saving up for the scooter shown. She has saved $63 already. She earns $7 a week for doing chores around the house. How many weeks will it take for Gloria to save at least enough money to buy the scooter? Write the inequality to represent the situation. Do not solve the inequality.

$150

_____

2. Write an inequality that represents 54 less than $\frac{1}{2}$ of a number is more than 233.

_____

3. Suppose Mario either wants to earn *no more than* $500 or *more than* $500 to afford his phone. How would the inequalities be different based on these two phrases?

_____

On Your Own

4. (MP) **Model with Mathematics** Saleem has $20. A fish tank that he wants to buy costs $140. He earns $23 per day at a restaurant. Saleem wants to know how many days he has to work to have at least enough money to buy the tank. What is an inequality statement that represents this situation?

_____

5. **Open Ended** Consider the inequality $3x + 7 \geq 25$. Write a word problem that represents this inequality.

6. (MP) **Model with Mathematics** There was a big snowstorm overnight that dumped 12 inches of snow on Math Town. Luckily, it got a lot warmer, and 0.5 inch is melting each hour. The snow is now less than 5 inches deep. Write an inequality to determine how many hours have passed since the snow started melting.

_____

For Problems 7–10, indicate whether each value of x is a *solution* or is *not a solution* of the inequality $33x + 55 > 17$.

7. $x = -2$

8. $x = 0$

9. $x = -1$

10. $x = 44$

For Problems 11–14, indicate whether each value of x is a *solution* or is *not a solution* of the inequality $-9x - 4 \leq 23$.

11. $x = 3$

12. $x = -5$

13. $x = 0$

14. $x = 26$

15. **(MP) Model with Mathematics** The vet says that George's cat Milo has to lose weight, so George is going to portion out Milo's meals and stop giving Milo table scraps. If Milo loses 0.25 pound every week, write an inequality to determine how many weeks it will take Milo to drop below 18 pounds.

22 lb

_____

16. Reiko's goal is to practice the drums for at least 800 minutes per week. This week, Reiko already has practiced for 175 minutes. If she practices for 35 minutes each session, Reiko wants to know how many sessions are left for her to make her goal.

A. **(MP) Model with Mathematics** Write an inequality for the situation.

_____

B. **(MP) Construct Arguments** Explain why you chose the inequality sign that you inserted.

_____

For Problems 17–19, write an inequality based on the statement.

17. Twice a number plus four is at most twelve.

_____

18. Three less than a quarter of a number is less than six.

_____

19. The sum of five and twenty-five times a number is at least one hundred.

_____

20. Alejandro is renting a car to visit his cousin for seven days. The rental car company charges him $199 for the week plus $0.32 per mile driven. Alejandro has $350 to spend on the rental car fees. Write an inequality to determine how many miles Alejandro can afford to drive.

_____

 **I'm in a Learning Mindset!**

Do I recognize any obstacles to understanding two-step inequalities? Can those obstacles be changed? Why or why not?

_____

_____

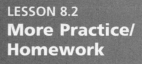
Write Two-Step Inequalities for Situations

1. **Music** Jason is a skilled rapper. He has already rapped a 40-word intro to a song and continues to rap 5 words per second. Write an inequality to determine how many more seconds t he will rap to complete the song if the total song including the intro is at least 500 words.

_____

2. A team can spend no more than $300 on shirts. The team has already spent $80. How many shirts for $15 each can they still buy?

   A. Write the inequality that represents the situation. _____

   B. Explain why you chose the inequality sign.

   _____

   C. Without solving, explain how you know that 20 is not a solution.

   _____

3. (MP) **Model with Mathematics** Felicia spends $50 on materials to make jewelry, and she plans on selling the pieces for $7 each. A friend donates $5 to get her started. Write an inequality to find the number of pieces of jewelry Felicia can sell and make a profit.

   _____

4. **Math on the Spot** Write a real-world problem that could be represented by $5x + 30 \geq 90$.

   _____
   _____
   _____

5. Write the inequality in words: $\frac{1}{3}n - 10 > 22$.

   _____

6. Rania is playing with her friend Arun, and they are setting up dominoes across the room. Each domino is 2 inches long. They have already placed 10 dominoes in a row. The room is 10 feet long and they want to know how many more dominoes they can set up before they reach all the way across the room. Does the inequality $2d + 20 < 120$ model this situation? Explain why or why not.

   _____
   _____
   _____
   _____

Test Prep

7. Raphael is flying a small plane that has a weight limit of 1,200 pounds. The plane is already carrying a combined weight of 800 pounds. Each bag weighs 75 pounds. Write an inequality to find the number of bags *b* that can be taken on board.

_____

8. Select an inequality that represents 3 less than 5 times a number is no more than 63.

   Ⓐ $5n - 3 \geq 63$ Ⓒ $5n - 3 \leq 63$

   Ⓑ $5n \geq 63 - 3$ Ⓓ $5n \leq 63 - 3$

9. Match the words with the inequality.

   $4n - 4 > 10$ •   • 4 times a number is greater than 10.

   $4n + 4 < 10$ •   • 4 less than 4 times a number is greater than 10.

   $4n > 10$ •   • 4 less than 4 times a number is no more than 10.

   $4n - 4 \geq 10$ •   • The sum of 4 and 4 times a number is less than 10.

   $4n + 4 \geq 10$ •   • The sum of 4 and 4 times a number is at least 10.

   $4n - 4 \leq 10$ •   • 4 less than 4 times a number is 10 or more.

10. Olivia is organizing a bake sale, and their goal is to raise at least $500. So far they have raised $210. If the items are all $5 each, which inequality represents how many more items they need to sell to meet Olivia's goal?

    Ⓐ $5b + 210 \geq 500$ Ⓒ $b + 500 \geq 210$

    Ⓑ $5b \geq 500 + 210$ Ⓓ $5b + 210 \leq 500$

Spiral Review

11. Max had *d* dollars and spent $31 but has at least $15 left. Write and solve an inequality to find *d*.

    _____

12. Write a simplified expression for the perimeter of the polygon shown.

    _____

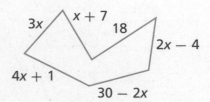

Apply Two-Step Inequalities to Solve Problems

(I Can) write and solve two-step inequalities for real-world scenarios.

Step It Out

1 ▶ A population study was performed to find the number of deer in two parks. The study found that twice the number of deer in Maple Park is at least 20 more than the number of deer in Smith Park. The study found that there are 50 deer in Smith Park.

A. Write an expression to represent the difference between twice the number of deer in Maple Park and the number of deer in Smith Park. Use *x* for the number of deer in Maple Park.

_____

B. What do you know is true about this difference?

The difference is _____ than or equal to _____.

C. Write and solve the inequality to determine the possible number of deer in Maple Park.

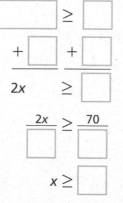

$$\boxed{} \geq \boxed{}$$

$$+\boxed{} \quad +\boxed{}$$

$$2x \quad \geq \boxed{}$$

$$\frac{2x}{\boxed{}} \geq \frac{70}{\boxed{}}$$

$$x \geq \boxed{}$$

D. Graph the solution of the inequality. Do all the values make sense? Explain.

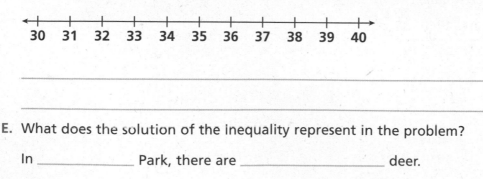

+—+—+—+—+—+—+—+—+—+—+—+—→
30 31 32 33 34 35 36 37 38 39 40

_____

_____

E. What does the solution of the inequality represent in the problem?

In _____ Park, there are _____ deer.

2

Rosina and Asia collect stamps. The number of stamps Rosina has is 7 more than 3 times the number of stamps Asia has. Rosina has less than 85 stamps. How many stamps can Asia have?

A. Asia has x stamps. Write an expression to represent how many stamps Rosina has.

_____

B. What do you know about the number of stamps Rosina has in her collection?

Rosina has $\boxed{\text{less / more}}$ than _____ stamps.

C. Write and solve an inequality to find the number of stamps Asia has in her collection.

$$3x + \boxed{} < \boxed{}$$
$$\underline{-\boxed{} \qquad -\boxed{}}$$
$$3x \qquad < \quad 78$$

$$\frac{3x}{\boxed{}} < \frac{78}{\boxed{}}$$

$$x < \boxed{}$$

D. Graph the solution of the inequality. Do all the values make sense? Explain.

20 21 22 23 24 25 26 27 28 29 30

_____

E. What does the solution of the inequality represent in the problem?

The number of stamps that Asia has is $\boxed{\text{less / greater}}$ than _____.

Solve the inequality: $-3b - 2 \leq 13$.

A. $-3b - 2 \leq 13$
$$\underline{+\boxed{} \qquad +\boxed{}}$$
$$-3b \quad \leq \quad \boxed{}$$

$$\frac{-3b}{\boxed{}} \geq \frac{15}{\boxed{}}$$

$$b \geq \boxed{}$$

B. Graph the solution of the inequality.

$-10 \quad -9 \quad -8 \quad -7 \quad -6 \quad -5 \quad -4 \quad -3 \quad -2 \quad -1 \quad 0$

Turn and Talk Is -5 a solution of the inequality in Problem 3? Explain.

4. Monica and Lucy are participating in a scavenger hunt. The number of items Monica found is 7 more than $\frac{1}{2}$ the number of items Lucy found. The number of items Monica found is at least 17.

A. Lucy found x items. Write an expression to represent how many items Monica found. Then complete the sentence about the number of items.

_____ The number of items Monica found is boxed(less / greater) than or equal to _____.

B. Write and solve the inequality to find what you know about the number of items Lucy found.

$$\frac{1}{2}x + 7 \geq 17$$

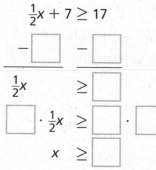

$$\frac{}{\frac{1}{2}x \quad \geq \quad \square}$$

$$\square \cdot \tfrac{1}{2}x \geq \square \cdot \square$$

$$x \geq \square$$

C. Graph the solution. Do all the values make sense? Explain.

$14 \quad 15 \quad 16 \quad 17 \quad 18 \quad 19 \quad 20 \quad 21 \quad 22 \quad 23 \quad 24$

_____

D. What does the solution of the inequality mean in the problem?

Lucy found boxed(less / greater) than or equal to _____ items.

Check Understanding

1. Solve the inequality $-7m + 4 < -45$. Graph the solution.

_____
$0 \quad 1 \quad 2 \quad 3 \quad 4 \quad 5 \quad 6 \quad 7 \quad 8 \quad 9 \quad 10$

2. The number of students using the cafeteria's healthy lunch line can be found by solving the inequality $\frac{1}{2}s - 51 \leq 20$. How many students use this lunch line?

_____

On Your Own

3. **(MP) Attend to Precision** A warehouse has 2,100 tables packaged in boxes. The daily shipment is shown. After how many days will there be fewer than 1,500 tables in the warehouse?

25 tables shipped daily

A. Write and solve an inequality for this situation.

_____

B. Graph the solution of the inequality.

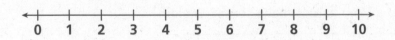

C. Do all the values make sense? What does the solution of the inequality represent in this context?

_____

_____

4. **(MP) Attend to Precision** Zachary and Dovante deliver packages. Dovante delivers 9 less than 4 times the number of packages Zachary delivers in one day. Dovante delivers no more than 11 packages in one day.

A. Write and solve an inequality to find the number of packages Zachary delivers in one day. Graph the solution of the inequality.

_____

```
<----+----+----+----+----+----+----+----+----+----+---->
     0    1    2    3    4    5    6    7    8    9   10
```

B. Do all the values make sense? What does the solution of the inequality represent in this context?

_____

For Problems 5–8, solve the inequality. Graph the solution.

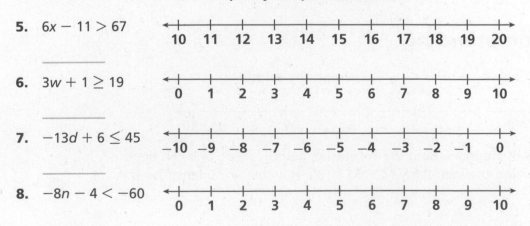

5. $6x - 11 > 67$

```
<---+----+----+----+----+----+----+----+----+----+---->
   10   11   12   13   14   15   16   17   18   19   20
```

_____

6. $3w + 1 \geq 19$

```
<---+----+----+----+----+----+----+----+----+----+---->
    0    1    2    3    4    5    6    7    8    9   10
```

_____

7. $-13d + 6 \leq 45$

```
<---+----+----+----+----+----+----+----+----+----+---->
  -10  -9   -8   -7   -6   -5   -4   -3   -2   -1    0
```

_____

8. $-8n - 4 < -60$

```
<---+----+----+----+----+----+----+----+----+----+---->
    0    1    2    3    4    5    6    7    8    9   10
```

_____

9. Felipe is distributing discount coupons for a concert. He starts with 25 coupons. He gives 2 coupons to each person he sees. He will leave to get more coupons when he has fewer than 4 coupons left. How many people will Felipe give coupons to before he leaves to get more?

A. What is an inequality for this situation? What is the solution?

_____

B. What does the solution of the inequality mean in this context? Explain.

_____

10. (MP) **Attend to Precision** Alicia is mixing paint. She has a bucket that contains $5\frac{1}{2}$ pints of paint. She adds $\frac{1}{4}$-pint containers of paint to the bucket until she has at most $8\frac{3}{4}$ pints of paint in the bucket. How many containers of paint can she add to the bucket?

_____

11. **Open Ended** Write a two-step inequality whose solution is represented by the number line.

<---+----+----+----+----+----+--->
    0   1   2   3   4   5   _____

For Problems 12–17, solve the inequality. Graph the solution.

12. $\frac{2}{3}t - \frac{1}{6} \leq \frac{5}{6}$

<---+----+----+----+----+----+----+----+----+----+----+--->
    0   1   2   3   4   5   6   7   8   9   10

_____

13. $-\frac{3}{4}m + \frac{1}{4} \geq 4\frac{3}{4}$

<---+----+----+----+----+----+----+----+----+----+----+--->
   -10 -9   -8   -7   -6   -5   -4   -3   -2   -1   0

_____

14. $-\frac{1}{10}a - \frac{2}{5} > \frac{3}{10}$

<---+----+----+----+----+----+----+----+----+----+----+--->
   -10 -9   -8   -7   -6   -5   -4   -3   -2   -1   0

_____

15. $\frac{3}{8}w + 5 < 11$

<---+----+----+----+----+----+----+----+----+----+----+--->
   10   11   12   13   14   15   16   17   18   19   20

_____

16. $\frac{3}{4}r + 5 \leq 17$

<---+----+----+----+----+----+----+----+----+----+----+--->
   10   11   12   13   14   15   16   17   18   19   20

_____

17. $2\frac{2}{3}b + 8 \geq 0$

<---+----+----+----+----+----+----+----+----+----+----+--->
   -5   -4   -3   -2   -1   0   1   2   3   4   5

_____

18. **Financial Literacy** Ariana started a savings account with $240. She deposits $30 into her account at the end of each month. She wants to know how many months it will take for her account to have a balance greater than $500.

A. (MP) **Model with Mathematics** Write and solve an inequality that represents this situation.

_____

_____

B. (MP) **Reason** How many months will it take for her account to have a balance greater than $500? Explain.

_____

_____

_____

For Problems 19–22, solve the inequality. Graph the solution.

19. $-5y + 47 > -13$

<-+--+--+--+--+--+--+--+--+--+--+->
10 11 12 13 14 15 16 17 18 19 20

_____

20. $18 - 4z \geq 26$

<-+--+--+--+--+--+--+--+--+--+--+->
-10 -9 -8 -7 -6 -5 -4 -3 -2 -1 0

_____

21. $8g + 30 < -2$

<-+--+--+--+--+--+--+--+--+--+--+->
-10 -9 -8 -7 -6 -5 -4 -3 -2 -1 0

_____

22. $-7s - 4 \leq 10$

<-+--+--+--+--+--+--+--+--+--+--+->
-10 -9 -8 -7 -6 -5 -4 -3 -2 -1 0

_____

23. Colleen is attending a carnival. The price of admission into the carnival is shown. It costs $3 to play a game. Colleen has $35. What is the greatest number of games she can play?

_____

24. A gift shop at an amusement park sells key chains. The gift shop has 55 key chains. When the number of key chains is below 10, the manager will reorder. If the gift shop sells 4 key chains each day, how many days will it take before the manager has to reorder?

_____

Carnival Admission: $8

© Houghton Mifflin Harcourt Publishing Company • Image Credit: © Steve Hamblin / Alamy

Apply Two-Step Inequalities to Solve Problems

Solve the inequality. Graph the solution.

1. $5x + 13 \leq 48$

_____

0 1 2 3 4 5 6 7 8 9 10

2. $16 - 7v < 2$

_____

0 1 2 3 4 5 6 7 8 9 10

3. $9r - \frac{3}{5} > 3\frac{9}{10}$

_____

−5 −4 −3 −2 −1 0 1 2 3 4 5

4. $-8c + 13 \geq 47$

_____

−8 −7 −6 −5 −4 −3 −2 −1 0 1 2

5. Math on the Spot Members of the drama club plan to present its annual spring musical. They have $1,262.50 left from fundraising, but they estimate that the entire production will cost $1,600.00. How many tickets at the price shown must they sell to at least break even?

_____

Tickets: $6.75 each

6. (MP) **Model with Mathematics** Jenna has a collection of trading cards. She started her collection with 175 cards. She buys packs of cards that contain 15 cards each. Solve an inequality to determine how many packs of cards Jenna buys so that she will have over 400 cards in her collection.

A. What is an inequality that represents this situation? What is the solution?

_____

B. How many packs of cards does Jenna buy?

_____

7. (MP) **Model with Mathematics** Drew and Larry are working together on a jigsaw puzzle. Drew places 11 less than 3 times the number of pieces that Larry places. Drew places at least 10 pieces. How many pieces does Larry place?

_____

Test Prep

8. Dwight and Walt are building model cars. Dwight builds 7 fewer models than 4 times the number Walt builds. Dwight builds at most 9 models. Which inequality could be used to find the number of models Walt builds?

Ⓐ $4m - 7 < 9$

Ⓑ $4m - 7 \leq 9$

Ⓒ $4m - 7 > 9$

Ⓓ $4m - 7 \geq 9$

9. A truck rental company rents a truck for a one-time fee of $25 plus $1.50 per mile traveled. Kelly has $80 she can spend on the rental truck. What is the greatest number of miles that she can travel?

_____

10. Ricardo measured the temperature in the morning. The temperature was $-6\,°C$. The temperature is increasing $1\frac{1}{2}\,°C$ every hour. After how many hours will the temperature be at least $2\,°C$? Select the best answer.

Ⓐ less than $1\frac{1}{3}$ hours

Ⓑ more than $2\frac{1}{3}$ hours

Ⓒ less than 4 hours

Ⓓ $5\frac{1}{3}$ hours or more

Spiral Review

11. A football team earns 6 points for a touchdown and 3 points for a field goal. In one game, a team scored a touchdown and some field goals. The total points the team scored is 18 points. Write an equation that can be used to find the number of field goals the team scored.

_____

12. Scott makes and sells bracelets. He spends $28 on supplies, and he sells each bracelet for $6. Write an expression that represents his profit for selling b bracelets.

_____

Vocabulary

1. Complete the graphic organizer for the vocabulary term *solution of an inequality*.

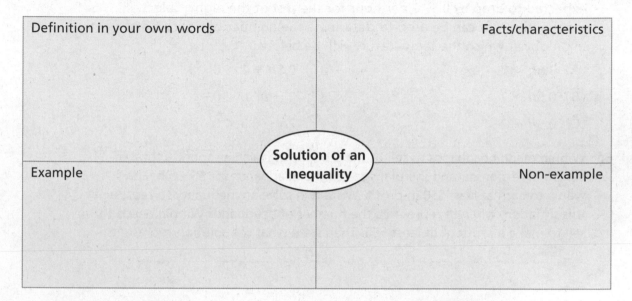

Definition in your own words	Facts/characteristics
Example	Non-example

Solution of an Inequality

Concepts and Skills

2. (MP) **Use Tools** Water is pumped out of a 500-gallon tank at a rate of 2.5 gallons per second. The inequality $500 - 2.5t < 100$ can be used to determine the time t, in seconds, after which there will be less than 100 gallons of water remaining in the tank. Solve the inequality, then state what the solution represents. State what strategy and tool you will use to answer the question, explain your choice, and then find the answer.

_____

_____

3. Faith wants to run at least 7 miles this week. She already has run $2\frac{1}{2}$ miles. She plans to run an equal distance on each of the last 3 days of this week. Write and solve an inequality to represent this situation, where d represents the distance in miles that Faith must run on each of the last 3 days to reach her goal. Graph the solution set of the inequality on the number line.

_____

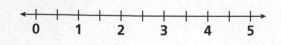

4. An airplane can carry a maximum of 36,600 pounds of cargo, passengers, and luggage. On the plane's next flight, it will carry 7,320 pounds of cargo. If each passenger with luggage weighs 220 pounds, what is the greatest number of passengers the plane can carry on its next flight?

(A) 33 passengers   (C) 166 passengers

(B) 133 passengers   (D) 199 passengers

5. At midnight, the outdoor temperature is 2 °C. The temperature is expected to drop by 0.5 °C per hour for the rest of the night. Select all inequalities that can be used to determine the number of hours h after midnight at which the temperature will be below 0 °C.

(A) $0.5h < 2$ (D) $0.5h + 2 < 0$

(B) $0.5h > 2$ (E) $2 - 0.5h < 0$

(C) $0.5h - 2 < 0$ (F) $2h - 0.5 < 0$

6. Winnie made headbands to sell at the school craft fair. She spent a total of $22.50 on expenses, and she plans to sell the headbands for $5 each. She wants to earn at least $50 in profit. Write and solve an inequality to represent this situation, where h represents the number of headbands Winnie needs to sell to make a profit of at least $50. Then state what the solution represents.

_____

_____

7. Marcus is ordering supplies online for his dog. He plans to order a collar for $6.76 and some bags of treats for $4.80 each. The total for his order must be more than $25 to qualify for free shipping.

A. Write an inequality that Marcus can use to determine the number of bags of treats t he must order to get free shipping.

_____

B. Marcus says that the minimum number of bags of treats he needs to order to get free shipping is 3. Do you agree? Explain your reasoning.

_____

_____

_____

8. Sarah begins the week with $21.55. A school lunch costs $2.75. How many school lunches can she buy and still have at least $10 left at the end of the week? Write and solve an inequality that Sarah can use to determine the number of lunches n that she can buy.

_____

Unit 4 Geometry

Data Analyst

A data analyst helps companies make good business decisions by collecting, analyzing, and storing data. The data may be related to sales, market research, costs, errors, or just about anything. A data analyst looks for patterns and trends in the data and then presents the results in a meaningful way.

STEM Task:

A rectangular electronic game board is 16.5 inches by 12 inches. It includes a grid with 8 rows of 8 squares, each 0.5 inch on a side. When you aim a laser at any of the red squares, data are collected on the accuracy of the hits. What are the ratios of (a) the area of one square to the area of the board, and (b) the combined area of the squares to the area of the board? Explain.

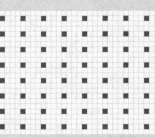

Learning Mindset

Perseverance Learns Effectively

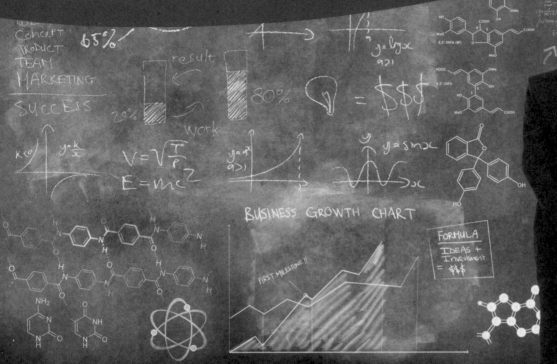

Perseverance is the ability to stick with a task until it is complete. But it can be difficult to persevere when a task seems too big or complicated. If you feel overwhelmed by a task, try dividing it into smaller, easier steps. Here's how:

- Identify the end goal of the task. Then work backward. What do you need to do before you can reach the end goal? What do you need to do before that? And before that?

- Alternatively, start by identifying just the first step. Sometimes completing the first step will help you see the second step.

- Each step should be specific and small enough to feel achievable. If a step feels overwhelming, break it down into even smaller steps.

Reflect

Q What steps were involved in completing the STEM Task?

Q Can you compute a ratio from the STEM Task more efficiently by refining how you used an area formula? Explain.

Draw and Analyze Two-Dimensional Figures

MOUSETRAP ON THE COORDINATE PLANE!

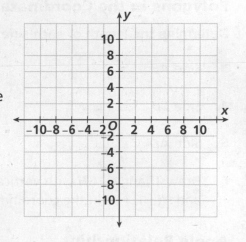

There is a mouse on the coordinate plane shown here. The mouse is at a location that has integer coordinates.

To find the mouse, first graph the following polygons.

A. Triangle *ABC* with vertices

   A(−7, 7), *B*(3, 7), and *C*(−2, 2)

B. Parallelogram *EFGH* with vertices *E*(−3, 5), *F*(6, 5), and *G*(3, 1). Where is vertex *H* located? _____

C. Square *KLMN* with vertices *K*(−1, 4), *L*(6, 4), and *M*(6, −3). Where is vertex *N* located?

   _____

D. Trapezoid *PQRS* with vertices

   P(−3, 4), *Q*(2, −1), *R*(2, −6), and *S*(−3, −9).

E. Now use these clues.

   The mouse is located inside Triangle *ABC*.

   The mouse is located inside Parallelogram *EFGH*.

   The mouse is located outside Square *KLMN*.

   The mouse is located outside Trapezoid *PQRS*.

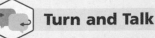 **Turn and Talk**

What are the coordinates of the location of the mouse? Explain how you know.

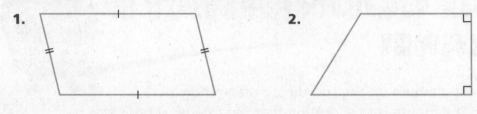
Are You Ready?

Complete these problems to review prior concepts and skills you will need for this module.

Quadrilaterals

Classify each quadrilateral in as many ways as possible. Write *parallelogram*, *rectangle*, *square*, or *trapezoid*. If the figure is a quadrilateral only, write *quadrilateral*.

1.

_____

2.

_____

Polygons in the Coordinate Plane

Determine the length of each side of Quadrilateral *ABCD*.

3. Side *AB* _____

4. Side *CD* _____

5. Side *AD* _____

6. Draw Triangle *FGH* with vertices *F*(−4, −4), *G*(−5, 2), and *H*(−1, −4) in the coordinate plane.

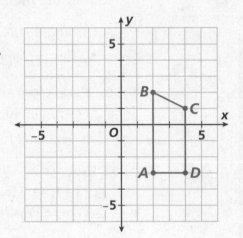

Angle Relationships

The figure includes Lines *l* and *m*. Use the information in the figure to determine the measure of each angle.

7. *x* _____

8. *y* _____

9. *z* _____

10. What is the relationship between the angles whose measures are *x*° and *y*°? Explain how you know.

_____

_____

_____

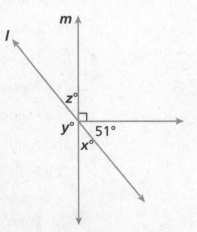

Name _____

Draw Circles and Other Figures

(**I Can**) inscribe triangles in circles and draw geometric figures meeting given conditions.

Spark Your Learning

Parker plans to build a circular fire pit in a square area. He is drawing a model on paper to confirm his plans before he starts to build. How can Parker use paper folding and a compass to draw the largest possible circular fire pit in the space he has staked off? Trace Parker's square to a piece of paper and draw the circle for the fire pit.

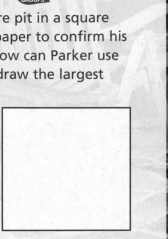

Turn and Talk Brainstorm a list of characteristics specific to squares and circles.

Build Understanding

1 A polygon is inscribed in a circle if every vertex of the polygon is on the circle. To investigate the kinds of triangles that can be inscribed in a circle, begin Parts A and B by using a compass to draw a circle with a radius of 0.5 inch. The **radius** of a circle is the distance from the circle's center to any point on the circle.

A. Draw a circle and inscribe a triangle in it. Inscribe more than one if you can.

B. Draw a circle and a **diameter**, which is a segment that passes through the circle's center and has endpoints on the circle. Use the endpoints of the diameter and a third point on the circle to inscribe a triangle in the circle.

C. Draw three circles, each with a diameter of 1 inch. Can you inscribe each triangle in one of the circles? If so, draw it. If not, justify your answer.

a triangle with a 50° angle

a triangle with a side of length 1.25 inches

a triangle with a 30° and a 60° angle

 Turn and Talk How many triangles can you draw in each of Parts A through C: none, only one, or more than one?

Step It Out

2 Draw a hexagon with side lengths 2, 3, 4, 5, 6, and 7 units. The two longest sides are **perpendicular**. The longest side and the third-longest side are **parallel**.

A. Begin by drawing the two longest sides perpendicular to each other. How can you draw two perpendicular segments?

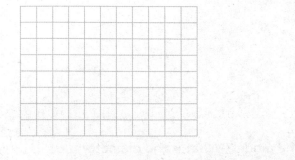

_____

_____

B. Draw the third-longest side parallel to the longest side and connected to the second-longest side. How can you draw two parallel segments?

_____

_____

C. Use a ruler or compass to draw the last three segments, or cut thin strips of paper. Use the segments to complete the hexagon.

The figure | does / does not | have at least one line of symmetry.

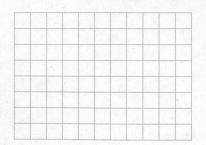

3 Kaylee has a square piece of wood with a side length of 48 inches. She wants to use it to build the largest circular tabletop that she can.

A. Draw a scale model of the piece of wood. Be sure to include the scale used in your model. Then draw the diagonals to find the center of the square, which will also be the center of the circle, and draw the circle.

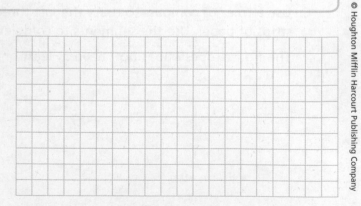

B. What is the diameter of the circle in the model? What is the diameter of the tabletop? How do you know?

_____

_____

_____

Check Understanding

1. Draw a circle. Can you inscribe an obtuse triangle? If so, inscribe an obtuse triangle and tell how many you can draw. If not, explain why not.

2. Use tools to draw a hexagon in which exactly three sides have a length of 3 units and there are two pairs of parallel sides.

3. A square has a side length of 2.5 meters. What is the radius of the largest circle that fits inside the square?

_____

On Your Own

4. (MP) **Use Tools** Draw an octagon with six sides of length 3 units, one side of length 4 units, and one side of length 10 units. Every pair of sides that meet are perpendicular. The figure should have symmetry.

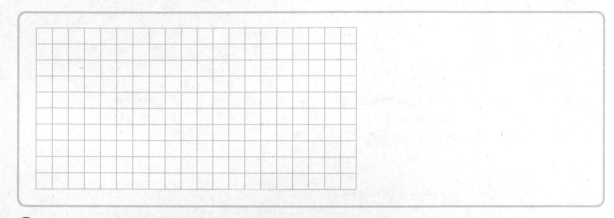

5. (MP) **Use Tools** Draw a quadrilateral with two pairs of opposite sides that are parallel and equal in length, no right angles, and no lines of symmetry. What is the quadrilateral?

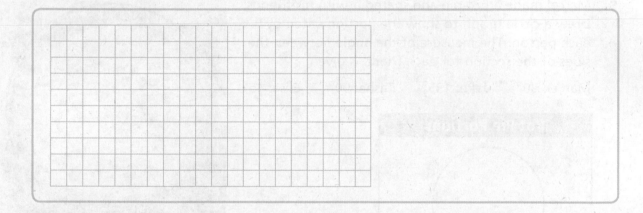

6. (MP) **Use Tools** Draw a circle and one of its diameters. Can you inscribe a triangle that has the diameter as a side and includes an obtuse angle? If so, draw the triangle. If not, justify your answer.

7. **Open Ended** Draw an octagon with seven sides of length 4 units and one side of length 12 units. The longest side should be perpendicular to at least two of the shorter sides and parallel to at least two of the shorter sides.

8. (MP) **Use Tools** Draw a quadrilateral with exactly one pair of parallel sides. What is the quadrilateral?

_____

_____

_____

9. Marcel made a pot pie and shared it with his friends. Draw a circle graph to show the portion eaten by each person. The measure of the angle between the sides of the section for each friend is given.

Marcel: 90°   Jake: 135°   Tasha: 90°   Elisa: 45°

Pot Pie Portions

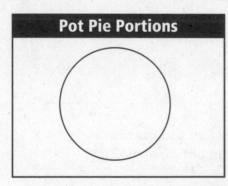

⊟ **I'm in a Learning Mindset!**

What can I apply from my knowledge of circles to better understand circle graphs?

_____

_____

Draw Circles and Other Figures

1. (MP) **Use Tools** Draw a decagon with eight sides of length 2 units and two sides of length 4 units. Any two sides that meet should be perpendicular, and the figure should contain parallel segments.

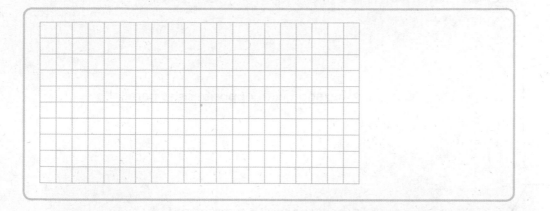

2. (MP) **Use Tools** Draw a quadrilateral with two pairs of congruent sides, no parallel sides, and one line of symmetry. What is the quadrilateral?

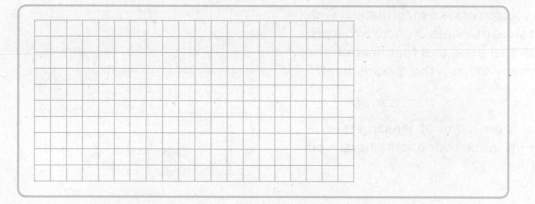

3. (MP) **Use Tools** Draw a circle with a radius of $\frac{3}{4}$ inch and a horizontal diameter. Inscribe a triangle that has the diameter as a side and a vertical line of symmetry.

Test Prep

4. Match each figure with its description.

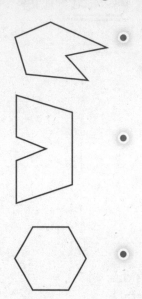

•   • hexagon with one line of symmetry

•   • hexagon with opposite sides parallel

•   • heptagon with symmetry

5. **A.** Use tools to draw a quadrilateral with four sides of length 3 units, two pairs of parallel sides, and four lines of symmetry. What is the quadrilateral?

_____

B. What is the radius of the largest circle that fits inside your quadrilateral from Part A?

_____

Spiral Review

6. Betty is 5 more than 3 times Jadyn's age. Betty is 41 years old. Write and solve an equation to find Jadyn's age.

_____

_____

7. Angles 1 and 2 are complementary. The measure of Angle 2 is two times the measure of Angle 1. Write and solve an equation to find the measure of both angles.

_____

_____

Name _____

Draw and Construct Triangles Given Side Lengths

(I Can) determine whether three lengths could be side lengths of a triangle, and, given two side lengths, I can find the range of possible lengths for the third side.

Spark Your Learning

Martina is building a wind chime. She has pieces of metal pipe 2, 3, 4, and 5 inches long that she is going to use to make a triangular top for the wind chime. Which combinations of three lengths will **not** work to make the top?

Turn and Talk What do you notice about the set of lengths that did not make a triangle?

Build Understanding

1   Can you draw a triangle with side lengths of 3, 4, and 8 units? There are different ways to model the situation and investigate. You can use thin strips of paper cut to the correct lengths, or you can use tools such as a ruler and compass, or geometry software.

A. Use the longest side of your model as the possible base. Use your model to view the shorter sides in different positions. Can you draw a triangle? If so, draw one. If not, explain why you cannot.

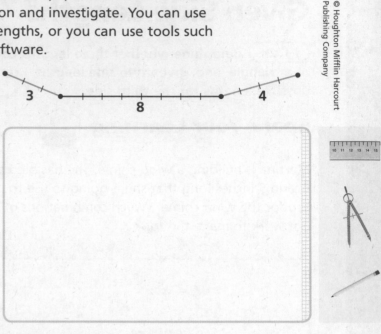

B. Repeat Part A using the shortest segment as the possible base. Can you draw a triangle? If so, draw one. If not, explain why you cannot.

C. Complete the statements describing the relationship among the three side lengths that do **not** form a triangle. Use *less than, equal to,* or *greater than.*

> The sum of the lengths of the two shorter sides is _____ the length of the longer one.

2   Can you draw a triangle with side lengths of 3, 4, and 6 units?

A. Use the 6-unit segment of your model as the possible base. Can you make a triangle? If so, draw it. If not, explain why you cannot.

_____

B. Use the 3-unit segment as the possible base. Can you make a triangle? If so, draw it. If not, explain why you cannot.

_____

C. Use the 4-unit segment as the possible base. Can you make a triangle? If so, draw it. If not, explain why you cannot.

_____

D. How are the triangles you made in Parts A–C alike?

E. Complete the statements describing the relationships between the three side lengths that form a triangle. Use *less than, equal to,* or *greater than.*

The sum of the lengths of the two shorter sides is _____ the length of the longest side.

F. Complete the summary of what you have discovered so far for three segments with lengths *a, b,* and *c,* where *c* is the greatest length.

If $a + b$ is equal to or _____ than *c*, the segments cannot form a triangle. If $a + b$ is _____ than *c*, the segments form one triangle.

3 ▶ Can you draw a quadrilateral with side lengths of 2, 3, 4, and 5 units?

A. Make and use a model. Can you connect the endpoints to form a quadrilateral? If so, draw a quadrilateral. If not, explain why you cannot.

B. Using the same side lengths, can you make a quadrilateral that is different than the one you drew in Part A? If so, draw it. If not, explain why you cannot.

C. Make a conjecture about the number of quadrilaterals that can be made using four different segment lengths. Support your conclusion.

_____

_____

_____

_____

_____

Turn and Talk Is it possible that four segments cannot form a quadrilateral?

Step It Out

4 In Parts A–C, let a and b be the shorter lengths and c be the longest length. Compare $a + b$ to c to determine if a triangle can be made. Write $<$, $=$, or $>$.

A. Nia wants to make a triangular picture frame from strips of wood that are 9 centimeters, 11 centimeters, and 15 centimeters long.

$9 + 11$ ☐ 15

Since the sum of the lengths of two shorter strips is _____ the length of the longest strip, Nia ⸢can / cannot⸥ make a triangle.

B. Gerard has pieces of string 6 inches, 5 inches, and 11 inches in length that he plans to use as a border for a collage.

$6 + 5$ ☐ 11

Since the sum of the lengths of two shorter pieces is _____ the length of the longest piece, Gerard ⸢can / cannot⸥ make a triangle.

C. Olivia gives her niece leftover pieces of ribbon from her art supplies. They are 12 inches, 10 inches, and 24 inches long.

$12 + 10$ ☐ 24

Since the sum of the lengths of two shorter pieces of ribbon is _____ the length of the longest, Olivia's niece ⸢can / cannot⸥ make a triangle.

D. Amil is making a bamboo picture frame. Given the side lengths shown for the first two sides, what is one possible side length that will form a triangular picture frame?

$5 + 8 =$ _____, so one side length that will make a triangle is _____ inches.

8 in.   5 in.

Check Understanding

1. Max has three pieces of oak trim that are 7 inches, 11 inches, and 18 inches long. He wants to use them to make a triangular base for a candleholder. Will the pieces make a triangle? Explain your answer.

_____

_____

2. Bella is making a sculpture. She has pieces of copper pipe that are 4 centimeters long and 13 centimeters long. What is a possible third length of copper pipe that will make a triangle? Justify your answer.

_____

On Your Own

3. Horace is making a shadow box in the shape of a triangle to hold his homerun baseballs. He has pieces of wood 12 inches, 12 inches, and 26 inches long. Show whether these pieces will make a triangle.

_____

4. **Art** An artist is going to make triangle earrings from glass rods with the lengths shown. Show whether these rods will make a triangle.

_____

_____

Pieces to use:
1 cm
2 cm
2.5 cm

5. Alan makes triangular potholders and sews edging around the outside. He has pieces of edging 5 inches, 5 inches, and 10 inches long. Show whether these pieces will make a triangle.

_____

_____

6. **Open Ended** The volleyball team is making a triangular banner for their last home game. They want two of the sides to be 4 feet long each. Determine one possible length for the third side. Justify your answer.

_____

_____

7. (MP) **Reason** Dante is constructing a quadrilateral with four sides, each 2 inches long. How many different quadrilaterals can he make? Explain.

_____

_____

_____

Determine whether each set of numbers could be lengths of the sides of a triangle.

8. 17, 13, 11 _____   **9.** 11, 19, 35 _____   **10.** 6, 7, 13 _____

Two side lengths of a triangle are given. Find a possible third length.

11. 5 meters, 12 meters   **12.** 3 feet, 9 feet   **13.** 23 miles, 31 miles

_____   _____   _____

14. A craftsman makes stained glass crafts. He has metal strips of lengths 5 inches, 8 inches, and 11 inches. Show whether these strips will make a triangle.

_____

_____

15. Karissa is building a triangular landscape border around her mailbox. She has logs 4 feet, 5 feet, and 10 feet long. Show whether these logs will make a triangle.

_____

_____

16. Pierce is developing his own board game. The border of the board is going to be 3 pieces of cardboard, each 17 inches long. Show whether these lengths will make a triangle.

_____

17. (MP) **Construct Arguments** Risa has four sticks measuring 2 inches, 2.5 inches, 3 inches, and 8 inches. She wants to connect the sticks end to end to make a quadrilateral. Can she do it? Explain why or why not.

_____

_____

_____

Determine whether each set of numbers could be lengths of the sides of a triangle.

18. 8.5, 6, 10 _____   **19.** 2.5, 2.5, 4 _____   **20.** 5, 12, 18 _____

Two side lengths of a triangle are given. Find a possible third length.

21. 5 inches, 10 inches   **22.** 6 yards, 18 yards   **23.** 9 meters, 21 meters

_____   _____   _____

 **I'm in a Learning Mindset!**

Did I find a different or unique way to determine whether a set of side lengths could form a triangle? What is it?

_____

_____

LESSON 9.2
**More Practice/
Homework**

ONLINE

Video Tutorials and
Interactive Examples

Draw and Construct Triangles Given Side Lengths

1. Haley is making a triangle-shaped box garden. She has wooden pieces of lengths 6 feet, 8 feet, and 13 feet. Show whether these pieces will make a triangle.

_____

_____

2. Students are making shapes with string in an art class. Ben has pieces of string measuring 4 inches, 2 inches, and 1.5 inches long. Show whether these lengths will make a triangle.

_____

_____

3. (MP) **Construct Arguments** The Culinary Club is making a triangle-shaped sign showing a piece of pie for their pie-eating competition. Two of the sides measure as shown. Determine a possible length for the third side. Justify your answer.

_____

_____

_____

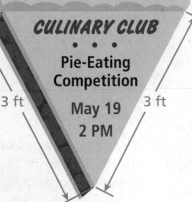

4. Seth wants to make a quadrilateral charm for a necklace. He has wire pieces with lengths 1 centimeter, 2 centimeters, 4 centimeters, and 5 centimeters. How many possible quadrilaterals are there with those side lengths?

_____

_____

Determine whether each set of numbers could be lengths of the sides of a triangle.

5. 2, 4, 6 _____   **6.** 16, 21, 33 _____   **7.** 1, 3, 3 _____

Two side lengths of a triangle are given. Find a possible third length.

8. 6 meters, 8 meters   **9.** 4 feet, 5 feet   **10.** 4.5 yards, 7 yards

_____   _____   _____

Test Prep

11. Lorelei is making decorative boxes in the shape of triangles. Which of the following could be the lengths of the sides of the boxes?

Ⓐ 12 cm, 13 cm, 24 cm

Ⓑ 12 cm, 13 cm, 25 cm

Ⓒ 10 cm, 10 cm, 24 cm

Ⓓ 10 cm, 10 cm, 22 cm

12. Lhu builds dollhouses with triangle-shaped roofs. Which of the following could be lengths of the edges of the roof of a dollhouse?

Ⓐ 10 in., 10 in., 20 in.

Ⓑ 10 in., 12 in., 24 in.

Ⓒ 11 in., 12 in., 24 in.

Ⓓ 11 in., 11 in., 20 in.

13. Select all the sets of numbers that could be lengths of the sides of a triangle.

Ⓐ 2, 7, 9

Ⓑ 4, 11, 13

Ⓒ 6, 9, 12

Ⓓ 6, 6, 14

Ⓔ 8, 15, 21

Ⓕ 9, 17, 27

14. An artist gets strips of metal from a salvage yard to make decorative wall art. He finds strips that are 2.5 feet and 3.5 feet long. Determine one possible length for the third strip if the artist wants to make a triangle.

_____

Spiral Review

15. Kevin wants to buy a video game for $45. He also wants to buy 2 game controllers. Each controller costs the same amount. He has a total of $120 to spend. Write and solve an inequality to find how much Kevin can spend on each controller.

_____

_____

16. Sofia has 16 hours to paint a living room and 2 bedrooms. She spends 7 hours painting the living room. Write and solve an inequality to find how much time she can spend on each bedroom if she splits her time equally.

_____

_____

Name _____

Draw and Construct Triangles Given Angle Measures

(**I Can**) determine whether it is possible to draw a triangle with three given angle measures. If it is, I can construct such a triangle.

Spark Your Learning

A town is designing triangular flower beds for a park. Is it possible to choose three angle measures that will **not** form a triangle? If so, draw several examples.

Turn and Talk Pick one of your examples above and describe how you could revise your drawing to form a triangle.

Build Understanding

1 ▸ Antonio and Karen are making quilts.
They are cutting triangle shapes for their
quilt. The triangles have angle measures
of 45°, 45°, and 90°. The pattern for the
triangles Karen is using is shown.

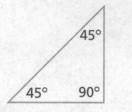

A. Antonio wants his triangles to be larger than Karen's. Is it possible for
Antonio to make larger triangles with the same angle measures? If so,
draw sample triangles. If not, explain why he cannot.

B. Amie is given three angle measures that form a triangle. How many
different triangles can Amie make, one or more than one? Explain.

C. Jess is given three segments that form a triangle. How many different
triangles can Jess make, one or more than one? Explain.

 Turn and Talk Is there a maximum number of different triangles that can be
made given three angle measures? Explain.

© Houghton Mifflin Harcourt Publishing Company • **Image Credit:** ©John Teate/Shutterstock

2 ▶ You can use tools to determine whether you can construct a triangle with three given angle measures.

A. Is it possible to construct a triangle with angle measures of 25°, 75°, and 80°? If so, draw the triangle.

B. Is it possible to construct a triangle with angle measures of 35°, 70°, and 90°? If so, draw the triangle.

C. Is it possible to construct a triangle with angle measures of 45°, 60°, and 55°? If so, draw the triangle.

D. Find the sum of the angle measures in Parts A–C. For the sets of angles that do not form triangles, what do their sums have in common?

_____

_____

_____

_____

Step It Out

3 Jenny draws a triangle that includes one angle that has a measure of 30°, one angle that has a measure of 90°, and one side that has a length of 1 inch. Without seeing her triangle, can you draw it?

A. Can the 1-inch side of Jenny's triangle be a side of both the 30° and 90° angles of the triangle? Can it be a side of only one of the angles? _____

B. Think about how the given side and the given angles might be positioned. Draw all the triangles you can using the information given for Jenny's triangle. Label the known measures on your drawings.

C. Can Jenny's triangle be found among your drawings? Explain.

_____

_____

D. Can you draw a triangle with one 90° angle and one 100° angle so that the side between the angles is 2 inches long? Why or why not?

_____

_____

_____

Check Understanding

1. Cliff wants to draw a triangle with a 30° angle and a 60° angle so that the side between them is 2 inches long. How many triangles can he draw?

_____

2. A. If possible, construct a triangle with angle measures of 45°, 65°, and 70°.

B. How many triangles are possible, none, one, or many?

_____

On Your Own

3. Kara is making a picture out of tiles. One tile will be triangular with angle measures of 25°, 25°, and 130°.

A. (MP) **Use Tools** Sketch a triangle with those angle measures.

B. Do you have enough information to make Kara's triangle? Explain.

(MP) **Use Tools** For Problems 4–7, determine whether it is possible to draw a triangle with the given angle measures. If it is possible, use tools to draw the triangle.

4. 55°, 60°, 70°

5. 30°, 40°, 110°

6. 45°, 65°, 70°

7. 25°, 85°, 75°

8. (MP) **Use Tools** Maurice is making blocks for a children's toy set. The instructions call for triangles with angle measures of 60°, 60°, and 60°. Draw a triangle with these angle measures.

9. **(MP) Use Tools** Kate is drawing a house. For the top of the house, she wants to make a triangle with angle measures of 30°, 30°, and 120°. Can Kate form a triangle with these angle measures? If so, use tools to draw the triangle. If not, explain why not.

10. **STEM** An engineer is designing a building that is shaped like a triangle and wants to know whether the angles of the triangle can be 50°, 50°, and 70°. Can these be the angles of the triangle? Use tools to draw a diagram that supports your answer.

11. **Open Ended** Eduardo is building a triangular sandbox for a playground. He wants the triangle to include a 65° angle, a 50° angle, and at least one side that is 12 feet long. Draw at least one possible triangle on a separate piece of paper and estimate possible lengths of the other two sides of the triangle.

I'm in a Learning Mindset!

How effective were the tools I used to construct triangles? How did I apply my knowledge of properties of triangles to the task?

Draw and Construct Triangles Given Angle Measures

1. (MP) **Use Tools** Vanessa wants to build a triangular table. Can she build a table with angle measures of 15°, 55°, and 110°? If so, draw the triangle.

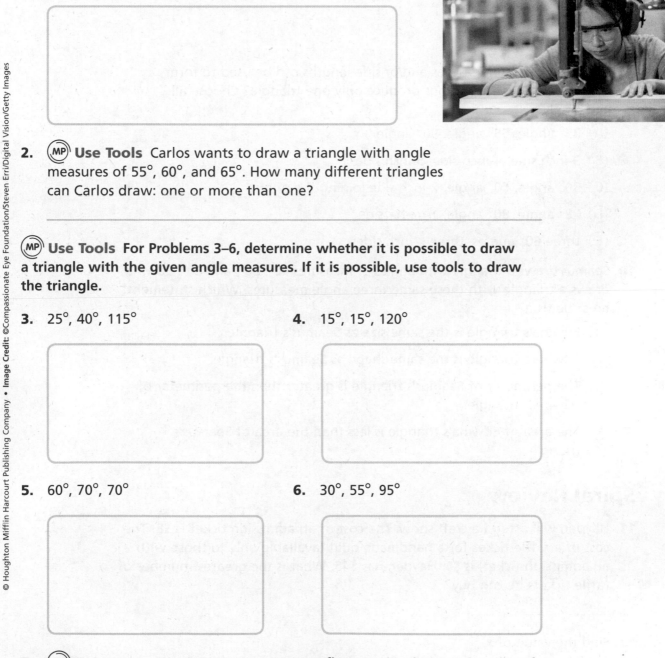

2. (MP) **Use Tools** Carlos wants to draw a triangle with angle measures of 55°, 60°, and 65°. How many different triangles can Carlos draw: one or more than one?

_____

(MP) **Use Tools** For Problems 3–6, determine whether it is possible to draw a triangle with the given angle measures. If it is possible, use tools to draw the triangle.

3. 25°, 40°, 115°

4. 15°, 15°, 120°

5. 60°, 70°, 70°

6. 30°, 55°, 95°

7. (MP) **Construct Arguments** James sees a floor made of triangular tiles of different sizes. He notices that two triangles each have one angle with a measure of 35°, another with a measure of 45°, and one side with a length of 6 inches. Are the two triangles the same? Explain.

_____

_____

Test Prep

8. How many different triangles can be made with the angle measures 30°, 60°, and 90°?

   Ⓐ none

   Ⓑ one

   Ⓒ exactly two

   Ⓓ more than two

9. Each set of angle measures and/or side lengths can be used to form a triangle. Which conditions produce only one triangle? Choose all that apply.

   Ⓐ 35° angle, 55° angle, 90° angle

   Ⓑ 3-inch side, 4-inch side, 5-inch side

   Ⓒ 30° angle, 60° angle, 2-inch side joining the angles

   Ⓓ 28° angle, 80° angle, 1-meter side

   Ⓔ three 60° angles, three $\frac{3}{4}$-inch sides

10. Seamus draws a triangle with angles of measures 40°, 60°, and 80°. Edwina draws a triangle with these same three angle measures. Which statement **must** be true?

    Ⓐ Edwina's triangle is the same size as Seamus's triangle.

    Ⓑ Edwina's triangle is the same shape as Seamus's triangle.

    Ⓒ The perimeter of Seamus's triangle is greater than the perimeter of Edwina's triangle.

    Ⓓ The area of Edwina's triangle is less than the area of Seamus's triangle.

Spiral Review

11. Hayden will attend a craft show. The cost of an admission ticket is $8. The cost of a raffle ticket for a handmade quilt (available only to those with an admission ticket) is $5. Hayden has $45. What is the greatest number of raffle tickets he can buy?

    _____

12. Find the value of x.

$(7x - 5)°$ $45°$

Name _____

Draw and Analyze Shapes to Solve Problems

(I Can) use tools to draw or construct figures that meet given criteria, and I can analyze the resulting figures.

Step It Out

1 ▶ Lucas is using strips of wood to construct a triangle. The first two strips are 4 feet long and 7 feet long. When Lucas nails them together, the two pieces of wood form a 50° angle.

A. Draw a model of the two strips after Lucas nailed them together.

B. Can he use a third strip to construct a triangle? If so, complete the model.

_____

C. How many triangles can be formed?

_____

2 ▶ In this task, you will draw triangles given the lengths of two sides and the measure of an angle that is **not** between them.

A. Side *AB*: 8 units; Side *BC*: 6 units; Angle *A*: 40°

To construct Triangle *ABC*, you need to draw Side *BC*. Because Side *BC* is 6 units long, put the point of the compass at Point *B* and draw part of a circle with radius 6 units. You can use this segment to help you open your compass to the correct radius.

|——————————|
  6 units

The circle intersects the other side of ∠*A* in _____ point(s). You can draw _____ triangle(s). Draw the triangle(s).

B. Side *AB*: 5 units; Side *BC*: 7 units; Angle *A*: 90°

To draw Side *BC*, put the point of the compass on Point *B*, and draw part of a circle with radius 7 units. Use this 7-unit segment to open your compass to the correct radius.

|————————————————|
　　　　7 units

The circle intersects the other side of ∠*A* at _____ point(s).

You can draw _____ triangle(s). Draw the triangle(s).

C. Side *AB*: 6 units; Side *BC*: 9 units; Angle *A*: 120°

Use this segment to help you draw Side *BC*.

|————————————————|
　　　　9 units

The circle intersects the other side of ∠*A* at _____

point(s). You can draw _____ triangle(s). Draw the

triangle(s).

D. How many triangles did you draw in Parts A–C given two sides and the measure of an angle that is not between them?

_____

_____

  Turn and Talk How are the situations in Step It Out 1 and Step It Out 2 different? How are they the same?

Check Understanding

1. Draw a right triangle with two sides of lengths 4 units and 5 units and the 90° angle between them.

2. Draw a right triangle with two sides of lengths 4 units and 5 units with the 90° angle not between them.

On Your Own

3. A triangle with the largest possible base is drawn inside a circle. What part of the circle must coincide with the base of the triangle?

_____

4. (MP) **Use Tools** Use the diagram shown. Construct two different triangles that each have Side *AB* with a length of 8 units, Side *BC* with a length of 5 units, and a 35° angle that is not between them. Use the segment below to help you draw Side *BC*.

5 units

5. STEM An ethologist is a scientist who studies animal behavior. One ethologist studied the play behavior of a group of infant lowland gorillas and measured the portion of play time given to three types of play. Draw a circle graph to show the portion of the day for each type. The measure of the angle between the sides of the section for each behavior is given.

Solitary play: 150°
Social play: 195°
Mother-infant play: 15°

Gorilla Play-Time

6. Travis draws a triangle with three 60° angles and three sides of length 5 inches.

A. Can Margarita draw a triangle with the same angle measures as Travis's triangle but with different side lengths? Why or why not?

_____

_____

B. Can she draw a triangle with the same side lengths as Travis's triangle but with different angle measures? Explain.

_____

_____

7. (MP) **Use Tools** Students were surveyed about the number of siblings they have. Draw a circle graph to show the part of the group surveyed that has each given number of siblings. The table shows the measure of the angle between the sides of the section for each number of siblings.

Siblings	0	1	2	3	4	5 or more
Angle measure	40°	85°	95°	50°	50°	40°

Numbers of Siblings

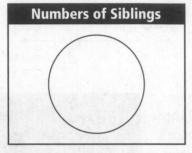

8. (MP) **Use Tools** Draw a triangle that has two sides of lengths 7 units and 5 units with a 42° angle between them. Can you draw more than one triangle?

9. **Open Ended** Draw a figure that has at least one pair of parallel sides and at least one side that is 6 units long. The figure should also have at least one line of symmetry.

LESSON 9.4
**More Practice/
Homework**

ONLINE

🍊Ed Video Tutorials and
Interactive Examples

Draw and Analyze Shapes to Solve Problems

1. **Open Ended** Draw a figure that has at least one pair of perpendicular sides, at least one side that is 4 units long, and at least one line of symmetry.

2. (MP) **Use Tools** How many triangles can you draw that have two sides of lengths 5 units and 2 units and a 68° angle between them? Draw the triangle(s).

3. A. (MP) **Use Tools** Complete the drawing to make Triangle(s) *ABC* with Side *AB* of length 9 units, Side *BC* of length 7 units, and Angle *A* with measure 45°. Use this segment to help you draw side *BC*.

   ⊢————⊣
   7 units

   B. How many triangles with these measurements can you draw?

   _____

   B

   9

   A 45°

4. (MP) **Reason** The two longest sides of a triangle are 7 inches and 10 inches long. Describe a possible length for the shortest side. Explain your reasoning.

   _____
   _____
   _____

Test Prep

5. Indicate whether one, no, or many triangles can be drawn with the given side lengths and/or angle measures.

	None	One	Many
6 feet, 6 feet, 8 feet	☐	☐	☐
40°, 40°, 112°	☐	☐	☐
68°, 22°, 90°	☐	☐	☐
7 meters, 6 meters, 12 meters	☐	☐	☐
6 inches, 10 inches, 45° angle between	☐	☐	☐
3 feet, 5 feet, 10 feet	☐	☐	☐

6. A triangle has two sides of lengths 20 centimeters and 8 centimeters. Which can be the length of the third side of the triangle? Select all that apply.

Ⓐ 30 centimeters   Ⓓ 8 centimeters

Ⓑ 22 centimeters   Ⓔ 6 centimeters

Ⓒ 14 centimeters

7. A road worker wants to place a circular map on a square sign that has a perimeter of 240 inches. What is the greatest possible radius of the circular map?

Ⓐ 15 inches   Ⓒ 60 inches

Ⓑ 30 inches   Ⓓ 120 inches

Spiral Review

8. It has been raining for hours, and 0.75 inch of rain has fallen. If there are 1.5 inches of rain in a single storm, Carmen knows that the basement of the building she is in will flood. The rain begins falling at a rate of 0.175 inch per hour. Write an inequality to represent how long it can continue to rain at this rate before the basement floods.

_____

9. Two complementary angles have measures of $(4x + 5)°$ and $(2x + 7)°$. What is the value of x? What are the measures of the angles?

_____

_____

Review

Vocabulary

Choose the correct term from the Vocabulary box.

Vocabulary
diameter
parallel
perpendicular
radius

1. The distance from the center of a circle to any point on the circle is the _____ of the circle.

2. Two lines that never intersect are _____.

3. A _____ of a circle is a line segment that passes through the center of the circle and has its endpoints on the circle.

Concepts and Skills

For Problems 4–5, draw a figure on the grid that matches each description.

4. A polygon with at least one pair of perpendicular sides, a side with a length of 8 units, and a side with a length of 6 units

5. An acute triangle with exactly one line of symmetry and one side with a length of 4 units

6. (MP) **Use Tools** Alisa drew the triangle shown. She claims it is the only distinct triangle that can be drawn with a 90° angle and two sides that measure 5 inches and 7 inches. Is Alisa correct? Why or why not? State what strategy and tool you will use to answer the question, explain your choice, and then find the answer.

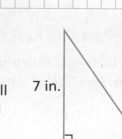

7 in.

5 in.

_____

_____

_____

_____

7. An artist is designing a logo for a new business. She starts by drawing a rectangle with a length of 10 centimeters and a width of 6 centimeters. What is the radius of the largest circle the artist can draw inside the rectangle if points on the circle can touch the sides of the rectangle?

_____ centimeters

8. Two of the sides of a triangle measure 6 inches and 10 inches. Select all measurements that could be the length of the third side of the triangle.

- (A) 4 inches
- (B) 5 inches
- (C) 8 inches
- (D) 10 inches
- (E) 12 inches
- (F) 18 inches

9. Colin draws two sides of a triangle so they measure 12 centimeters and 4 centimeters. What is a possible length of the third side?

_____ centimeters

10. How many unique quadrilaterals can be constructed from sides measuring 9 inches, 9 inches, 12 inches, and 12 inches?

- (A) none
- (B) exactly one
- (C) exactly two
- (D) more than two

11. For each set of measurements, tell whether exactly one triangle, more than one triangle, or no triangle can be constructed.

	Exactly one triangle	More than one triangle	No triangle
Angles that measure 60°, 60°, and 60°	☐	☐	☐
Angles that measure 30°, 90°, and 90°	☐	☐	☐
Sides that measure 4 cm, 8 cm, and 9 cm	☐	☐	☐
Sides that measure 15 mm, 20 mm, and 35 mm	☐	☐	☐

12. Ernesto drew a quadrilateral that has exactly one pair of parallel sides and exactly one line of symmetry. Which shape could he have drawn?

(A) (B) (C) (D)

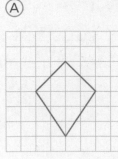
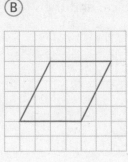
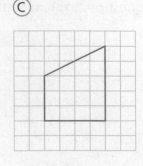

Analyze Figures to Find Circumference and Area

What Comes Next in the Pattern?

The figures shown are squares, non-square rectangles, and triangles.

Find the area of each figure in square centimeters. Look for patterns.

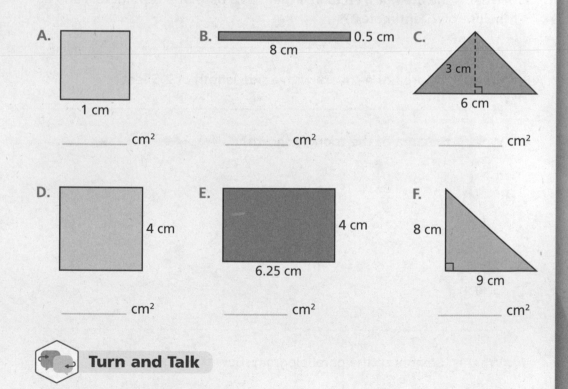

A.

1 cm

_____ cm²

B.

8 cm   0.5 cm

_____ cm²

C.

3 cm

6 cm

_____ cm²

D.

4 cm

_____ cm²

E.

4 cm

6.25 cm

_____ cm²

F.

8 cm

9 cm

_____ cm²

Turn and Talk

If the pattern continues, what three figures will appear in the next row? What will the areas of the figures be?

Are You Ready?

Complete these problems to review prior concepts and skills you will need for this module.

Solve One-Step Equations

Solve the equation.

1. $\frac{x}{2} = 5$ for x _____

2. $2w = \frac{10}{3}$ for w _____

3. $\frac{h}{20} = \frac{5}{4}$ for h _____

Evaluate Algebraic Expressions

Evaluate each given expression for $n = -3$.

4. $4n + n$ _____

5. $-n + n^2$ _____

6. $3 - n^2$ _____

Area of Quadrilaterals and Triangles

7. What is the area of a rectangle that has a base of 5 centimeters and a height of 2 centimeters?

_____

8. What is the area of a square with a side length of 2.5 feet?

_____

9. What is the area of the triangle shown?

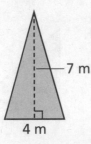

7 m

4 m

_____

10. What is the area of the parallelogram shown?

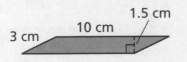

1.5 cm

10 cm

3 cm

_____

Name _____

Derive and Apply Formulas for Circumference

1 ft

I Can use the circumference formulas $C = \pi d$ and $C = 2\pi r$ to solve for C, r, or d when the value of the other variable is given.

Spark Your Learning

PAIRS

A woodworker has twelve spokes. To make the wheel's rim, there are two pieces of wood that can be curved using steam. They are 6 feet and 8 feet long.

The measure along the spokes from the center to the inside of the rim is shown. Is the 6-foot piece of wood long enough to curve around for the wheel's rim? Is the 8-foot piece of wood long enough? Use measuring tools, large paper, and string to help solve.

 Turn and Talk Did this experiment give you an idea of how much longer a string that makes up the rim of a wheel must be than one of the spokes? Explain.

Build Understanding

1 Find circular objects or objects that have a circular face. For each object, follow the steps to complete the table.

A. List the name of the object in the table.

B. Measure and record the circumference of the circular face.

C. Measure and record the diameter of the circular face.

D. Calculate the ratio of the circumference to the diameter. Write the ratio as a decimal in the table.

Object	Circumference, C	Diameter, d	Ratio, $\frac{C}{d}$
small bowl	about 16 in.	5 in.	

5 in.

 Turn and Talk Describe what you notice about the ratio $\frac{C}{d}$ in your table. Does the relationship between the circumference and diameter of a circle appear to be proportional? Explain.

2 Pi, represented by the symbol π, is the ratio of a circle's circumference to its diameter. You can use this relationship to find a formula for circumference.

A. Write an equation for π using C for circumference and d for diameter.

$$\pi = \frac{\boxed{}}{\boxed{}}$$

B. How can you rewrite the equation as a formula for circumference C?

$$C = \boxed{} \cdot \boxed{}$$

C. How are diameter and radius related?

The diameter is equal to _____ times the radius.

D. Rewrite your equation for C in terms of the radius r.

$$C = \boxed{} \cdot 2 \boxed{}$$

Step It Out

3 Juanita wants to put a circular fence around the edge of the circular garden shown. How much fencing will she need to the nearest foot? Use 3.14 for π.

14 ft

$C = \pi d$

$C \approx 3.14 \cdot \boxed{}$

$C \approx \boxed{}$

Juanita will need about _____ feet of fencing.

4 The circumference of a men's adult basketball hoop is about 56.52 inches. The diameter of a basketball is about 9.55 inches. Show that the ball can fit through the hoop. Use 3.14 for π.

Find the diameter of the hoop using $C = \pi d$.

$C = \pi d$

$\boxed{} \approx \boxed{} \cdot d$

$\dfrac{\boxed{}}{\boxed{}} \approx d$

$\boxed{} \approx d$

The diameter of the hoop is about _____ inches, which [is / is not] greater than the diameter of the basketball.

Check Understanding

1. At a park, the jogging trail is a circle with a radius of 200 meters. How far is it around the trail? Use 3.14 for π. Show your work.

_____

2. A contractor is installing a semicircular window with a radius of 3.5 feet. Find the distance around the window. Use $\frac{22}{7}$ for π. Explain your answer.

3.5 ft

_____

_____

_____

_____

On Your Own

56 ft

3. Toni rides the Ferris wheel shown for 15 revolutions.

    A. How far does Toni travel in one revolution?
Use $\frac{22}{7}$ for π.

    _____

    B. How far does Toni travel for the entire ride?

    _____

4. (MP) **Reason** Paul is making a ball-toss game for his club booth at the fair. He wants to make the circumference of the holes at least 3 inches greater but not more than 4 inches greater than the circumference of the ball. One person suggests that Paul can make the diameter of the hole 1 inch greater than that of the ball. Another suggests the diameter should be 2 inches greater. Which suggestion should Paul choose? Explain.

_____

_____

_____

_____

_____

5. **Health and Fitness** Juan runs a total of 11,775 feet around a circular track, burning 12 calories each lap. The track's diameter is 150 feet. How many calories does Juan burn? Round your answer to the nearest whole number. Use 3.14 for π.

_____

For Problems 6–7, find the circumference. Round your answer to the nearest hundredth. Use 3.14 for π.

6.

10 m

7.

21 cm

I'm in a Learning Mindset!

Did my strategy for deriving and applying circumferences work? How did I adjust my strategy when I got stuck?

_____

_____

LESSON 10.1
**More Practice/
Homework**

ONLINE

Video Tutorials and
Interactive Examples

Derive and Apply Formulas for Circumference

1. **Math on the Spot** A counter recorded 254 revolutions of the bicycle wheel shown. How far did the bicycle travel? Use $\frac{22}{7}$ for π.

   A. How far does the wheel roll for one tire revolution?

   _____

   B. What is the total distance recorded?

   _____

diameter $\frac{5}{4}$ ft

2. (MP) **Use Structure** Hans opens a circular window that is 3.5 feet across at its widest point. What is the circumference of the window to the nearest whole number? Use 3.14 for π.

   _____

3. (MP) **Use Structure** Ting is making a circular garden with a radius of 6 feet. How far across is the garden at its widest point? What is the length of edging material to the nearest hundredth needed to enclose the garden? Use 3.14 for π.

   _____

   _____

For Problems 4–9, find the circumference. Round your answer to the nearest hundredth. Use 3.14 for π.

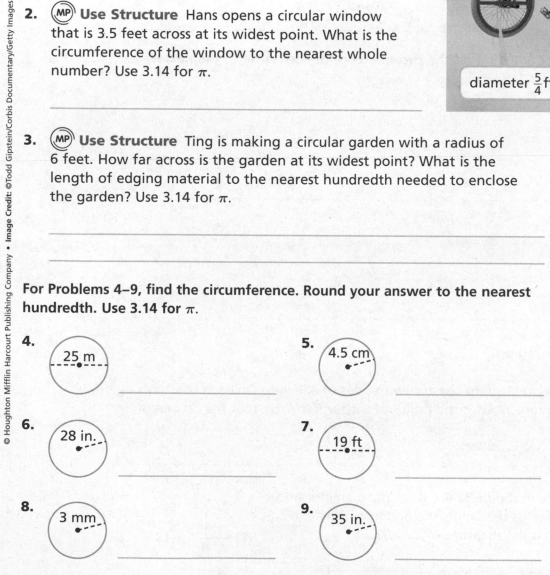

4. 25 m   _____

5. 4.5 cm   _____

6. 28 in.   _____

7. 19 ft   _____

8. 3 mm   _____

9. 35 in.   _____

Test Prep

10. What is the circumference of the circle to the nearest hundredth? Use 3.14 for π.

Ⓐ 26.69 in.

Ⓑ 53.38 in.

Ⓒ 106.76 in.

Ⓓ 907.46 in.

17 in.

11. Randy is designing a circular garden that is 18 feet in diameter. He is buying plastic edging that costs $1.50 per foot. He can only buy edging in whole-foot amounts. How much does it cost Randy to buy edging for his garden? Use 3.14 for π.

_____

For Problems 12 and 13, find the circumference of each circle to the nearest hundredth. Use 3.14 for π.

12.

49 cm

_____

13.

4.4 in.

_____

Spiral Review

14. Nada is making square coasters with sides of 3 inches. On each coaster is a circular design. What is the radius of the largest circle that fits on one of the coasters?

_____

15. In the circle in the diagram, $\overline{AC}$ is the diameter and $\overline{BD}$ is the radius that splits the upper semicircle in half. What is the measure of ∠ABD?

_____

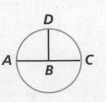

Name _____

Derive and Apply a Formula for the Area of a Circle

(I Can) use the area formulas for a circle to find the area of a circle if I know its radius or circumference or to find the radius or circumference if I know the area.

Spark Your Learning

A designer plans for a circular rug in a 9-foot by 9-foot square bedroom. What is the largest area of a rug that can fit in the bedroom?

 Turn and Talk How close do you think your estimate of the rug's area was? Explain.

Build Understanding

1 Use a parallelogram to find the area of a circle.

A. Use a compass to draw a circle on a piece of paper. Cut out the circle. Fold the circle in half three times as shown to get wedges of equal size.

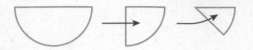

B. Cut the circle along the folded lines to separate the circle into eight equal wedges.

C. Arrange the wedges to form a figure resembling a parallelogram. Label the **base** of the parallelogram in terms of the circumference C. Label the **height** of the parallelogram in terms of the radius r.

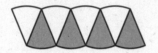

D. Use the labels on your parallelogram of wedges to substitute for b and h in the formula for area of a parallelogram.

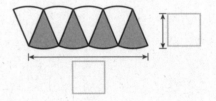

$A = b \cdot h$

$A = \boxed{} \cdot \boxed{}$

E. The formula for the circumference of a circle is $C = \pi \boxed{}$.

So half of the circumference can be written in terms of the radius as:

$\frac{1}{2}C = \pi \boxed{}$

F. Finally, complete the formula for the area of your parallelogram of wedges.

$A = \frac{1}{2}C \cdot r$

$A = \boxed{} \cdot r$ Substitute for $\frac{1}{2}C$.

$A = \boxed{}$ Write using an exponent.

G. The parallelogram of wedges is made from a circle, so the formula for the area of a circle is:

$A = \boxed{}$

 Turn and Talk How could you make your parallelogram of wedges look more like a parallelogram with straight edges?

Step It Out

2 ▸ The formula for the area of a circle is $A = \pi r^2$. This formula allows you to find the area of a circle if you know the radius or diameter. How can you find the area if you know only the circumference?

A. Write the formula for circumference using r. Then solve for r.

$$C = \pi d$$

$$C = \boxed{}$$

$$\dfrac{C}{\boxed{}} = r$$

B. Substitute the expression for r into the formula for the area of a circle and simplify.

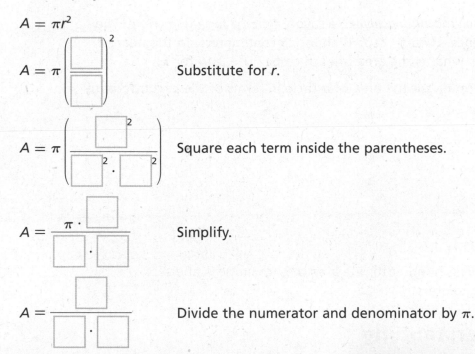

$$A = \pi r^2$$

$$A = \pi \left(\dfrac{\boxed{}}{\boxed{}} \right)^2 \qquad \text{Substitute for } r.$$

$$A = \pi \left(\dfrac{\boxed{}^2}{\boxed{}^2 \cdot \boxed{}^2} \right) \qquad \text{Square each term inside the parentheses.}$$

$$A = \dfrac{\pi \cdot \boxed{}}{\boxed{} \cdot \boxed{}} \qquad \text{Simplify.}$$

$$A = \dfrac{\boxed{}}{\boxed{} \cdot \boxed{}} \qquad \text{Divide the numerator and denominator by } \pi.$$

C. Tomas visits the circular play yard for pets, as shown. Use your formula to find the area, to the nearest square meter, of this pet play yard. Use 3.14 for π.

65 m of fencing

$$A = \dfrac{\boxed{}}{\boxed{}}$$

$$A = \dfrac{\boxed{}^2}{4\pi} \approx \boxed{}$$

The area is about $\boxed{}$ square meters.

3 ▶ Davonte wants to install a circular pool like the one shown. What is the area of the bottom of the pool to the nearest square foot? Use 3.14 for π.

A circle with a diameter of 18 feet has a radius of ⬚ feet.

$A = \pi r^2$

$A = \pi \left(\boxed{} \right)^2$

$A \approx \boxed{} \cdot \boxed{} \approx \boxed{} \ ft^2$

The bottom of the pool has an area of about ⬚ square feet.

4 ▶ Louisa is making *okonomiyaki*, a savory type of Japanese crepe. The circumference of each crepe is about 25 centimeters. To the nearest hundredth, what is the area of each crepe? Use 3.14 for π.

Use the formula for the area of a circle in terms of the circumference.

$A = \dfrac{C^2}{4\pi}$

$A = \dfrac{\boxed{}^2}{4\pi}$

$A \approx \dfrac{\boxed{}}{4 \cdot 3.14} \approx \boxed{}$

To the nearest hundredth, the area of each crepe is about ⬚ square centimeters.

Check Understanding

1. The new circular community swimming pool has a diameter of 64 feet.

A. What is the radius of the community pool?

_____

B. What is the area of the surface of the pool? Use 3.14 for π.

_____

2. To the nearest square centimeter, what is the area of a circle with a circumference of 75.36 centimeters? Use 3.14 for π.

_____

On Your Own

For Problems 3–5, use the circular mirror shown.

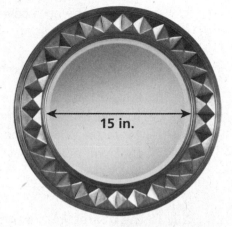

15 in.

3. To the nearest hundredth, what is the area of the mirror? Use 3.14 for π.

   _____

4. The mirror has a frame. The diameter of the mirror with the frame is 17 inches. To the nearest hundredth, what is the area of the mirror with the frame?

   _____

5. (MP) **Reason** To the nearest hundredth, what is the area of the frame?

   _____

6. A disk is shaped like a flat circular plate. Its radius is 4.25 inches. To the nearest hundredth, what is the area of the disk? Use 3.14 for π.

   _____

7. (MP) **Critique Reasoning** A classmate states that if the radius of a circle is doubled, then its area is doubled. Do you agree or disagree? If you disagree, how much larger do you think the area will be?

   _____

   _____

   _____

For Problems 8–9, find the area to the nearest hundredth. Use 3.14 for π.

8. 4 ft

   _____

9. 9 m

   _____

For Problems 10–11, find the area. Use $\frac{22}{7}$ for π.

10. 8 ft

   _____

11. 3 yd

   _____

12. **(MP)** **Use Repeated Reasoning** A lawn sprinkler waters a lawn in a circle as shown. Use $\frac{22}{7}$ for π.

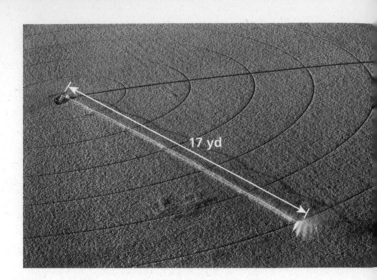

17 yd

A. What is the area covered by the sprinkler?

_____

B. Suppose the water pressure is reduced so that the radius of coverage is now 11 yards. What is the area of the lawn that will now be covered?

_____

13. To the nearest hundredth, find the area of a circle with a circumference of 69.08 feet. Use 3.14 for π.

_____

14. **(MP)** **Reason** A circular garden with a radius of 20 meters is surrounded by a walkway that measures 1 meter in width. Find the area of the walkway to the nearest hundredth. Use 3.14 for π.

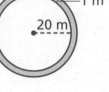

1 m

20 m

_____

15. Workers on a factory floor are painting one side of circular discs that will be placed on an assembly line. For every gallon of paint, a worker can paint an area that measures 1,256 square feet. If each disc has a radius of 2 feet, how many discs can they paint with one gallon of paint? Use 3.14 for π.

_____

For Problems 16–19, find the area, to the nearest hundredth, of the circle with the given circumference. Use 3.14 for π.

16. 19 centimeters

17. 132 millimeters

_____

18. 6.28 miles

19. 43.96 inches

_____

I'm in a Learning Mindset!

How effective were the strategies I used to find the area of a circle using the circumference of the circle?

_____

Name _____

Derive and Apply a Formula for the Area of a Circle

1. To make grape juice, water is added to a large cylindrical vat of grapes. If the diameter of the vat is 16 feet, what is the area of the base of the vat? Use 3.14 for π.

_____

2. **Math on the Spot** A group of historians is building a tepee to display at a local multicultural fair. The tepee has a height of 7 feet 4 inches at its center, and it has a circular floor of radius 14 feet. What is the area of the floor of the tepee to the nearest square foot? Use $\frac{22}{7}$ for π.

_____

3. The face of a clock has a circumference of 14π inches. What is its area? Use 3.14 for π.

_____

4. A carpenter cuts a circle out of a piece of wood. The radius of the circle is about 23 inches. The carpenter cuts the circle into two semicircles. What is the area of one semicircle? Use 3.14 for π.

_____

5. (MP) **Use Structure** Four identical circles are lined up in a row with no gaps between them such that the diameters form a segment that is 68 centimeters long. What is the combined area of all the circles to the nearest hundredth? Use 3.14 for π.

_____

6. Ms. Flynn's class is painting a circular canvas for the upcoming school dance. The class is estimating the area they need to paint. Its diameter is 5 feet. What is the area of the canvas to the nearest whole number? Use 3.14 for π.

_____

For Problems 7–12, find the area of each circle described. Use 3.14 for π.

7. radius of 10 centimeters

_____

8. diameter of 2 feet

_____

9. circumference of 62.8 inches

_____

10. diameter of 8 inches

_____

11. circumference of 18.84 miles

_____

12. radius of 99 millimeters

_____

Test Prep

13. Larry drew a circle with a circumference of 40.82 centimeters. What is the area of the circle? Use 3.14 for π.

_____

14. Safeta put a circular placemat on a table. The radius of the placemat is 7.5 inches. What is the area of the placemat? Use 3.14 for π.

_____

15. The length of the curved part of a semicircle is 25.12 inches. What is the approximate area of the semicircle? Use 3.14 for π.

Ⓐ 25.12 in²

Ⓑ 50.24 in²

Ⓒ 100.48 in²

Ⓓ 200.96 in²

16. On a middle school basketball court, there is a large circle painted on the floor. The diameter of the circle is 12 feet. What is the area of the circle? Use 3.14 for π.

Ⓐ 18.84 ft²

Ⓑ 113.04 ft²

Ⓒ 452.16 ft²

Ⓓ 1,808.64 ft²

17. Find the area of a circle with a radius of 33 millimeters. Use 3.14 for π.

_____

Spiral Review

18. Carlos drew a figure on the smartboard and said it was a triangle with angles of 100°, 35°, and 55°. Nate said that was impossible. Who is correct? Explain.

_____

_____

19. The diameter of a wheel is 3 feet. What is the circumference? Use 3.14 for π.

_____

Name

Describe and Analyze Cross Sections of Circular Solids

(I Can) identify the shapes of cross sections of circular solids and solve problems involving the areas of cross sections.

Spark Your Learning

Cassie and Amanda are making a cylindrical layer cake with four different-flavored layers. Amanda wants a circular piece of cake with only one flavor. Cassie wants a piece of cake with a rectangular face and all four flavors. Show how each girl could make a single cut to the cake to get the piece each one wants. Can both girls get the piece of cake they want from the same cake? Explain.

Turn and Talk For each type of cut, does the location where the cake is cut change the shape of the piece of cake?

Build Understanding

1 An art class is cutting foam figures for a project.

2 cm

5 cm

A. Jerome has two identical cylinders with the dimensions shown. He cuts one horizontally and one vertically through the centers of the bases. What are the figures and dimensions of the cross sections? Make sketches of the cross sections.

B. Jana has two identical cones like the one shown. She cuts one horizontally and one vertically through the center of the base. What are the figures and the given dimensions of the cross sections? Make sketches of the cross sections.

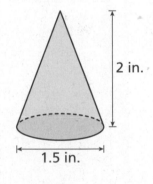

2 in.

1.5 in.

C. Javier has two identical spheres like the one shown. He cuts one horizontally through the center and one vertically through the center. What are the figures and dimensions of the cross sections? Make sketches of the cross sections.

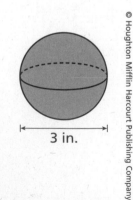

3 in.

 Turn and Talk Does the location of a horizontal cross section of the cylinder change the dimensions of the cross section? Explain.

Step It Out

2 A cylindrical barrel that is used to collect rainwater is shown.

A. Sketch the horizontal cross section. Label the radius. Find the circumference and the area, to the nearest hundredth, of the horizontal cross section of the barrel. Use 3.14 for π.

radius 11.25 in.

33.5 in.

B. Sketch the vertical cross section through a diameter of the base and label the length and width. Find the area of this vertical cross section of the barrel.

 Turn and Talk What do you notice about the width of a vertical cross section through the centers of the bases and the diameter of the horizontal cross section? Is this true for all cylinders? Explain.

3 Kia has a funnel shaped like a cone. The cone has a diameter of $2\frac{5}{8}$ inches and is 6 inches tall.

A. Sketch the vertical cross section through the center of the base of the cone and label its height and base.

B. Find the area of the vertical cross section of the cone. Explain how you arrived at your answer.

_____

_____

_____

Check Understanding

1. Ralph has a cylindrical container of parmesan cheese. The diameter of the base of the container is 2.75 inches, and the height is 6 inches. What is the area of a horizontal cross section of the cylinder to the nearest tenth of a square inch? Use 3.14 for π.

_____

2. Tori has a paper cup that is shaped like a cone. The radius of the base is 2.5 centimeters and the height is 11 centimeters. What are the shape and dimensions of the vertical cross section through the center of the base?

_____

_____

3. Tito builds a model of the solar system. In his model, the diameter of the sphere representing Jupiter is 7 inches. What is the circumference of a cross section through the center of the model of Jupiter? Use 3.14 for π.

_____

On Your Own

4. (MP) **Use Repeated Reasoning** Brock has a cylindrical metal tin where he keeps his coins. The radius of the base is 5.5 inches, and the height is 4 inches.

    A. What is the circumference of a horizontal cross section of the cylinder? Use 3.14 for π.

    _____

    B. What is the area of a horizontal cross section of the cylinder to the nearest hundredth? Use 3.14 for π.

    _____

    C. What is the area of a vertical cross section of the cylinder through the center of the base?

    _____

5. Find the circumference of a horizontal cross section of the cylinder. Use 3.14 for π.

6. Find the area of a vertical cross section through the center of the base of the cone.

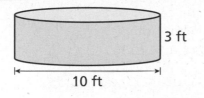

3 ft

10 ft

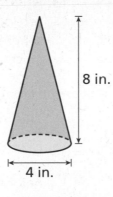

8 in.

4 in.

_____   _____

7. Find the area of a vertical cross section through the center of the base of the cylinder.

8. Find the area of a cross section through the center of the sphere. Use 3.14 for π.

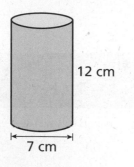

12 cm

7 cm

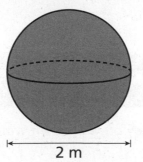

2 m

_____   _____

9. **(MP)** **Reason** Why can't the dimensions of a horizontal cross section of a cone be determined from just the dimensions of the cone?

_____

_____

_____

10. A cone-shaped paperweight is 5 inches tall, and the base has a circumference of about 12.56 inches. What is the area of a vertical cross section through the center of the base of the paperweight? Use 3.14 for π.

_____

32.5 mm

98 mm

11. Rosalie has a can of soup that is shaped like a cylinder. The measurements of the can are shown. Find the areas of a vertical cross section through the centers of the bases and a horizontal cross section of the can. Use 3.14 for π.

_____

_____

_____

12. Find the area of a vertical cross section through the center of the base of a cone with a height of 5 feet and a circumference of about 28.26 feet. Use 3.14 for π.

_____

13. Find the area of a vertical cross section through the center of a sphere with a diameter of 16 centimeters. Use 3.14 for π.

_____

14. Find the area of a vertical cross section through the centers of the bases of a cylinder with a height of 24 inches and a circumference of about 43.96 inches. Use 3.14 for π.

_____

15. Find the area of a horizontal cross section of a cylinder with a height of 34 centimeters and a circumference of about 131.88 centimeters. Use 3.14 for π.

_____

I'm in a Learning Mindset!

What strategies do I use to stay on task when working on my own?

_____

_____

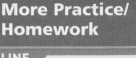

Describe and Analyze Cross Sections of Circular Solids

1. Clyde has a cone-shaped party hat. The height of the hat is 10 inches, and the radius of the base of the hat is 4 inches. What is the area of a vertical cross section through the center of the base of the party hat?

_____

2. A cylindrical swimming pool has a height of 4 feet and a circumference of about 75.36 feet. What is the area of a vertical cross section through the center of the pool? Use 3.14 for π.

_____

3. **Open Ended** Alexandra is working on a float for a parade. She is making a sphere out of papier-mâché. She knows the circumference of a cross section through the center of a sphere. How can Alexandra find the radius of the sphere?

_____

_____

_____

4. Find the area of a vertical cross section through the center of the base of the cone.

32 cm

12 cm

_____

5. Find the area of a cross section through the center of the sphere. Use 3.14 for π.

10 in.

_____

6. Find the area of a vertical cross section through the centers of the bases of a cylinder with a height of 27 inches and a circumference of about 47.1 inches. Use 3.14 for π.

_____

7. Find the area of a horizontal cross section of a cylinder with a height of 11 meters and a circumference of about 81.64 meters. Use 3.14 for π.

_____

Test Prep

8. Two chefs are working on cylindrical cakes. David wants to make a stripe of frosting in his cake, and he makes a cut that shows a rectangle. Terri wants to put a layer of frosting in the middle of her cake, so she makes a cut that shows a circle. How was Terri's cut different from David's?

_____

_____

9. Name the figure that represents the two-dimensional cross section of the cylinder cut by the plane.

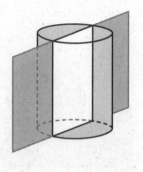

10. The cone is sliced horizontally, parallel to its base, as shown. Choose the figure that represents the two-dimensional cross section of the cone.

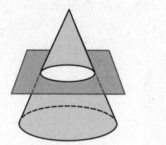

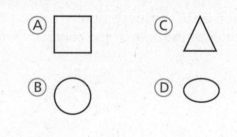

Spiral Review

11. A straight path from the edge of a circular garden to the center of the garden is 7 meters long. What is the area of the garden? Use 3.14 for π.

_____

12. How many unique triangles can be made with the angle measures 48°, 64°, and 68°: none, one, or infinitely many?

_____

Name

Areas of Composite Figures

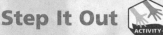 break a composite figure into simple shapes and use area formulas to find its area.

Step It Out

1 Rahim drew an outline of the front of a house on grid paper. He wants to find the area of his model.

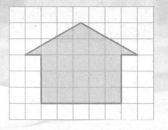

A. Separate the composite figure into simple geometric figures. What simple geometric figures are used to form the outline?

_____

B. Determine the dimensions and then find the area of each of the simple geometric figures.

_____

_____

_____

C. Find the area of the composite figure.

_____

_____

Turn and Talk Can you separate the composite figure into different simple geometric figures? Explain.

2 A section of a basketball court is shown.

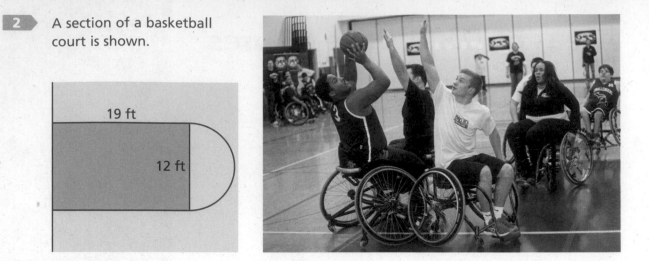

19 ft

12 ft

A. Determine the simple geometric figures that are used in the composite figure.

_____

B. Find the dimensions of the simple geometric figures.

_____

_____

C. How is the area of a semicircle related to the area of a circle with the same radius?

_____

_____

_____

D. Find the area of the simple geometric figures to the nearest square foot. Use 3.14 for π.

_____

_____

E. Find the area of the composite figure.

_____

_____

 Turn and Talk What method do you use to determine the simple geometric figures of a composite figure?

3 The manager of a hotel wants to put new carpet in the lobby. The dimensions of the lobby are shown. There is a statue with a circular base in the lobby that does not need to have carpet under it.

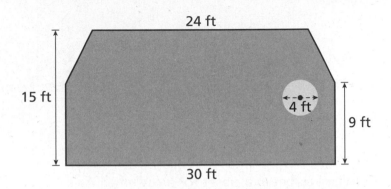

A. Determine the simple geometric figures that are in the composite figure. Find the dimensions of the simple geometric figures.

_____

_____

_____

B. Find the areas of the simple geometric figures. Use 3.14 for π.

_____

_____

_____

C. Find the area of the lobby that needs carpet. Explain how you found the area.

_____

_____

_____

Check Understanding

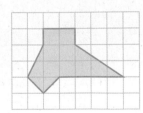

1. Find the area of the composite figure.

_____

2. Farrah has a piece of paper that is 11 inches long and 8 inches wide. She cuts a semicircle with a radius of 4 inches out of the piece of paper. What is the area of the piece of paper she has left after the cut to the nearest hundredth? Use 3.14 for π.

_____

On Your Own

3. Greg designed a trophy using grid paper. What is the area of the drawing of the trophy shown?

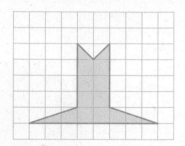

_____

4. (MP) **Attend to Precision** Clara is making a pennant. She attaches a rectangle that is 1 inch wide and 6 inches long to a triangle that has a base of 6 inches and a height of 28 inches. What is the area of the pennant?

_____

5. Financial Literacy Mary is installing carpet in a closet for a customer. A floor plan of the closet is shown. Mary charges $5.60 per square foot of carpet, plus a $150 installation fee.

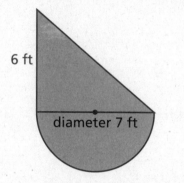

6 ft

diameter 7 ft

How much should Mary charge the customer to the nearest cent? Use 3.14 for π.

_____

For Problems 6–9, find the area of the composite figure shown to the nearest half unit. Use 3.14 for π.

6.

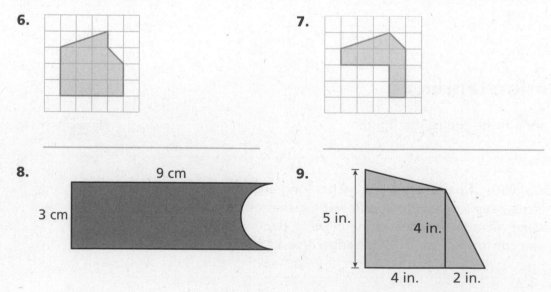

7.

8.

9 cm

3 cm

9.

5 in.

4 in.

4 in.   2 in.

_____

Areas of Composite Figures

1. A driveway consists of two rectangles. One rectangle is 80 feet long and 15 feet wide. The other is 30 feet long and 30 feet wide. What is the area of the driveway?

_____

2. (MP) **Use Tools** A patio is made of two sections. One is shaped like a trapezoid, and the other like a semicircle. The bases of the trapezoid are 12 feet and 8 feet. The height of the trapezoid is 4 feet. The diameter of the semicircle is the same as the trapezoid's shorter base. Use geometry software or another tool to draw a model of the patio. Find the patio's area. Use 3.14 for π.

_____

3. **Open Ended** Juanita is making a ribbon as shown.

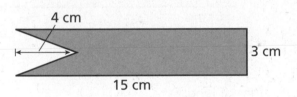

Explain two different ways you can find the area of the ribbon. Then find the area of the ribbon.

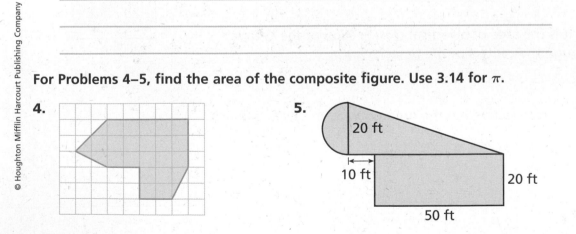

_____

_____

_____

_____

_____

For Problems 4–5, find the area of the composite figure. Use 3.14 for π.

4.

5.

_____   _____

© Houghton Mifflin Harcourt Publishing Company • Image Credit: ©haveseen/iStock/Getty Images Plus/Getty Images

Test Prep

6. A plot of grass behind a building is shown. What is the area of the plot of grass?

_____

7. Eric is designing a logo for a company. The logo consists of two identical parallelograms joined at their longest sides. One of the parallelograms has a base of 2.5 centimeters and a height of 1.25 centimeters. What is the area of the logo?

_____

8. Find the approximate area of the composite figure. Use 3.14 for π.

Ⓐ 174.96 cm²

Ⓑ 231.48 cm²

Ⓒ 288 cm²

Ⓓ 344.52 cm²

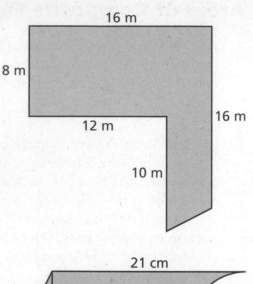

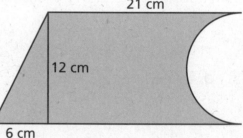

Spiral Review

9. How many unique triangles can be made with sides of lengths 4 cm, 7 cm, and 12 cm: none, one, or many?

_____

10. A cylindrical garbage can has the dimensions shown.

A. What is the area of a horizontal cross section of the cylinder? Use 3.14 for π.

_____

B. What is the area of a vertical cross section of the cylinder through the centers of the bases?

_____

C. Which cross section has the greater area, and by how much?

_____

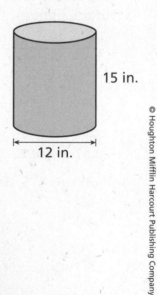

Vocabulary

Choose the correct term from the Vocabulary box.

Vocabulary
circumference
cross section
pi (π)
plane

1. the distance around a circle _____

2. a flat surface that has no thickness and extends forever

_____

3. the intersection of a three-dimensional figure and a plane

_____

Concepts and Skills

Use the circle for Problems 4–5.

4. Calculate the circumference of the circle in terms of π.

_____

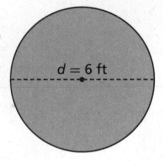

$d = 6$ ft

5. What is the area of the circle in terms of π?

_____

6. Given that $\pi \approx 3.14$, which values are reasonable for the area of a circle with radius 5 inches? Select all that apply.

Ⓐ 10π in^2

Ⓑ 15.7 in^2

Ⓒ 25π in^2

Ⓓ 31.4 in^2

Ⓔ 78.5 in^2

7. Ⓜ️Ⓟ **Use Tools** Given that the circumference of a circle is 8π centimeters, calculate the area of the circle in terms of π. State what strategy and tool you will use to answer the question, explain your choice, and then find the answer.

_____

_____

_____

8. The cylinder is being sliced horizontally by a plane as shown. Select all reasonable statements for the figure.

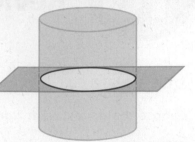

Ⓐ The cross section is parallel to the base of the cylinder.

Ⓑ The cross section is a rectangle.

Ⓒ The cross section is a circle.

Ⓓ The cross section has the same dimensions as the base of the cylinder.

Ⓔ The cross section would be the same if the cylinder were sliced vertically instead of horizontally.

For Problems 9–10, calculate the area for the given figure.

9.

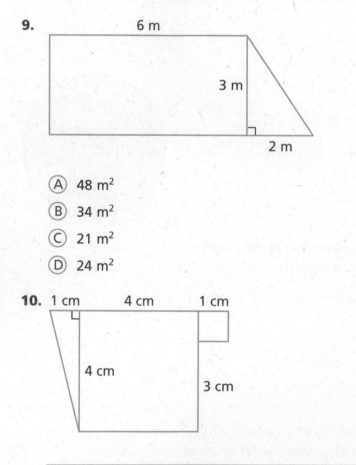

Ⓐ 48 m²

Ⓑ 34 m²

Ⓒ 21 m²

Ⓓ 24 m²

10. 1 cm   4 cm   1 cm

4 cm

3 cm

_____

11. The new circular community water fountain has a diameter of 192 feet. What is the area of the surface of the circular community water fountain? Use 3.14 for π.

_____

Analyze Surface Area and Volume

The Prism Family

Each of the rectangular prisms shown is made from cubes with an edge length of 1 centimeter. All of the prisms in this family have something in common.

Investigate by finding the dimensions, surface area, and volume of each prism. How are they all related?

A.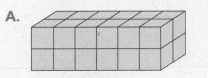

Dimensions:

_____, _____, _____

Surface area: _____

Volume: _____

B.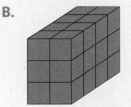

Dimensions:

_____, _____, _____

Surface area: _____

Volume: _____

C.

Dimensions:

_____, _____, _____

Surface area: _____

Volume: _____

Turn and Talk

Describe the family of rectangular prisms.

Are You Ready?

Complete these problems to review prior concepts and skills you will need for this module.

Explore Volume

Each rectangular prism is composed of cubes with an edge length of 1 inch. Determine the volume of each prism.

1. _____ in³

2. _____ in³

Nets and Surface Area

Draw a net of each prism. Then use the net to determine the surface area of the prism.

3. 3 cm
    2 cm
    5 cm

    _____ cm²

4. 10 m
    8 m
    6 m
    5 m

    _____ m²

Cross Sections of Circular Solids

5. A horizontal plane slices a cylinder as shown. Draw the cross section of the cylinder.

6. Can a plane slice a cone so that the cross section of the cone is a triangle? Explain.

    _____

    _____

Name _____

Describe and Analyze Cross Sections of Prisms and Pyramids

(I Can) describe and analyze the cross sections of pyramids and prisms of all types, with or without a diagram.

Spark Your Learning

PAIRS

Brittany bought a candle in the shape of a square pyramid. She wants to know what the inside of the candle looks like. She wonders what figures would be formed if she slices the candle. How could Brittany slice the candle to make a figure with a square face? A triangular face?

Turn and Talk How can you move the slice of the candle to get a smaller or larger square face?

Build Understanding

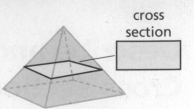

cross section

A **cross section** is an inside view produced by making a cut or slice. In this lesson, only cuts made parallel or perpendicular to the base will be shown.

1 ▶ Analyze the shipping box shown, which is in the shape of a **rectangular prism** with two square faces. What are the figures formed when slicing the box from different directions?

A. The box is a prism. What polygon describes the two-dimensional bases of this prism? What polygon describes the other faces?

_____

_____

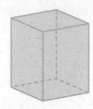

B. Suppose you slice the prism parallel to its base as shown. What two-dimensional figure is the cross section?

_____

C. Suppose you slice the prism perpendicular to its base as shown. What two-dimensional figure is the cross section?

_____

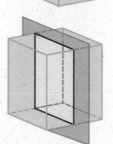

D. Consider the **pyramid** shown. Identify the two-dimensional base and faces. What is the name of this pyramid?

_____

_____

_____

E. Suppose you slice the pyramid shown parallel to its base. What two-dimensional figure is the cross section?

_____

F. Suppose you slice the pyramid shown perpendicular to its base, through the **vertex**. What two-dimensional figure is the cross section?

_____

G. Suppose you slice the pyramid perpendicular to its base through one edge. What shape is the cross section?

_____

© Houghton Mifflin Harcourt Publishing Company • **Image Credit:** ©realperson/Shutterstock

Step It Out

2 ► Rajesh is doing a research project on the Pentagon, which is located near Washington, D.C. Rajesh sketched a pentagonal prism to help him model the Pentagon.

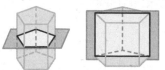

A. When Rajesh slices the pentagonal prism parallel to the bases, the result is a plane figure that has the same shape as the | bases / faces connecting the bases |. So the figure is a _____.

B. When Rajesh slices the pentagonal prism perpendicular to the bases, the result is a figure of the same type as the | bases / faces connecting the bases |. So the figure of this cross section is a _____.

C. Now consider a hexagonal pyramid. The two-dimensional figure that results from slicing the hexagonal pyramid shown parallel to the base is a _____.

D. The figure that results from slicing the hexagonal pyramid perpendicular to the base but not through the vertex, as shown, is a _____.

> **Turn and Talk** What other shape can be produced by slicing a hexagonal pyramid perpendicular to the base? Explain.

Check Understanding

1. A triangular prism is sliced parallel to its base. What two-dimensional figure is the cross section? Use a sketch to support your answer.

2. What cross section is made when a hexagonal pyramid like the one in Task 2 is sliced perpendicular to its base, through its vertex?

_____

3. Suppose the box of cereal shown is sliced parallel to its base. What is the resulting cross section?

_____

4. Compare the cross sections made from slicing the cereal box parallel to its base and slicing it perpendicular to its base.

_____

_____

On Your Own

For Problems 5–7, use the picture of the hotel with a roof in the shape of a regular pentagonal pyramid.

Pentagon Hotel
OPENS JUNE 2020

5. **(MP) Use Structure** Describe how the roof can be sliced to make a cross section in the shape of a pentagon.

_____

6. **(MP) Use Structure** Describe how the roof can be sliced to make a cross section in the shape of a triangle.

_____

7. **(MP) Reason** Describe how the location of a slice parallel to the base can affect the size of the resulting pentagon. Explain your reasoning.

_____

_____

For Problems 8–13, identify the shape of the two-dimensional cross section shown.

8. perpendicular to base of a rectangular prism

9. perpendicular to base not through vertex of a rectangular pyramid

10. perpendicular to base and through vertex of a square pyramid

11. parallel to base of a pentagonal prism

12. parallel to base of a hexagonal prism

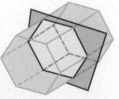

13. parallel to base of a square pyramid

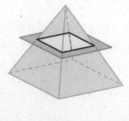

I'm in a Learning Mindset!

What methods are most effective for analyzing cross sections of prisms and pyramids?

Name

LESSON 11.1
**More Practice/
Homework**

ONLINE

Video Tutorials and
Interactive Examples

Describe and Analyze Cross Sections
of Prisms and Pyramids

**For Problems 1–3, describe the two-dimensional figure that results
from slicing the given three-dimensional figure.**

1. Slice parallel to the base

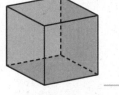

_____

2. Slice perpendicular to the base,
through the vertex

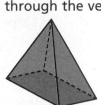

_____

3. Slice perpendicular to the base, not through the vertex

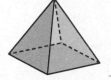

_____

**For Problems 4–6, tell whether the slice must be parallel or perpendicular to
the base to make the given cross section.**

4. A slice of a pentagonal pyramid results in a pentagon.

_____

5. A slice of a triangular prism results in a triangle.

_____

6. A slice of a hexagonal pyramid results in a triangle.

_____

7. (MP) **Use Repeated Reasoning** A sphere has a radius of 12 inches.

A. Describe the cross section formed by slicing the sphere through the
sphere's center.

_____

B. Describe the cross sections formed by slicing the sphere many times,
each time farther from the center of the sphere.

_____

_____

_____

8. (MP) **Use Structure** What cross sections might you see when slicing a cone
that you would **not** see when slicing a pyramid or a prism?

Test Prep

9. Select all of the following three-dimensional figures that could have a cross section of a triangle when sliced parallel to the base, perpendicular to the base through the vertex, or perpendicular to the base *not* through the vertex.

Ⓐ cube

Ⓑ triangular prism

Ⓒ rectangular prism

Ⓓ triangular pyramid

Ⓔ pentagonal prism

10. Match each description of slicing a three-dimensional figure with the resulting two-dimensional figure shown.

Slice a square pyramid parallel to base　●　　　●　　☐ A

Slice a non-square rectangular prism parallel to base　●　　　●　　⬠ B

Slice a square pyramid perpendicular to base through the vertex　●　　　●　　☐ C

Slice a pentagonal prism parallel to base　●　　　●　　△ D

11. Describe the cross sections made by slicing a hexagonal prism parallel to and perpendicular to its base.

_____

_____

Spiral Review

12. Draw a quadrilateral with two pairs of parallel, congruent sides and four right angles.

13. Find the area of the composite figure.

_____

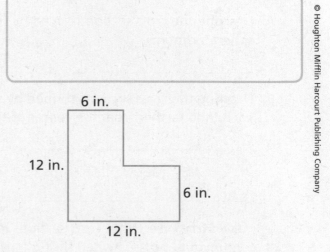

6 in.

12 in.

6 in.

12 in.

Name _____

Derive and Apply Formulas for Surface Areas of Cubes and Right Prisms

(I Can) derive and apply the formulas for surface area of any right prism.

Spark Your Learning

Sara is wrapping a gift box with dimensions 10 inches by 14 inches by 5 inches with wrapping paper. What is the least amount of wrapping paper she will need to cover the gift box without any overlap?

Turn and Talk What is the difference between area and surface area?

© Houghton Mifflin Harcourt Publishing Company • Image Credit: ©JGI/Jamie Grill/Blend Images/Getty Images

Build Understanding

1 A wooden toy box is represented by the **net** shown with it.

A. How many faces make up the toy box? What does the net show about these faces?

_____

_____

B. Are any of the faces congruent? If so, which ones?

_____

_____

C. What is the shape of the two bases? What is their combined area?

_____

D. What is the combined area of the front and back faces?

_____

E. What is the combined area of the left and right faces?

_____

F. How can you find the total **surface area** of the toy box? What is this value?

_____

G. Use the net to derive a formula for surface area of a box with length ℓ, width w, and height h:

Surface area = $2\ell w +$ ☐ $+$ ☐

Since ℓw is the area of a _____, replace ℓw with B: $2B + 2\ell h + 2wh$.

Both parts of the expression $2\ell h + 2wh$ contain an h, so factor it out: $2B + h($ ☐ $+$ ☐ $)$.

Since $2\ell + 2w$ represents the _____ of the base, replace $2\ell + 2w$ with P:

Surface Area = $2B +$ ☐ h

> **Turn and Talk** How could you change the surface area formula for a cube to make it simpler?

Step It Out

The surface area of a right prism is $S = 2B + Ph$, where B is the base area, P is the base perimeter, and h is the height of the prism.

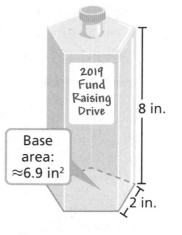

2 ▶ A foundation has the water bottles shown as giveaways for its annual fundraiser. What is the approximate surface area of the water bottle, treating the top surface as flat and ignoring the spout?

2019 Fund Raising Drive

8 in.

Base area: ≈6.9 in²

2 in.

A. From the picture, the area of the base is approximately ☐ square inches and the height is ☐ inches.

The perimeter of the base is ☐ × ☐ = ☐ inches.

B. Find the approximate surface area.

$S = 2B + Ph$

$S \approx 2\boxed{} + \boxed{} \left(\boxed{} \right)$

$S \approx \boxed{} + \boxed{}$

$S \approx \boxed{}$

The surface area of the water bottle is approximately ☐ square inches.

Check Understanding

1. A couch cushion needs to be covered with fabric. The dimensions of the cushion are 1.5 feet long by 1.5 feet wide by 0.5 foot high. What is the least amount of fabric that will be needed to cover the couch cushion?

_____

2. Bobby is sanding a five-sided storage chest with the dimensions shown. The base is a regular pentagon. If he sands only the outside of the chest, approximately how much area must he sand?

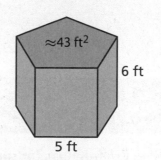

≈43 ft²

6 ft

5 ft

_____

3. A photographer's darkroom needs a new coat of black paint on all surfaces of the room, including the ceiling and the floor. The room is a cube with edge length 11 feet. How much surface area must be painted?

_____

On Your Own

4. Lily is using wrapping paper to cover a box with dimensions 7 centimeters by 10 centimeters by 5 centimeters. What is the least amount of paper Lily will need to cover the box? _____

5. (MP) **Use Structure** Gavin is making a scale replica of a tent for his social studies project. The replica is in the shape of a triangular prism. It has an isosceles triangle base with side lengths 6 inches, 5 inches, and 5 inches. The height of the triangle is 4 inches, and the depth of the tent is 7 inches. How much fabric will Gavin need to make the outside of the replica, including the "floor"? _____

6. Blake made a storage bin out of poles in the shape of a regular hexagonal prism, as shown. He wants to cover the surface area of the prism, including the floor, with a tarp to protect his things from the weather. What is the approximate surface area that the tarp will cover? Explain.

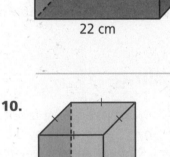

$B \approx 93.6$ ft^2

10 ft

6 ft

_____

_____

_____

Find the surface area of each prism.

7.

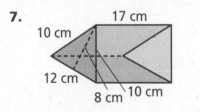

17 cm
10 cm
12 cm
8 cm
10 cm

_____

8.

7.5 cm
5.5 cm
22 cm

_____

9. 14 in.

≈ 509 in^2

_____

10.

6.5 cm

_____

➗ I'm in a **Learning Mindset!**

How does using the formulas for surface area of right prisms help me find surface area more efficiently?

_____

_____

Derive and Apply Formulas for Surface Area of Cubes and Right Prisms

1. (MP) **Use Structure** Melissa baked a cake. The box for the cake is in the shape of a cube with edges 9 centimeters in length. Draw a supporting picture and find how many square centimeters of cardboard are needed to make the box.

2. Sue is upholstering a rectangular ottoman that measures 21 centimeters by 18 centimeters by 15 centimeters. What will be the total square centimeters of fabric that Sue must use to cover all faces of the ottoman?

   _____

3. A drawing of the attic in a house is shown. It needs insulation on all sides. How many square feet of insulation are needed?

   _____

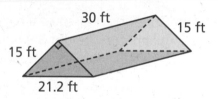

30 ft   15 ft
15 ft
21.2 ft

For Problems 4–7, find the surface area of each prism. Round to the nearest tenth if necessary.

4. **Math on the Spot**

   3 cm
   10 cm   4 cm

   _____

5.

   5 in.
   4 in.   10 in.
   5 in.   6 in.

   _____

6. Regular pentagon base
   B ≈ 61.94 cm²

   5 cm
   6 cm

   _____

7.

   20 cm
   16 cm
   12 cm   10 cm

   _____

Test Prep

8. Find the surface area of the figure.

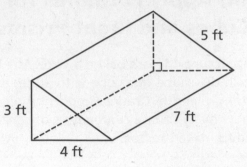

(A) 41 ft²

(B) 69 ft²

(C) 75 ft²

(D) 96 ft²

9. Mark bought a jewelry box in the shape of a cube. The jewelry box has edge lengths of 6 inches. What is the total surface area of the jewelry box?

(A) 36 in²

(B) 108 in²

(C) 216 in²

(D) 1,296 in²

10. Find the surface area of a rectangular prism with length of 4.7 inches, width of 6.4 inches, and height of 8.2 inches. Round to the nearest tenth.

_____

11. Find the surface area of a regular hexagonal prism with side length 4.2 millimeters, height 3.9 millimeters, and base area of approximately 45.8 square millimeters. Round to the nearest tenth.

_____

Spiral Review

12. Identify the two-dimensional figure that results from slicing a cylinder parallel to its base.

_____

13. Find the area of the composite figure.

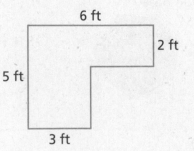

_____

Name

Derive and Apply a Formula for the Volume of a Right Prism

(I Can) accurately apply the formula to find the volume of right prisms.

Spark Your Learning

Use unit cubes or graph paper to find how many 1-inch cubes could fit into a rectangular prism with edge lengths shown. Describe how you found your answer.

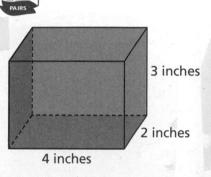

3 inches

2 inches

4 inches

Turn and Talk How are the dimensions of the box related to the number of unit cubes required to fill it?

Build Understanding

1 To derive the formula for **volume** of any right prism, imagine filling a right rectangular prism with 1-inch cubes.

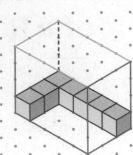

A. How many 1-inch cubes can be placed along the length of the prism shown here? The width of the prism?

_____

B. How many cubes are needed to make one horizontal layer in the prism? Explain how you found your answer.

_____

_____

C. How is completing the first layer like finding the area of a rectangle or a cross section of the prism? How is it different?

_____

_____

_____

D. How will the number of cubes needed to make the first layer compare to the number of cubes needed to complete any other layer?

_____

E. How many layers will it take to fill the prism shown? How did you find your answer?

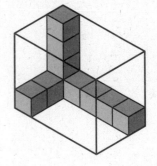

_____

_____

F. Using the concept of "layers," how can you determine the number of cubes it will take to fill up the entire volume of the prism? What is the volume of the prism?

_____

_____

G. Using Parts A through F, complete the statements to derive the formula for the volume *V* of a right prism.

V = (length × _____) × _____

V = area of the _____ × _____

Turn and Talk Using what you know about the formulas for area of triangles and trapezoids, will this same formula work for other types of prisms?

Step It Out

The formula for volume, $V = Bh$, is the area of the base (B) of a prism multiplied by its height (h).

 Find the volume of the tent shown.

A. Since the tent is shaped like a prism, the base of the prism is a | triangle / rectangle |.

B. Write an expression for the area of the base of the prism.

$B = (\boxed{})(\boxed{})(\boxed{})$

C. The length of the tent is $\boxed{}$ feet. This represents the | base / height | of the prism.

D. Use the formula.

$V = Bh$

$V = (\boxed{} \cdot \boxed{} \cdot \boxed{}) \boxed{} = \boxed{}$ ft³

3 A hexagonal prism has a volume of 60 cubic centimeters. The hexagonal base has an area of 12 square centimeters. Find the height of the prism.

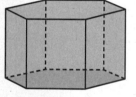

A. The base of this prism is a | hexagon / rectangle |.

B. Use the formula.

$V = Bh$

$\boxed{} = \boxed{} h$

$\boxed{} = h$ The height of the hexagonal prism is $\boxed{}$ centimeters.

Check Understanding

1. A rectangular sandbox measures 4 feet by 7 feet by 2 feet. How many cubic feet of sand can the sandbox hold?

2. A triangular prism has a base length of 1.5 centimeters, a base height of 3 centimeters, and a height of 12 centimeters.

   A. Find the volume of the prism.

   B. A pentagonal prism has the same volume as the triangular prism in Part A. Its base has an area of $4\frac{1}{2}$ centimeters. Find its height.

On Your Own

3. Leah is filling a cube-shaped box with packing material and gift items. Each edge length of the box is 20 inches. What is the greatest possible volume of all the presents and packing material inside the cube?

_____

4. (MP) **Use Structure** A lantern is represented by the pentagonal prism shown. What is the area of the base of the lantern? Explain your reasoning. Round to the nearest tenth.

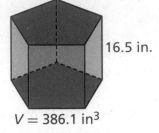

16.5 in.

$V = 386.1$ in³

_____

_____

_____

5. A rectangular water tank can hold 142.5 cubic meters of water. Its base is 9.5 meters by 5 meters. What is its height?

_____

6. A triangular prism has the dimensions shown. What is the length x if its volume is 72 cubic feet?

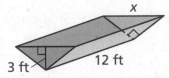

x

3 ft   12 ft

_____

For Problems 7–8, find the volume of each figure.

7.

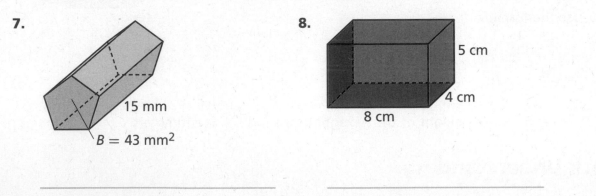

15 mm

$B = 43$ mm²

8.

5 cm

4 cm

8 cm

_____   _____

I'm in a Learning Mindset!

Did I manage my time well when I applied the formulas for volumes of right prisms? What can I do to manage my time better?

_____

_____

Derive and Apply a Formula for the Volume of a Right Prism

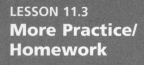

1. The Truit family rented the cabin shown in the shape of a triangular prism. The cabin is 30 feet deep. What is its volume?

_____

25 ft

15 ft

2. A piece of copper tubing is in the shape of a hexagonal prism. The area of the base of the prism is 3 square centimeters. The volume of the prism is 51 cubic centimeters. What is the height of the tubing?

_____

3. **Open Ended** A restaurant's walk-in commercial refrigerator has a capacity of 120 cubic feet. It is a rectangular prism 6 feet tall. Using graph paper, model the possible dimensions of the length and width of the refrigerator's footprint. (*Hint*: Have each square on the graph paper represent one square foot.) Are your answers reasonable? Explain.

_____

_____

_____

_____

_____

4. **Math on the Spot** Find the volume of the triangular prism.

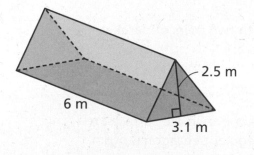

2.5 m

6 m

3.1 m

_____

Find the volume of each figure.

5.

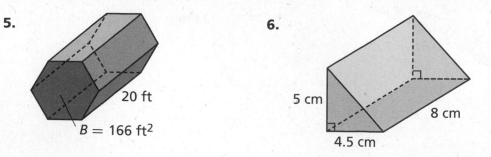

20 ft

B = 166 ft²

6.

5 cm

8 cm

4.5 cm

_____   _____

Test Prep

7. Jerome photographed an aquarium that measured 12 inches by 18 inches by 24 inches. Lim photographed an aquarium that was 12 inches by 30 inches by 12 inches. Both aquariums are rectangular prisms. How much more volume does Jerome's aquarium have than Lim's?

_____

8. An attic for a dollhouse is represented by a triangular prism with the dimensions shown. What is the volume of the attic?

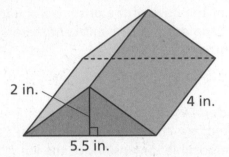

Ⓐ 11.5 in³   Ⓒ 44 in³

Ⓑ 22 in³   Ⓓ 88 in³

9. The volume of an octagonal prism is 1,260 cubic meters. The base has an area of 28 square meters. Write and solve an equation to find the height of the prism.

_____

10. A rectangular prism has a volume of 98 cubic feet, a width of 2 feet, and a length of 7 feet. Find the height of the rectangular prism.

_____

Spiral Review

11. Use geometry software to draw a quadrilateral with two pairs of parallel sides and four right angles. What is the quadrilateral?

_____

12. Find the surface area of the right triangular prism.

13. Find the approximate surface area of the regular pentagonal prism.

Name _____

Solve Multi-step Problems with Surface Area and Volume

(I Can) solve multi-step surface area and volume problems.

Step It Out

1 ▷ A toy manufacturer makes a game that they package in a cube-shaped carton with a surface area of 54 square inches. What is the volume of the shipping carton?

A. What information is given?

| surface area / volume |

What information is needed?

| surface area / volume |

B. Write the formulas for surface area and volume of a cube, where *s* is the length of an edge.

Surface area = 6 ☐² and Volume = ☐³

What do the two formulas have in common?

_____

C. Use the given surface area to find the edge length *s*.

Surface area = 6 ☐²

Substitute the surface area. ☐ = 6 ☐²

Divide both sides by 6. ☐ = s^2

Find the number whose square is 9. ☐ = *s*

D. Use the edge length to find the volume.

Volume = ☐³

Volume = ☐³ = ☐ in³

The volume is _____ cubic inches.

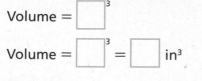

Turn and Talk If the carton were a rectangular prism instead of a cube, could you find its edge lengths from its surface area? Explain.

© Houghton Mifflin Harcourt Publishing Company • **Image Credits:** (tl) ©artpritsadee/Shutterstock, (tr) ©Sergei Kardashev/Shutterstock

2 Use what you know about surface area and volume to solve each problem.

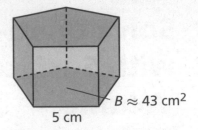

B ≈ 43 cm²

5 cm

A. The regular pentagonal prism shown has a surface area of approximately 191 square centimeters. Find the approximate volume of the prism.

Use the surface area to find the approximate height.

Surface Area = 2B + Ph $\boxed{}$ ≈ 2 ($\boxed{}$) + $\boxed{}$ h

191 ≈ $\boxed{}$ + 25h

Subtract 86 from both sides: $\boxed{}$ ≈ 25h

Divide both sides by 25: $\boxed{}$ ≈ h

The approximate height h is _____ centimeters. Use the approximate height to find the volume.

Volume = Bh ≈ $\boxed{}$ × $\boxed{}$ = $\boxed{}$ cm³

The volume is approximately _____ cubic centimeters.

B. Find the surface area of the rectangular prism with a square base.

First use the volume to find the _____.

Volume   = Bh

Substitute known values: $\boxed{}$ = ($\boxed{}$)h

Divide both sides by $\boxed{}$: $\boxed{}$ = h

The height is _____ inches.

Use the height you found to determine the surface area.

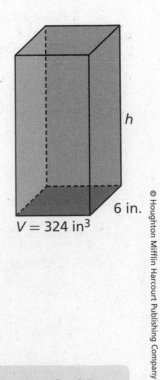

h

6 in.

V = 324 in³

Surface Area = 2B + Ph

= 2($\boxed{}$) + ($\boxed{}$) ($\boxed{}$) = $\boxed{}$

The surface area is _____ square inches.

Turn and Talk Make a list of strategies that help with setting up and solving word problems relating to surface area and volume. Explain each strategy.

3 Reggie built the doghouse shown. He will cover the outside with weatherproof paper, then cut out the entrance. How much weatherproof paper will he need?

First use one of the given prism volumes to find its height. Then find the combined surface area.

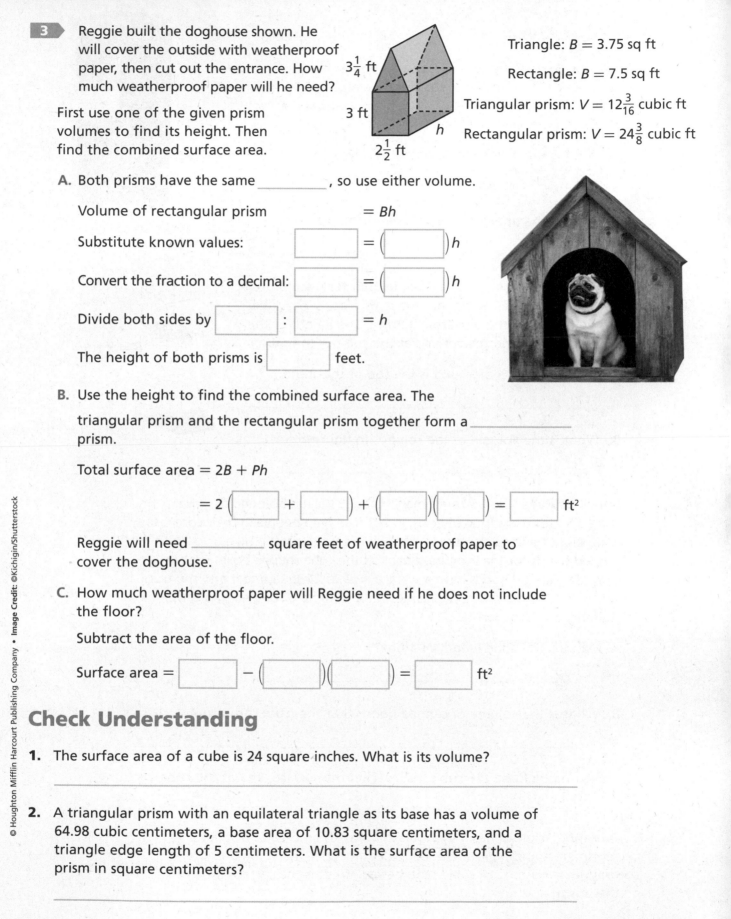

$3\frac{1}{4}$ ft

3 ft

h

$2\frac{1}{2}$ ft

Triangle: $B = 3.75$ sq ft

Rectangle: $B = 7.5$ sq ft

Triangular prism: $V = 12\frac{3}{16}$ cubic ft

Rectangular prism: $V = 24\frac{3}{8}$ cubic ft

A. Both prisms have the same _____, so use either volume.

Volume of rectangular prism = Bh

Substitute known values: ⬚ = (⬚) h

Convert the fraction to a decimal: ⬚ = (⬚) h

Divide both sides by ⬚ : ⬚ = h

The height of both prisms is ⬚ feet.

B. Use the height to find the combined surface area. The triangular prism and the rectangular prism together form a _____ prism.

Total surface area = $2B + Ph$

= 2 (⬚ + ⬚) + (⬚)(⬚) = ⬚ ft²

Reggie will need _____ square feet of weatherproof paper to cover the doghouse.

C. How much weatherproof paper will Reggie need if he does not include the floor?

Subtract the area of the floor.

Surface area = ⬚ − (⬚)(⬚) = ⬚ ft²

Check Understanding

1. The surface area of a cube is 24 square inches. What is its volume?

_____

2. A triangular prism with an equilateral triangle as its base has a volume of 64.98 cubic centimeters, a base area of 10.83 square centimeters, and a triangle edge length of 5 centimeters. What is the surface area of the prism in square centimeters?

_____

On Your Own

3. **(MP) Use Structure** Lonnie makes a regular hexagonal prism as shown with a surface area of approximately 244.8 square inches to collect his change. What is the approximate volume of change the prism will hold?

3 in.

   A. What is the approximate height of the prism?

   _____

   B. What is the approximate volume of the prism?

   _____

$B = 23.4$ in²

4. **(MP) Use Structure** A stand is being built for a sculpture at a school art show. The stand is made by placing the cube shown on top of the trapezoidal prism. The height of the prism is 3 feet. Find the volume of the composite figure.

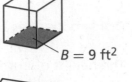

$B = 9$ ft²

   A. How high off the ground is the top of the stand?

   _____

   B. What is the volume of the composite figure?

   _____

$B = 15.6$ ft²

5. **Social Studies** The USDA estimates that 15 million households in the United States were food insecure in 2017. To help people in their community who might be food insecure, a school has a fundraiser to fill a truck with canned goods for the local food bank. If the cube-shaped boxes used to store the canned goods have a surface area of 24 square feet and the truck will hold 128 boxes, what is the maximum volume of canned goods the students can transport?

   A. What is the edge length of 1 box?

   _____

   B. What is the volume of canned goods that the truck can carry?

   _____

6. A cube has volume 216 cubic inches. Find the surface area of the cube.

   _____

7. A triangular prism has a triangular base with an area of 6 square centimeters and a perimeter of 12 centimeters. The volume of the triangular prism is 18 cubic centimeters. What is the surface area of the prism?

   _____

8. An ice cube from this ice tray has a surface area of 6 square inches. What is the total volume of all the ice in the tray?

   A. What is the edge length of one ice cube?

   _____

   B. (MP) **Use Structure** What is the total volume of all the ice in the tray?

   _____

9. (MP) **Attend to Precision** Maribelle decorates molds for making candles. The molds have the shape of open-topped regular pentagonal prisms. Each mold holds an approximate volume of 275 cubic centimeters of wax. The area of the base of a mold is approximately 27.5 square centimeters and the edge length of the base is 4 centimeters. What is the approximate surface area of a mold (not including a top)?

   A. What is the approximate height of a mold?

   _____

   B. How should the formula for surface area be changed for this situation?

   _____

   _____

   C. What is the approximate surface area of a mold?

   _____

10. STEM Noah is building a scale model of a barn for an architecture project. It is made from a trapezoidal prism on top of a rectangular prism. The volume of the barn is 390 cubic inches. The area of the base of the rectangular prism is 30 square inches, and the area of the base of the trapezoidal prism is 9 square inches. The dimensions of the front face of the barn are shown.

   3 in.
   2.5 in.   2.5 in.
   5 in.
   6 in.

   A. What is the depth of the barn model (height of the prism)?

   _____

   B. What is the surface area of the model of the barn?

   _____

11. (MP) **Reason** A rectangular prism has a 10-inch by 2-inch base and a surface area of 424 square inches. What is the volume of a column of 8 rectangular prisms with these dimensions, stacked base-to-base?

   _____

12. (MP) **Use Structure** The tent shown is a triangular prism. What is the amount of space inside the tent?

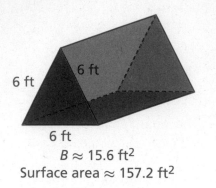

6 ft

6 ft

6 ft

6 ft

$B \approx 15.6 \text{ ft}^2$
Surface area $\approx 157.2 \text{ ft}^2$

A. About how long is the tent from the front to the back?

_____

B. What formula will find the space inside the tent? What is the space inside the tent?

_____

13. (MP) **Use Structure** Kristoff has a wooden cube with a volume of 1,000 cubic inches. He is going to make paper signs for each face of the cube for advertising.

A. What is the edge length of the wooden block?

_____

B. What amount of paper will he need for the signs?

_____

14. (MP) **Use Structure** A company stores supplies in cube-shaped boxes in a warehouse. They are stored on pallets that hold 4 boxes wide, deep, and high. The total volume of boxes is 512 cubic feet. Find the surface area of 1 box.

A. What is the volume of one cube? What is its edge length?

_____

B. What is the surface area of one box?

_____

15. A trapezoidal prism has a volume of 585 cubic centimeters. The area of the base is 39 square centimeters. If the base has sides measuring 4, 6.5, 6.5, and 9 centimeters, what is the surface area of the prism?

_____

Name _____

LESSON 11.4
More Practice/ Homework

ONLINE
😊Ed
Video Tutorials and Interactive Examples

Solve Multi-step Problems with Surface Area and Volume

1. (MP) **Use Structure** Holly is using wood to build the base and sides of a regular hexagonal prism-shaped herb garden with a volume of 4.3875 cubic feet. The area of the base is 5.85 square feet, and the side length of the hexagon is $1\frac{1}{4}$ feet long. Find the amount of wood Holly will need to complete the project.

   A. What is the height of the herb garden?

   _____

   B. What amount of wood, in square feet, does Holly need?

   _____

2. (MP) **Use Structure** The cargo area of the moving truck shown will be completely filled by 45 identical cube-shaped boxes. What will be the surface area of one layer of boxes on the floor of the truck bed?

   A. What is the edge length of one box?

   _____

   B. What is the surface area of one layer of boxes on the floor of the truck bed?

   _____

   C. How many boxes make up this one layer?

   _____

6 ft   6 ft   10 ft

3. A regular hexagonal prism has a surface area of 1,714.56 square centimeters. If the area of the base is 665.28 square centimeters and the side length is 16 centimeters, what is the volume of the prism?

   _____

4. A cube has a surface area of 96 square inches. If 16 cubes are combined to make a rectangular prism, what is the volume of the rectangular prism?

   _____

5. **Math on the Spot** Find the volume of milk, in cubic inches, that the carton shown can hold when it is filled up to the top of the rectangular part of the carton.

   _____

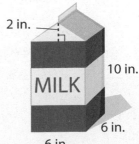

2 in.

10 in.

MILK

6 in.

6 in.

Test Prep

6. A cube has a surface area of 1,176 square inches. What is the volume of the cube?

Ⓐ 14 in³

Ⓑ 196 in³

Ⓒ 1,728 in³

Ⓓ 2,744 in³

7. Ina makes cakes in a pan shaped like a rectangular prism. The base of the pan is an 8-inch by 12-inch rectangle, and the volume of the pan is 288 cubic inches. Find the surface area of a cheesecake baked in this pan.

_____

_____

8. Suppose you are given the base area and surface area of a triangular prism and the side lengths of the triangular base. Select all the steps needed to find the volume of the prism.

Ⓐ Find the height of the prism using the surface area formula.

Ⓑ Find the height of the prism using the volume formula.

Ⓒ Find the height of the triangle.

Ⓓ Use the area of the base and the height to find the volume.

Ⓔ Use the height of the base and the height of the prism to find the volume.

Spiral Review

9. How many triangles can be drawn with side lengths 8 feet, 10 feet, and 21 feet?

_____

10. Jared works as a landscaper. He installs a sprinkler that sprays water in a circle with an 8-foot radius. What is the approximate area covered by the sprinkler? Use 3.14 for π.

_____

11. A bike wheel has a 16-inch diameter. Approximately how far will the wheel travel in three rotations? Use 3.14 for π.

_____

Vocabulary

Tell whether each statement is true or false. If it is false, tell what word could replace the underlined word to make the statement true.

1. A cross section is a <u>two</u>-dimensional figure formed when a three-dimensional figure is cut. _____

2. A <u>pentagon</u> is a polygon with six sides. _____

3. A triangular prism has three faces that are <u>triangles</u>. _____

Concepts and Skills

Draw a figure that represents the cross section of each three-dimensional figure.

4. A pyramid is sliced vertically from the vertex.

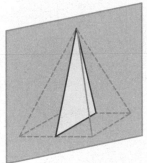

5. A prism is sliced horizontally.

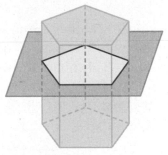

6. Darren and Riya each cut the prism shown to make a cross section. The cross section from Darren's cut is a triangle. The cross section from Riya's cut is a rectangle. How did each of them cut the prism?

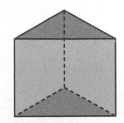

_____

_____

7. (MP) **Use Tools** A gift box made from cardboard is shaped like a trapezoidal prism. It takes 84 square centimeters of cardboard to make the flaps needed to glue the box together. How many square centimeters of cardboard are needed to make the box and the flaps? State what strategy and tool you will use to answer the question, explain your choice, and then find the answer.

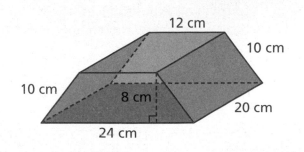

_____

_____

8. The square prism and equilateral triangular prism shown have bases that have the same side measures, 4 inches. About how much greater is the surface area of the square prism than the surface area of the triangular prism?

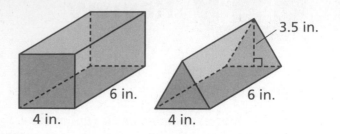

Ⓐ 21 in²

Ⓒ 28 in²

Ⓑ 24 in²

Ⓓ 42 in²

9. A school garden club is making the garden bed shown. It needs to hold 24 cubic feet of soil when full. Draw a rectangle on the grid that represents a possible length and width of the bed.

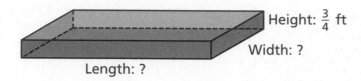

Height: $\frac{3}{4}$ ft

Width: ?

Length: ?

1 ft

10. Wes is making 20 candles in the shape of hexagonal prisms with the dimensions shown. The base of each candle is a regular hexagon with an area of 10.4 square inches. The wax Wes is using to make the candles costs $0.10 per cubic inch. To the nearest cent, how much will the wax cost for all 20 candles cost?

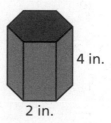

4 in.

2 in.

$ _____

11. The surface area of a cube is 150 square meters. What is the volume of the cube?

Ⓐ 25 m³

Ⓒ 15,625 m³

Ⓑ 125 m³

Ⓓ 625 m³

12. Amber is making a scratching post for her cat. The scratching post is composed of two rectangular prisms with the dimensions shown. Amber plans to cover all exposed faces, except for the bottom face, with carpet. How many square inches of carpet does she need?

_____ in²

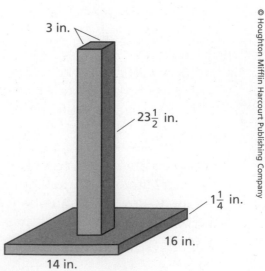

3 in.

$23\frac{1}{2}$ in.

$1\frac{1}{4}$ in.

16 in.

14 in.

Sampling and Data Analysis

Research Assistant

A research assistant collects or verifies information in a laboratory setting, or even in an office for a field such as law or media. Responsibilities of a research assistant may include conducting surveys, analyzing data, providing quality control, managing information storage, and preparing results for presentation or publication. Research assistants often use computers to help them perform these tasks.

STEM Task:

Work as a class to record the birth month of each class member. Assign the number 1 to represent January, the number 2 to represent February, and so on. Use the class data to make a dot plot. What observations and conclusions can you make by looking at the dot plot? What questions do the data raise? Explain your thinking.

Learning Mindset

Resilience Manages the Learning Process

Resilience is the ability to move forward when obstacles arise. Developing resilience allows you to identify a barrier, learn from it, and overcome the challenges it presents. Here are some ways you can increase your resilience.

- Consider where you are within the learning process. Do you think you may encounter barriers to completing a task? If so, try to identify them.

- Review the steps you are taking to direct your learning. Monitor your feelings, motivation, and interest level to keep yourself on task.

- If necessary, modify learning situations and activities so that they lead to successful conclusions.

Reflect

Q What strategies did you use to overcome barriers you encountered during the STEM Task?

Q What steps can you take to direct your learning and better understand how to collect and analyze data?

Proportional Reasoning with Samples

Which One Doesn't Belong?

WHICH FRACTION DOES *NOT BELONG?*

Each diagram represents a fraction. All but one of the fractions can be matched with a partner, but not based on the shapes of the models.

Write the fraction that each model represents.

A. ☐

B. ☐

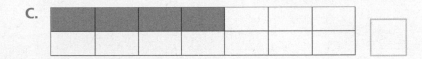

C. ☐

D. ☐

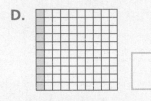

E. ☐

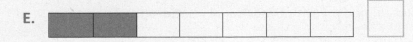

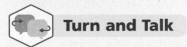 **Turn and Talk**

How can you pair up the fractions? Which is the fraction that does not belong? Explain your answers.

Are You Ready?

Complete these problems to review prior concepts and skills you will need for this module.

Statistical Data Collection

For Problems 1 and 2, tell whether the question is a statistical question. Explain your reasoning.

1. How many days are in the month of March?

_____

_____

2. How tall are the giraffes at the zoo?

_____

3. Write a statistical question about your school.

_____

Representing Equivalent Ratios

Complete the table of equivalent ratios.

4.

Size (oz)	Price ($)
4	1.00
	2.00
10	
12	

5.

Time (h)	Distance (mi)
	84
3	126
5	
	336

Use Ratio and Rate Reasoning

Write an equation to model each proportional relationship. Then solve the problem.

6. The ratio of tables x to chairs y in a restaurant is 2 to 7. The restaurant has a total of 12 tables. How many chairs does it have?

Equation: _____ Solution: _____ chairs

7. Let x represent the number of batteries and y represent the cost of the batteries. A package of 8 rechargeable batteries costs $12. At this rate, how much would a package of 20 rechargeable batteries cost?

Equation: _____ Solution: $_____

Name

Understand Representative Samples

I Can identify the population and sample of given survey scenarios, and determine whether the sample is random and/or representative of the population.

Spark Your Learning

In the fall, the residents of a large city will be voting on whether to use state funding to build a new football stadium. A research analyst wants to know the opinion of all the registered voters of the city in order to predict the outcome of the upcoming vote. Without polling all of them, how can the research analyst be sure that the poll represents the opinion of the registered voters?

Turn and Talk Does it make sense for the research analyst to poll every registered voter in the city about using state funding to build a stadium? Explain.

Build Understanding

1 ▷ A chain restaurant is thinking of entering a city for the first time. The owners want to determine if the teenagers in the city like the kind of food served by the restaurant.

A. In this case, what is the *population* the restaurant needs to survey? Is it reasonable for them to survey the entire population? Why or why not?

_____

_____

_____

> **Connect to Vocabulary**
>
> When information is being gathered about a group, the entire group of objects or individuals considered for a survey is the **population.**

When a population is too large to survey, a subset of the population, or a *sample*, is used to represent the population. If the sample is representative, it can be used to infer data about the population. The restaurant owners made a list of possible samples.

List of potential samples of the population:
1. Survey every 10th person coming out of a competitor's restaurant.
2. Call every 100th person in the local phonebook.
3. Survey 10% of the students at the city's middle schools and high schools.
4. Survey teenagers leaving a local theatre.

> **Connect to Vocabulary**
>
> A **sample** is part of the population that is chosen to represent the entire group.
> A **representative sample** is a sample that has the same characteristics as the population.
> When a sample does not accurately represent the population, it has **bias**.

B. Which of the potential samples are more likely to be representative of the population? Why?

_____

_____

C. Of the representative samples of the population, which is most representative of the population? Explain.

_____

_____

_____

D. Which of the potential samples are *biased*? Explain.

_____

_____

_____

_____

392

A sample in which every member of the population has an equal chance of being selected is a **random sample**.

2 ▸ Aiden asks the survey question shown to determine what genre of music to play at an employee event.

SURVEY
What is your favorite genre of music?
?_____

A. He asks every tenth employee on a list of all employees. Is this sample random? Explain.

_____

B. Is the sample in Part A representative of the population? Explain.

_____
_____

C. On Thursday, he asks every third employee that gets off the elevator on the fifth floor the survey question. Is this sample biased? Explain.

_____
_____

D. Is the sample in Part C a random sample? Explain.

_____
_____

 Turn and Talk Does a random sample always generate a representative sample? Explain.

Check Understanding

1. Isabella wants to know the favorite sport of the students in her school. She randomly asks every fifth person entering the football game Friday night. Is this sample biased? Explain.

_____
_____

2. Noah assigned a number to each of the 200 students in seventh grade. He put the numbers in a bag. Noah randomly chose 30 numbers and surveyed those students. Identify the population and sample.

_____
_____

3. Wyatt wants to poll the opinion of a neighborhood about safety. Give an example of a biased sample. Justify your answer.

_____
_____
_____

On Your Own

For Problems 4–5, use this survey information; every hundredth resident of voting age listed on the county census was surveyed about building a library.

4. Identify the population and sample.

   A. Population: _____

   B. Sample: _____

5. (MP) **Reason** Is the sample random? Is the sample representative of the population? Explain.

   _____

   _____

For Problems 6–7, identify the population and sample. Determine whether each sample is random and whether it is biased. Explain your reasoning.

6. Juanita surveys 50 adults at a local swimming pool during the summer to determine the favorite month of adults in her city.

   A. Population: _____

   B. Sample: _____

   C. Random? _____

   D. Representative? _____

7. Cameron surveys every tenth student who walks into school to determine the favorite type of movie of students in his school.

   A. Population: _____

   B. Sample: _____

   C. Random? _____

   D. Representative? _____

8. (MP) **Construct Arguments** Addison surveys every 25th customer who leaves a grocery store to determine whether students at her school prefer to pack a lunch or purchase a lunch. Is her sample biased? Explain.

   _____

   _____

I'm in a Learning Mindset!

What barriers block my understanding of representative samples?

_____

Understand Representative Samples

For Problems 1–3, use the following information.

The president of a national soccer fan club, Abdul, wants to determine if the club's 10,000 members are in favor of using club dues to make a new online video to support their team in the upcoming championship. He assigns a number to each member and uses a random number generator to choose 250 members to survey.

1. Identify the population and sample.

   _____

   _____

2. Is the sample representative of the entire population? Explain.

   _____

   _____

3. Suppose 212 of the 250 members in a random sample are in favor of using club dues to make a new video for their team. What can Abdul conclude about the results of the survey? Explain.

   _____

   _____

   _____

4. **Math on the Spot** Determine whether the sample is representative or biased. Explain.

   A. A teacher chooses the grades of 50 students at random from his classes to calculate the average grade earned in his class.

   _____

   _____

   B. Seventy-five people exiting a bookstore are surveyed to find out the average amount of time spent reading each day by people in the area.

   _____

   _____

5. **Open Ended** A random sample of 10 students and a random sample of 200 students are chosen from a student population of 1,200 students. Which sample do you think is more likely to be representative of the population? Explain.

   _____

   _____

Test Prep

6. Jayla wants to know the favorite sports team of the adults in her city. Which survey method is representative of the population?

   Ⓐ Randomly survey 1,000 adults as they leave a professional basketball game.

   Ⓑ Randomly survey 2,000 adults in one neighborhood.

   Ⓒ Survey every 100th adult customer who enters the local grocery store.

   Ⓓ Survey every 20th student who enters the high school.

For Problems 7 and 8, determine whether each situation *does* or *does not* show bias.

7. Haley wants to know if people use the store's bags or bring their own reusable bags. She surveys every tenth person who leaves a grocery store.

   This situation | does / does not | show bias.

8. Josiah wants to know the favorite pet of adults in his city. Josiah assigned a number to each of the 200 people on the list to adopt a dog from a dog shelter. He puts the numbers in a hat. Josiah randomly chose 40 numbers and surveyed those people.

   This situation | does / does not | show bias.

9. Fayard wants to know the favorite instrument for students in his school. He puts the names of all the students in a jar, draws 5 names, and surveys those students. Suppose that Julia conducts the same survey in the same way, but she draws 15 names. Which method is more representative? Explain.

_____

_____

_____

Spiral Review

10. The drawing is a scale drawing of a house. If the scale is 2 inches = 4.5 feet, what is the actual height of the house? Round to the nearest hundredth.

_____

9 in.

11. The circumference of a circle is 50.24 centimeters. What is the area of the circle? Use 3.14 for π. Round to the nearest hundredth.

_____

Make Inferences from a Random Sample

(**I Can**) use proportional reasoning to make inferences about populations based on the results of a random sample.

Spark Your Learning

At a grocery store, a bin is filled with trail mix made by mixing raisins with a large 30-pound bag of nuts. Zane buys a small bag of a trail mix that contains $1\frac{1}{2}$ pounds of nuts and $\frac{1}{2}$ pound of raisins. If the nuts and raisins in Zane's bag are proportional to the nuts and raisins in the bin of trail mix, how many pounds of raisins do you think the store used to make the entire bin of trail mix?

Turn and Talk How is the connection between the sample (small bag) and population (large bin) of trail mix similar to the sample and population of a survey?

Build Understanding

1▸ To estimate the number of pets that students in your school have, conduct a survey of ten randomly selected students in your class.

A. Plot the results of your survey on the grid provided.

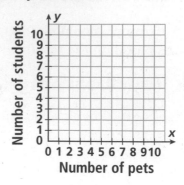

B. According to my survey, most students in my school have _____ pets.

C. According to my survey, about _____% of the students in my school have more than two pets.

D. According to my survey, about _____% of the students in my school have zero pets.

Conduct the same survey again using a second set of ten randomly selected students in your class.

E. Plot the results of your survey on the grid provided.

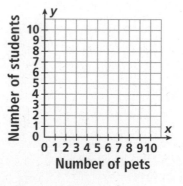

F. According to my survey, most students in my school have _____ pets.

G. According to my survey, about _____% of the students in my school have more than two pets.

H. According to my survey, about _____% of the students in my school have zero pets.

I. Compare the results from both of your samples.

- Are the results from the two samples exactly the same?

  _____

- Will a different sample give a different estimate?

  _____

A sample ratio can be used to estimate a population ratio. However, because different samples will likely vary, a sample ratio must be considered as only an estimate of the population ratio.

 Turn and Talk Discuss how samples from random surveys can be improved to obtain better estimates about a population.

Step It Out

To make inferences about a population based on a random representative sample, you can use proportional reasoning.

2 ▶ Javier randomly selects 12 cartons of eggs from the grocery store. He finds that 2 cartons have at least one broken egg.

Suppose there are 144 cartons of eggs at the grocery store. What is an estimate of the total number of those 144 cartons that have at least one broken egg?

A. Identify the sample.

_____

B. Identify the population.

_____

C. Write the ratio of cartons with at least one broken egg to the total number of cartons in the sample.

$$\frac{\boxed{}}{\boxed{}}$$

D. Use the sample ratio to write an equation for the proportional relationship.

$$y = \frac{\boxed{}}{\boxed{}} \cdot 144$$

E. Use your equation in Part D to estimate the number of cartons in the population that have at least one broken egg.

_____

_____

_____

Turn and Talk Discuss how to write an equation for the proportional relationship using a decimal or a percent for the sample ratio.

3 A worker randomly selects one out of every 7 sets from the 3,500 sets of headphones produced. The results are shown.

4 of 500 defective

A. The population / sample is the total of 3,500 sets of headphones produced. The 500 selected for testing is the population / sample .

B. Write the ratio of defective headphones to total headphones in the sample. Then write the ratio as a decimal and as a percent.

$$\frac{\boxed{}}{\boxed{}} = \boxed{} = \boxed{} \%$$

C. Write and solve an equation to find the number of headphones in the population that can be estimated to be defective.

$$y = \frac{\boxed{}}{\boxed{}} \cdot 3{,}500$$

There would be about $\boxed{}$ defective headphones.

Check Understanding

1. William conducted a random survey of the students in his school regarding the number of hours of sleep they got last night. The box plot shows the results of his survey. Make an inference about the entire population.

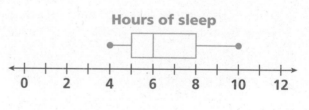

Hours of sleep

0   2   4   6   8   10   12

_____

_____

2. Hazel assigned a number to each of the 100 students in the band and put the numbers in a bag. She randomly chose 20 numbers and found that 3 students did not complete their homework for today. Make an inference about the number of students in the band that did not do their homework. If Hazel randomly chose 20 more numbers, what results would you expect? Explain.

_____

_____

_____

On Your Own

For Problems 3–5, make an inference about the ages of all drama club students at a theater conference using the dot plot showing the ages of students in a random sample of conference attendees.

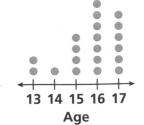

13 14 15 16 17
Age

3. Most drama club students at the conferenece are _____ 15 years old.

4. About _____% of the students at the conference plays are 16 years old or older.

5. (MP) **Construct Arguments** Would you think that it is likely for the number of 16-year-old students and the number of 17-year-old students to be almost equal in another random sample of conference attendees? Explain.

_____

_____

6. A manager randomly selects 1,500 ink pens produced today and finds 12 of them defective. There were 12,000 ink pens produced today. Make an inference about the number of ink pens produced today that are defective.

The sample ratio of defective pens is $\dfrac{\boxed{}}{\boxed{}}$ or $\boxed{}$%.

Inference: In the 12,000 population, the number of defective pens is

estimated to be $\boxed{}$ · 12,000 = $\boxed{}$.

7. Gabby assigned a number to each of the 120 athletes at her school and put the numbers in a box. She randomly chose 25 numbers and found that 10 athletes were female. Use this sample to make an inference about how many athletes at Gabby's school are female.

_____

8. A random sample of dry-erase board markers at Juan's school shows that 9 of the 60 dry-erase board markers do not work. There are 200 dry-erase board markers at Juan's school. Make an inference about the number of dry-erase board markers at Juan's school that do not work.

_____

9. A mail carrier randomly inspects every 20th letter being mailed. Out of 600 letters in the sample, 3 were open. There were 18,000 letters being mailed. Make an inference about the number of all the letters being mailed that were open.

_____

The box plot shows the results of a survey of the number of minutes that people at a variety of randomly selected gyms exercise. For Problems 10–13, make an inference about the number of minutes that people at gyms exercise according to this survey.

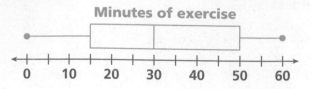

Minutes of exercise

10. According to the survey, 75% of people at gyms exercise for _____ minutes or longer.

11. According to the survey, 25% of people at gyms exercise for more than

_____ minutes.

12. According to the survey, _____% of people at gyms exercise from 15 to 50 minutes.

13. According to the survey, _____% of people at gyms exercise from 15 to 30 minutes.

14. **Health and Fitness** Would the owners of another gym be able to use data from a survey like the one in Problems 10–13 to make inferences about the number of minutes people exercise at their gym? Explain your reasoning.

_____

_____

_____

_____

15. A wildlife park manager is working on a request to expand the park. In a random selection during one week, 3 of every 5 cars have more than 3 people inside. If about 5,000 cars come to the park in a month, estimate how many cars that month would have more than 3 people inside. Show your work.

_____

_____

_____

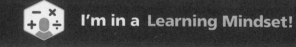

I'm in a Learning Mindset!

How is making inferences from random samples similiar to the way I make decisions when I am learning something new?

_____

_____

Name _____

Make Inferences from a Random Sample

Xavier surveyed a random sample of the grade levels of the Spanish Club members in the county. The bar graph shows the results of his survey. Use this information for Problems 1–5.

1. The largest number of students in the Spanish Club are in _____ grade.

2. The same number of students in the Spanish Club are in the _____ grade as are in the 11th and 12th grades combined.

3. If there are 300 students in the Spanish Club in the county, predict how many are 10th graders.

_____

4. Of the 300 students, predict about how many are 9th graders.

_____

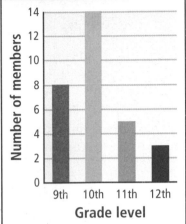

Random Sample of Spanish Club Members

5. Xavier conducted another random survey of the grade levels of the Spanish Club members in the county. In what grade would you expect to find the most students in Spanish Club? Explain.

_____

_____

_____

6. A manager at a factory finds that in a random sample of 200 clocks, 15 are defective.

   A. What percent of the clocks are defective?

   _____

   B. Of the 10,000 clocks from which the sample was chosen, about how many clocks are probably not defective?

   _____

   C. The next day the manager finds only 8 of the 200 randomly selected clocks are defective. About how many clocks out of the 10,000 produced that day are probably defective?

   _____

7. (MP) **Use Structure** Based on a sample survey, a tutoring company claims that 90% of their students pass their classes. Out of 300 students, how many would you predict will pass?

   _____

© Houghton Mifflin Harcourt Publishing Company

Test Prep

8. Ronnie surveyed a random selection of realtors in his town about the number of bedrooms in the houses for sale that week. The dot plot shows the results. Which inference is correct?

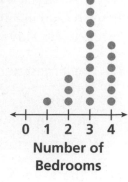

Number of
Bedrooms

(A) Most of the houses have fewer than 3 bedrooms.

(B) Some houses have 0 bedrooms.

(C) More than 50% of the houses have exactly 3 bedrooms.

(D) 80% of the houses have 3 or 4 bedrooms.

9. A random sample of laptop computers at an electronics store shows that 1 of the 25 sampled laptop computers has a malfunction. There are 300 laptop computers at the electronics store. Estimate the number of laptop computers at the electronics store that have malfunctions.

_____

_____

10. Jaylen used the seat number for each of the 6,500 fans' seats in the stands at a college football game and put the numbers in a computer program. He randomly chose 200 numbers and found that 36 of those people had also purchased a parking voucher. Estimate the number of fans in the stands at a sold-out football game that purchased a parking voucher. Explain.

_____

_____

_____

Spiral Review

11. Ricardo jogged up 864 steps in $13\frac{1}{2}$ minutes. What is Ricardo's average number of steps per minute?

_____

_____

12. Imani wants to know the favorite day of the week of adults in the town where she lives. Imani surveys every tenth adult that enters a convenience store between 4:00 p.m. and 8:00 p.m. Identify the population and sample.

_____

_____

_____

_____

Name _____

Make Inferences from Repeated Random Samples

(**I Can**) calculate sample ratios, and I can make inferences about the populations from the samples.

Step It Out

1 ▶ The results of a school-wide survey of all students at a middle school about renaming the school mascot to Bears from Grizzlies, are shown at the right. Since all students in the school were surveyed, these ratios are the population ratios. The students in a math class had an assignment to collect random samples of 20 students in the school and compare the sample ratio to the population ratio. The results are shown below. Find each sample ratio for those who prefer "Bears," and write it as a percent.

Bears   Grizzlies

BEARS Mascot **70%**   GRIZZLIES Mascot **30%**

A. Sample 1: 13 students prefer "Bears"

Sample ratio of those who prefer "Bears": $\dfrac{\boxed{}}{20} = \boxed{}$ %

B. Sample 2: 16 students prefer "Bears"

Sample ratio of those who prefer "Bears": $\dfrac{\boxed{}}{20} = \boxed{}$ %

C. Sample 3: 15 students prefer "Bears"

Sample ratio of those who prefer "Bears": $\dfrac{\boxed{}}{20} = \boxed{}$ %

D. Do these sample ratios support the findings that 70% of the entire school population prefer the mascot name "Bears"? Explain.

_____

_____

_____

_____

 Turn and Talk Why are the sample ratios different from the population ratio?

2 A bagel shop offering regular or toasted bagels makes the claim shown. Use each method to explore how much variation can be expected from a sample.

60% prefer toasted bagels

A. Construct a mock population. Place 60 red pieces of paper (for toasted) and 40 blue pieces of paper (for not toasted) in a bag.

B. Randomly select 10 pieces of paper from the bag and record the results in the column for Sample 1. Be sure to return each piece of paper to the bag before you draw another piece.

C. Repeat Step B nine more times, recording your results in the table.

	Samples									
	1	2	3	4	5	6	7	8	9	10
Red paper										
Blue paper										
Sample ratio of red paper										

D. Plot the results in the dot plot.

E. How do the sample ratios compare with the population ratio?

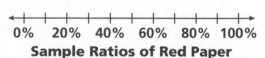

Sample Ratios of Red Paper

_____

_____

_____

Turn and Talk How can repeated random samples of the same size from a population help you to understand the variation in the sample ratios?

Check Understanding

1. A company manager takes a random sample of 20 employees and finds that 16 employees prefer day shifts to night shifts. Does this support the claim that 75% of employees prefer day shifts? Explain.

_____

2. With repeated samples, is the average of sample ratios more likely to approximate the population ratio than a single sample? _____

On Your Own

65%

35%

3. Health and Fitness The results of a survey about whether students at a middle school prefer to participate in basketball or football are shown.

Bella used a random number generator to generate 10 samples of the population.

Numbers 1–65: basketball
Numbers 66–100: football

Sample 1	62	1	73	53	85	31	79	68	8	14	13	29	30	25	61	28	26	67	24	80
Sample 2	48	66	65	59	58	21	85	92	34	56	67	76	82	26	28	18	93	39	73	97
Sample 3	99	12	92	45	13	2	62	40	96	64	100	69	35	70	93	14	78	48	67	15
Sample 4	85	32	25	37	8	49	28	24	60	31	43	61	94	16	58	63	59	12	52	1
Sample 5	28	36	3	78	46	6	54	52	99	59	39	65	84	80	81	98	75	14	53	79
Sample 6	60	66	53	40	18	55	72	38	44	69	49	51	93	17	34	67	64	89	91	13
Sample 7	28	56	93	7	84	29	57	11	35	74	87	65	78	80	27	85	99	41	91	40
Sample 8	58	46	82	56	24	26	12	67	73	61	6	52	68	29	48	21	43	85	49	2
Sample 9	3	43	98	76	17	88	44	13	65	23	87	2	18	93	49	60	58	57	86	29
Sample 10	57	11	8	3	68	98	1	67	97	29	23	99	59	56	65	72	60	79	89	30

A. Use the random numbers from each sample to complete the table.

	Samples									
	1	**2**	**3**	**4**	**5**	**6**	**7**	**8**	**9**	**10**
Numbers 1–65										
Numbers 66–100										
Sample ratio of numbers 1–65										

B. Plot the results from the table in the dot plot.

C. How does the Sample 9 ratio compare to the population ratio?

_____

_____

```
←——+——+——+——+——+——+——+——+——+——+——→
  50%  60%  70%  80%  90%  100%
```

Sample Ratios of Numbers 1–65

D. (MP) Construct Arguments How do the sample ratios compare to the population ratio?

_____

_____

4. A factory owner surveyed employees about whether they prefer working 5 regular workdays or 4 longer workdays. The results are shown.

20% prefer 5 workdays

80% prefer 4 workdays

A. Construct a mock population using blue paper and green paper.

Blue: prefer 5 regular workdays
Green: prefer 4 longer workdays.

Place 10 blue paper and 40 green paper in a hat. Randomly select a sample of 10 paper from the hat, and record the ratio. Replace the paper, and repeat for 10 samples.

	Samples									
	1	2	3	4	5	6	7	8	9	10
5 workdays										
4 workdays										
Sample ratio of 5 workdays										
Sample ratio of 4 workdays										

B. Plot the ratios of those who prefer 5 workdays in the dot plot.

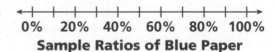

0%   20%   40%   60%   80%   100%
Sample Ratios of Blue Paper

C. How do the sample ratios of those who prefer 5 workdays compare to the population ratio?

_____

_____

D. (MP) **Attend to Precision** Plot the ratios of those who prefer 4 workdays in the dot plot.

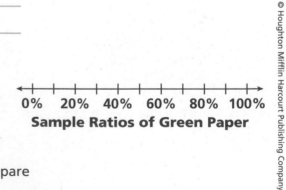

0%   20%   40%   60%   80%   100%
Sample Ratios of Green Paper

E. How do the sample ratios of green paper compare to the population ratio?

_____

_____

Make Inferences from Repeated Random Samples

Name _____

A poll was conducted among all students at a middle school about whether they prefer blue or red. Use the resulting estimated population ratios shown for Problems 1 and 2.

1. Glen used a random number generator to generate the sample ratios shown in the chart.

   Numbers 1–55: students who prefer blue
   Numbers 56–100: students who prefer red

	Samples									
	1	**2**	**3**	**4**	**5**	**6**	**7**	**8**	**9**	**10**
Blue preference	12	11	13	8	11	12	10	9	10	9
Red preference	8	9	7	12	9	8	10	11	10	11
Sample ratio of blue preference	60%	55%	65%	40%	55%	60%	50%	45%	50%	45%

   The sample ratio for blue preference in Sample 1 is ⟨ above / below ⟩ the population ratio.

   The sample ratio for blue preference in Sample 8 is ⟨ above / below ⟩ the population ratio.

2. **A.** Plot the results for blue preference from the table on the dot plot.

   30% 40% 50% 60% 70% 80%
   Sample Ratios of Blue Preference

   B. Open Ended How do the sample ratios Glen generated compare to the population ratio?

   _____

   _____

   C. (MP) **Reason** Predict what would happen to the sample ratios in the dot plot as more samples are taken.

   _____

   _____

Test Prep

3. Abner researched and found that 60% of students in his school ride the bus to school. Abner took a random sample of 50 students and found that 38 ride the bus to school. Which statement correctly describes the sample ratio?

Ⓐ The sample ratio is 38%, which is below the population ratio.

Ⓑ The sample ratio is 38%, which is above the population ratio.

Ⓒ The sample ratio is 76%, which is below the population ratio.

Ⓓ The sample ratio is 76%, which is above the population ratio.

4. The population ratio of male employees in a large office is 55%. Random samples of 20 employees are taken. Select how the sample ratio varies in relation to the actual ratio of the population.

	5% Above	10% Above	5% Below	10% Below
45% of employees are male.	☐	☐	☐	☐
10 out of 20 employees are male.	☐	☐	☐	☐
60% of employees are male.	☐	☐	☐	☐
13 out of 20 employees are male.	☐	☐	☐	☐

5. Research claims that 30% of dental customers have had braces. Julie used a random number generator to generate samples, where numbers 1–3 represent having braces and numbers 4–10 represent not having braces. One sample is shown. How does the sample compare to the population?

Sample 5: 2 1 7 5 8 3 9 6 8 4 3 2 3 5 6 8 6 7 2 8

_____

_____

_____

Spiral Review

6. The results of a random survey about number of siblings of students are shown in the box plot. Make an inference about the larger student population.

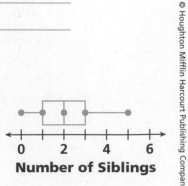

_____

_____

7. Libby bought 224 ounces of flour. If each bag contains 32 ounces of flour, how many bags of flour did Libby buy?

_____

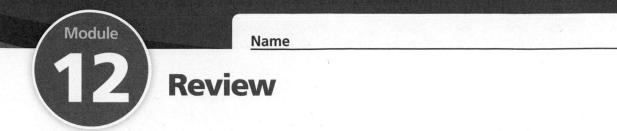
Vocabulary

Dana wants to know how many students at her school watch sports on television. She selects 40 students from her school to survey. Use this information to answer each question.

1. What is the population in this situation?

_____

2. What is the sample?

_____

3. What is the difference between a representative sample and a biased sample in this situation?

_____

_____

_____

_____

Concepts and Skills

4. A theater owner wants to survey the audience about the types of plays they want to see. At a sold-out show, there are 100 people in VIP seats, 700 on the main floor, and 400 in the balcony. Which sample can best help the owner see the preferences of all the audience members?

Ⓐ 5 people in VIP seats, 20 on the main floor, and 35 in the balcony

Ⓑ 5 people in VIP seats, 35 on the main floor, and 20 in the balcony

Ⓒ 20 people in VIP seats, 20 on the main floor, and 20 in the balcony

Ⓓ 10 people in VIP seats, 7 on the main floor, and 4 in the balcony

5. ⓂⓅ **Use Tools** There are 580 students at Alejandro's school. He surveys a random sample of 60 students and finds that 21 of them regularly bring their lunch. Based on these results, estimate how many students at Alejandro's school regularly bring their lunch. State what strategy and tool you will use to answer the question, explain your choice, and then find the answer.

_____

_____

6. A city librarian wants to see if visitors want to add a cafe to the library. On a Monday morning, the librarian surveys every fourth visitor to the library. Is this sample likely to be representative of all library visitors? Explain.

_____

_____

_____

_____

7. A factory produces a batch of 4,800 pens. The company dictates that if a random sample of the batch shows that more than 2% of the pens are defective, the batch needs additional testing. A worker checks a random sample of 60 pens from the batch and finds that 2 are defective. Based on this information, which statement(s) about the sample are true? Select all that apply.

Ⓐ It indicates the batch needs additional testing.

Ⓑ It indicates probably about 96 pens in the batch are defective.

Ⓒ It indicates there are probably about 160 defective pens in the batch.

Ⓓ It indicates probably about 4,580 pens in the batch have no defects.

Ⓔ It indicates that about 1.25% of the pens in the batch are defective.

8. A company makes short-sleeved and long-sleeved T-shirts. The company checks a random sample of 60 T-shirts of each type. It finds that 4 short-sleeved shirts have problems and 1 long-sleeved shirt has problems. How many T-shirts should the company predict have problems in a shipment of 3,000 shirts of each type? _____ total T-shirts

9. An inspector takes 20 different random samples of 25 apples each from a shipment of 2,000 apples. Based on the data, which is the most reasonable prediction of the number of apples in the shipment that weigh more than 7 ounces?

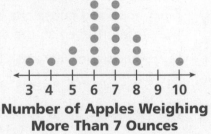

Number of Apples Weighing More Than 7 Ounces

Ⓐ about 200 apples   Ⓒ about 520 apples

Ⓑ about 320 apples   Ⓓ about 560 apples

10. Karen and Zeb each use a computer program to randomly select 50 students from the school directory. They ask the students about the school rules. They find that 68% from Karen's sample and 72% from Zeb's sample say the rules are fair. Explain why Karen and Zeb likely got different results, even though they used the same sampling method.

_____

_____

_____

_____

And the Best Player Is...

Three friends have a tournament to see who is best at playing a popular game on their phones. They each play the game 9 times. Their scores are shown.

Find the mean, median, range, and interquartile range for each player. Who is the best player?

A.

Arianna's Scores		
68	88	89
90	77	75
67	41	98

Mean: _____

Median: _____

Range: _____

Interquartile range: _____

B.

Deshauna's Scores		
98	79	41
93	24	93
91	31	35

Mean: _____

Median: _____

Range: _____

Interquartile range: _____

C.

Mayumi's Scores		
90	65	78
10	67	71
97	81	80

Mean: _____

Median: _____

Range: _____

Interquartile range: _____

Turn and Talk

Which player do you think is the best player? Justify your answer.

Are You Ready?

Complete these problems to review prior concepts and skills you will need for this module.

Mean

Find the mean of each set of data.

1. The table lists the weights of a random sample of 11 tents from an outdoor store. What is the mean weight?

   _____

Tent Weights (ounces)		
79	73	77
81	76	50
64	56	47
59	75	

2. 17, 25, 22, 18, 18, 20 _____

3. 48, 12, 35, 57, 42, 15, 74, 29 _____

4. 24, 27, 29, 31, 8, 16, 24, 19, 11 _____

Dot Plots

Rosa is growing pea plants for a science experiment. The dot plot shows the heights of her 11 plants. Use the dot plot to determine each measure of center or variability.

5. Mean _____

6. Median _____

7. Range _____

Height of Pea Plants (cm)

Box Plots

A karate studio offers 10 classes per week for middle school students. The numbers of students in the classes are listed below.

13, 15, 14, 10, 12, 10, 13, 16, 15, 13

8. Use the number line to make a box plot of the data set. Be sure to label what the number line represents.

9. Median _____

10. Range _____

11. Interquartile range _____

9 10 11 12 13 14 15 16 17

Name _____

Compare Center and Spread of Data Displayed in Dot Plots

(I Can) compare important characteristics of data sets displayed in dot plots to draw conclusions based on data.

Step It Out

1 At the end of the first week of school, Mr. Parrish asked 15 freshman students how much time they spent studying that week. He also surveyed 15 sophomore students to investigate whether their habits were different.

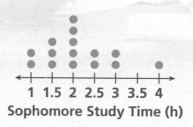

0 0.5 1 1.5 2 2.5 3
Freshman Study Time (h)

1 1.5 2 2.5 3 3.5 4
Sophomore Study Time (h)

A. Compare the shapes of the dot plots by describing where the values are clustered in each plot.

_____

_____

_____

B. Find the **median** and **mean** of each set of data.

Freshman: median = _____   Sophomore: median = _____

Freshman: mean = _____   Sophomore: mean = _____

C. Find the **range** of each set of data.

Freshman range: 3 − _____ = _____ hours

Sophomore range: 4 − _____ = _____ hours

Both data sets have a range of _____ hours.

D. What do the data tell you about study habits?

_____

_____

  Turn and Talk How does a dot plot help you look at trends in data?

© Houghton Mifflin Harcourt Publishing Company • Image Credit: ©Blend Images - Moxie Productions/Brand X Pictures/Getty Images

2 Bill grows oranges and Carla grows apples. Each farmer selected 13 trees at random and counted the pieces of fruit they produced to the nearest hundred.

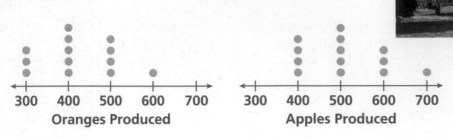

A. How are the shapes of the dot plots alike in terms of their peaks?

_____

_____

B. What is the median of each data set? Compare the medians of the plots.

_____

_____

C. Use the dot plots to compare the ranges of the data.

_____

_____

 Turn and Talk What information can you find by comparing the ranges of two data sets? Explain.

Check Understanding

The members of two book clubs kept track of how many hours they spent reading over one weekend. Use the dot plots for Problems 1–3.

1. Compare the means of the data sets and draw one conclusion.

_____

_____

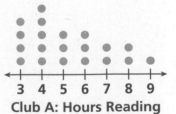

Club A: Hours Reading

2. Compare the ranges of the data sets and draw one conclusion.

_____

_____

3. Draw one conclusion from the shape of the data distribution.

_____

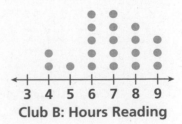

Club B: Hours Reading

On Your Own

4. The dot plots show recorded wait times for two food trucks.

Burgerama Wait Times (min)   Rodeo Burger Wait Times (min)

A. (MP) **Use Structure** Visually compare the spreads of the data sets.

_____

_____

B. (MP) **Use Structure** Visually compare the centers of the data sets.

_____

C. Complete the table to verify your visual assessments.

	Burgerama	Rodeo Burger
Number of observations		
Median		
Range		

D. Do you expect the means to be about the same or to be different for each data set? Explain your visual assessment.

_____

_____

_____

_____

E. Find the mean to the nearest tenth to check your visual assessment.

Burgerama mean: _____   Rodeo Burger mean: _____

F. (MP) **Construct Arguments** Based on the data, which food truck would have more predictable wait times? Explain.

_____

_____

5. Fabulous Fashions selected employees at random to review salary distribution for the company.

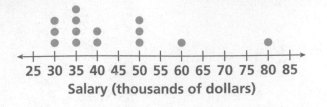

Salary (thousands of dollars)

A. What is the median? Describe the shape of the data, including any clusters.

_____

_____

B. What is the range of the data?

_____

C. What do the data in the dot plot tell you about what most employees earn?

_____

_____

6. The dot plots show the ages in years of the players for both the Wolves and the Jets basketball teams.

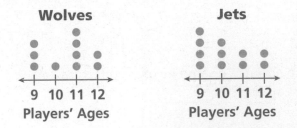

A. Compare the shapes of the set of data.

_____

B. Compare the modes and medians of the data sets.

_____

C. What is the range of each data set?

_____

D. (MP) **Reason** What do the dot plots tell you about the ages of the players on the two teams?

_____

_____

Compare Center and Spread of Data Displayed in Dot Plots

Tallahassee and Key West are at opposite ends of the state of Florida. The dot plots show high temperatures recorded in each city in May. Use this information for Problems 1–7.

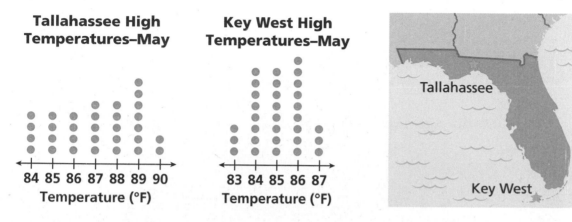

1. Calculate the ranges of both sets of data.

_____

2. Which city's temperatures have the greater spread?

_____

3. Calculate the medians of both sets of data.

_____

4. Which city's temperatures have the greater median?

_____

5. What was the mean high temperature in May for each city, rounded to the nearest degree?

_____

6. What was the difference between the median and the mean for each city?

_____

7. **Geography** What do you learn about the temperatures for May in these cities by comparing their dot plots?

_____

_____

_____

_____

Test Prep

Use the dot plots for Problems 8–11.

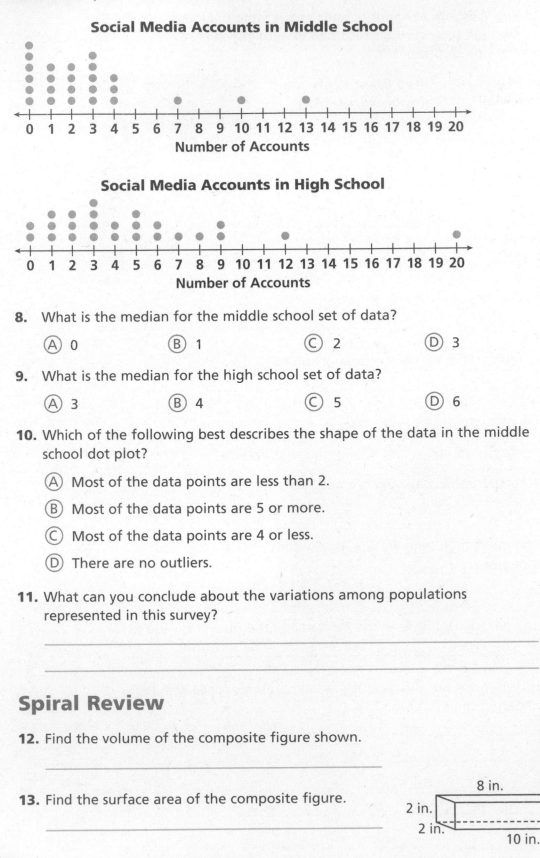

Social Media Accounts in Middle School

Number of Accounts

Social Media Accounts in High School

Number of Accounts

8. What is the median for the middle school set of data?

   (A) 0   (B) 1   (C) 2   (D) 3

9. What is the median for the high school set of data?

   (A) 3   (B) 4   (C) 5   (D) 6

10. Which of the following best describes the shape of the data in the middle school dot plot?

   (A) Most of the data points are less than 2.

   (B) Most of the data points are 5 or more.

   (C) Most of the data points are 4 or less.

   (D) There are no outliers.

11. What can you conclude about the variations among populations represented in this survey?

_____

_____

Spiral Review

12. Find the volume of the composite figure shown.

_____

13. Find the surface area of the composite figure.

_____

2 in.

8 in.

8 in.

2 in.

2 in.

10 in.

Compare Center and Spread of Data Displayed in Box Plots

(**I Can**) make box plots and draw inferences about populations based on displayed data.

Step It Out

1 ▷ The sixth- and seventh-grade students are having a reading contest. Their progress is shown.

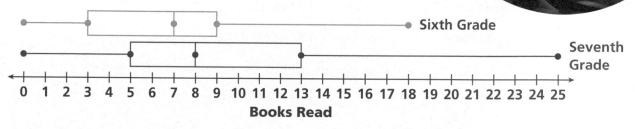

Books Read

A. Describe the shapes of the box plots.

_____

_____

_____

B. Compare the *centers* of the box plots by comparing their medians.

_____

C. Find the ranges and the **interquartile ranges.** Complete the table.

	Sixth grade	Seventh grade
Range		
Interquartile range		

D. Why would the data sets appear to have similar spreads using interquartile range and very different spreads using the range?

_____

_____

E. Explain what the left whiskers of the box plots tell you about the data sets.

_____

_____

_____

 Turn and Talk Can you project the winner of the contest based on this data?

2 The times for students to take a test on paper and the same test on a computer are shown.

Paper: 42, 48, 52, 54, 59, 61, 61, 64, 65, 67, 68, 70, 72, 75, 80	Computer: 46, 47, 48, 50, 52, 55, 58, 60, 62, 64, 64, 64, 69, 73, 74

A. Find the five key values that describe the test scores collected from pencil-and-paper exams.

The minimum is _____. The maximum is _____.

The median, or middle value, is _____.

The **lower quartile** is the median of values less than the median, $Q_1 = $ _____.

The **upper quartile** is the median of the top half of the data, $Q_3 = $ _____.

B. Identify the five key values for the sample of computer exam scores.

Minimum: _____   Median: _____   Maximum: _____

Q_1: _____ Q_3: _____

C. Sketch box plots to represent each sample.

Paper

Computer

```
←┼─┼─┼─┼─┼─┼─┼─┼─┼─┼─┼─┼─┼─┼─┼─┼─┼─┼─┼─┼→
  42 44 46 48 50 52 54 56 58 60 62 64 66 68 70 72 74 76 78 80
```
Time to Complete Exam (min)

D. Compare the centers and spreads of the box plots. Which testing format takes students longer to complete?

_____

_____

Check Understanding

1. Two groups of 8 violin students kept track of the hours they practiced in a week. The results were:
A: 0, 1, 3, 5, 5, 6, 6, 8   B: 2, 3, 3, 3, 5, 6, 9, 10
Sketch box plots representing each data set. Draw one conclusion based on the plots.

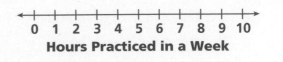

Group A

Group B

```
←┼─┼─┼─┼─┼─┼─┼─┼─┼─┼─┼→
  0  1  2  3  4  5  6  7  8  9  10
```
Hours Practiced in a Week

_____

_____

2. About how many data points fall below the median of a data set?

_____

On Your Own

3. The box plots below show the distribution of ages for players on two football teams.

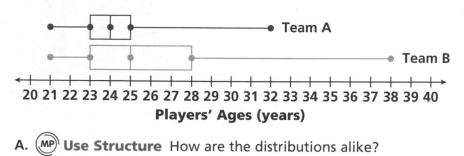

Players' Ages (years)

A. **(MP) Use Structure** How are the distributions alike?

_____

_____

B. Which measure of spread would you choose to describe these data sets? Use it to compare the spread of the data in these sets.

_____

_____

_____

_____

C. Use the box plots to complete the table.

D. Compare the centers of the box plots.

_____

_____

	Team A	Team B
Minimum		
Lower quartile		
Median		
Upper quartile		
Maximum		

E. Explain the significance of the age 25 years in each box plot.

_____

_____

F. **(MP) Reason** Where is the greatest difference in the box plots? Justify your choice.

_____

_____

_____

_____

4. Each year the Academy Awards honor excellence in film, including awards for Best Actor and Best Actress. The data sets shown are random samples of the ages, in years, at which these awards have been won.

A. Find the five key values for each data set.

_____

_____

_____

_____

_____

_____

Best actor: 29, 53, 40, 62, 36, 49, 53, 37, 44, 31, 41, 49, 51, 48, 32

Best actress: 22, 41, 27, 22, 38, 60, 62, 30, 36, 49, 21, 33, 26, 38, 28

B. Sketch box plots to represent each sample.

Best Actor

Best Actress

20 22 24 26 28 30 32 34 36 38 40 42 44 46 48 50 52 54 56 58 60 62
Age at Receiving Award (yr)

C. Compare the centers and spreads of the box plots.

_____

_____

_____

D. (MP) **Critique Reasoning** After looking at the box plots, Tomás expresses surprise that most award-winning actresses are under the age of 40. Martha disagrees, pointing out that the right whisker is the longest part of the Best Actress box plot. Therefore, she argues, there are more winners from ages 41 to 62 than in the other intervals. Determine which friend is correct, and explain why.

_____

_____

_____

E. (MP) **Reason** What do the box plots for the samples tell you about the populations?

_____

_____

_____

Compare Center and Spread of Data Displayed in Box Plots

Ms. Horvat is investigating prices of laptop computers at her local stores. She visits two different stores and selects a random sample of computers, recording their prices.

1. The box plot representing the data from Store A is shown.

    The five key values for the data from Store B are:

    minimum = $300, Q_1 = $500, median = $800,
    Q_3 = $1,000, maximum = $1,500

    A. Use the key values to sketch the box plot for Store B.

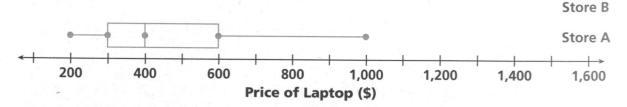

Store B

Store A

200   400   600   800   1,000   1,200   1,400   1,600
Price of Laptop ($)

B. Compare the centers and shapes of the box plots.

_____

_____

C. Compare the spreads of the box plots.

_____

_____

_____

D. (MP) **Use Structure** The price $1,000 is a key value for each box plot. Explain the significance of this price for each store's data.

_____

_____

_____

E. For each store, compare the spread of the lower half of the data with the upper half of the data.

_____

_____

_____

_____

Test Prep

2. Which measures are used to make a box plot? Select all that apply.

  Ⓐ maximum   Ⓓ minimum

  Ⓑ mean   Ⓔ mode

  Ⓒ median

3. When comparing two sets of data represented by box plots, compare the

shape, _____ , and _____ .

4. Which is the preferred measure of spread for a data set with outliers?

  Ⓐ interquartile range   Ⓒ median

  Ⓑ mean   Ⓓ range

5. Moesha and Justin are competing in an online game to see who can solve puzzles in less time. The dot plots show the distribution of their times. Compare the centers and shapes of the box plots.

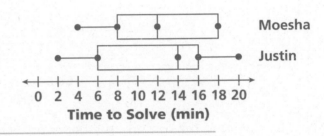

_____

_____

_____

_____

Spiral Review

6. Describe the cross section made from slicing the right triangular prism perpendicular to its base and the cross section made from slicing the right prism parallel to its base.

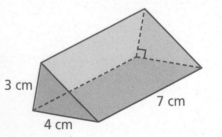

_____

_____

_____

7. What is the volume of the right triangular prism shown?

_____

8. How many triangles can you construct with side lengths 5 inches, 8 inches, and 20 inches?

_____

Name _____

Compare Means Using Mean Absolute Deviation and Repeated Sampling

(I Can) use the means and MADs to assess the amount of visual overlap of two numerical data distributions.

Step It Out

1 ▶ Elia collected data from 10 randomly selected seventh-graders about the number of text messages they sent in one day. Results are shown in the table.

104	92	107	83	96
98	70	91	119	90

Recall that the **mean absolute deviation (MAD)** is the average distance from the data points to the mean. It is a measure of the spread of data because it describes the variation of data values from the mean.

A. What is the range of the data? What is the mean number of messages sent in this sample?

_____

B. Complete the table to show each data point's absolute deviation, or difference, from the mean.

$\lvert 104 - 95 \rvert = 9$	$\lvert 92 - 95 \rvert = 3$	$\lvert 107 - 95 \rvert =$ ___	$\lvert 83 - 95 \rvert =$ ___	$\lvert 96 - 95 \rvert =$ ___
$\lvert 98 - 95 \rvert =$ ___	$\lvert 70 - 95 \rvert =$ ___	$\lvert 91 - 95 \rvert =$ ___	$\lvert 119 - 95 \rvert =$ ___	$\lvert 90 - 95 \rvert =$ ___

C. Find the sum of the absolute deviations. _____

D. Find the mean absolute deviation by finding the mean of these absolute deviations. Divide the sum in Part C by the total number of data points.

The mean absolute deviation is _____ messages.

E. Which data points have an absolute deviation that is less than or equal to the MAD? These data points are said to be *within* the MAD.

_____

 Turn and Talk How does the mean absolute deviation describe data differently than the mean of the data?

2 Quentin collected data about the numbers of minutes students spent completing a math puzzle at the beginning of the year and at the end of the year.

Beginning of Year				
12	18	20	16	11
14	16	22	17	14

End of Year				
12	6	3	4	9
4	5	8	9	10

A. Complete the table.

	Beginning of Year	End of Year
Mean		
MAD		

B. The MAD for these data sets happens to be the same. Compare the difference of the means to the MAD. Round to the nearest tenth.

$$\frac{\text{difference of the means}}{\text{MAD}} = \frac{\boxed{}}{\boxed{}} = \underline{\hspace{2cm}}$$

The difference of the means is _____ times the MAD.

C. When two data sets are displayed in dot plots, the points might overlap a lot, a little, or not at all. The centers might appear to be close or far apart. The ratios of the difference of the means to the MADs can help you predict how much separation there will be between the two distributions. The greater the ratio, the greater the separation. When the MADs of the data sets are similar, these ratios will be similar.

These plots show the puzzle-solving data. The yellow shading shows values within the mean absolute deviation.

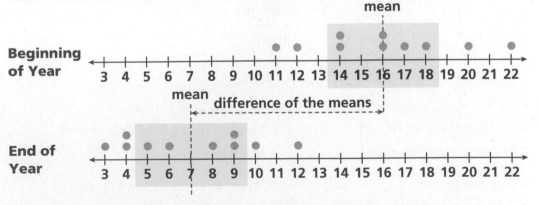

What does the ratio you calculated in Part B tell you about the separation between the two distributions?

_____

_____

_____

3 The first plot shows the heights in inches of sixth-grade students in the orchestra. The second shows the heights in inches of eighth grade students in the orchestra.

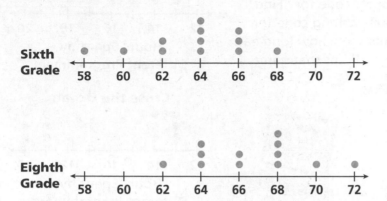

A. Complete the table. Round to the nearest tenth.

B. For each plot, draw a dashed vertical segment to show the mean. Then, shade the region that shows the values that are within the MAD.

	6th Grade	8th Grade
Mean		
MAD		

C. Find the ratio of the difference of the means to the MAD for each data set. Round to the nearest tenth.

6th Grade: $\dfrac{\text{difference of the means}}{\text{MAD}}$ = _____   8th Grade: $\dfrac{\text{difference of the means}}{\text{MAD}}$ = _____

D. What do the ratios you calculated in Part C tell you about the separation between the two distributions?

_____

_____

_____

Check Understanding

1. The difference of the means of two data sets is 0.5. Both data sets have a MAD of 1. How does the difference of the means compare to the MADs? If the data were displayed in dot plots, how much overlap would you expect to see? Explain.

_____

_____

2. A survey of adults and teens recorded the daily time in minutes each person spent messaging on a cell phone. These are the results:

   Adults: 5, 10, 20, 15, 10   Teens: 50, 60, 40, 10, 80

   The MAD for _____ is more than _____ times the MAD for

   _____, so the variation for _____ is much greater than for

   _____ .

On Your Own

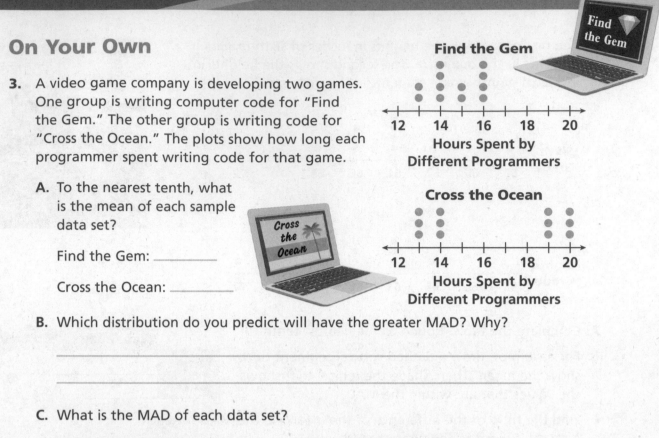

Find the Gem

Hours Spent by
Different Programmers

Cross the Ocean

Hours Spent by
Different Programmers

3. A video game company is developing two games. One group is writing computer code for "Find the Gem." The other group is writing code for "Cross the Ocean." The plots show how long each programmer spent writing code for that game.

A. To the nearest tenth, what is the mean of each sample data set?

Find the Gem: _____

Cross the Ocean: _____

B. Which distribution do you predict will have the greater MAD? Why?

_____

_____

C. What is the MAD of each data set?

MAD of "Find the Gem" _____   MAD of "Cross the Ocean" _____

D. (MP) **Attend to Precision** Complete the statement.

The MAD for "Cross the Ocean" is _____ times the MAD for "Find the Gem."

For Problems 4–7, write the approximate ratio of the difference of the means to the MADs for the given data sets. Then tell how much overlap you would expect to see in dot plots of the sample data.

4.

	Sample A	Sample B
Mean	45	48
MAD	1.5	1.5

_____

5.

	Sample A	Sample B
Mean	112	107
MAD	4.8	5.2

_____

6.

	Sample A	Sample B
Mean	36	43
MAD	14	14

_____

7.

	Sample A	Sample B
Mean	27.5	27.2
MAD	0.09	0.09

_____

8. **(MP) Reason** Randomly selected high
school students with summer jobs and
adult workers were surveyed about
their hourly wages in dollars. The data
are shown.

Hourly Wage of Students ($)				
8.50	8.50	9.00	9.00	9.00
10.00	10.00	10.00	10.00	10.00
11.00	11.00	11.50	12.00	15.00

A. What are the mean and MAD of
each sample data set rounded
to the nearest hundredth?

Hourly Wage of Adults ($)				
14.00	15.00	16.00	17.50	18.00
19.00	21.00	22.00	24.00	25.00
27.00	28.00	28.00	31.50	32.00

High school students:

The mean is _____.

The MAD is _____.

Adults: The mean is _____. The MAD is _____.

B. The MAD for adults is about _____ times the MAD for the students.
This means the variation in the wages for adults is much _____ than
the variation in the wages for the students.

C. **Open Ended** Suggest a change to one hourly wage in the student
table so that the MAD will be less than before.

_____

9. Two groups are each given a bag of beads with letters. Each group
randomly selects 20 beads and records the number of vowels in the sample.
They each perform the process 8 times. Their data are shown below.

Group A	3	1	0	2	3	4	1	2
Group B	3	0	4	4	2	1	4	2

A. What are the mean and MAD, to the nearest hundredth, of each data set?

Group A:

The mean is _____.

The MAD is _____.

Group B:

The mean is _____.

The MAD is _____.

B. **(MP) Construct Arguments** If the data for the two groups were
displayed in dot plots, how much separation would you expect to
see in the distributions? Explain. Support your answer by finding the
difference of the means and comparing it to the MADs.

_____

_____

_____

10. Randomly selected seventh graders in two classes are each asked to measure the entire length of their pointer finger and its length from the tip to the middle joint. The ratio of the lengths is recorded. The data are then organized for each class.

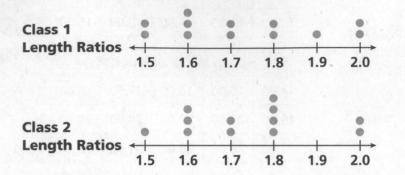

A. Do the two data sets overlap a lot, a little, or not at all?

_____

B. What is the mean of each data set to the nearest hundredth?

Class 1: _____

Class 2: _____

C. What is the MAD of each data set to the nearest thousandth?

Class 1: _____

Class 2: _____

D. Use the means and MADs above to approximate the ratio of the difference of the means to the MADs for each data set. Round your ratios to the nearest hundredth.

Class 1: _____

Class 2: _____

E. Do your answers to Part D support your answer to Part A? Explain.

_____

_____

F. Do you think there are meaningful differences in the two data sets? Explain.

_____

_____

_____

_____

Name

LESSON 13.3
**More Practice/
Homework**

ONLINE

Video Tutorials and
Interactive Examples

Compare Means Using Mean Absolute Deviation and Repeated Sampling

1. **STEM** Akuchi is experimenting with the effect of using plant food on the growth of sunflowers. The dot plots show the heights in inches of randomly selected sunflowers.

A. What is the mean height of sunflowers in each sample data set?

Without food, the mean height is _____ inches.

With food, the mean height is _____ inches.

B. What is the mean absolute deviation in height for each data set?

The MAD without food is _____. The MAD with food is _____.

C. Are the data distributions visually separate? Explain why you would or would not expect them to be.

_____

_____

2. **Math on the Spot** The tables show the number of minutes per day students spend outside of school reading and doing their math homework.

Number of minutes reading	Number of minutes doing math homework
15, 15, 15, 20, 30, 30, 30, 30, 45, 60	25, 30, 30, 30, 30, 40, 45, 45, 55, 60

What is the difference of the means as a multiple of the approximate mean absolute deviations? _____

Test Prep

Use this information for Problems 3 and 4.

Aubree recorded the duration in minutes of randomly selected hit songs from two different years. Her data are represented in the dot plots below.

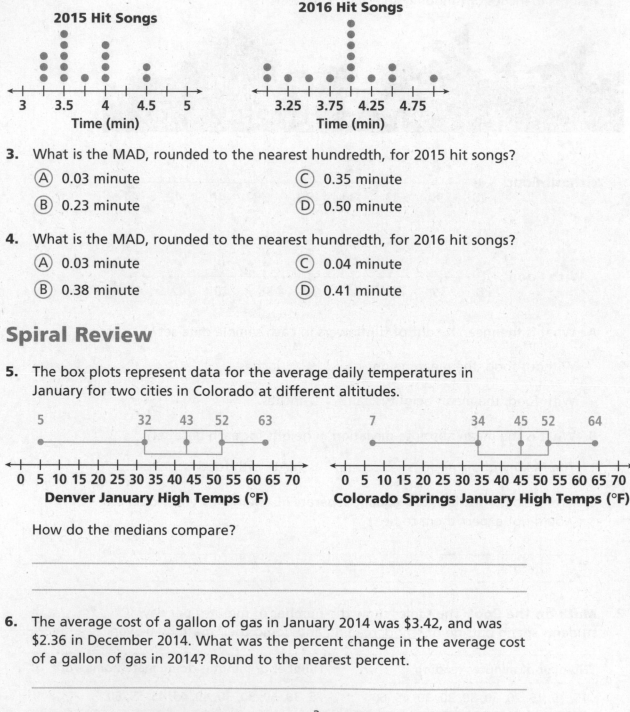

3. What is the MAD, rounded to the nearest hundredth, for 2015 hit songs?

Ⓐ 0.03 minute   Ⓒ 0.35 minute

Ⓑ 0.23 minute   Ⓓ 0.50 minute

4. What is the MAD, rounded to the nearest hundredth, for 2016 hit songs?

Ⓐ 0.03 minute   Ⓒ 0.04 minute

Ⓑ 0.38 minute   Ⓓ 0.41 minute

Spiral Review

5. The box plots represent data for the average daily temperatures in January for two cities in Colorado at different altitudes.

How do the medians compare?

_____

_____

6. The average cost of a gallon of gas in January 2014 was $3.42, and was $2.36 in December 2014. What was the percent change in the average cost of a gallon of gas in 2014? Round to the nearest percent.

7. A recipe for one batch of dough calls for $2\frac{3}{4}$ cups of flour. Thomas is making $2\frac{1}{2}$ batches of the recipe. How many cups of flour does he need?

_____

Vocabulary

1. How is a dot plot similar to a box plot? How are they different?

_____

_____

2. How are the median and upper quartile of a data set related?

_____

_____

Concepts and Skills

3. Cheri skated 10 laps and Kristen skated 9 laps on a skating rink. The dot plots show the time it took them to skate each lap. Plot a dot on Kristen's dot plot to show a time she must get on her tenth lap so that her median time is equal to Cheri's median time.

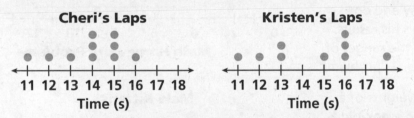

Cheri's Laps

11 12 13 14 15 16 17 18
Time (s)

Kristen's Laps

11 12 13 14 15 16 17 18
Time (s)

4. (MP) **Use Tools** A shipment includes 500 boxes of wheat cereal and 500 boxes of corn cereal. The dot plots show the masses of a random sample of 20 boxes of each type. Which cereal has a greater median mass? How much greater? State what strategy and tool you will use to answer the question, explain your choice, and then find the answer.

_____

_____

_____

_____

_____

_____

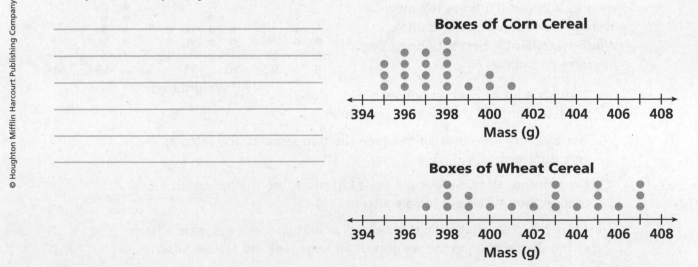

Boxes of Corn Cereal

394 396 398 400 402 404 406 408
Mass (g)

Boxes of Wheat Cereal

394 396 398 400 402 404 406 408
Mass (g)

5. The box plot shows the numbers of students in a random sample of 30 classes at Lincoln Middle School and a random sample of 30 classes at Fairview Middle School. Which statements about the classes at the two schools are supported by the random samples? Select all that apply.

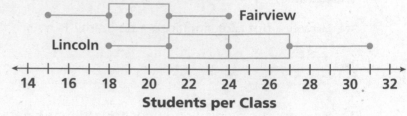

Ⓐ There is little overlap in the distributions of the samples.

Ⓑ The number of students per class is more variable at Lincoln than at Fairview.

Ⓒ A typical class at Lincoln has about 10 more students than a typical class at Fairview.

Ⓓ About half the sampled classes at Lincoln have more students than the largest sampled class at Fairview.

Ⓔ The interquartile range for the number of students per class at Fairview is about 3 times the interquartile range at Lincoln.

6. Ignacio surveyed a random sample of students at his school about the number of math problems they had for homework on Monday and on Friday. The box plot shows his results. What is the difference in the ranges of the two data sets? _____ problems

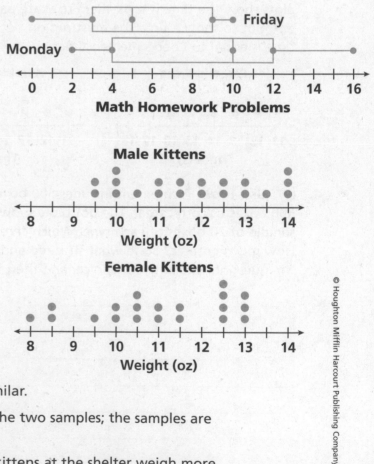

7. The dot plots show the weights of a random sample of 20 two-week-old male kittens and 20 two-week-old female kittens at a shelter. The mean weight of the males is 11.75 ounces, and the mean weight of the females is 11 ounces. The difference in the mean weights is about 0.6 times the mean average deviation of either sample. Which statement is best supported by the random samples?

Ⓐ There is a lot of overlap between the two samples; the samples are similar.

Ⓑ There is very little overlap between the two samples; the samples are very different.

Ⓒ On average, all two-week-old male kittens at the shelter weigh more than all two-week-old female kittens.

Ⓓ There is more variation in the weights of all two-week-old male kittens at the shelter than in the weights of all two-week-old female kittens.

Probability

Game Designer

A game designer usually works as part of a team that designs and makes games. Video game designers help develop computer games for a variety of platforms, from large consoles to mobile phones. Shigeru Miyamoto, sometimes called the father of modern video games, is a Japanese game designer who has invented some of the world's most famous and successful video games.

STEM Task:

Work with a partner to invent a simple board game for two players. Your game should use up to ten cards and/or one or two number cubes. Choose the goal of the game and decide how players move on the board. Then play the game with your partner several times. Do you think you designed a fair game? Explain why or why not.

Learning Mindset

Challenge-Seeking Defines Own Challenges

A challenge is a problem that requires work and determination to solve. A challenging project may include both short- and long-term tasks. By definition, a challenge is not easy—that is why mastering a challenge is such a rewarding experience. You can feel a sense of pride because you know you accomplished something difficult. Here are some tips for tackling a challenge.

- Divide the challenge into smaller steps. Think about how each step leads to completion of the entire project or task.

- Decide how and where to find the information and knowledge you need to complete each step.

- Work with others to brainstorm, check work, share knowledge, and give and receive support.

Reflect

Q What steps did you take to complete the STEM Task?

Q What challenges did you and your partner identify while working on the STEM Task? How did you address them?

Understand and Apply Experimental Probability

Go for the Gold!

In the first four levels of a video game, players roam through a castle collecting gold coins and bars. To reach Level D, a player must have a total of at least 10 more gold bars than coins. The table shows the number of coins or gold bars that Miguel collected in each of the first three levels.

Complete the table by sketching the missing gold coins and gold bars.

Level	Ratio of Coins to Gold Bars	Number of Coins Collected	Number of Gold Bars Collected
A	2:3	○ ○ ○ ○	
B	6:8	○ ○ ○ ○ ○ ○ ○ ○ ○ ○	
C	4:10		▭▭▭▭▭ ▭▭▭▭▭ ▭▭▭▭▭

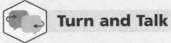 **Turn and Talk**

Does Miguel advance to Level D? Justify your answer.

© Houghton Mifflin Harcourt Publishing Company • Image Credit: ©Sergey Novikov/Shutterstock

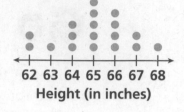

Are You Ready?

Complete these problems to review prior concepts and skills you will need for this module.

Statistical Data Collection

The dot plot shows the heights of students in one class. Use this information for Problems 1–2.

1. What unit of measure was used? How was it measured?

   _____

2. How many students are in the class? Explain.

   _____

   _____

Find a Percent or a Whole

Find each value.

3. What is 45% of 200?

   _____

4. 19 is 20% of what number?

   _____

5. 42 is 14% of what number?

   _____

6. What is 58% of 60?

   _____

7. What is 90% of 560?

   _____

8. 85.5 is 45% of what number?

   _____

Use Ratio and Rate Reasoning

9. One out of every 3 players on a soccer team is new this season. There are 15 players on the team in all. How many of the players are new?

   _____ new players

10. There are 515 students who attend Central Middle School. Three out of every 5 students live within 1 mile of the school. How many students at Central Middle School live within 1 mile of the school?

    _____ students

11. How can you use proportional reasoning to write a ratio that is equivalent to another ratio?

    _____

    _____

Name _____

Understand Probability of an Event

(I Can) describe the likelihood of an event.

Spark Your Learning

A gumball machine contains 50 gumballs. There are 25 blue, 10 red, 12 green, and 3 yellow gumballs in the machine. Bart puts a coin in and turns the wheel to receive a gumball. What is an outcome that is likely to occur? Not likely? As likely as not? Certain? Impossible?

Turn and Talk How would you describe the likelihood of receiving a red gumball, using the given phrases? Explain.

Build Understanding

Probability describes how likely an event is to occur. It is a measure between 0 and 1 as shown on the number line, and can be written as a fraction, a decimal, or a percent. The probability of an event is written as *P*(event).

Connect to Vocabulary

The **probability of an event** measures the likelihood that an event will occur.

The closer the probability of the event is to 0, the less likely the event is to occur. The closer the probability of the event is to 1, the more likely the event is to occur. An event with probability 0 is impossible. An event with probability 1 is certain.

Impossible	Unlikely	As likely as not	Likely	Certain
0		$\frac{1}{2}$		1
0		0.5		1.0
0%		50%		100%

1 ▶ Tell whether each event is impossible, unlikely, as likely as not, likely, or certain. Then tell whether the probability is 0, close to 0, $\frac{1}{2}$, close to 1, or 1.

A. A bag contains pieces of paper labeled with the numbers 1 through 100. A piece of paper with the number 13 is selected at random.

_____

B. Two standard number cubes are rolled. The sum of the numbers is 1.

_____

C. A standard number cube is rolled, and the result is an even number.

_____

D. A bowl contains 26 disks. Each disk is labeled with a different letter of the alphabet. A consonant is selected at random.

_____

E. Twelve middle-school students are selected to complete a survey. None of the students are in tenth grade.

_____

 Turn and Talk What do you know about the value of the probability of an event that is likely? Explain.

Often the same experiment is repeated many times. Each repetition of an experiment is called a **trial**, and each result of a trial is an **outcome**. A set of one or more possible outcomes for a trial is an **event**. A **sample space** is the set of all possible outcomes for an experiment.

Connect to Vocabulary

An **experiment** is an activity involving chance in which results are observed.

2 ▶ Roll a number cube 10 times. How likely is each event in the table?

A. What is the sample space of all possible outcomes when you roll the number cube once?

_____

B. Roll a number cube 10 times and record the number of times each event occurs in the table.

Event	Frequency
Roll a 2	
Roll a 1, 3, 4, 5 or 6	
Roll an odd number	
Roll a number less than 7	

C. How many trials did you perform? How many events did you record?

_____

D. Judging from the results of your trials, which events are certain when rolling a number cube?

_____

E. Judging from the results of your trials, which events are likely? Which events are unlikely? Which events are as likely as not?

_____

_____

> **Turn and Talk** Based on your results from the table, what number or number range might you use to describe the probability of rolling a 2? Explain.

Check Understanding

1. Tell whether choosing a blue marble from a jar containing 4 blue marbles and 12 red marbles is unlikely, as likely as not, or likely. Is the probability closer to 0 or 1?

_____

2. What number and what percent describe the probability of a certain event? What number and what percent describe the probability of an impossible event?

_____

On Your Own

3. Mina opens a book 15 times and records whether the page number is even or odd. How many trials did she conduct? Name two events that she recorded.

_____

4. Krisha has a bowl with 12 green disks and 8 yellow disks. Is the probability of randomly selecting a green disk unlikely, as likely as not, or likely?

_____

5. (MP) **Reason** A container holds 20 red, 20 blue, and 10 green marbles. Is the probability of choosing a blue marble greater than or less than the probability of not choosing a blue marble? Explain.

_____

_____

_____

For Problems 6–7, describe the probability of each event in words. Then describe each probability with a number or a number range.

6. Roll a number greater than 5 on a standard number cube.

_____

7. Pick a number less than or equal to 30 from a bag with 40 pieces of paper numbered 1 through 40.

_____

8. **Open Ended** Ask 6 students their age and record the results. Pick one age from the results. How many students stated this age? Describe in words the probability that a student in your class is this age, judging from the results.

_____

 I'm in a Learning Mindset!

Did I select appropriate challenges as part of learning how to describe the probability of an event?

_____

_____

LESSON 14.1
**More Practice/
Homework**

Understand Probability of an Event

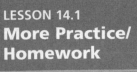

ONLINE Video Tutorials and
Interactive Examples

1. Roberta rolls two standard number cubes. Tell whether a sum greater than 12 is impossible, unlikely, as likely as not, likely, or certain.

_____

2. A machine makes 50 parts. Out of the 50 parts, 3 are defective. Using a number or a number range, describe the probability that a randomly selected part is *not* defective.

_____

3 out of 50 parts
are defective.

3. **Open Ended** Write a situation where the probability of an event occurring is unlikely.

_____

_____

_____

4. Rocky has a box of pens. He has 11 black pens, 8 blue pens, and 6 red pens. He randomly selects a pen from the box. Describe the probability that the pen he selects is blue, using a number or a number range.

_____

Flip a coin eight times and record the results of *heads* or *tails*. Use the results for Problems 5–9.

5. List the sample space of all possible outcomes when you flip a coin once.

_____

6. What experiment did you perform? How many trials of the experiment did you conduct? What events did you record?

_____

7. How many times did the coin land heads up? Based only on these results, does getting *heads* seem to be impossible, unlikely, as likely as not, likely, or certain?

_____

8. How many times did the coin land tails up? Based only on these results, does getting *tails* seem to be impossible, unlikely, as likely as not, likely, or certain?

_____

9. (MP) **Reason** Are the results of your experiment what you would expect? Explain.

_____

Test Prep

10. Adam has 10 blocks numbered 1 through 10. Which describes the probability of randomly choosing a block that has an even number?

(A) impossible

(B) unlikely

(C) as likely as not

(D) likely

(E) certain

11. Bella finds some beach glass. She finds 14 pieces of brown beach glass, 12 pieces of white beach glass, 12 pieces of green beach glass, and 2 pieces of blue beach glass. She lets her sister pick one piece at random to keep. Describe the probability, using a number or a number range, that her sister picks a piece of blue beach glass.

_____

12. A bowl contains 4 blue marbles and 12 red marbles. Soo-jin picks a marble from the bowl. Describe a likely event.

_____

13. A community service club has 12 seventh-graders and 12 eighth-graders. The name of each student is put in a hat, and a name is drawn at random. Which number or number range describes the probability that the student selected is an eighth-grader?

(A) a number greater than 0 and less than $\frac{1}{2}$

(B) a number greater than $\frac{1}{2}$ and less than 1

(C) 1

(D) $\frac{1}{2}$

Spiral Review

14. A patio is shaped as a composite figure consisting of two rectangles. One part of the patio is 20 feet long and 15 feet wide. The other part is 15 feet long and 10 feet wide. What is the area of the patio?

_____

15. An aquarium is a rectangular prism. The volume of the aquarium is 6,480 cubic inches. The length of the aquarium is 30 inches, and the height is 18 inches. What is the width of the aquarium?

_____

Name _____

Find Experimental Probability of Simple Events

(I Can) find an experimental probability and its complement.

Spark Your Learning

SMALL GROUPS

Toss a paper cup a number of times and record the different ways that the cup lands on a table. Describe each way that the cup lands as likely or unlikely. Organize your results in a table.

Outcome	Frequency
Open end up	
Open end down	
On its side	

 Turn and Talk How do you think increasing the number of times you toss the cup would change your results?

Build Understanding

1 ▶ Conduct an experiment by flipping a coin. Record your results in the table. Repeat until you have conducted the experiment 20 times.

Outcome	Frequency
Heads	
Tails	

A. How many trials did you conduct? Do the outcomes appear to be equally likely based on your results? Explain.

_____

_____

B. Use the number of times each event occurs compared to the number of trials to approximate the probability of each event.

Outcome	Probability
Heads	$\dfrac{\text{Heads}}{20} = \dfrac{\Box}{20}$
Tails	$\dfrac{\text{Tails}}{20} = \dfrac{\Box}{20}$

C. If you flip the coin only four times, do you think it is possible that you might record only *tails* and no *heads*? What if you flip a coin 100 times? Compare the chances of the two possibilities.

_____

_____

_____

D. What happens to the number of times each outcome occurs as you perform more trials?

_____

_____

_____

E. What is the sum of the probabilities in Part B?

_____

 Turn and Talk Are there any outcomes that did not occur in your set of trials? Why is this so?

Step It Out

The **experimental probability** of an event is found by comparing the number of times an event occurs to the total number of trials.

$$\text{experimental probability} = \frac{\text{number of times the event occurs}}{\text{total number of trials}}$$

2 ▸ Muriel has a spinner with red, blue, and green sections. She spins the spinner 50 times and records the results in a table.

Event	Frequency
Red	14
Blue	12
Green	24

A. Find the experimental probability of each outcome.

_____

B. What conclusions can you make about the spinner using the experimental probabilities?

_____

_____

_____

C. How would you find the experimental probability of the spinner landing on a color that is not red, and what is that experimental probability in this example?

_____

_____

D. How is the experimental probability of the spinner landing on a color that is not red related to the experimental probability of the spinner landing on red?

_____

Connect to Vocabulary

The **complement** of an event is the set of all outcomes in the sample space that are *not* included in the event. The sum of the probability of an event and the probability of its complement is 1.

E. Muriel spins the spinner another 50 times and records the outcomes. Do you think the experimental probabilities based on the results will be the same as the ones in Part A? Explain.

_____

_____

_____

A **simulation** is a model of an experiment that would be difficult to actually perform. A simulation can be used to find an experimental probability and make a prediction.

 A softball player hits the ball and reaches base safely about 30% of the time. The player hits the ball but is called "out" about 50% of the time. The player strikes out about 20% of the time.

A. How could you use a random number generator to simulate the next 25 times the player comes up to hit the ball?

_____

_____

B. Perform the simulation. Record your results.

Event	Frequency
Hit - Safe	
Hit - Out	
Strikeout	

C. Make a prediction based on your simulation.

_____

D. Combine the results of your simulation with the results of all the simulations. How do the total results of the class compare to your simulation?

_____

_____

_____

Check Understanding

1. Allison rolls a standard number cube 30 times and records her results. The number of times she rolled a 4 is 6. What is the experimental probability of rolling a 4? What is the experimental probability of not rolling a 4?

_____

2. Kelly averages 90% correct on her math assignments. She wants to perform a simulation to predict the number of questions she will answer correctly out of her next 70 questions. What is a simulation she could use to make this prediction?

_____

_____

_____

On Your Own

3. Andreas is performing an experiment involving rolling a number cube. He rolls the number cube 60 times and records the results in the table.

   A. (MP) **Construct Arguments** Do you think the outcomes are equally likely? Explain.

   _____

   _____

   B. Find the experimental probabilities to complete the table.

Outcome	Frequency	Experimental Probability
1	8	
2	11	
3	10	
4	7	
5	11	
6	13	

4. **Open Ended** Ask 8 students how many letters are in their first name. Record the number of letters for each answer. Describe one event from your experiment and find the experimental probability of this event.

   _____

5. (MP) **Use Tools** A football quarterback completes 60% of attempted passes. Describe a simulation that you can perform in order to predict how many passes out of 40 this quarterback will complete.

   _____

   _____

6. Jean estimates that her friend completes a new level of a video game on the first try 20% of the time. She conducts a simulation to predict how many times out of 80 her friend would complete a new level on the first try. Jean uses a random number generator. Every digit that is 8 or 9 represents completing the level. What is the probability that her friend completes a new level on the first try, written as a percent?

Digit	0	1	2	3	4	5	6	7	8	9
Frequency	10	9	6	7	8	12	4	6	7	11

7. Diego has a spinner that is divided into four sections labeled A, B, C, and D as shown. He spins the spinner many times and records the results. The results are shown in the table.

Letter	A	B	C	D
Frequency	14	24	14	12

A. Add the frequency of each event to find the total number of times that he spun the spinner. Then find the experimental probability of spinning each letter.

_____

B. What is the probability of the complement of spinning D?

_____

C. (MP) **Construct Arguments** What conclusion can Diego make about the bias of the spinner he used, based on the experimental probabilities? Explain your reasoning.

_____

_____

_____

_____

_____

8. Dustin buys packs of trading cards. He reads that half of the packs contain a bonus card. Dustin uses a coin to perform a simulation to estimate how many packs will contain a bonus card if he buys 20 packs. He uses heads to represent a pack with a bonus card. The results of his simulation are shown.

H, H, T, H, T, T, T, H, T, H, H, T, T, H, T, H, H, T, H, H

How many packs in this simulation did not contain a bonus card?

_____

I'm in a Learning Mindset!

Am I willing to accept new challenges while learning about probability?

_____

_____

Find Experimental Probability of Simple Events

1. Luther is performing an experiment involving a triangular pyramid with faces labeled 1–4. He shakes it in a jar and empties the jar without looking 80 times. He records the number of the face it lands on in a table. Find the experimental probabilities to complete the table.

Outcome	Frequency	Experimental Probability
1	19	☐/80
2	17	☐/80
3	23	☐/80
4	21	☐/80

2. (MP) **Use Tools** Marcela gets to school later than her friend Kim about half the time. Describe a way to simulate this event for 10 school days. Then perform the simulation. How many times does it show Marcela arriving later than Kim? What is the experimental probability of this event?

_____

_____

3. **Math on the Spot** For one month, Terry recorded the time at which her school bus arrived. She organized her results in a frequency table. Find the experimental probability that the bus will arrive between 8:20 and 8:24. Find the experimental probability that the bus will arrive after 8:19.

Time	8:15–8:19	8:20–8:24	8:25–8:30
Frequency	10	11	3

_____

4. (MP) **Model with Mathematics** Wei has two different routes he takes to a park. He labels the routes A and B. He takes route B about 33% of the time. Describe a simulation Wei could perform using a number cube to estimate the number of times he will take route B to get to the park if he goes to the park 60 times.

_____

_____

_____

Test Prep

5. Asia has a jar of marbles. She randomly selects a marble from the jar, records its color, and returns it to the jar. She repeats this 74 times. Her results are shown in the table.

Outcome	Frequency
Red	13
Blue	20
Green	22
Yellow	19

What is the experimental probability of Asia choosing a green marble?

_____

6. Jordan performed an experiment using a number cube. He rolled a number cube 50 times. He found that he rolled a 6 a total of 8 times. What is the experimental probability that he did *not* roll a 6?

Ⓐ $\frac{3}{25}$

Ⓑ $\frac{4}{25}$

Ⓒ $\frac{21}{25}$

Ⓓ $\frac{22}{25}$

7. Juan rolls a number cube 40 times. He rolls a 3 on the number cube 6 times. What is the experimental probability that he rolls a 3?

_____

Spiral Review

8. Emma selects coins at random from a jar, putting the coin back each time after selecting it. She conducts 28 trials and selects 7 pennies, 12 nickels, and 9 dimes. Based on the results, describe in words the likelihood that she selects a penny.

_____

9. Claire wants to start a stamp collection. She spends $15 on an album to hold her stamps and $1.25 for each stamp. If she has $40, what is the maximum number of stamps she can buy?

_____

© Houghton Mifflin Harcourt Publishing Company

Name _____

Find Experimental Probability of Compound Events

(**I Can**) find the experimental probability of a compound event.

Spark Your Learning

Felix was attending an awards dinner and the menu had the choices shown for appetizer and entrée. What is the sample space for his dinner selection?

> **Awards Dinner**
>
> *Appetizers:*
> · Shrimp Cocktail
> · Garden Salad
>
> *Entrees:*
> · Roast Beef
> · Chicken Marsala
> · Vegetarian Lasagna

x	*y*

 Turn and Talk The menu also had a choice of two drinks. When considering that choice, how does that affect the total number of combinations that are available to order?

Build Understanding

At Felix's awards dinner, T-shirts were being handed out to the award winners. The choices for the shirts are shown. The selection of a shirt is a compound event due to the available choices in different categories.

1 Define the sample space of the shirt choices.

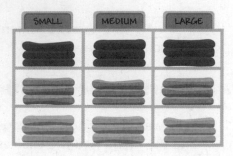

A. How many colors are there? What are the choices?

_____

B. How many sizes are there? What are the choices?

_____

C. Write all the possible combinations of sizes and colors.

_____

_____

_____

D. There are _____ possible outcomes for this compound event.

E. In the table, fill out the shaded boxes with headings for the possible sizes and colors of the shirts. Then fill in the table to show the sample space, all the possible outcomes when a shirt is selected.

F. Suppose a compound event includes two simple events. Explain how many rows and columns are needed in a table of the sample space.

_____

_____

_____

_____

_____

Turn and Talk Does it matter whether sizes or colors are listed in rows or columns? Explain.

456

Step It Out

Conducting a survey is a type of experiment. Each time a question is asked of one person counts as one trial. Each answer is an outcome. Compare the number of times one answer is given to the total number of times a question is asked to find the experimental probability that a new, randomly chosen person, if asked, will give this answer.

2 ▸ Guests at the awards were asked for their dinner order. The number of people who gave each answer are shown. Find the experimental probability that a dinner guest orders roast beef and salad.

	Roast beef	Chicken marsala	Vegetarian lasagna
Shrimp cocktail	15	32	12
Garden salad	24	22	15

Awards Dinner

Appetizers:
· Shrimp Cocktail
· Garden Salad

Entrees:
· Roast Beef
· Chicken Marsala
· Vegetarian Lasagna

A. Find the total number of dinner orders.

$15 + 32 +$ ☐ $+ 24 + 22 + 15 =$ ☐

B. Find the experimental probability.

$$P(\text{roast beef, salad}) = \frac{\text{number of orders for roast beef with salad}}{\text{total number of orders (total trials)}}$$

$$= \frac{☐}{☐}, \text{ or } \frac{☐}{☐}$$

3 ▸ The T-shirt choices of some award winners are shown in the table. What is the experimental probability that an award winner does NOT select a medium green T-shirt?

	Small	Medium	Large
Red	4	8	8
Green	2	5	7
Blue	3	4	9

A. Find the experimental probability of choosing a medium green T-shirt.

$$P(\text{medium, green}) = \frac{\text{number of medium green T-shirts selected}}{\text{total number of T-shirts selected (total number of trials)}}$$

$$= \frac{☐}{☐} = \frac{☐}{☐}, \text{ or } ☐ \%$$

B. Find the complement of the event in Part A, the experimental probability of NOT choosing a medium green T-shirt.

$$P(\text{NOT medium, green}) = 1 - P(\text{medium, green})$$

$$= 1 - \frac{☐}{☐} = \frac{☐}{☐}, \text{ or } ☐ \%$$

4 A party bundle sold by an event planning company contains party favors and table decorations. The party favor choices are key chains, pens, or wristbands. The table decoration choices are flowers or candles. The company packs party bundles and stores them in a warehouse, choosing the party favor and decorations for each bundle at random. Tatiana simulates choosing a bundle from the warehouse and checking its contents.

A. List the compound events that occur when checking the bundles.

_____

_____

_____

B. Describe the two choices that together make up each compound event.

_____

C. How can you use a number cube and a coin to simulate the experiment?

_____

_____

D. Tatiana simulates 100 trials of the experiment and records the results shown in the table. What is the experimental probability that the next choice of a bundle includes pens and candles?

	Key chain	Pen	Wristband
Flowers	21	19	18
Candles	18	14	10

$P(\text{pens, candles}) = \dfrac{\text{number of pens/candles bundles selected}}{\text{total number of party bundles selected (total trials)}}$

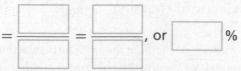

$= \dfrac{\boxed{}}{\boxed{}} = \dfrac{\boxed{}}{\boxed{}}$, or $\boxed{}$ %

Check Understanding

A restaurant manager records the choices made at breakfast. The table shows the average daily breakfast orders for toast.

	Wheat	White	Rye
Butter	20	32	8
Dry	7	10	3

1. How many possible outcomes are in the sample space of toast choices?

_____

2. What is the experimental probability that a new customer orders buttered white toast? Write your answer as a fraction and a percent.

_____

© Houghton Mifflin Harcourt Publishing Company • Image Credits: (t)©Vasilixa/Shutterstock; (b)©Susan Kinast/The Image Bank/Getty Images

On Your Own

3. A tea bar offers tea in the varieties shown.

   A. How many rows and columns represent the sample space?

   _____

   B. How many possible outcomes are in the sample space?

   _____

Teas
• Hibiscus tea
• Macha tea
• Black tea
Sizes
• Small
• Large

4. (MP) **Model with Mathematics** Sabah works at a movie theater. One evening, she tracks the popcorn orders at the concessions stand.

   A. Sabah sold 125 orders of popcorn. Complete the table to show the number of times a large popcorn without butter was sold.

	Small	Medium	Large
With butter	18	15	36
Without butter	19	22	

   B. Find the experimental probability of a new customer ordering a

   large popcorn without butter. _____

5. (MP) **Construct Arguments** When simulating a compound event by rolling a number cube and flipping a coin, does it matter which one is done first? Explain your answer.

   _____

   _____

The table shows activities chosen. For Problems 6–9, use the table to determine the experimental probability of the choice and its complement.

	Swimming	Boating	Arts & Crafts	Field Sports
Morning	48	36	16	25
Afternoon	45	30	40	35

6. swimming in the afternoon _____

7. field sports in the morning _____

8. boating in the morning _____

9. arts & crafts in the afternoon _____

(MP) Use Tools For Problems 10–12, tell how you could use the tools shown to simulate each compound event.

Random Number Generator

10. Choosing a pet at the animal shelter: a male or female; a cat, a dog, or a rabbit

_____

_____

_____

11. Choosing colors for a shed: a red, blue, or yellow shed with white, gray, or black trim

_____

_____

_____

12. Choosing an activity: going hiking or going swimming; traveling by bus or traveling by bicycle

_____

_____

_____

13. Open Ended Write a word problem that includes finding the possible outcomes, and the size of the sample space, for a compound event. Then find the size of the sample space described in your problem.

_____

_____

_____

_____

_____

_____

_____

© Houghton Mifflin Harcourt Publishing Company

 **I'm in a Learning Mindset!**

If you want to adjust the level of challenge in a simulation, would changing the order of simple events work? Why or why not?

_____

_____

LESSON 14.3
**More Practice/
Homework**

ONLINE
Ed   Video Tutorials and
Interactive Examples

Find Experimental Probability
of Compound Events

1. **Math on the Spot** A compound event is simulated by flipping
   a coin (H or T) and rolling a number cube (1–6).

   A. List all the different possible outcomes.

   _____

   B. Represent the sample space using the table.

	1	2	3	4	5	6
H						
T						

(MP) **Model with Mathematics** Nico rolled two number cubes 250 times.
The table shows his results. Use the table for Problems 2–4.

NC1 / NC2	1	2	3	4	5	6
1	6	7	3	8	9	7
2	4	8	6	5	10	2
3	7	6	11	9	8	7
4	6	7	6	8	9	5
5	3	5	9	7	6	4
6	6	8	5	3	4	26

2. Find the experimental probability of rolling a 5 on the first
   number cube and a 2 on the second number cube.

   _____

3. **A.** Find the experimental probability of rolling a 1 on the second number cube.

   _____

   B. Use the complement to find the experimental probability of NOT
   rolling a 1 on the second number cube.

   _____

4. (MP) **Reason** Find the experimental probability of rolling double sixes. Is
   this experimental probability close to what you would expect? Explain.

   _____

   _____

Test Prep

5. Carlotta is doing an experiment by flipping a coin and rolling a number cube. Select all that apply to the sample space of the experiment.

(A) The possible outcomes for the simulation can be represented in a table with 2 rows and 6 columns.

(B) The possible outcomes for the simulation can be represented in a table with 6 rows and 2 columns.

(C) The sample space of the simulation can only be represented by a table.

(D) The sample space has 36 total possible outcomes.

(E) The sample space has 8 total possible outcomes.

6. Ali runs a simulation using a coin and random number generator with output from 1 to 5. The table shows the results of the simulation.

	1	2	3	4	5
Heads (H)	12	8	11	14	8
Tails (T)	9	10	9	7	12

A. Find the experimental probability of the outcome H-4.

_____

B. Use the complement to find the experimental probability of NOT H-4.

_____

Spiral Review

7. John is using a number cube to simulate the outcome of rain or no rain with a 50% chance of rain forecast. Describe how he can interpret the outcome from each roll of the number cube to perform his simulation.

_____

_____

8. Using a number or a number range, describe the probability of rolling a 3 on a number cube.

_____

9. Describe the graph of a proportional relationship on a coordinate plane.

_____

_____

Name _____

Use Experimental Probability and Proportional Reasoning to Make Predictions

(**I Can**) use proportional reasoning or percent expressions to make a prediction based on an experimental probability.

Step It Out

1 Jessica bowls in several leagues, and she is very good at closing out frames. Over the past few years, she has closed out 8 of every 10 frames she has bowled. This season Jessica will bowl 35 games, or 350 frames. How many frames can Jessica expect to close out this season?

A. Method 1: Use a proportion.

Write a proportion: 8 out of 10 is how many out of 350?

$$\frac{8}{10} = \frac{x}{\boxed{}}$$

Multiply $\frac{8}{10}$ by a form of 1 to keep the equation true and to find the value of x.

$$\frac{8}{10} \cdot \frac{\boxed{}}{\boxed{}} = \frac{x}{\boxed{}}$$

The value of x is $8 \cdot \boxed{} = \boxed{}$.

B. Method 2: Use a percent expression.

Write $\frac{8}{10}$ as a percent and a decimal: $\boxed{}$ % and $\boxed{}$.

Find $\boxed{}$ % of 350: $\boxed{}$ · 350, or $\boxed{}$.

So Jessica can expect to close out about _____ frames.

C. If Jessica closes out 288 frames this season, was her average over the past few years a good predictor of her performance?

_____

Connect to Vocabulary

A **proportion** is an equation that states that two ratios are equivalent. Multiplying the numerator and denominator of one of the ratios by the same, correctly chosen number will yield the other ratio.

 Turn and Talk Which method do you prefer for making a prediction, using a proportion or a percent? Explain.

2 ▸ The middle school that Carmen and Richard attend has 925 students. The schedule options for first period include only math and English. In order to find out whether students prefer first period math or first period English, Carmen and Richard took a poll of 100 randomly selected students. The results are shown.

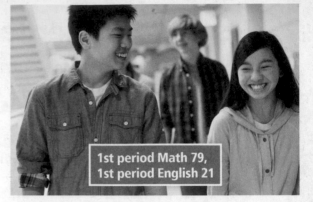

1st period Math 79,
1st period English 21

A. Method 1

Use proportional reasoning to predict the number of students in the whole school who will state that they prefer first period math.

_____ out of 100 is how many out of 925?

$$\frac{\boxed{}}{100} = \frac{x}{\boxed{}}$$

Multiply by a form of 1: $\frac{79}{100} \cdot \frac{\boxed{}}{\boxed{}} = \frac{x}{925}$.

The value of x is $79 \cdot \boxed{} = \boxed{}$.

About _____ students will state that they prefer first period math.

B. Method 2

Use a percent to predict the number of students in the whole school who will state that they prefer first period math.

79 out of 100 is _____%, so find _____% of _____, the number of students in the whole school.

$$\boxed{} \cdot 925 = \boxed{}$$

About _____ students will state that they prefer first period math.

C. Find the number of students who will state that they prefer first period English without using proportional reasoning or a percent. This is the complement of the event from Parts A and B.

Subtract the number of students who will state that they prefer first period math from the total number of students in the school.

$$925 - \boxed{} = \boxed{}$$

A reasonable prediction of students in this school who will state that they prefer first period English is _____ students.

 Turn and Talk Explain why the answers were rounded to whole numbers in this task.

3 A company analyzes the page views of visitors that come to its website. Based on a sample, the company determines that 30% of all visitors click away from the site after viewing only the home page. The company gets an average of 1,173 visitors per week. Use proportional reasoning to predict how many visitors will leave the website next week after visiting only the home page.

$$\frac{\boxed{}}{100} = \frac{x}{1{,}173}$$

$$\frac{30}{100} \cdot \frac{\boxed{}}{\boxed{}} = \frac{x}{1{,}173}$$

The value of x is $30 \cdot \boxed{} = \boxed{}$.

Because the number describes the number of people, it should be a whole number. So the prediction is that about $\boxed{}$ people leave the site after visiting only the home page.

🗨 **Turn and Talk** The company's president claims that they are losing about 450 visitors per week who click away after seeing only the home page. Is this a reasonable claim? Explain.

Check Understanding

1. A random sample of patients at a medical office found that 40% were in the age range 13–21. There are 1,100 patients in total. Use the experimental probability from the survey to predict about how many patients are in the age range 13–21.

_____

Use the following information for Problems 2–3.

A company sold 660 watches. A consumer advocate group found that 5% of this particular type of watch was defective when they conducted a random survey of 100 watches.

2. Estimate the number of watches sold that were defective.

_____

3. Estimate the number of watches sold that were not defective.

_____

On Your Own

4. **(MP) Model with Mathematics** In a sample of 100 randomly selected concert attendees, the concert organizers find that 11 of them left the show early. The concert originally had 2,040 attendees.

   A. Use proportional reasoning to estimate how many of the total number of attendees left the concert early.

   B. **(MP) Attend to Precision** Explain why the answer in Part A cannot be a decimal.

   _____

   C. Suppose there are 3 concerts at this hall next week, and the total attendance will be 5,500. Use a percent expression to predict the number of these attendees who will leave a concert early next week.

5. **(MP) Model with Mathematics** In D'Andre's class, 5 of the 25 students are 5 feet tall or shorter. There are 400 students in D'Andre's grade at his school.

   A. Set up a proportional relationship to estimate the total number of students who are 5 feet tall or shorter in D'Andre's grade, based on the experiment probability from the survey of his class.

   _____

   B. Estimate how many students in D'Andre's grade are *over* 5 feet tall.

   _____

6. **STEM** According to the US Forest Service, the most common tree type found in timberlands in the state of Florida is the longleaf pine tree. In a sample population, 35% of trees were of this type.

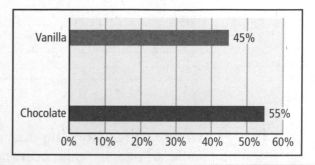

There are approximately 17.4 million acres of forested land in Florida.

A. Write a percent expression to estimate the number of acres of longleaf pine trees in Florida.

_____

B. Evaluate the percent expression to estimate how many acres of longleaf pine trees there are in Florida.

_____

7. A survey was conducted among middle school students asking, "Do you prefer vanilla or chocolate ice cream?" The results are shown.

A. Write both a proportion and a percent expression to estimate how many students prefer chocolate in a population of 700.

_____

```
Vanilla    |███████████████| 45%
Chocolate  |████████████████████| 55%
          0%  10%  20%  30%  40%  50%  60%
```

B. Estimate how many students out of 700 prefer chocolate ice cream.

_____

For Problems 8–11, the following samples were taken to see how many people preferred Candidate A. Estimate the number of people who prefer Candidate A based on the information given.

8. Sample size: 200
   Number of favorable responses: 100
   Population: 1,000

   _____

9. Sample size: 100
   Percent favorable: 35%
   Population: 1,800

   _____

10. Sample size: 100
    Number of favorable responses: 22
    Population: 450

    _____

11. Sample size: 10
    Percent favorable: 90%
    Population: 2,100

    _____

12. **(MP) Construct Arguments** Steven tossed a coin 100 times. It came up heads 52 times and tails 48 times. Based on this sample, write a percent expression and predict how many times heads would occur if Steven tossed the coin 1,000 times. This is not the expected 500 times (or 50%). Explain the discrepancy.

_____

_____

_____

13. Aman sometimes receives undeliverable messages on her e-mail. Of the last 100 e-mails that she sent, 6 of them came back as undeliverable. She sends an average of 750 e-mails in a month. How many undeliverable messages should Aman expect to receive in one month?

_____

14. Social Studies Jiang was concerned about a particularly busy intersection because it did not have a stop sign. She took a survey of 100 people who used that intersection. Seventy-five people she spoke to support putting in a stop sign. The town's population is 4,480. Write a percent expression and a proportion to estimate how many people in the town support the stop sign. Then make an argument as to why Jiang's survey results may not be a good predictor of town opinion.

_____

_____

_____

15. (MP) **Attend to Precision** Luis used proportional reasoning to predict that the number of people riding buses past his window each day would be 100.6 people. How should he express his answer? Explain.

_____

For Problems 16–17, use this information.

Of 100 students and teachers in Claire's school, the number of people who have each birthstone are shown. The school has 510 teachers and students.

Garnet (January): 6   Ruby (July): 11

Amethyst (February): 15   Peridot (August): 6

Aquamarine (March): 8   Sapphire (September): 8

Diamond (April): 9   Opal (October): 4

Emerald (May): 9   Topaz (November): 10

Pearl (June): 7   Tanzanite (December): 7

16. Write and evaluate a percent expression to estimate the total number of teachers and students at the school who have amethyst as their birthstone.

_____

17. Write and solve a proportion to estimate how many more teachers and students at the school have garnets than opals as their birthstone.

_____

© Houghton Mifflin Harcourt Publishing Company • Image Credit: ©Derek Anderson/Alamy

LESSON 14.4
**More Practice/
Homework**

ONLINE

Video Tutorials and
Interactive Examples

Use Experimental Probability and
Proportional Reasoning to Make Predictions

1. Ms. Kalidova asked her class to use a percent expression to predict the result of the upcoming election for class president of the seventh grade. Results of a poll conducted of 50 students are provided in the graph. Assume the seventh grade has 350 students and everyone votes for one of the two candidates. Write a percent expression and evaluate it to find the number of votes Andrew should expect to receive.

   _____

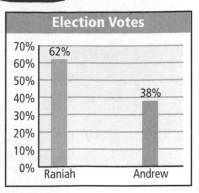

2. **Open Ended** Write a real-world problem involving a sample and a population that can be modeled by the proportion: $\frac{66}{100} = \frac{x}{2,500}$.

   _____

   _____

   _____

3. Shane plays baseball. The chart shows the results of his first 100 times at bat. Write a proportion and solve it to predict the number of home runs Shane will hit in his next 460 times at bat.

Out	63
Walk	8
Single	15
Double	8
Triple	1
Home run	5

   _____

4. **Math on the Spot** Professor Burger found that the experimental probability of his making a strike in bowling is 20%. Out of 400 throws, about how many could he predict would be strikes?

   _____

(MP) **Model with Mathematics** For Problems 5–6, use the following scenario.

In one weekend, 1,200 people attend a play at the theater downtown. A survey of 100 people who attended found that 45 gave the play at least 4 stars out of 5. Write and use the indicated model to estimate how many people in all would give the play at least 4 stars.

5. Solve using a proportion.   6. Solve using a percent expression.

   _____   _____

7. The chart shows the number of hours each student spends training for their favorite sport, per 100 hours.

Simone	12
Javier	9
Robert	15
Natasha	8

A. Write a proportion and make a prediction for the number of hours Simone will spend training over a 2,000-hour period.

_____

B. Write and use a percent expression to predict the number of hours Javier will spend training over a 2,000-hour period.

_____

8. Jabrin was tossing a ball up in the air and catching it. He found that in 50 tries, he could catch it 45 times. He is going to do this 33 more times. Predict how many times Jabrin will catch the ball out of these 33 tosses.

_____

_____

9. Considering the proportions/percent equations and the corresponding values of x given, which combination is correct?

Ⓐ $\frac{40}{100} = \frac{x}{900}$; $x = 49$ Ⓒ $\frac{25}{100} = \frac{x}{750}$; $x = 175$

Ⓑ $0.20(1,200) = x$; $x = 300$ Ⓓ $0.70(500) = x$; $x = 350$

Spiral Review

10. A vegetarian restaurant offers 52 vegetarian meals on its menu. Four of the meals include eggplant. Shan picks a dish at random from the menu with his eyes closed. What is the probability that he orders a meal that does *not* include eggplant? Write the probability as a fraction.

_____

11. Jake is saving for a new tablet. It costs $250, and he has $100. He earns $5 per week for doing chores. Jake wants to figure out how many weeks it will take for him to have at least enough money to buy a new tablet. Write an inequality and solve it to determine the number of weeks it will take.

_____

Name _____

Review

Vocabulary

Complete each sentence using terms from the Vocabulary box.

<table>
<tr><td colspan="2">Vocabulary</td></tr>
<tr><td>event</td></tr>
<tr><td>experiment</td></tr>
<tr><td>outcome</td></tr>
<tr><td>probability</td></tr>
<tr><td>sample space</td></tr>
<tr><td>trial</td></tr>
</table>

1. The _____ of an experiment is the set of all possible outcomes of the experiment.

2. The _____ of an event is a number from 0 to 1, or from 0% to 100%, that describes its likelihood.

3. Each repetition of a probability _____ is called a _____.

4. Rolling a number less than 4 on a number cube is an _____ that consists of more than one _____.

Concepts and Skills

5. The chance that a baseball player will get a hit is estimated to be 23%. How would you describe this likelihood?

   Ⓐ certain   Ⓑ likely   Ⓒ unlikely   Ⓓ as likely as not

6. A news report states that a hurricane will reach land on Monday or Tuesday, but Tuesday is more likely. Give a number or number range to describe the probability that the hurricane will reach land on Tuesday.

   _____

7. Indira drew 3 animals: an eagle, a snake, and a shark. She drew each animal twice, once with green eyes and once with red eyes. Ten students chose their favorite drawing. Three of them chose the shark with red eyes. How many possible outcomes are there in the sample space of her experiment? Based on the results, what is the experimental probability that a shark with red eyes is *not* picked, written as a percent?

   _____

8. (MP) **Use Tools** Sophia randomly selects a marble from a bag of marbles and then replaces it. The results of 300 trials are shown. Based on this data set, what is the experimental probability of selecting a red marble from the bag? State what strategy and tool you will use to answer the question, explain your choice, and then find the answer.

Red	57
White	105
Blue	138

   _____

9. In each cycle of a stoplight, the light is green for 30 seconds, yellow for 5 seconds, and red for 85 seconds. Liam conducts 500 trials of a simulation to estimate the likelihood that the stoplight will be a particular color when a car reaches it. Use the results to find the experimental probability of each event.

Event	Experimental Probability
Getting a green light	
Getting a yellow light	
Not getting a red light	

Simulation Results	
Outcome	Frequency
Green light	115
Yellow light	15
Red light	370

10. A bag holds 6 plain bagels, 3 raisin bagels, 2 cheddar bagels, and 1 onion bagel. Grace chooses 4 bagels from the bag at random without replacing them. Select all possible compound events.

   (A) All of the bagels are raisin bagels.

   (B) There are exactly 2 plain bagels.

   (C) More than half the bagels are cheddar bagels.

   (D) There are more onion bagels selected than raisin bagels.

   (E) The number of cheddar bagels is equal to the number of plain bagels.

11. The experimental probability that Teresa will make a free-throw shot in basketball is 50%. Describe a simulation that can be used to estimate the probability that Teresa will make both of her next 2 free-throw shots.

_____

_____

_____

12. The table shows the blood types of the last 300 people to donate blood at a blood bank. Use this information to answer each question.

Blood Donations	
Blood type	Frequency
O	144
A	93
B	49
AB	14

   A. What is the experimental probability that the next person to donate blood will have type O blood?

   _____

   B. If 50 people donate blood on Friday, how many can be expected to have type O blood? _____ people

13. The experimental probability of winning a prize when playing a carnival game is estimated to be 4%. Based on this information, approximately how many times would a player need to play the game to win 10 prizes?

   (A) 25 times   (B) 40 times   (C) 250 times   (D) 400 times

472

Understand and Apply Theoretical Probability

ANALYZING ROCK-PAPER-SCISSORS

Destiny and Mateo are in the semi-finals of a Rock-Paper-Scissors tournament. Rock-Paper-Scissors is a game for two players, using the three hand signals shown. Players count, "1, 2, 3, go!" and then each player makes a hand signal for rock, paper, or scissors. Each player has an equal chance of winning.

Rock (R) beats scissors (S); Scissors (S) beat paper (P); Paper (P) beats rock (R)

A. The table shows the results of Destiny and Mateo's match. Complete the table by filling in the missing entries.

Destiny	R	P	S	S	S	P	P	P	P	R
Mateo	P	R	P	S	R	S	R	P	R	R
Winner	M	D	D	X						

The winner of this round of the semi-finals is _____!

B. Complete the statements. Write each experimental probability as a fraction and as a decimal.

- Destiny(D) chose Rock _____ times. $P(DR) = \dfrac{\boxed{}}{10}$ or _____

- Mateo(M) chose Rock _____ times. $P(MR) = \dfrac{\boxed{}}{10}$ or _____

- Destiny chose Paper _____ times. $P(DP) = \dfrac{\boxed{}}{10}$ or _____

- Mateo chose Paper _____ times. $P(MP) = \dfrac{\boxed{}}{10}$ or _____

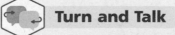 **Turn and Talk**

Calculate each player's experimental probability of choosing scissors. Explain your method of calculation.

Are You Ready?

Complete these problems to review prior concepts and skills you will need for this module.

More Likely, Less Likely, Equally Likely

Use the spinner to answer the questions.

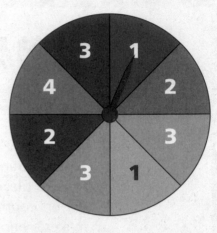

1. Which event is more likely than spinning a 1?

_____

2. Which event is less likely than spinning a 1?

_____

3. Which event is equally likely as spinning a 1?

_____

Experimental Probability

The number of each type of bar in a variety pack of granola bars can vary. The table shows the number of peanut butter bars in a random sample of 300 variety packs. Use this information for Problems 4–6.

Number of Peanut Butter Bars per Pack	Frequency
0	11
1	29
2	60
3	75
4	71
5	39
6	15

4. What is the experimental probability that a variety pack will have exactly 3 peanut butter bars?

_____

_____

5. What is the experimental probability that a variety pack will have at most 4 peanut butter bars?

_____

_____

6. Esme buys 15 variety packs. How many packs can she expect to have more than 2 peanut butter bars? Explain your reasoning.

_____

_____

_____

_____

Name _____

Find Theoretical Probability of Simple Events

(I Can) find the theoretical probability of a simple event.

Spark Your Learning

Dominic wants to play a balloon dart game at the county fair. He can play Game 1 or Game 2. If he pops a blue balloon with a dart, he wins a prize. Which game should Dominic play if he wants a better chance of winning a prize? Assume that Dominic gets one throw, and it will hit a balloon in either game.

Turn and Talk Explain what changes could be made to Game 1 so that Dominic has the same chance of winning a prize when playing either game.

Build Understanding

1 Clara is playing a game where she chooses to spin one of the spinners shown. If the spinner lands on a section labeled "A," she wins a pair of headphones. Which spinner will give her the best chance of winning?

Spinner 1

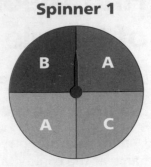

A. Total number of sections for each spinner:

Spinner 1 has a total of _____ sections of the same area.

Spinner 2 has a total of _____ sections of the same area.

B. Number of sections labeled "A" for each spinner:

Spinner 2

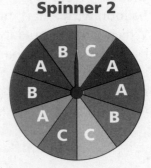

Spinner 1 has _____ sections labeled "A".

Spinner 2 has _____ sections labeled "A".

C. What is the ratio of sections labeled "A" to total number of sections for each spinner?

Spinner 1: $\dfrac{\boxed{}}{4}$ Spinner 2: $\dfrac{\boxed{}}{10}$

D. How can you make the ratios in Part C easier to compare?

_____

_____

E. What is the ratio of sections labeled "A" to total number of sections for each spinner, written as fractions with a common denominator?

Spinner 1: $\dfrac{\boxed{}}{20}$ Spinner 2: $\dfrac{\boxed{}}{20}$

F. Which spinner should Clara spin to give her the best chance of winning a pair of headphones? Explain.

_____

_____

G. Which spinner should Clara spin to give her the best chance of landing on "C"? Explain.

_____

_____

 **Turn and Talk** Describe another way to compare the ratios in Part C.

Step It Out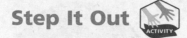

If the outcomes of an experiment are equally likely, you can find the theoretical probability of an event without performing the experiment.

$P(\text{event}) = \dfrac{\text{number of equally likely outcomes in the event}}{\text{total number of equally likely outcomes in the sample space}}$

When a probability is given as a fraction, it is usually written in simplest form.

Connect to Vocabulary

If all possible outcomes are equally likely, the **theoretical probability** of an event is the ratio of the number of possible outcomes in the event to the total number of possible outcomes in the sample space.

2 ▶ Lindsay is going to draw one tile from the bag shown without looking. The tiles are the same size and cannot be told apart by touch, so each tile has an equal chance of being chosen. What is the theoretical probability that she selects a red tile?

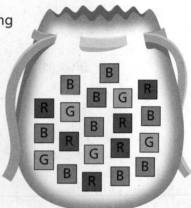

A. Identify the sample space.

5 | red / blue / green | tiles

6 | red / blue / green | tiles

9 | red / blue / green | tiles

B. Find the total number of equally likely possible outcomes in the sample space by adding.

green tiles + red tiles + blue tiles = total number of tiles

□ + □ + □ = □

There are _____ equally likely outcomes in the sample space.

C. Identify the total number of possible outcomes included in the event "select a red tile." Is each possible outcome equally likely?

There are _____ red tiles in the bag, so there are _____ possible outcomes included in this event. Each of these possible outcomes | is / is not | equally likely.

D. Find the theoretical probability that Lindsay will select a red tile. Then, write the ratio in simplest form.

$P(\text{red tile}) = \dfrac{\text{number of red tiles}}{\text{total number of tiles}} = \dfrac{\square}{\square} = \dfrac{\square}{\square}$

E. Probability can be written as a fraction, decimal, or percent. Write the theoretical probability that Lindsay draws a red tile from the bag as a fraction, a decimal, and a percent.

3 ▸ Miguel is deciding if he should do his chores or homework first. To help him decide, he flips a coin.

A. Miguel flips the coin once. Find the theoretical probability of the coin landing on heads and the theoretical probability of the coin landing on tails. Write each as a decimal.

$P(\text{Heads}) = \boxed{}$ $P(\text{Tails}) = \boxed{}$

B. Predict the number of times the coin will land on heads and tails out of 20 flips using the theoretical probability.

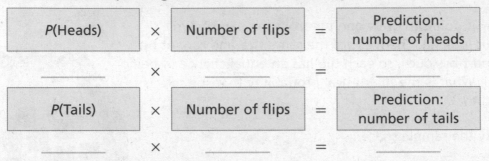

Outcome	Heads	Tails
Frequency		
Experimental probability		

C. Flip a coin 20 times. Record the outcomes in the frequency column. Then give the experimental probability to the nearest percent.

D. Compare the theoretical and experimental probabilities of the coin landing on heads and tails. Are the probabilities equal? Why isn't experimental probability always the same as theoretical probability?

_____

_____

_____

Check Understanding

1. Eric's coach said he could spin a spinner with 4 equal sections labeled 1–4, or roll a number cube labeled 1–6. If Eric gets a 1, he does not have to run a sprint. If Eric does not want to run a sprint, which should he pick? Explain.

_____

_____

2. Pam tossed a coin 50 times and found the probability of getting heads was 45%. Was this a theoretical or experimental probability? Explain.

_____

On Your Own

3. (MP) **Use Structure** Amara has the choice to select one card from Pile 1 or Pile 2 without looking. If she selects a yellow card, she wins the game. Which pile should Amara pick from to give her a better chance of winning? Explain your reasoning.

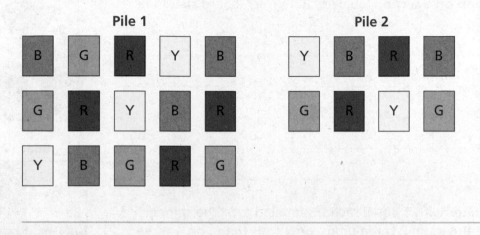

Pile 1

| B | G | R | Y | B |

| G | R | Y | B | R |

| Y | B | G | R | G |

Pile 2

| Y | B | R | B |

| G | R | Y | G |

_____

_____

_____

4. (MP) **Reason** The table shows the results of rolling a number cube 50 times. Compare the experimental probability and theoretical probability of rolling a 5. Give a possible reason why the probabilities are different.

Outcome	1	2	3	4	5	6
Frequency	10	9	5	6	7	13

_____

_____

_____

_____

For Problems 5–8, use the gift boxes shown. Find the theoretical probability of randomly selecting each gift box. Write the probability as a fraction in simplest form.

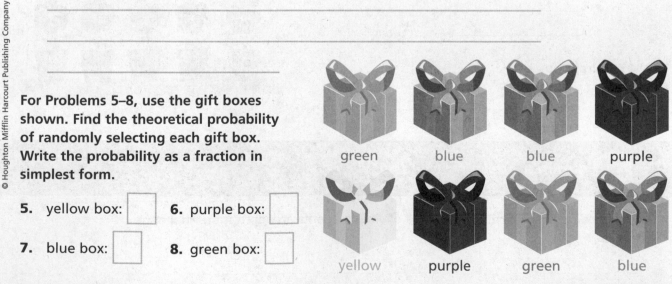

green   blue   blue   purple

yellow   purple   green   blue

5. yellow box: ☐

6. purple box: ☐

7. blue box: ☐

8. green box: ☐

9. A bag contains 5 red balls, 8 white balls, and 7 black balls. What is the theoretical probability of randomly selecting a black ball from the bag?

_____

10. Chase can spin a spinner centered on Board 1 or Board 2. He wants the spinner to land on a section labeled "R." Which board should he choose? Explain.

_____

_____

_____

_____

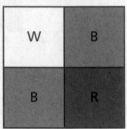

Board 1

Board 2

11. Edith spun a spinner with 5 equal sections labeled 1–5. The spinner landed on 1 five times, on 2 three times, on 3 four times, on 4 three times, and on 5 five times. For which number is the experimental probability the same as its theoretical probability? Explain.

_____

_____

_____

_____

(MP) **Use Structure** For Problems 12–13, use the flowers shown. Find the theoretical probability of selecting the color listed. Write the probability as a fraction in simplest form, a decimal, and a percent.

12. orange flower

_____

13. purple flower

_____

⊟×⊡÷ **I'm in a Learning Mindset!**

Was finding theoretical probabilities of simple events an appropriate challenge for me?

_____

Name _____

LESSON 15.1
More Practice/
Homework

ONLINE

Ed
Video Tutorials and
Interactive Examples

Find Theoretical Probability of Simple Events

Without looking, Luke picks necklace beads from a bag of 52 beads. Half the beads are rough. The other half are smooth. There are 13 red beads, 13 blue beads, 13 green beads, and 13 black beads. Use this information for Problems 1–5. Write each probability as a fraction in simplest form.

1. What is the theoretical probability of selecting a smooth bead?

   _____

2. What is the theoretical probability of selecting a blue bead?

   _____

3. What is the theoretical probability of selecting a rough bead?

   _____

4. What is the theoretical probability of not selecting a red bead?

   _____

5. (MP) **Reason** One hundred times, Luke picks one bead then puts it back into the bag. The results are shown. What are the experimental probability and theoretical probability of picking a black bead? Name a possible reason why the probabilities are not the same.

Outcome	Red	Blue	Green	Black
Frequency	21	26	33	20

   _____

   _____

   _____

   _____

6. **Math on the Spot** Find the probability of the event. Write your answer as a fraction, as a decimal, and as a percent.

   A. draw one of the 4 *L*'s from a bag of 100 letter tiles

   _____

   B. roll a number less than 4 on a number cube

   _____

© Houghton Mifflin Harcourt Publishing Company • Image Credit: ©undefined undefined/iStock/Getty Images Plus/Getty Images

Test Prep

7. Brice can win a game by selecting a letter tile with the letter B from a bag. He wants to choose a bag that will give him the best chance of winning. Which statement is correct?

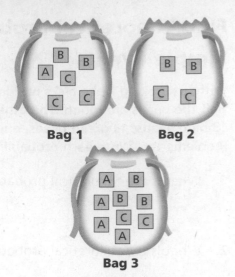

Bag 1   Bag 2

Bag 3

   (A) Brice has the best chance only with Bag 1.

   (B) Brice has the best chance only with Bag 2.

   (C) Brice has the best chance only with Bag 3.

   (D) Brice has the best chance with either Bag 1 or Bag 3.

8. Use the spinner to match the theoretical probability to the correct event.

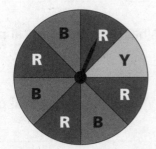

   $P(Y)$ •   • $\frac{1}{2}$

   $P(R)$ •   • 0.375

   $P(B)$ •   • 12.5%

9. The table shows the results of flipping a coin 10 times. How do the theoretical and experimental probabilities of the coin landing on heads compare?

Outcome	Heads	Tails
Frequency	3	7

_____

_____

_____

_____

Spiral Review

10. A soccer team made 2 goals out of 32 attempts in a game. What is the experimental probability that the team made a goal on any given shot? Write the probability as a decimal.

_____

11. The experimental probability that Jason makes a free throw is 72%. If Jason shoots 50 free throws, about how many can you expect him to make? Explain.

_____

Find Theoretical Probability of Compound Events

(I Can) find the theoretical probability of a compound event.

Step It Out

1 ▶ Lucas spins the two spinners shown labeled 1 through 4. Spinning each number on one spinner is equally likely. He wants to find the probability that the sum of the two numbers he spins is 3.

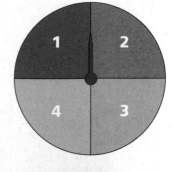

A. Lucas makes a table to represent the sample space of sums. Each entry in the table is the sum of the numbers in the corresponding row and column. Complete the remainder of the table.

+	1	2	3	4
1	2	3	4	
2	3	4		
3	4			
4				

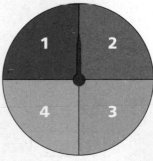

B. The table in Part A shows:

• There are _____ possible outcomes with a sum of 3.

• There are _____ equally likely outcomes in the sample space.

C. Find the theoretical probability of spinning a sum of 3.

$$P(\text{sum of 3}) = \frac{\text{number of equally likely outcomes that add to 3}}{\text{total number of equally likely outcomes in the sample space}}$$

$$= \frac{\boxed{}}{16}$$

$$= \frac{\boxed{}}{\boxed{}}$$

D. Determine another possible outcome in the sample space that has the same probability as that of spinning a sum of 3.

$P(\text{sum of 3}) = P(\underline{\hspace{2cm}})$

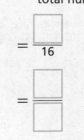

2 ▸ Aria can choose one pair of shorts (black or white), one shirt (red, blue, or green), and one pair of shoes (brown or tan) as her outfit. Find the probability of choosing an outfit at random and getting white shorts, a blue shirt, and tan shoes.

A. Complete the **tree diagram** to represent the sample space.

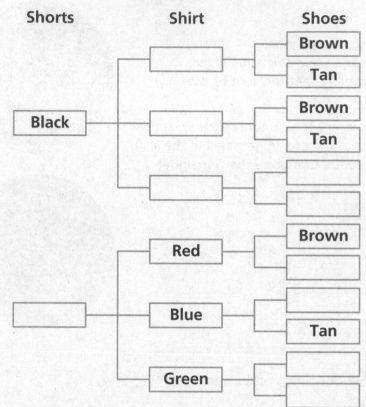

Shorts	Shirt	Shoes
		Brown
		Tan
Black		Brown
		Tan
	Red	Brown
	Blue	
		Tan
	Green	

B. The tree diagram shows that there are _____ equally likely outcomes in the sample space.

C. Find the probability P(white, blue, tan).

$$P(\text{white, blue, tan}) = \frac{\text{number of equally likely outcomes in the event (white, blue, tan)}}{\text{total number of equally likely outcomes in the sample space}}$$

$$= \frac{\ \ }{\ \ }$$

D. Find the probability of selecting white shorts and a blue shirt when selecting clothes at random.

$$P(\text{white, blue}) = \frac{\text{number of equally likely outcomes in the event (white, blue)}}{\text{total number of equally likely outcomes in the sample sapce}}$$

$$= \frac{\ \ }{\ \ }$$

3 Ali draws cards from a hat that contains three cards labeled A, B, and C. He has an equal chance of drawing each card. He draws one card at a time, records the result, and replaces it before the next draw. Ali wins a prize for drawing the A-card 3 times in a row. What is the probability that he wins a prize?

Winning Combination

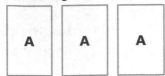

A. Complete the organized lists to represent the sample space.

A on first draw		
A	A	A
A	A	B
A	A	C
A	B	A
A	B	B
A	B	C
A	C	
A	C	
A	C	

B on first draw		
B	A	A
B	A	B
B	A	C
B	B	
B	B	
B	B	
B	C	
B	C	
B	C	

C on first draw		
C	A	
C	A	
C	A	
.	B	
C		A
C		B
C	C	C

B. The organized lists show that there are _____ equally likely outcomes in the sample space.

C. Find the probability $P(A, A, A)$. Write the probability as a fraction, decimal, and percent. Round to the nearest hundredth and whole percent.

$$P(A, A, A) = \frac{\text{number of equally likely outcomes in the event (A, A, A)}}{\text{total number of equally likely outcomes in the sample space}}$$

$$= \frac{\boxed{}}{\boxed{}} \text{ or } \boxed{} \text{ or } \boxed{} \%$$

The probability that Ali wins a prize is about _____ %.

Turn and Talk How do you think you could use the organized lists to find the probability of drawing 2 or more A-cards in any order?

Check Understanding

1. What are some ways that you can represent the sample space of a compound event?

_____

2. Mila spins two spinners. One spinner has two equal sections labeled 1 and 2. The other spinner has three equal sections labeled 1, 2, and 3. What is the probability that the sum of the two spins is 4?

_____

On Your Own

3. **MP Use Structure** Wyatt rolls two number prisms in the shape of triangular prisms, labeled 1 to 3 as shown.

A. Complete the table to represent the sample space for the sum of these two number prisms.

+	1	2	3
1			
2			
3			

B. What is the probability that Wyatt rolls a sum of 3?

_____

C. What event has the same probability as rolling a sum of 3? Explain.

_____

_____

_____

D. Name an event that is less likely than a sum of 3. Explain.

_____

_____

_____

E. Name an event that is more likely than a sum of 3. Explain.

_____

_____

_____

MP Model with Mathematics Find each probability. Give your answer as a simplified fraction, a decimal to the nearest hundredth, and a percent to the nearest whole percent.

F. *P*(sum of 4)   G. *P*(sum of 6)

_____   _____

H. *P*(sum < 10)   I. *P*(sum > 10)

_____   _____

4. (MP) **Use Structure** Layla tosses three coins.

A. Complete the tree diagram to show the sample space for how the coins can land. H represent heads and T represent tails.

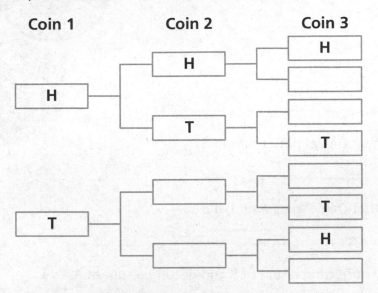

Coin 1	Coin 2	Coin 3

B. What is the probability that exactly two coins land heads up? Write the probability as a fraction, decimal, and percent.

_____

C. What is the probability that exactly two coins land tails up? Compare this probability to the probability that exactly two coins land heads up.

_____

D. What is the probability that exactly three coins land tails up? Write the probability as a fraction, decimal, and percent.

_____

E. Name an event with the same probability as that of three tails? Explain.

_____

_____

F. Compare the theoretical probability of getting at least one head and the theoretical probability of getting at least two tails.

_____

_____

_____

_____

5. **(MP) Use Structure** Daniel is going to spin the spinner shown and roll a number cube.

A. Make an organized list to show the sample space for spinning the spinner and rolling the number cube.

_____

_____

_____

_____

B. What is the probability that Daniel gets a sum of 5?

_____

C. What is the probability that Daniel gets a sum of 3?

_____

D. Compare the probability of getting a sum of 5 and getting a sum of 3.

_____

_____

E. **Open Ended** Give an example of an event that is more likely than getting a sum of 8. Explain your reasoning.

_____

_____

_____

F. **Open Ended** Give an example of an event that is as equally likely as getting a sum of 6. Explain your reasoning.

_____

_____

_____

6. **(MP) Reason** How is finding the theoretical probability of a compound event similar to finding the theoretical probability of a simple event?

_____

_____

_____

LESSON 15.2
**More Practice/
Homework**

ONLINE
😊Ed Video Tutorials and
Interactive Examples

Find Theoretical Probability of Compound Events

1. (MP) **Use Structure** Christian has a red box with tiles numbered from 1 to 5 and a green box with tiles numbered from 1 to 3. He draws a tile from each box, and then finds the sum.

   A. Make a table to represent the sample space for drawing a particular sum from the numbers in the two boxes.

   B. What is the probability of drawing a sum of 7?

   _____

   C. Name an event that is more likely than drawing a sum of 7.

   _____

2. (MP) **Use Structure** Lucy can choose one sandwich (ham or turkey), one side (apples or grapes), and one drink (milk or water). Lucy has an equally likely chance of choosing any combination.

   A. Make a tree diagram to find the sample space.

   Sandwich   **Side**   **Drink**

   B. What is the probability Lucy picks a ham sandwich and grapes?

   _____

   C. What is the probability Lucy chooses milk with a turkey sandwich and apples?

   _____

   D. (MP) **Reason** Name an event that is equally as likely as choosing ham and apples.

   _____

3. (MP) **Attend to Precision** How many different possible outcomes are there for the experiment described here?

   Step 1
   Toss a
   number
   cube.

   Step 2
   Toss
   a fair
   coin.

   Step 3
   Spin the
   spinner.

   There are _____ different possible outcomes.

Test Prep

4. Emma is going to flip a coin, resulting in H for heads or T for tails, and spin the spinner shown. Which list correctly represents the sample space?

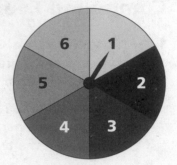

Ⓐ H, T, 1, 2, 3, 4, 5, 6

Ⓑ H-1, H-2, H-3, H-4, H-5, H-6

Ⓒ H-1, H-2, H-3, H-4, H-5, H-6, T-1, T-2, T-3, T-4, T-5, T-6

Ⓓ H-T-1, H-T-2, H-T-3, H-T-4, H-T-5, H-T-6

5. Luna rolls two number cubes labeled 1–6. Match the probability to the correct event.

P(sum of 5) •   • $\frac{1}{6}$

P(sum less than 4) •   • $\frac{1}{9}$

P(sum of 7) •   • $\frac{5}{18}$

P(sum greater than 8) •   • $\frac{1}{12}$

6. Carson can choose one vehicle (car or truck), one color (blue, red, or silver), and one type of transmission (standard or automatic). How many possible outcomes are there?

_____

Spiral Review

7. Aaliyah spins the spinner shown. What is the theoretical probability that the spinner will land on an even number?

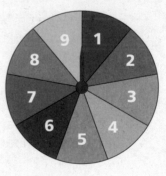

_____

8. Tell whether the following relationship is a proportional relationship. Explain why or why not. If it is, identify the unit rate.

Time (min)	3	5	8	10
Words Typed	120	200	320	400

_____

_____

_____

_____

Name _____

Use Theoretical Probability and Proportional Reasoning to Make Predictions

(I Can) use theoretical probability to make predictions about real-world situations.

Step It Out

1 ▶ Sadie spins the spinner shown 80 times. Predict how many times she will spin a 2 or 3.

A. The theoretical probability of spinning a 2 or 3 is _____, or _____%.

B. Solve by using proportional reasoning.

$$\frac{1}{2} = \frac{x}{\boxed{}}$$

$1 \times \boxed{} = x$
$2 \times 40 = 80$

So $x = \boxed{}$

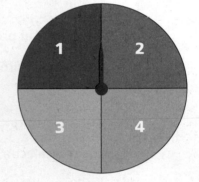

Sadie will spin a 2 or 3 about _____ times.

C. Solve by multiplying the probability by the number of trials.

P(spinning 2 or 3) × number of trials

$\boxed{}\%$ × $\boxed{}$ = $\boxed{}$

Sadie will spin a 2 or 3 about _____ times.

2 ▶ Bailey rolls a number cube 180 times. Predict how many times she will roll a 5 or 6.

A. The theoretical probability of rolling a 5 or 6 is _____, or _____.

B. Solve by using proportional reasoning.

$$\frac{1}{3} = \frac{x}{\boxed{}}$$

$1 \times \boxed{} = x$ So $x = \boxed{}$
$3 \times \boxed{} = 180$

Bailey will roll a 5 or 6 about _____ times.

C. Solve by multiplying the probability by the number of trials.

P(rolling 5 or 6) × number of trials

$\boxed{}$ × $\boxed{}$ = $\boxed{}$

Bailey will roll a 2 or 3 about _____ times.

3 Jamie works at a dog shelter. The types, colors, and genders of dogs are shown. Predict how many times out of 90 Jamie will randomly pick a tan, male pug to walk. Assume an equal chance for her to select each dog.

A. Make a tree diagram or organized list to represent the sample space.

Type	Color	Gender
Beagle (B)	Black (Bl)	Male (M)
Pug (P)	White (Wh)	Female (F)
Collie (C)	Tan (T)	

B. The theoretical probability of selecting a tan, male pug is _____.

C. Solve by using proportional reasoning.

$\frac{1}{18} = \frac{x}{\boxed{}}$ $1 \times \boxed{} = x$ So $x = \boxed{}$

$18 \times \boxed{} = 90$

Jamie will select a tan, male pug about _____ out of 90 times.

D. Solve by multiplying the probability by the number of times she picks.

P(tan, male, pug) × number of times

$\boxed{}$ × $\boxed{}$ = $\boxed{}$

Jamie will select a tan, male pug about _____ out of 90 times.

E. Predict how many times out of 90 Jamie will randomly select a tan pug or tan collie. Use the sample space to find the probability.

There are _____ tan pugs and tan collies in the sample space.

P(tan pug or tan collie) = $\frac{\boxed{}}{18}$, or $\frac{\boxed{}}{\boxed{}}$

Solve by using proportional reasoning.

$\frac{\boxed{}}{\boxed{}} = \frac{x}{\boxed{}}$ $\boxed{} \times \boxed{} = x$ So, $x =$ _____

$\boxed{} \times \boxed{} = 90$

Jamie will select a tan pug or tan collie about _____ out of 90 times.

Turn and Talk Describe an alternate solution method for Part E.

492

© Houghton Mifflin Harcourt Publishing Company • Image Credit: ©Camille Tokerud/The Image Bank/Getty Images

4 Ezekiel randomly draws a card from the stack shown. Which is more likely: drawing a card that is NOT red or drawing a green card?

A. First find P(red). Then find P(not red).

$$P(\text{red}) = \frac{\text{number of red cards}}{\text{total number of equally likely cards}} = \frac{\boxed{}}{\boxed{}}$$

$$P(\text{not red}) = 1 - P(\text{red}) = 1 - \frac{\boxed{}}{\boxed{}} = \frac{\boxed{}}{15}$$

B. Complete the inequality statement to compare P(not red) and P(green).

P(not red) ⬜ P(green)

⬜ ⬜ ⬜

So drawing | not red / green | is more likely.

5 Isla is resetting her door code. The code is a 3-digit number made up of the digits 0 through 9. The digits can be repeated. Isla used a random number generator to select a code so all possible codes are equally likely. Would you predict that the door code 567 will be generated more than 5 out of 8,000 times?

A. First find the number of equally likely outcomes in the sample space.

Imagine drawing a tree diagram. There are 10 possible outcomes for the first digit, and each of those has 10 possible outcomes for the second digit, and each of those 10 more.

The sample space has 10 × 10 × 10 = _____ equally likely outcomes.

B. Find the probability of randomly generating the code 567, and use it to predict the number of times out of 8,000 you would expect code 567 to be generated.

$$P(567) = \frac{\boxed{}}{1{,}000} \qquad \overset{\displaystyle P(567) \times \text{number of trials}}{\boxed{} \times \boxed{} = \boxed{}}$$

I | would / would not | predict that the code 567 will be generated more than 5 out of 8,000 times.

Check Understanding

1. A bag of marbles contains 5 red, 3 blue, and 12 yellow marbles. Predict the number of times Hazel will select a blue marble out of 500 trials.

_____

2. Kai flips a coin and spins a 3-sector spinner labeled 1–3. Predict the number of times Kai will get the outcome (heads, 2) in 300 trials.

_____

On Your Own

3. **(MP) Construct Arguments** Bryson selects a folder from a pile. The folder is blue. There are 8 blue folders, 9 yellow folders, and 3 orange folders left in the pile. He selects a second folder from the pile without looking. Is it likely that Bryson selects matching folders? Explain your reasoning.

_____

_____

_____

_____

(MP) Model with Mathematics An eight-sided game piece has 8 congruent triangular faces. The faces are labeled 1–8. Nevaeh rolls the game piece 400 times. Use this information for Problems 4–7.

4. Write and solve a proportion to predict how many times the game piece will land on 7.

_____

5. Write and solve a proportion to predict how many times the game piece will land on 3 or 5.

_____

6. Write and evaluate an expression to predict how many times the game piece will land on an even number.

_____

7. Write and evaluate an expression to predict how many times the game piece will land on a number less than or equal to 3.

_____

Liliana spins a spinner with equal-sized sections numbered 1 through 4. She spins the spinner a total of 300 times. Use this information for Problems 8–9.

8. Write and solve a proportion to predict the number of times Liliana can expect to spin a 3.

_____

9. Write and evaluate an expression to predict the number of times Liliana can expect to spin an even number.

_____

10. Ezra is resetting the code on his safe. The code is a 3-digit number made up of the digits 0 through 5. The digits can be repeated. Ezra will randomly draw numbers from a hat to select a code, replacing the number after each draw. Is it likely that Ezra will randomly select the safe code 123 more than 10 times out of 4,320 random codes drawn from the hat? Solve using an expression. Explain your reasoning.

_____

_____

_____

_____

11. Savannah is going to randomly select a block from a bag and return it to the bag 240 times. There are 3 colors (red, green, yellow) and two shapes (square and triangle). Explain how to find the sample space. Then predict how many times Savannah will select a red triangle. Solve using a proportion.

_____

_____

_____

(MP) **Model with Mathematics** **Elliot rolls two number cubes 900 times. Their faces are labeled 1–6. Use this information for Problems 12–15.**

12. Write and solve a proportion to predict the number of times Elliot can expect to roll a sum of 11.

_____

13. Write and solve a proportion to predict the number of times Elliot can expect to roll two odd numbers.

_____

14. Write and evaluate an expression to predict the number of times Elliot can expect to roll one even number and one odd number.

_____

15. Write and evaluate an expression to predict the number of times Elliot can expect to roll the same number on both cubes.

_____

16. Penelope selects an earring from a jewelry box. The earring color is gold. The colors of the remaining earrings are: 11 gold, 16 silver, and 13 black. She randomly selects a second earring from the jewelry box. Is it likely that Penelope selects earrings of the same color? Explain your reasoning.

_____

_____

_____

_____

17. (MP) **Construct Arguments** The security desk for an office building has visitor's badges with codes consisting of one letter (A–Z) and 1 digit (0 through 9). A visitor can select a badge at random and badges are returned at the end of each day. Is it likely that the badge L7 is the first badge selected more than 5 times in 365 days? Explain your reasoning. (_Hint:_ Imagine making a a rectangular array. There would be 26 × 10 different badge codes.)

_____

_____

_____

_____

(MP) **Model with Mathematics Ian is going to flip a coin and roll a number cube 3,000 times. Use this information for Problems 18–20.**

18. Write and solve a proportion to predict the number of times the coin lands on tails and the number cube lands on 5.

_____

19. Write and evaluate an expression to predict the number of times the coin lands on heads and the number cube lands on an even number.

_____

20. Write and evaluate an expression to predict the number of times the coin lands on tails and the number cube lands on a number greater than 2.

_____

21. A box had 12 red tiles, 15 blue tiles, and 23 purple tiles. LaTanisha randomly selects a tile without looking 2,000 times. Each time a tile is selected, it is replaced before the next selection. Predict the number of times LaTanisha selects a blue or red tile.

_____

Use Theoretical Probability and
Proportional Reasoning to Make Predictions

1. Oliver selects a glove from his drawer. The glove is blue. There are 3 red gloves, 6 black gloves, and 11 blue gloves left in the drawer. He selects a second glove from the drawer without looking. Is it likely that Oliver selects a glove of the same color? Explain your reasoning.

_____

_____

2. If you roll a number cube 20 times, about how many times do you expect to roll a number greater than 4?

_____

(MP) **Use Structure** Victoria spins the two spinners shown 500 times. Use this information for Problems 3–5.

3. Solve a proportion to predict the number of times the sum is 4.

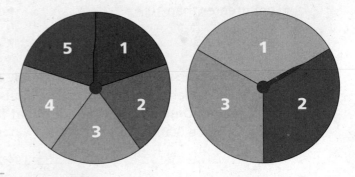

4. Solve a proportion to predict the number of times the sum is 4, 5, or 6.

_____

5. Solve a percent equation to predict the number of times the sum is less than or equal to 3.

_____

(MP) **Model with Mathematics** There are 5 red, 18 green, and 17 blue pens in a bag. Leah selects a pen 800 times without looking. Before each selection, she replaces the pen in the bag. Use this information for Problems 6–7.

6. Write and evaluate an expression to predict the number of times Leah selects a pen that is red or green.

_____

7. Write and evaluate an expression to predict the number of times Leah selects a pen that is not red.

_____

Test Prep

8. Leo has 10 red cards, 20 black cards, 20 yellow cards, and 25 white cards in a bag. He randomly selects a card 300 times. He replaces the card after each selection. Predict how often Leo will select a white card.

(A) about 12 times

(B) about 75 times

(C) about 100 times

(D) about 150 times

9. Scarlet rolls a number cube labeled 1–6 and spins the spinner shown 2,100 times. Match the prediction to the correct event.

sum of 5 •   • about 300 times

sum less than 7 •   • about 50 times

sum of 13 •   • about 200 times

sum greater than 10 •   • about 550 times

sum of 8 or 9 •   • about 750 times

10. All 3,000 lockers at a school are randomly assigned 3-digit combination codes. The codes are made up of the digits 0 through 9. The digits can be repeated. Describe the likelihood that fewer than 5 of the lockers will have the code 000.

_____

_____

_____

_____

Spiral Review

11. Levi rolled a number cube labeled 1–6. The number cube landed on 1 four times, 2 two times, 3 one time, 4 two times, 5 three times, and 6 six times. Which experimental probability is the same as the theoretical probability?

_____

_____

12. Brianna rolls two number cubes labeled 1–6. What is the probability that Brianna rolls a sum of 5?

_____

Name

Conduct Simulations

(I Can) use a simulation to test the probability of simple and compound events.

Step It Out

1 ▶ What is the experimental probability that you first find a winner on the second plate you check at the fundraiser dinner shown?

20% of the plates are winners!

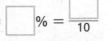

A. P(winning sticker) = ☐% = ☐/10

B. Carlos uses whole numbers from 1 to 10 to design a simulation. He generates one number at random to simulate checking one plate.

Winning: 1, 2

Non-winning: 3, 4, 5, 6, 7, 8, 9, 10

The table shows the results from Carlos's experiment: generating numbers for each trial until a winning number (1 or 2) appears. Complete the table.

Trial	Numbers generated	Plates checked
1	5, 8, 1	3
2	1	1
3	4, 8, 9, 2	4
4	5, 1	2
5	7, 8, 2	
6	8, 9, 10, 6, 2	
7	2	
8	3, 5, 7, 1	
9	9, 8, 2	
10	8, 6, 3, 4, 9, 2	

C. For Trial 1, a winning number appeared after _____ plate(s).

For Trial 2, a winning number appeared after _____ plate(s).

How many of the 10 trials showed a winner on the second plate?

_____

D. The experimental probability of first finding a winner on the second plate is

☐/☐, or _____ %.

2 Manufacturers of Crunchy Flakes place a prize in 25% of their cereal boxes. Use a simulation to find the experimental probability that you will get at least one prize if you buy 3 boxes of Crunchy Flakes.

A. Design the experiment using whole numbers from 1 to 4.

Getting a prize: 1   Not getting a prize: ☐

B. Label slips of paper with the whole numbers 1–4 and place them in a cup. Draw a number, record it, and place the number back in the cup. Use this process to generate 10 sets of 3 random whole numbers from 1 to 4. Record the results.

_____

C. The experimental probability is $\dfrac{\square}{\square}$ = ☐ %.

3 The chance that Amir will make a free throw at any given time is shown. Find the experimental probability that Amir will make at least 3 of the next 5 free throws he attempts.

60% free-throw success

A. Choose a model to simulate this compound event.

Use whole numbers from 1 to 5. Amir makes free throws _____ % of the time. Let 1, 2, and 3 represent a successful free throw, and let _____ and _____ represent a missed free throw.

B. Amir used a calculator to generate 10 trials of 5 random numbers from 1 to 5. Complete the table.

Trial	Numbers Generated	Successful Free Throws
1	3, 1, 4, 4, 5	2
2	5, 2, 1, 3, 2	4
3	2, 5, 4, 2, 4	
4	4, 3, 5, 4, 5	
5	2, 1, 3, 3, 4	
6	3, 4, 2, 3, 2	
7	1, 1, 5, 4, 5	
8	4, 5, 1, 2, 1	
9	3, 3, 3, 3, 4	
10	5, 4, 2, 4, 3	

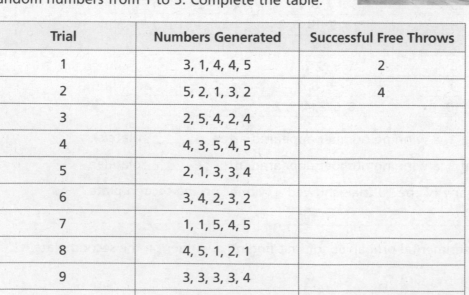

C. List trials that represent at least 3 successful free throws.

_____

D. Find the experimental probability that Amir makes at least 3 of the next 5 free throws he attempts.

$$\frac{\boxed{}}{10} = \boxed{}\ \%$$

 Turn and Talk Explain how the model changes if the whole numbers from 1 to 10 were used to simulate this situation.

Check Understanding

Suppose there is a 70% chance that Reagan will make a field goal at any given time. A computer was used to generate 10 sets of random numbers from 1 to 10, where the numbers 1–7 represent a successful field goal and numbers 8–10 represent a missed field goal. The results are shown. Use the table for Problems 1-2.

Trial	Numbers Generated
1	1, 9, 1, 2, 10, 6, 5, 2, 7, 2
2	8, 10, 4, 10, 2, 2, 3, 6, 7, 10
3	6, 9, 9, 10, 4, 10, 10, 2, 6, 6
4	8, 8, 2, 3, 4, 6, 5, 6, 5, 3
5	1, 10, 1, 2, 5, 6, 9, 4, 10, 3
6	7, 1, 9, 1, 6, 3, 3, 7, 5, 6
7	2, 5, 2, 7, 5, 5, 10, 5, 6, 3
8	9, 6, 10, 4, 9, 6, 8, 9, 9, 9
9	5, 1, 4, 5, 2, 8, 5, 7, 5, 6
10	7, 6, 5, 5, 1, 10, 9, 3, 9, 2

1. Find the experimental probability that Reagan will miss the first two field goals and make the third one.

_____

2. Each trial in the table shows a simulation of 10 field goal attempts. Which trials in the table show that Reagan made at least 7 of her field goal attempts? Use this information to find the experimental probability that Reagan will make at least 7 of the next 10 field goals attempted.

On Your Own

3. **(MP) Use Tools** Lindsay randomly answers the questions on a 10-question true or false quiz. By guessing, she will get a question correct half the time. Explain how to model a simulation to find the experimental probability that Lindsay will answer at least 7 questions correctly.

_____

_____

_____

_____

_____

_____

4. **(MP) Use Structure** At a new restaurant, 10% of the customers selected at random get a $5 coupon with their bill. Sasha wants to use a simulation to find the experimental probability that the second customer of the day gets a coupon with the bill. She uses a calculator to generate random numbers from 1 to 10. The number 1 represents a customer receiving a coupon and the numbers 2–10 represent a customer not receiving a coupon. The results of her simulation are shown in the table.

Trial	Numbers Generated
1	7, 5, 9, 9, 10, 10, 10, 7, 5, 1
2	4, 3, 3, 9, 1
3	5, 2, 1
4	6, 3, 9, 1
5	7, 4, 2, 5, 4, 1
6	7, 7, 2, 2, 9, 6, 2, 4, 6, 1
7	7, 8, 10, 4, 9, 7, 3, 7, 5, 1
8	10, 7, 4, 7, 9, 3, 8, 9, 4, 1
9	9, 9, 2, 3, 8, 3, 3, 5, 4, 1
10	7, 1

A. Which trials show the second customer getting a coupon? How many of the 10 trials show this event occuring? _____

B. Find the experimental probability that the second customer gets a coupon. Give your answer as a percent. _____

C. Find the experimental probability that the tenth customer is the first one to receive a coupon. Give your answer as a percent. _____

Use the table and the information given for Problems 5 and 6.

Geography Over a 100-year period, the probability that a hurricane struck Reyna's city in any given year was 20%. Reyna performed a simulation to find the experimental probability that a hurricane would strike the city in at least 4 of the next 10 years. In Reyna's simulation, 1 represents a year with a hurricane.

Trial	Numbers Generated
1	2, 5, 3, 2, 5, 5, 1, 4, 5, 2
2	1, 1, 5, 2, 2, 1, 3, 1, 1, 5
3	4, 5, 4, 5, 5, 4, 3, 5, 1, 1
4	1, 5, 5, 5, 1, 2, 2, 3, 5, 3
5	5, 1, 5, 3, 5, 3, 4, 5, 3, 2
6	1, 1, 5, 5, 1, 4, 2, 2, 3, 4
7	2, 1, 5, 3, 1, 5, 1, 2, 1, 4
8	2, 4, 3, 2, 4, 4, 2, 1, 3, 1
9	3, 2, 1, 4, 5, 3, 5, 5, 1, 2
10	3, 4, 2, 4, 3, 5, 2, 3, 5, 1

5. According to Reyna's simulation, what was the experimental probability that a hurricane would strike the city in at least 4 of the next 10 years?

_____

6. **MP** **Reason** Suppose that over the 10 years following Reyna's simulation, there was exactly 1 year in which a hurricane struck. How did this compare to the results of Reyna's simulation?

_____

_____

7. **Open Ended** Keith wants to use the spinner shown to simulate an event with a 75% chance of occurring. Describe a situation Keith could be simulating. Then describe how the spinner can be used.

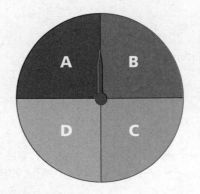

_____

_____

_____

8. (MP) **Use Tools** Dave wants to generate random numbers to simulate an event with a 25% chance of occurring. Describe a model he could use.

_____

_____

_____

9. (MP) **Reason** Is it possible to perform a simulation several times and get different experimental probabilities for the same event? Explain.

_____

_____

_____

10. **STEM** A quality control technician wants to determine how much variation can be expected in a random sample of light bulbs produced at a plant. The known rate of defective light bulbs is 5%. Describe a simulation the technician could use to find the experimental probability that a sample of 100 bulbs will include at least 5 defective bulbs.

_____

_____

_____

_____

_____

11. Allie is a softball player. She has a batting average of 0.600. This means that Allie gets a hit 60% of the time.

A. Design a simulation using slips of paper and a box to find the experimental probability of Allie getting a hit at least 2 out of 5 times.

_____

_____

_____

_____

B. (MP) **Use Tools** Perform the simulation. Describe your results. Use the results to predict the probability of Allie getting a hit at least 2 out of 5 times.

_____

_____

Conduct Simulations

1. There is a card under 30% of the chairs at a booster meeting. Finn wants to find the probability that the first card he finds will be under the third chair that he checks. He generates 10 sets of random numbers from 1 to 10. The numbers 1–3 represent a chair with a card and 4–10 represent a chair without a card. Complete the table, and find the experimental probability of the event.

Trial	1	2	3	4	5	6	7	8	9	10
Numbers Generated	6, 5, 1	8, 1	10, 1	7, 8, 4, 1	9, 3	5, 4, 2	3	9, 5, 8, 2	7, 3	9, 6, 8, 4, 7, 3
Chairs Checked										

2. **Math on the Spot** There is a 20% chance that a particular volcano will erupt during any given decade. A random number generator generated 10 sets of random numbers from 1 to 5 as shown. The number 1 represents the volcano erupting. Find the experimental probability that the volcano will erupt in 1 or 2 of the next 5 decades.

Trial	Numbers Generated
1	3, 1, 3, 4, 2
2	3, 2, 2, 4, 5
3	1, 3, 3, 2, 5
4	5, 3, 4, 5, 4
5	5, 5, 3, 2, 4
6	2, 3, 3, 4, 2
7	1, 2, 4, 1, 4
8	1, 3, 2, 1, 5
9	1, 2, 4, 2, 5
10	5, 5, 3, 2, 4

3. Sia makes 10% of the shots she attempts in soccer at any given time. A random number generator was used to generate 5 sets of random numbers from 1 to 10 as shown, where number 1 represents a successful shot and numbers 2–10 represent a missed shot. Find the experimental probability that Sia will make at least 2 of the next 10 shots attempted.

Trial	Numbers Generated
1	5, 4, 8, 4, 8, 6, 7, 1, 7, 4
2	6, 9, 4, 6, 6, 4, 6, 8, 8, 6
3	10, 1, 8, 2, 3, 2, 9, 3, 5, 7
4	3, 6, 10, 5, 5, 4, 10, 6, 1, 5
5	8, 1, 9, 9, 3, 7, 4, 5, 1, 10

Test Prep

4. There is a 25% chance that Jahil will hit an archery target on any given attempt. Which model can be used to find the experimental probability that Jahil will hit the target on at least 3 of the next 4 attempts?

   Ⓐ Use a computer to generate whole numbers from 1 to 8 where numbers 1–2 represent hitting the target and numbers 3–8 represent not hitting the target.

   Ⓑ Use a calculator to generate whole numbers from 1 to 8 where numbers 1–6 represent hitting the target and numbers 7–8 represent not hitting the target.

   Ⓒ Use a computer to generate whole numbers from 1 to 4 where numbers 1–2 represent hitting the target and numbers 3–4 represent not hitting the target.

   Ⓓ Use a calculator to generate whole numbers from 1 to 4 where numbers 1–3 represent hitting the target and number 4 represents not hitting the target.

5. At a gym, 50% of the customers get a free training session. Let the number 1 represent a customer receiving a free training session and the number 2 represent not receiving a free training session. A calculator generated random numbers, 1 and 2, until a number that represents a customer receiving a free training session appeared. The results are shown in the table. Find the experimental probability that you must ask exactly 2 customers before you find a customer that received a free training session.

   _____ %

Trial	Numbers Generated
1	1
2	2, 2, 1
3	2, 1
4	1
5	2, 2, 1

6. Out of 12 trials, a simulation showed Ming getting a place in a summer art program 10 times. What is the experimental probability of the event, according to the simulation?

   _____

Spiral Review

7. Vera is going to flip a coin 50 times. Write and evaluate an expression to predict the number of times the coin lands on heads.

   _____

   _____

8. Juan spins two spinners each with 4 equal sections labeled 1–4. What is the probability that Juan spins a sum greater than 3?

   _____

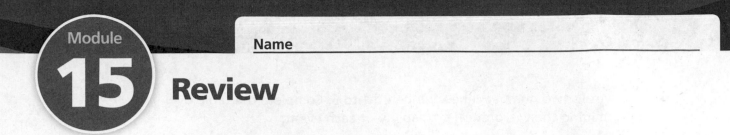
Vocabulary

1. How is theoretical probability different from experimental probability?

_____

_____

_____

_____

_____

2. What is a *simulation* in probability? Write a definition in your own words.

_____

_____

Concepts and Skills

3. A box contains 4 red pencils, 6 yellow pencils, and 5 blue pencils. What is the probability of randomly selecting a yellow pencil from the box?

_____

4. Select the situation with a $\frac{1}{3}$ probability of randomly selecting a blue marble from a bag.

(A) A bag containing 1 white, 4 red, 3 blue, 2 green, and 4 black marbles

(B) A bag containing 2 white, 6 red, 8 blue, 5 green, and 5 black marbles

(C) A bag containing 3 white, 2 red, 5 blue, 3 green, and 2 black marbles

(D) A bag containing 3 white, 3 red, 3 blue, 3 green, and 3 black marbles

5. (MP) **Use Tools** A stack of cards contains 25 red cards, 25 blue cards, 25 green cards, and 25 yellow cards. A card is drawn from the stack at random and then replaced 300 times. The results are shown. Which experimental probability from this experiment is closest to the expected theoretical probability based on the sample space? State what strategy and tool you will use to answer the question, explain your choice, and then find the answer.

Experimental Results	
Outcome	Frequency
Red	74
Blue	68
Green	78
Yellow	80

_____

6. Ginny rolls two number cubes numbered 1 to 6. Complete the table by determining the theroretical probability of each event.

Event	Probability
Rolling double 3s	
Rolling a sum of 7	
Rolling two even numbers	

7. Harry spins the spinner shown 60 times. How many times can he be expected to get a number less than 3?

_____ times

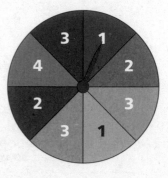

8. A restaurant serves buttermilk, gingerbread, and pecan pancakes with strawberry, banana, or blueberry topping. Each week, the manager randomly selects one pancake type and one topping to be the breakfast special. There is an equal chance that each type and topping is picked. For about how many of the 52 weeks in a year can the restaurant be expected to have banana pecan pancakes as the breakfast special?

Ⓐ 6 weeks   Ⓑ 9 weeks   Ⓒ 12 weeks   Ⓓ 17 weeks

9. Sula designs greeting cards for her friends. Each friend has a 30% chance to get a musical greeting card. Design a simulation that can be used to estimate the probability that a friend who receives 2 greeting cards will receive at least one musical greeting card.

_____

_____

_____

_____

10. A kitten has an equal chance of being male or female. In a litter of 3 kittens, the outcomes {MMM, MMF, MFM, MFF, FMM, FMF, FFM, FFF} are theoretically equally likely. Jaime used random numbers to simulate 400 litters of 3 kittens each. The table shows the result of the simulation. For which type of litter of 3 kittens is the frequency from the simulation less than the expected theoretical frequency?

Simulation Results	
Outcome	Frequency
3 males	63
2 males, 1 female	151
1 male, 2 females	130
3 females	56

Ⓐ 3 male kittens   Ⓑ exactly 2 male kittens

Ⓑ 3 female kittens   Ⓓ exactly 2 female kittens

UNIT 1

MODULE 1, LESSON 1

On Your Own
3. 6 (min); 20 (gal); yes
5. Yes

More Practice/Homework
1. Yes 3. No 5. Yes 7. A
9. $94.20

MODULE 1, LESSON 2

On Your Own
5. yes; $k = 21$ 7. yes; $y = 7x$
9. No 11. $k = 42$; $y = 42x$
13. 100; 300; 2

More Practice/Homework
1. yes; $k = 9$ 3. The table represents a proportional relationship; $k = 24$; $y = 24x$
5. $k = 8$; $y = 8x$ 7. Table 2
9. It takes 24 h to build each chair. 11. A 13. Yes

MODULE 1, LESSON 3

On Your Own
5. 110 beats per min 7A. 12 min
B. 3 mi in 36 min C. Naomi
9. 4:1; No 11. $y = \frac{1}{60}x$; $\frac{5}{12}$ c
13. $8/h 15. $3\frac{1}{3}$ mi/h

More Practice/Homework
1. 3.8 g/cm³ 3. Maria's
5. $2.60 per lb 7. $3\frac{1}{2}$ ft²/h 9. $9/h
11. 17 mi/h 13. 20 min/lb 15. B
17. up to 14 bracelets

MODULE 1, LESSON 4

On Your Own
3A. It takes Yazmin 16 min to jog 1 mi. B. Yes; 16; $y = 16x$
5. Proportional

More Practice/Homework
1A. Yes B. $k = 15$ yd² per gal; $y = 15x$ 5. B 7. $3.50 per sandwich

MODULE 1, LESSON 5

On Your Own
3A. 30 ft³/min B. 1,800 ft³/h
C. $y = 1,800x$; 10,800 ft³ of water D. 15,300 ft³ of water
5A. 384,000 ft/h B. 72.7 mi/h
C. $y = 72.7x$; 218.1 mi

More Practice/Homework
1. 5.7 mi/h 3. 5.5 mi/h
5. 84.48 km 7. $15 9. B 11. >
13. −15, −5, −2, 1, 3, 8 15. 8

MODULE 1, LESSON 6

On Your Own
3B. $\frac{5 \text{ ft}}{1 \text{ in.}}$ C. $y = 5x$ D. 17.5 ft
E. 8 in. 5A. 7.5 feet per unit
B. $y = 7.5x$; about 47 ft

More Practice/Homework
1A. $y = 22.5x$ B. length:18 m; width: 9 m 3. 14.7 in. 5. 10; 18
7.

Hours	Parts
2	40
3	60
5	100
8	160

MODULE 2, LESSON 1

On Your Own
7. 69 students 9. 2.5% increase
11A. 54 feet B. 354 feet C. No
13. 56%; decrease 15. 75%; increase 17. 5%; decrease
19. 50%; increase 21. 146.25 yd to 153.75 yd 23. 14.7 to 15.3
25. 28.8 to 33.2 27. 45.0 to 53.0
29. No 31. 44% increase

More Practice/Homework
1. 30% 3. 217 bacteria
5. 147 orders to 153 orders
7. increase of 87.5% 9. between 150 and 170 successful attempts
11. 7.76; 8.24 13. C 15. 20 in²

MODULE 2, LESSON 2

On Your Own
5. $42 7. $133,860 9. $85
11. $9.74 13. $87.84 15. 150%
17A. 3.4 B. $y = 3.4x$ C. $204
D. $264 E. 70% F. The sale price is 30% less than the retail price. The markdown rate is 30%.
G. $y = 0.7x$ 19. $35 21. $398.75

More Practice/Homework
1. 25% 5. $3.38 7. $352.00
9. C 11. Possible answer:
$p = (1 − 0.18) \times 55$
13. proportional

MODULE 2, LESSON 3

On Your Own
5. $290 7. $33.59 9. $900
11. $24.44 13. $250 15. $32.50
17. $676.18 19. $5.54
21. $14,242.50 23A. $y = 0.062x$;
$41.85 C. $y = 1.15x$; 25.30
25. $y = 1.085x$ 27. $88.42

More Practice/Homework
1. $89.10 3. $16.32 5. 7%
7. $166.07 9. $126.36
11. $256.10 13. $600 15. D
17. 384 students

MODULE 2, LESSON 4

On Your Own
5. $121,000 7. $61,500
9. $141.60 11. $39,600
13. $9,600 15. $17,160 17. $573
19. $4,920 21A. Irma also gets $11 for each delivery.
B. $4,044.80 C. In addition to a different base salary and a different commission rate for groceries, she will earn a commission rate for pet supplies instead of a fixed delivery fee.
D. $3,597.26

More Practice/Homework
1. $6,500 **3.** $64,700 **5.** $1,925
7. $80,425 **9.** A, C, E **11.** $1,215
13. 7.5% **15.** $28.20

MODULE 2, LESSON 5
On Your Own
3. principal: 3,000; interest rate:
0.035; time: 4 years **5A.** $I = 28.6t$
B. $200.20 **C.** 1.75% **7A.** 11 yr
B. $26,000.00 **C.** $314.42; $355.57
9A. $30 **B.** $2,150 **C.** 17 yr
11A. $13,750 **B.** 10 yr

More Practice/Homework
1. $3,955.00 **3.** $15,225 **5.** B
7. 9 years **9.** −1

UNIT 2

MODULE 3, LESSON 1
On Your Own
3. on the 31-yd marker; 6 yards
to the right **5.** lost ground; 4 yd
7.

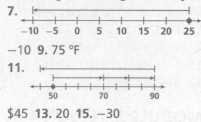

−10 **9.** 75 °F
11.

$45 **13.** 20 **15.** −30

More Practice/Homework
1. $750 **3.** decrease; 10 degrees;
endothermic **5.** No **7.** $47
9. positive **11.** 1:4 **13.** $68.70

MODULE 3, LESSON 2
On Your Own
3.

$4
5.

4
7. 30; (−40); (−20); −40; −40 m
9. agree **11.** 40 °C **13.** −50 **15.** 9
17. 0

More Practice/Homework
1. −4
3.

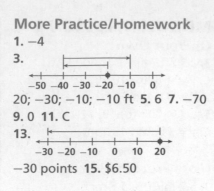

20; −30; −10; −10 ft **5.** 6 **7.** −70
9. 0 **11.** C
13.

−30 points **15.** $6.50

MODULE 3, LESSON 3
On Your Own
5. −5 + 13 + (−5) = 3 **7.** 40 °F
9.

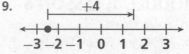

11B. $19.25 **13.** Possible answer:
$-1\frac{1}{4}, \frac{1}{2}$ **15.** Possible answer: −5, 5
17. increase 7 °F

More Practice/Homework
1.

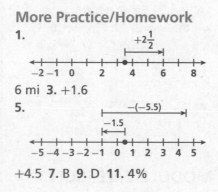

6 mi **3.** +1.6
5.

+4.5 **7.** B **9.** D **11.** 4%

MODULE 4, LESSON 1
On Your Own
3. −10 + (−15); −$25
5. 15 + (−30); −15 pencils
7. −100 + 33; −$67 **9.** −48
11. −26 **13.** −9 **15.** 76 + (−42);
$34 **17.** 10 + (−17); −7 yd
19. −46 **21.** 15 **23.** −14

More Practice/Homework
1A. 230 + (−300) **B.** −70 ft or 70 ft
below **3.** 28 + (−9); $19 profit
5. 15 **7.** −44 **9.** −31 **11.** 33
13. 327 + (−243); 84 car radios
remaining **15.** C **17.** 1:18
19. $535.00

MODULE 4, LESSON 2
On Your Own
5. −15 − 2; −17 °F **7.** 45 − 70;
$25 more **9.** −12 + 10; −2
11. 0 + 13; 13 **13.** −15 + (−12);
−27 **15.** −150 points **17.** 65 −
(−10); $75 **19.** 41 + (−41); 0
21. −13 + 10; −3 **23.** 21 + (−6); 15
25. 0 + 5; 5

More Practice/Homework
1A. 4 − (−2) **B.** 6 points **5.** −2
7. −19 **9.** −108 **11.** 0 **13.** 6
15. 61 **17.** 15 + (−21); −6
19. B **21.** C **23.** 6.8 mi/h
25. increase of 30.8%

MODULE 4, LESSON 3
On Your Own
3A. −56.2 − 27.7; −83.9 strokes
B. Yes **5.** 33.6 + (−5.5);
28.1 points **7.** 15.50 − 5.37;
$10.13 **9.** 6.4 **11.** −9.03
13. $5\frac{37}{40}$ or 5.925 miles **15.** 24.01
17. $-3\frac{1}{4}$ **19.** 22.13

More Practice/Homework
1. $22.11 **3.** $1\frac{2}{3}$ mi **5.** $\frac{5}{12}$ **7.** $-1\frac{3}{4}$
9A. change of −1.7
11. $37.81 **13.** 7.5%

MODULE 4, LESSON 4
On Your Own
3A. 95.25 cm **B.** 10.35 cm more
5. 4.2 °F **7.** −17.05 **9.** −12.89
11. 5.4 **13.** $64.47 **15.** −37.2 ft
17. −3.5 **19.** −6.1 **21.** −2.8
23. −7.7 **25.** $65.77 **27.** 56 in.
29. 5.55 **31.** 17.24 **33.** −9.56
35. −10.78

More Practice/Homework
1. $11\frac{3}{4}$ ft or 11.75 ft
3. Commutative Property of
Addition; Associative Property
of Addition; $\frac{1}{8}$ **5.** −7.7 **7.** −32.95
9. 3.9 **11.** −1.69 **13.** 1.05
15. −9.925 ft, −12.05 ft **17.** C
19. −21.1 °F

MODULE 5, LESSON 1

On Your Own

5. The balance in his checking account decreases by $500.
7. 10; 10 9. negative
11. negative 13. negative
15A.

−2 B. negative

More Practice/Homework

1. Overall, missed landings on aerial cartwheels lowered the scores by 10 points.
3. top: −4; −4, bottom: 3; 8; 8
5. negative 7. disagree
9. A, B, E, F 11. B 13. $188.50

MODULE 5, LESSON 2

On Your Own

7. positive 9. Assoc. Prop. of Mult.; 7 11. 120 13. −9 15. 7
17. $-\frac{2}{15}$

More Practice/Homework

1A. 3 B. −72; At the end of two days, the temperature in the freezer has decreased by 72 °F.
3. −900 5. $-\frac{3}{5}$ 7. 4
9. B 11. products in order: $\frac{1}{3}$, $-\frac{1}{3}$, $\frac{2}{3}$, $\frac{1}{3}$ 13. $1,649.60

MODULE 5, LESSON 3

On Your Own

5. −2; The temperature fell by 2 °F every hour.
7A.

Fraction	Decimal
$\frac{1}{8}$	0.125
$\frac{2}{8}$	0.250
$\frac{3}{8}$	0.375

Possible answer: Each decimal is 0.125 more than the previous decimal. B. yes 9. −8.5; Each charge decreased the value of the gift card by $8.50. 11. 0.625
13. 0.777…, or $0.\overline{7}$
15. 10.3636…, or $10.\overline{36}$
17. Possible answer: $\frac{3}{-5}$, $-\left(\frac{3}{5}\right)$

19. Possible answer: $-7\frac{3}{5} =$ $-\frac{38}{5} = \frac{-38}{5}$, −38 and 5 are integers.
21. 13 23. −7.5

More Practice/Homework

1A. 0.5625 pound B. $13.50
3. 4.875 5. −6 7. −5.4
9A.

Fraction	Decimal
$\frac{1}{9}$	0.111…
$\frac{2}{9}$	0.222…
$\frac{3}{9}$	0.333…

Possible answer: Each decimal is 0.111… more than the previous decimal. B. yes 11. The values, in order, are −8, 8, 6, and −6.
13. −11 + (−13) = −24; The price decreased by $24 over the two years.

MODULE 5, LESSON 4

On Your Own

3A. −3.76 °F; When elevation increases by 0.2 mile, temperature drops about 3.76 °F.
B. 3.76 °F; When elevation decreases by 0.2 mile, temperature increases about 3.76 °F. C. The temperature changes are opposites. 5. $-12\frac{1}{2}$ feet per minute 7. 5 containers; Possible answer: The quotient is $5\frac{1}{4}$ containers. So he can fill 5 whole containers and he'll have $\frac{1}{4} \times \frac{2}{3} = \frac{1}{6}$ cup of blueberries left over.

9. $\frac{-\frac{2}{4}}{-\frac{3}{4}}$, or $\frac{-\frac{1}{2}}{-\frac{3}{4}}$; $\frac{-\frac{1}{2}}{-\frac{3}{4}} = \frac{-1}{2} \div \frac{-3}{4} =$ $\frac{-1}{2} \times \frac{4}{-3} = \frac{2}{3}$, and 2 and 3 are integers. 11. $\frac{35}{36}$ 13. −0.7
15. −0.8

More Practice/Homework

1. −20 ft 3A. 4(3)(−12.50) = −150; −$150 B. 1 and 7, 2 and 6, 3 and 5, 4 and 4, 5 and 3, 6 and 2, 7 and 1 C. 9; Possible answer: Tanisha was dividing the total charge on her account by the charge per class. 5. $\frac{3}{2}$, or $1\frac{1}{2}$

7. −20 9. B
11.

(−1.4) + (−1.4) + (−1.4) + (−1.4) + (−1.4) = −7

MODULE 6, LESSON 1

On Your Own

5A. $\frac{1}{3}(18) + (18) + \left[3 + \frac{18}{2}\right]$ B. 36
7. 16 · 16; 256 9. $\frac{1}{2} - \frac{3}{4}$; $-2\frac{1}{2}$ 11. 8

More Practice/Homework

1. 60 − 6 − 18 − [4 · (3 + 6)]; 0
3. 15.6 5. $\left(-\frac{3}{2} + 2\frac{1}{8} - \frac{5}{8}\right)$; 0
7. C 9. 10 students 11. 8
13. no; $20

MODULE 6, LESSON 2

On Your Own

3A. 15 vans B. overestimate; overestimate, so there are enough vans. 5A. Possible answer: about $1\frac{1}{2}$ mi B. exact
7. Possible answer: $35.00; underestimate

More Practice/Homework

1. Possible answer: $3,300; underestimate 3. Possible answer: 24; underestimate 5. Possible answer: 200; yes 9. 39 doses
11. Commutative Property of Multiplication

MODULE 6, LESSON 3

On Your Own

3A. 1.47 h 5. 4 batches
7A. 6 batches B. $1.44/batch
9. 4%

More Practice/Homework

1A. 10 cakes B. $0.88 per cake
3A. 23.9 min 5. C 7. C
9. Nicolas; 7 ft 11. $y = 23x$

UNIT 3

MODULE 7, LESSON 1
On Your Own
3. $40h + 15h + 50$ and $55h + 50$
5. $3f + 0.25f$ and $3.25f$ 7. no; $1.8m$

More Practice/Homework
1. Possible answer: $62h + 15h + 79$ and $77h + 79$ 3. Possible answer: $2L + 0.7L$ and $2.7L$
5. Possible answer: $8w + 10w + 50$
7. yes 9. yes 11. $4b + 0.8b$ and $4.8b$ 13. B, C 15. 1 and 3

MODULE 7, LESSON 2
On Your Own
5A. $10(5 - 1\frac{1}{3}t)$ B. $10 \cdot 5 - 10 \cdot 1\frac{1}{3}t$; $50 - 13\frac{1}{3}t$ 7. $60 + 20x$ 9. $3(x + 5)$
11. $8t - 3$ 13. $9(3y) - (9)(5)$; $27y - 45$ 15A. $28.8t + 17.7$
B. Commutative and Associative Properties of Addition
17. $3y - 44$ 19. $42b + 28$
21. $6g + 9$; $3(2g + 3)$

More Practice/Homework
1. $9\frac{3}{4}t - 1$ 3. $6y - 5$ 5. $13t + 5$
7. $-x - 8$ 9. $r - 1$ 11. $42y - 48$
13. $-2\frac{1}{6}x - 35$ 15. C 17. positive

MODULE 7, LESSON 3
On Your Own
3. Possible answer: $2x + 48 = 120$
5. Possible answer: $2(x + 2\frac{1}{2}) = 6\frac{1}{3}$
7. Possible answer: $0.70(x + 35) = \$44.80$

More Practice/Homework
1. Possible answer: $2x + 40.6 = 72.2$ 3. Possible answer: $0.85x + 2.95 = \$8.05$ 5. Possible answer: $0.20(x + 25) = 13$

7. Possible answer: $19.50(x + 3) = 146.25$ 9. Possible answer: $0.10x + 2 = 2.8$ 11. A 13. \$26.39

MODULE 7, LESSON 4
On Your Own
5A. $(43 - 7) \div 2 = 36 \div 2 = 18$ memberships B. $2m + 7 = 43$; $m = 18$ memberships C. Both use subtraction and then division. 7. $-3x + 52 = 37$; 5 misses 9. $a = -36$ 11. $f = 10$
13. $p = -14$ 15. $k = 42$
17. $17.50h + 200 = 637.50$; 25 hours 19. $n = -9$
21. $h = -12$ 23. $n = -69\frac{1}{3}$
25. $y = -\frac{7}{15}$

More Practice/Homework
1. $0.50b + 4.50 = 22$; 35 bulbs
3. $2(x + 1\frac{1}{2}) = 4\frac{1}{2}$; $\frac{3}{4}$ c nuts
5. $z = 3$ 7. $g = 8$ 11. B 13. D
15. 40 miles per hour

MODULE 7, LESSON 5
On Your Own
3A. $3x + 10 + 12x + 35 = 180$
B. $x = 9$ C. $37°$ 5. $8x + 12 + \frac{1}{2}(8x + 12) = 90$; $x = 6$ 7. They are vertical angles, so their measures are equal. 9A. $122°$
B. adjacent angles 11. $3x + 8 + x + 4 = 180$ 15. $x = 10$; $43°$ and $47°$ 17. $x = 15$; $97°$ and $83°$
19. $x = 16$; $37°$ and $53°$

More Practice/Homework
1. $45°$ 3A. $5x + 5 = 30$; $x = 5$
B. $150°$ 5. $75°$ 7. C 9. false
11. 4 apples

MODULE 8, LESSON 1
On Your Own
5. $4x \leq 24$; $x \leq 6$ ft 7. $x \geq 3$

9. $x > -10$

11. $4x \leq 24$; $x \leq 6$ 13. No

15. $x > 11.2$

17. $x < -3\frac{3}{5}$

More Practice/Homework
1A. $12x > 72$; $x > 6$ ft
B. $12x \leq 156$; $x \leq 13$ ft C. Longer than 6 ft and no longer than 13 ft
3. $-3t > -24$; $t < 8$ min
5. B 7. at least; 8 9. $x = 65°$

MODULE 8, LESSON 2
On Your Own
7. not a solution 9. solution
11. solution 13. solution
15. $22 - 0.25w < 18$
17. $2x + 4 \leq 12$ 19. $25x + 5 \geq 100$

More Practice/Homework
1. $5t + 40 \geq 500$ 3. Possible answer: $7x + 5 > 50$ 5. 10 less than a third of a number is greater than 22. 7. $75b + 800 \leq 1,200$ 9. $4n - 4 > 10$, 4 less than 4 times a number is greater than 10.; $4n + 4 < 10$, The sum of 4 and 4 times a number is less than 10.; $4n > 10$, 4 times a number is greater than 10.; $4n - 4 \geq 10$, 4 less than 4 times a number is 10 or more.; $4n + 4 \geq 10$, The sum of 4 and 4 times a number is at least 10.; $4n - 4 \leq 10$, 4 less than 4 times a number is no more than 10.
11. $d - 31 \geq 15$; $d \geq 46$

MODULE 8, LESSON 3
On Your Own
3A. $2,100 - 25d < 1,500$; $d > 24$
B.

C. No, only whole numbers. The number of tables will be less than 1,500 after more than 24 days.

5. $x > 13$

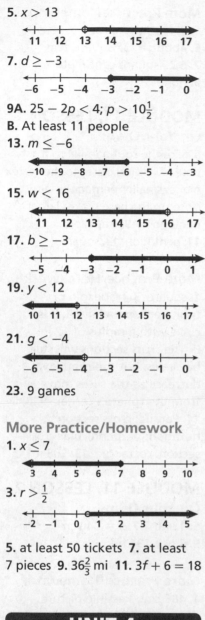

7. $d \geq -3$

9A. $25 - 2p < 4$; $p > 10\frac{1}{2}$
B. At least 11 people

13. $m \leq -6$

15. $w < 16$

17. $b \geq -3$

19. $y < 12$

21. $g < -4$

23. 9 games

More Practice/Homework
1. $x \leq 7$

3. $r > \frac{1}{2}$

5. at least 50 tickets **7.** at least
7 pieces **9.** $36\frac{2}{3}$ mi **11.** $3f + 6 = 18$

UNIT 4

MODULE 9, LESSON 1
On Your Own
5. The quadrilateral is a
parallelogram. Possible answer:

7. Possible answer:

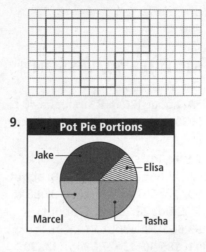

9.

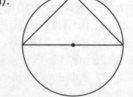

Pot Pie Portions
Jake
Elisa
Marcel
Tasha

More Practice/Homework
1. Possible answer:

3. Possible answer shown
(reduced):

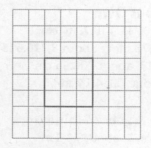

5A. The quadrilateral is a square.
Possible answer:

5B. 1.5 units **7.** $2x + x = 90$;
$x = 30$; Angle 1 measures 30°
and Angle 2 measures 60°.

MODULE 9, LESSON 2
On Your Own
3. $12 + 12 < 26$, so the pieces
will not make a triangle.
5. $5 + 5 = 10$, so these pieces

will not make a triangle. **7.** an
infinite number of different
quadrilaterals **9.** no **11.** 7 m <
length < 17 m **13.** 8 mi <
length < 54 mi **15.** $4 + 5 < 10$,
so these logs will not make a
triangle. **17.** no **19.** yes
21. 5 in. < length < 15 in.
23. 12 m < length < 30 m

More Practice/Homework
1. $6 + 8 > 13$, so these pieces will
make a triangle. **3.** One possible
side length is 5 ft. **5.** no **7.** yes
9. 1 ft < length < 9 ft **11.** A
13. B, C, E **15.** $2x + 45 \leq 120$; $x \leq$
37.50; Kevin can spend at most
$37.50 on each controller.

MODULE 9, LESSON 3
On Your Own
3A.

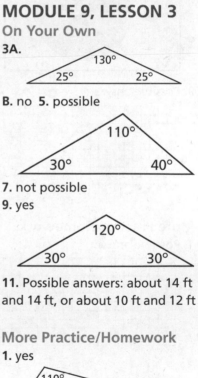

B. no **5.** possible

7. not possible
9. yes

11. Possible answers: about 14 ft
and 14 ft, or about 10 ft and 12 ft

More Practice/Homework
1. yes

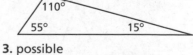

3. possible

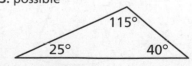

5. not possible

Selected Answers

7. They may or may not be the same. **9.** B, C, E **11.** 7 raffle tickets

MODULE 9, LESSON 4
On Your Own
3. a diameter of the circle
5.

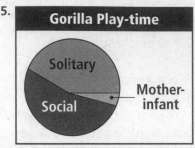

Gorilla Play-time

Solitary

Social

Mother-infant

7.

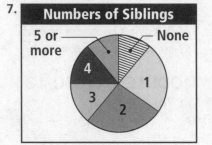

Numbers of Siblings

5 or more

None

4

1

3

2

9. Possible answer:

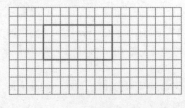

More Practice/Homework
1. Possible answer:

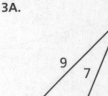

3A.

B

9

7

7

45°

A   C₁   C₂

B. 2 5. one; none; many; one; one; none **7.** B **9.** $x = 13$; 57° and 33°

MODULE 10, LESSON 1
On Your Own
3A. about 176 ft **B.** about 2,640 ft
5. 300 calories **7.** about 131.88 cm

More Practice/Homework
1A. about $\frac{55}{14}$ ft or 3.9 ft **B.** about $997\frac{6}{7}$ or 997.9 ft **3.** 12 ft; 37.68 ft
5. about 28.26 cm **7.** about 59.66 ft **9.** about 219.8 in.
11. $85.50 **13.** 27.63 in. **15.** 90°

MODULE 10, LESSON 2
On Your Own
3. 176.63 in² **5.** 50.24 in²
7. disagree; 4 times as large
9. 254.34 m² **11.** about $28\frac{2}{7}$ yd²
13. 379.94 ft² **15.** 100 discs
17. 1,387.26 mm² **19.** 153.86 in²

More Practice/Homework
1. 200.96 ft² **3.** 153.86 in²
5. 907.46 cm² **7.** 314 cm² **9.** 314 in²
11. 28.26 mi² **13.** 132.665 cm²
15. C **17.** 3,419.46 mm²
19. 9.42 ft

MODULE 10, LESSON 3
On Your Own
5. about 31.4 ft **7.** 84 cm²
11. 6,370 mm²; about 3,316.625 mm² **13.** about 200.96 cm²
15. about 1,384.74 cm²

More Practice/Homework
1. 40 in² **5.** about 78.5 in²
7. about 530.66 m²
9. rectangle **11.** about 153.86 m²

MODULE 10, LESSON 4
On Your Own
3. 12 square units **5.** $375.30
7. 8 square units
9. 22 square inches

More Practice/Homework
1. 2,100 square feet **3.** 39 cm²
5. about 1,757 square feet
7. 6.25 square centimeters
9. none

MODULE 11, LESSON 1
On Your Own
5. Slice the roof parallel to the base. **7.** Slicing closer to the vertex makes smaller pentagons, and closer to the base makes larger pentagons. **9.** trapezoid
11. pentagon **13.** square

More Practice/Homework
1. square **3.** trapezoid or triangle **5.** parallel **7A.** It is a circle with a radius of 12 in.
B. The cross sections will still be circles, but their radii will decrease as the slices move away from the sphere's center. **9.** B, D
11. Parallel cross section: hexagon; perpendicular cross section: rectangle **13.** 108 in²

MODULE 11, LESSON 2
On Your Own
5. 136 in² **7.** $S = 640$ cm²
9. $S \approx 2,194$ in²

More Practice/Homework
1. 486 cm²; Possible picture:

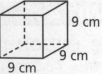

9 cm

9 cm

9 cm

3. 1,761 ft²
5. $S = 184$ in² **7.** $S = 672$ cm²
9. C **11.** 189.9 mm² **13.** 21 ft²

MODULE 11, LESSON 3
On Your Own
3. 8,000 in³ **5.** 3 m **7.** 645 mm³

More Practice/Homework
1. 5,625 ft³ **5.** 3,320 ft³ **7.** 864 in³ more **9.** $V = Bh$; 1,260 = 28h; $h = 45$ m **11.** rectangle **13.** about 818.8 mm²

MODULE 11, LESSON 4
On Your Own
3A. 11 in. **B.** 257.4 in³ **5A.** 2 ft
B. 1,024 ft³ **7.** 48 cm² **9A.** 10 cm
B. Only one base should be included. **C.** 227.5 cm²
11. 2,560 in³ **13A.** 10 in.
B. 600 in² **15.** 468 cm²

More Practice/Homework
1A. $\frac{3}{4}$ ft **B.** 11.475 ft²
3. 2,661.12 cm³ **5.** 360 in³
7. 312 in² **9.** none **11.** 150.72 in.

UNIT 5

MODULE 12, LESSON 1
On Your Own
5. yes; yes **7A.** all students in Cameron's school **B.** every tenth student that walks into school **C.** yes **D.** yes

More Practice/Homework
1. Population: 10,000 members of the fan club; Sample: the 250 members chosen at random
3. The response is overwhelmingly in support of making the video.
5. The larger sample **7.** does not
9. Julia's **11.** 200.96 cm²

MODULE 12, LESSON 2
On Your Own
3. at least **5.** yes **7.** 48 female athletes **9.** 90 letters **11.** 50
13. 25 **15.** 3,000 cars

More Practice/Homework
1. 10th **3.** 140 tenth graders
5. 10th grade **7.** 270 students

9. 12 laptop computers
11. 64 steps per minute

MODULE 12, LESSON 3
On Your Own
3A. Possible answers: From left to right, top: 14, 11, 11, 18, 12, 13, 11, 15, 14, 12; middle: 6, 9, 9, 2, 8, 7, 9, 5, 6, 8; bottom: 70%, 55%, 55%, 90%, 60%, 65%, 55%, 75%, 70%, 60%
B.

Sample Ratios of Numbers 1–65

C. slightly above
D. Most sample ratios are close to the population ratio.

More Practice/Homework
1. above; below **3.** D **5.** The sample ratio is slightly above the population ratio. **7.** 7 bags

MODULE 13, LESSON 1
On Your Own
5A. $37,500; clustered from $30,000 to $40,000 **B.** $50,000
C. Most earn salaries from $30,000 to $40,000.

More Practice/Homework
1. Tallahassee: 6°F, Key West: 4°F
3. Tallahassee: 87°F, Key West: 85°F **5.** Tallahassee: 87°F, Key West: 85°F **7.** Possible answer: The temperatures in Key West were more consistent and cooler than those in Tallahassee. Although Tallahassee is farther north, it got hotter in May than Key West. **9.** B **11.** Possible answer: HS students have more variation in the number of accounts than do MS students.
13. 136 in²

MODULE 13, LESSON 2
On Your Own
3A. Possible answer: On both teams, 25% of the players are ages 21–23, and 75% or more of the players are under 29 years.
B. IQR; Possible answer: Range is not an appropriate measure of spread, because this data set is likely to contain outliers. The interquartile range for Team A is 2 years, and the IQR for Team B is 5 years. Team B has a greater variability in players' ages.
C.

	Team A	Team B
Minimum	21	21
Lower quartile	23	23
Median	24	25
Upper quartile	25	28
Maximum	32	38

D. The centers are similar.
F. Highest 50%

More Practice/Homework
1B. Possible answer: Median A < Median B; Store B prices vary more, but both stores have outlier high prices. **C.** Possible answer: The interquartile range for Store B is greater than the interquartile range for Store A. Both box plots have long right whiskers, so there may be high outliers at both stores. **D.** 75% of the prices in the sample from Store B ≤ $1,000, while all prices in the sample from Store A ≤ $1,000. **E.** Possible answer: For Store A, the spread of the upper half of the data is 3 times the spread of the lower half. For Store B, the spread of the upper half of the data is a little less than $1\frac{1}{2}$ times the spread of the lower half. **3.** center; spread

5. Possible answer: The medians are close, but Moesha's median is less. Justin's times tend to be more varied. **7.** 42 cm³

MODULE 13, LESSON 3
On Your Own
3A. 14.7 h; 16.5 h **B.** Cross the Ocean **C.** 1h; 3h **5.** 1; some overlap **7.** 3; little or no overlap **9A.** Group A: 2, 1; Group B: 2.5, 1.25

More Practice/Homework
1A. 32; 39.4 **B.** 2 in.; 2.2 in. **C.** yes **3.** C **5.** The median temperature in Colorado Springs is 2 °F higher. **7.** $6\frac{7}{8}$ c

UNIT 6

MODULE 14, LESSON 1
On Your Own
3. 15 trials; opening to an odd page, opening to an even page **5.** less **7.** likely, a number greater than $\frac{1}{2}$ and less than 1

More Practice/Homework
1. impossible **5.** Possible answer: {heads, tails} or {heads, tails, lands on side} **11.** a number greater than 0 and less than $\frac{1}{2}$ **13.** D **15.** 12 in.

MODULE 14, LESSON 2
On Your Own
3A. Yes **B.** The probabilities, in order, are $\frac{2}{15}$, $\frac{11}{60}$, $\frac{1}{6}$, $\frac{7}{60}$, $\frac{11}{60}$, and $\frac{13}{60}$. **5.** Possible answer: Use random integers 1–10, where 1–6 represent completed passes. Perform 40 trials. **7A.** $P(A) = \frac{7}{32}$; $P(B) = \frac{3}{8}$; $P(C) = \frac{7}{32}$; $P(D) = \frac{3}{16}$ **B.** $\frac{13}{16}$ **C.** The spinner is somehow biased in favor of the section labeled B.

More Practice/Homework
1. The probabilities, in order, are $\frac{19}{80}$, $\frac{17}{80}$, $\frac{23}{80}$, and $\frac{21}{80}$. **3.** between: $\frac{11}{24}$; after: $\frac{7}{12}$ **5.** $\frac{11}{37}$ **7.** $\frac{3}{20}$ **9.** 20 stamps

MODULE 14, LESSON 3
On Your Own
3A. 2 by 3 or 3 by 2 **B.** 6 possible outcomes **5.** No **7.** $\frac{1}{11}$, $\frac{10}{11}$ **9.** $\frac{8}{55}$, $\frac{47}{55}$ **11.** Possible answer: Random number generator, 1-2 for red, 3-4 for blue, 5-6 for yellow; Random number generator, 1-2 for white trim, 3-4 for gray trim; 5-6 for black trim

More Practice/Homework
1A. 1H, 1T, 2H, 2T, 3H, 3T, 4H, 4T, 5H, 5T, 6H, 6T **3A.** $\frac{4}{25}$ **B.** $\frac{21}{25}$ **5.** A, B **7.** Possible answer: Rolling a 1, 2, or 3 represents rain. **9.** The graph is a line that passes through the origin and has a positive or negative slope.

MODULE 14, LESSON 4
On Your Own
5A. $\frac{5}{25} = \frac{x}{400}$; about 80 students **B.** about 320 students **7A.** $\frac{55}{100} = \frac{x}{700}$; 0.55(700) **B.** About 385 students **9.** 630 people **11.** 1,890 people **13.** 45 undeliverable messages **15.** 101 people **17.** About 10 more

More Practice/Homework
1. 0.38(350); 133 votes **3.** $\frac{5}{100} = \frac{x}{460}$; 23 home runs **5.** $\frac{45}{100} = \frac{x}{1,200}$; $x = 540$ people **7A.** $\frac{12}{100} = \frac{x}{2,000}$; $x = 240$ h **B.** 0.09(2,000); 180 h **9.** D **11.** $100 + 5w \geq 250$; $w \geq 30$; at least 30 weeks

MODULE 15, LESSON 1
On Your Own
3. Pile 2 **5.** $\frac{1}{8}$ **7.** $\frac{3}{8}$ **9.** 35% or $\frac{7}{20}$ **11.** landing on 3 **13.** $\frac{3}{5}$, 0.6, 60%

More Practice/Homework
1. $\frac{1}{2}$ **3.** $\frac{1}{2}$ **5.** The theoretical probability of selecting a black bead is $\frac{13}{52}$ or $\frac{1}{4}$. The experimental probability is $\frac{1}{5}$. **7.** B **9.** The theoretical probability is greater. **11.** 36

MODULE 15, LESSON 2
On Your Own
3A. From left to right, top: 2, 3, 4; middle: 3, 4, 5; bottom: 4, 5, 6 **B.** $\frac{2}{9}$ **C.** rolling a sum of 5 **D.** Possible answer: rolling a sum of 2 **E.** Possible answer: rolling a sum of 4 **F.** $\frac{1}{3}$, 0.33, 33% **G.** $\frac{1}{9}$, 0.11, 11% **H.** $\frac{9}{9}$, 1.0, 100% **I.** $\frac{0}{9}$, 0.0, 0% **5A.** 1, 1; 1, 2; 1, 3; 1, 4; 1, 5; 1, 6; 2, 1; 2, 2; 2, 3; 2, 4; 2, 5; 2, 6; 3, 1; 3, 2; 3, 3; 3, 4; 3, 5; 3, 6 **B.** $\frac{3}{18}$ or $\frac{1}{6}$ **C.** $\frac{2}{18}$ or $\frac{1}{9}$ **D.** The probability of getting a sum of 5 is greater.

More Practice/Homework
1A.

+	1	2	3	4	5
1	2	3	4	5	6
2	3	4	5	6	7
3	4	5	6	7	8

B. $\frac{2}{15}$ **C.** Possible answer: drawing a sum of 6 **3.** 48 **5.** P(sum of 5) is $\frac{1}{9}$, P(sum less than 4) is $\frac{1}{12}$, P(sum of 7) is $\frac{1}{6}$, P(sum greater than 8) is $\frac{5}{18}$. **7.** $\frac{4}{9}$

MODULE 15, LESSON 3
On Your Own
3. not likely **5.** $\frac{2}{8} = \frac{x}{400}$; about 100 times **7.** $\frac{3}{8} \times 400$; about 150 times **9.** $\frac{2}{4} \times 300$;

about 150 times **11.** $\frac{1}{6} = \frac{x}{240}$; 40 times **13.** $\frac{1}{4} = \frac{x}{900}$; about 225 times **15.** $\frac{1}{6} \times 900$; about 150 times **17.** not likely **19.** 25% × 3,000; about 750 times **21.** about 1,080 times

More Practice/Homework
1. yes **3.** $\frac{3}{15} = \frac{x}{500}$; about 100 times **5.** 20% × 500 = 100; about 100 times **7.** $\frac{35}{40} \times 800$; about 700 times **9.** sum of 5: about 200 times; sum less than 7: about 750 times; sum of 13: about 50 times; sum greater than 10: about 300 times; sum of 8 or 9: about 550 times **11.** landing on 5

MODULE 15, LESSON 4
On Your Own
5. 20% **7.** Possible answer: Suppose a store gives out a free sticker to 75% of its customers. Keith can use the spinner to simulate whether a customer gets a sticker (A, B, or C) or does not get a sticker (D). **9.** yes

More Practice/Homework
1. Chairs Checked: 3; 2; 2; 4; 2; 3; 1; 4; 2; 6; experimental probability: 20% **3.** 20% **5.** 20% **7.** $\frac{1}{2} \times 50$; 25 times

Interactive Glossary

As you learn about each new term, add notes, drawings, or sentences in the space next to the definition. Doing so will help you remember what each term means.

Pronunciation Key

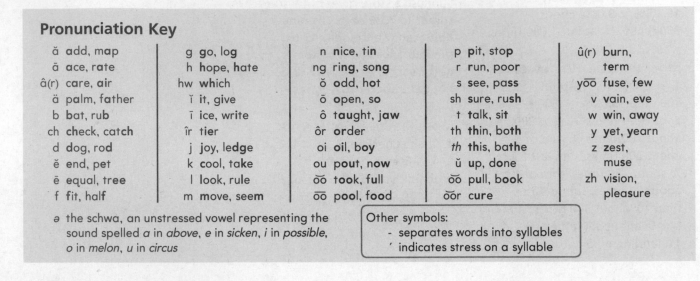

ă add, map
ā ace, rate
â(r) care, air
ä palm, father
b bat, rub
ch check, catch
d dog, rod
ĕ end, pet
ē equal, tree
f fit, half

g go, log
h hope, hate
hw which
ĭ it, give
ī ice, write
îr tier
j joy, ledge
k cool, take
l look, rule
m move, seem

n nice, tin
ng ring, song
ŏ odd, hot
ō open, so
ô taught, jaw
ôr order
oi oil, boy
ou pout, now
o͝o took, full
o͞o pool, food

p pit, stop
r run, poor
s see, pass
sh sure, rush
t talk, sit
th thin, both
th this, bathe
ŭ up, done
o͝o pull, book
o͝or cure

û(r) burn, term
yo͞o fuse, few
v vain, eve
w win, away
y yet, yearn
z zest, muse
zh vision, pleasure

ə the schwa, an unstressed vowel representing the sound spelled *a* in *above*, *e* in *sicken*, *i* in *possible*, *o* in *melon*, *u* in *circus*

Other symbols:
- separates words into syllables
′ indicates stress on a syllable

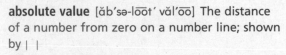
A

My Vocabulary Summary

absolute value [ăb′sə-lo͞ot′ văl′o͞o] The distance of a number from zero on a number line; shown by | |

valor absoluto Distancia a la que está un número de 0 en una recta numérica. El símbolo del valor absoluto es | |

accuracy [ăk′yər-ə-sē] The closeness of a given measurement or value to the actual measurement or value

exactitud Cercanía de una medida o un valor a la medida o el valor real

acute angle [ə-kyo͞ot′ ăng′gəl] An angle that measures greater than 0° and less than 90°

ángulo agudo Ángulo que mide más de 0° y menos de 90°

My Vocabulary Summary

acute triangle [ə-kyo͞ot′ trī′ăng′gəl] A triangle with all angles measuring less than 90°

triángulo acutángulo Triángulo en el que todos los ángulos miden menos de 90°

addend [ăd′ĕnd′] A number added to one or more other numbers to form a sum

sumando Número que se suma a uno o más números para formar una suma

Addition Property of Equality [ə-dĭsh′ən prŏp′ər-tē ŭv ĭ-kwŏl′ĭ-tē] The property that states that if you add the same number to both sides of an equation, the new equation will have the same solution

Propiedad de igualdad de la suma Propiedad que establece que puedes sumar el mismo número a ambos lados de una ecuación y la nueva ecuación tendrá la misma solución

Addition Property of Opposites [ə-dĭsh′ən prŏp′ər-tē ŭv ŏp′ə-zĭt] The property that states that the sum of a number and its opposite equals zero

Propiedad de la Suma de los Opuestos Propiedad que establece que la suma de un número y su opuesto es cero

additive inverse [ăd′ĭ-tĭv ĭn-vûrs′] The opposite of a number, such that the sum of the number and its additive inverse is 0

inverso aditivo El opuesto de un número, tal que la suma del número y su inverso aditivo es 0

Interactive Glossary

adjacent angles [ə-jā′sənt ăng′gəls] Two angles in the same plane with a common vertex and a common side but no common interior points

ángulos adyacentes Dos ángulos en el mismo plano con el vértice y un lado común, pero sin puntos internos comunes

algebraic expression [ăl′jə-brā′ĭk ĭk-sprĕsh′ən] An expression that contains at least one variable

expresión algebraica Expresión que contiene al menos una variable

algebraic inequality [ăl′jə-brā′ĭk ĭn′ĭ-kwŏl′ĭ-tē] An inequality that contains at least one variable

desigualdad algebraica Desigualdad que contiene al menos una variable

arc [ärk] A part of a circle named by its endpoints

arco Parte de un círculo que se nombra por sus extremos

area [âr′e-ə] The number of square units needed to cover a given surface

área El número de unidades cuadradas que se necesitan para cubrir una superficie dada

Associative Property of Addition [ə-sō′shə-tĭv prŏp′ər-tē ŭv ə-dĭsh′ən] The property that states that for all real numbers *a*, *b*, and *c*, the sum is always the same, regardless of their grouping

Propiedad asociativa de la suma Propiedad que establece que para todos los números reales *a*, *b* y *c*, la suma siempre es la misma sin importar cómo se agrupen

Associative Property of Multiplication [ə-sō′shə-tĭv prŏp′ər-tē ŭv mŭl′tə-plĭ-kā′shən] The property that states that for all real numbers *a*, *b*, and *c*, their product is always the same, regardless of their grouping

Propiedad asociativa de la multiplicación Propiedad que para todos los números reales *a*, *b* y *c*, el producto siempre es el mismo sin importar cómo se agrupen

asymmetry [ă-sĭm′ĭ-trē] Not identical on either side of a central line; not symmetrical

asimetría Ocurre cuando dos lados separados por una línea central no son idénticos; falta de simetría

axes [ăk′sēz′] The two perpendicular lines of a coordinate plane that intersect at the origin

ejes Las dos rectas numéricas perpendiculares del plano cartesiano que se intersecan en el origen

Interactive Glossary

B

base (**of a three-dimensional figure**) [bās (ŭv ā thrē-dǐ-měn′shə-nəl fǐg′yər)] A face of a three-dimensional figure by which the figure is measured or classified

base (**de una figura tridimensional**) Cara de una figura tridimensional a partir de la cual se mide o se clasifica la figura

bias [bī′əs] When a sample does not accurately represent the population

sesgada Cuando una muestra no representa precisamente la población

bisect [bī′sěkt′] To divide into two congruent parts

trazar una bisectriz Dividir en dos partes congruentes

box-and-whisker plot [bŏks-ănd-wǐs′kər plot] A graph that shows how data are distributed by using the median, quartiles, least value, and greatest value; also called a box plot

gráfica de mediana y rango Gráfica que muestra los valores máximo y mínimo, los cuartiles superior e inferior, así como la mediana de los datos

C

capacity [kə-păs′ĭ-tē] The amount a container can hold when filled

capacidad Cantidad que cabe en un recipiente cuando se llena

Celsius [sĕl'sē-əs] A metric scale for measuring temperature in which 0 °C is the freezing point of water and 100 °C is the boiling point of water; also called *centigrade*

Celsius Escala métrica para medir la temperatura, en la que 0 °C es el punto de congelación del agua y 100 °C es el punto de ebullición. También se llama *centígrado*

---

circle graph [sûr'kəl grăf] A graph that uses sectors of a circle to compare parts to the whole and parts to other parts

gráfica circular Gráfica que usa secciones de un círculo para comparar partes con el todo y con otras partes

---

circumference [sər-kŭm'fər-əns] The distance around a circle

circunferencia Distancia alrededor de un círculo

---

clockwise [klŏk'wīz'] A circular movement in the direction of the typical forward movement of the hands of a clock

en el sentido de las manecillas del reloj Movimiento circular en la dirección típica de las manecillas de un reloj

---

coefficient [kō'ə-fĭsh'ənt] The number that is multiplied by the variable in an algebraic expression

coeficiente Número que se multiplica por la variable en una expresión algebraica

Interactive Glossary

commission [kə-mĭsh'ən] A fee paid to a person for making a sale

comisión Pago que recibe una persona por realizar una venta

commission rate [kə-mĭsh'ən rāt] The fee paid to a person who makes a sale expressed as a percent of the selling price

tasa de comisión Pago que recibe una persona por hacer una venta, expresado como un porcentaje del precio de venta

common denominator [kŏm'ən dĭ-nŏm'ə-nā'tər] A denominator that is the same in two or more fractions

denominador común Denominador que es común a dos o más fracciones

Commutative Property of Addition [kŏm'yə-tā'tĭv prŏp'ər-tē ŭv ə-dĭsh'ən] The property that states that two or more numbers can be added in any order without changing the sum

Propiedad conmutativa de la suma Propiedad que establece que sumar dos o más números en cualquier orden no altera la suma

Commutative Property of Multiplication [kŏm'yə-tā'tĭv prŏp'ər-tē ŭv mŭl'tə-plĭ-kā'shən] The property that states that two or more numbers can be multiplied in any order without changing the product

Propiedad conmutativa de la multiplicación Propiedad que establece que multiplicar dos o más números en cualquier orden no altera el producto

compatible number [kəm-păt′ə-bəl nŭm′bər]
Numbers that are close to the given numbers
that make estimation or mental calculation
easier.

números compatibles Números que están cerca
de los números dados y hacen más fácil la
estimación o el cálculo mental.

complement of an event [kŏm′plə-mənt ŭv ən
ĭ-věnt′] The set of all outcomes in the sample
space that are *not* included in the event

complemento de un evento Conjunto de todos
los resultados del espacio muestral que *no* están
incluidos en el evento

complementary angles [kŏm′plə-měn′tə-rē
ăng′gəls] Two angles whose measures add to 90°

ángulos complementarios Dos ángulos cuyas
medidas suman 90°

complex fraction [kəm-plĕks′ frăk′shən] A fraction
that contains one or more fractions in the
numerator, the denominator, or both

fracción compleja Fracción que contiene
una o más fracciones en el numerador, en el
denominador, o en ambos

composite figure [kəm-pŏz′ĭt fĭg′yər] A figure
made up of simple geometric shapes

figura compuesta Figura formada por figuras
geométricas simples

composite number [kəm-pŏz′ĭt nŭm′bər] A
number greater than 1 that has more than two
whole-number factors

número compuesto Número mayor que 1 que
tiene más de dos factores que son números
cabales

Interactive Glossary

compound event [kŏm-pound′ ĭ-věnt′] An event made up of two or more simple events

suceso compuesto Suceso que consista de dos o más sucesos simples

---

compound inequality [kŏm-pound′ ĭn′ĭ-kwŏl′ĭ-tē] A combination of more than one inequality

desigualdad compuesta Combinación de dos o más desigualdades

---

cone [kōn] A three-dimensional figure with one vertex and one circular base

cono Figura tridimensional con un vértice y una base circular

---

congruent [kŏng′grōō-ənt] Having the same size and shape; the symbol for congruent is ≅

congruentes Que tiene el mismo tamaño y la misma forma, expresado por ≅

---

constant of proportionality [kŏn′stənt ŭv prə-pôr-shə-năl′ĭ-tē] A constant ratio of two variables related proportionally

constante de proporcionalidad Razón constante de dos variables que están relacionadas en forma proporcional

coordinate plane [kō-ôr′dn-ĭt plān] A plane formed by the intersection of a horizontal number line called the *x*-axis and a vertical number line called the *y*-axis

plano cartesiano Plano formado por la intersección de una recta numérica horizontal llamada eje *x* y otra vertical llamada eje *y*

cost [kôst] The amount paid or required in payment for a purchase, a price

costo El monto pagado o requerido en el pago de una compra, un precio

counterclockwise A circular movement in the direction opposite of the typical forward movement of the hands of a clock

en sentido contrario a las manecillas del reloj Un movimiento circular en la dirección opuesta al moviemiento típico de las manecillas del reloj

cross section [krôs sĕk′shən] The intersection of a three-dimensional figure and a plane

sección transversal Intersección de una figura tridimensional y un plano

cube (in numeration) [kyo͞ob] A number raised to the third power

cubo (en numeración) Número elevado a la tercera potencia

Interactive Glossary

cylinder [sil′ən-dər] A three-dimensional figure with two parallel, congruent circular bases connected by a curved lateral surface

cilindro Figura tridimensional con dos bases circulares paralelas y congruentes, unidas por una superficie lateral curva

D

denominator [dĭ-nŏm′ə-nā′tər] The bottom number of a fraction that tells how many equal parts are in the whole

denominador Número de abajo de una fracción que indica en cuántas partes iguales se divide el entero

dependent events [dĭ-pĕn′dənt ĭ-vĕnts′] Events for which the outcome of one event affects the probability of the second event

sucesos dependientes Dos sucesos son dependientes si el resultado de uno afecta la probabilidad del otro

diameter [di-am′i-tər] A line segment that passes through the center of a circle and has endpoints on the circle, or the length of that segment

diámetro Segmento de recta que pasa por el centro de un círculo y tiene sus extremos en la circunferencia, o bien la longitud de ese segmento

dimension [dĭ-mĕn′shən] The length, width, or height of a figure

dimensión Longitud, ancho o altura de una figura

Distributive Property [dĭ-strĭb′yə-tĭv prŏp′ər-tē]
For all real numbers, *a*, *b*, and *c*, $a(b + c) =$
$ab + ac$ and $a(b - c) = ab - ac$

Propiedad distributiva Dado números reales *a*, *b*,
y *c*, $a(b + c) = ab + ac$ y $a(b - c) = ab - ac$

---

dividend [dĭv′ĭ-dĕnd′] The number to be divided
in a division problem

dividendo Número que se divide en un problema
de división

---

divisible [dĭ-vĭz′ə-bəl] Can be divided by a
number without leaving a remainder

divisible Que se puede dividir entre un número
sin dejar residuo

Division Property of Equality [dĭ-vĭzh′ən prŏp′ər-tē
ŭv ĭ-kwŏl′ĭ-tē] The property that states that if you
divide both sides of an equation by the same
nonzero number, the new equation will have the
same solution

Propiedad de igualdad de la división
Propiedad que establece que puedes dividir
ambos lados de una ecuación entre el mismo
número distinto de cero, y la nueva ecuación
tendrá la misma solución

---

divisor [dĭ-vī′zər] The number you are dividing by
in a division problem

divisor El número entre el que se divide en un
problema de división

Interactive Glossary

My Vocabulary Summary

equation [ĭ-kwā′zhən] A mathematical sentence that shows that two expressions are equivalent

ecuación Enunciado matemático que indica que dos expresiones son equivalentes

equilateral triangle [ē′kwə-lăt′ər-əl trī′ăng′gəl] A triangle with three congruent sides

triángulo equilátero Triángulo con tres lados congruentes

equivalent [ĭ-kwĭv′ə-lənt] Having the same value

equivalentes Que tienen el mismo valor

evaluate [ĭ-văl′yōō-āt] To find the value of a numerical or algebraic expression

evaluar Hallar el valor de una expresión numérica o algebraica

event [ĭ-vĕnt′] An outcome or set of outcomes of an experiment or situation

suceso Un resultado o una serie de resultados de un experimento o una situación

experiment [ĭk-spĕr′ə-mənt] In probability, any activity based on chance, such as tossing a coin

experimento En probabilidad, cualquier actividad basada en la posibilidad, como lanzar una moneda.

experimental probability [ĭk-spĕr′ə-mĕn′tl prŏb′ə-bĭl′ĭ-tē] The ratio of the number of times an event occurs to the total number of trials, or times that the activity is performed

probabilidad experimental Razón del número de veces que ocurre un suceso al número total de pruebas o al número de veces que se realiza el experimento

exponent [ĭk-spō′nənt] The number that indicates how many times the base is used as a factor

exponente Número que indica cuántas veces se usa la base como factor

F

factor tree [făk′tər trē] A diagram showing how a whole number breaks down into its prime factors

árbol de factores Diagrama que muestra cómo se descompone un número cabal en sus factores primos

factor [făk′tər] A number that is multiplied by another number to get a product

factor Número que se multiplica por otro para hallar un producto

Fahrenheit [făr′ən-hīt′] A temperature scale in which 32 °F is the freezing point of water and 212 °F is the boiling point of water

Fahrenheit Escala de temperatura en la que 32 °F es el punto de congelación del agua y 212 °F es el punto de ebullición

fee [fē] A fixed amount or a percent of an amount

tarifa Cantidad fija o porcentaje de una cantidad

first quartile [fûrst kwôr til] The median of the lower half of a set of data; also called *lower quartile*

primer cuartil La mediana de la mitad inferior de un conjunto de datos; también llamado *cuartil inferior*

Interactive Glossary

My Vocabulary Summary

formula [fôr′myə-lə] A rule showing relationships among quantities

fórmula Regla que muestra relaciones entre cantidades

frequency [frē′kwən-sē] The number of times the value appears in the data set

frecuencia Cantidad de veces que aparece el valor en un conjunto de datos

gratuity [grə-t′ĭ-tē] A tip, or monetary percentage that is given or paid in addition to the price of a service

gratificación Una propina o porcentaje monetario, que se da o paga además del precio de un servicio

greatest common factor (GCF) [grāt·est kŏm′ən făk′tər] The largest common factor of two or more given numbers

máximo común divisor (MCD) El mayor de los factores comunes compartidos por dos o más números dados.

height [hīt] In a pyramid or cone, the perpendicular distance from the base to the opposite vertex

altura En una pirámide o cono, la distancia perpendicular desde la base al vértice opuesto.

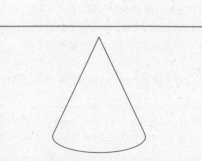

hypotenuse [hi-pŏt′n-ōōs′] In a right triangle, the side opposite the right angle

hipotenusa En un triángulo rectángulo, el lado opuesto al ángulo recto

I

Identity Property of Addition [ĭ-dĕn′tĭ-tē prŏp′ər-tē ŭv ə-dĭsh′ən] The property that states that the sum of zero and any number is that number

Propiedad de identidad de la suma Propiedad que establece que la suma de cero y cualquier número es ese número

Identity Property of Multiplication [ĭ-dĕn′tĭ-tē prŏp′ər-tē ŭv mŭl′tə-plĭ-kā′shən] The property that states that the product of 1 and any number is that number

Propiedad de identidad de la multiplicación Propiedad que establece que el producto de 1 y cualquier número es ese número

independent events [ĭn′dĭ-pĕn′dənt ĭ-vĕnts′] Events for which the outcome of one event does not affect the probability of the other

sucesos independientes Dos sucesos son independientes si el resultado de uno no afecta la probabilidad del otro

independent variable [ĭn′dĭ-pĕn′dənt vâr′ē-ə-bəl] In a relationship between variable quantities, a variable whose value determines the value of another quantity

variable independiente En una relación entre cantidades que varían, variable cuyo valor determina el valor de otra cantidad

inequality [ĭn′ĭ-kwŏl′ĭ-tē] A mathematical sentence that shows the relationship between quantities that are not equivalent

desigualdad Enunciado matemático que muestra una relación entre cantidades que no son equivalentes

Interactive Glossary

integers [ĭn′tĭ-jərs] The set of whole numbers and their opposites

enteros Conjunto de todos los números cabales y sus opuestos

interquartile range [ĭn′tər-kwôr′tīl′ rănj] The difference between the upper and lower quartiles in a box-and-whisker plot

rango entre cuartiles La diferencia entre los cuartiles superior e inferior en una gráfica de mediana y rango

inverse operations [ĭn-vûrs′ ŏp′ə-rā′shəns] Operations that undo each other: addition and subtraction, or multiplication and division

operaciones inversas Operaciones que se cancelan mutuamente: suma y resta, o multiplicación y división

Inverse Property of Addition [ĭn-vûrs′ prŏp′ər-tē ŭv ə-dĭsh′ən] The sum of a number and its opposite, or additive inverse, is 0

propiedad inversa de la suma La suma de un número y su opuesto, o inverso aditivo, es cero

Inverse Property of Multiplication [ĭn-vûrs′ prŏp′ər-tē ŭv mŭl′tə-plĭ-kā′shən] The product of a nonzero number and its reciprocal, or multiplicative inverse, is 1

Propiedad inversa de la multiplicación El producto de un número distinto a cero y su recíproco, o inverso multiplicativo, es uno

isosceles triangle [ī-sŏs′ə-lēz′ trī′ăng′gəl] A triangle with at least two congruent sides

triángulo isósceles Triángulo que tiene al menos dos lados congruentes

L

legs [lĕgs] In a right triangle, the sides that include the right angle; in an isosceles triangle, the pair of congruent sides

catetos En un triángulo rectángulo, los lados adyacentes al ángulo recto. En un triángulo isósceles, el par de lados congruentes

like terms [līk tûrms] Terms with the same variables raised to the same exponents

términos semejantes Términos que contienen las mismas variables elevada a las mismas exponentes

line graph [līn grăf] A graph that uses line segments to show how data changes

gráfica lineal Gráfica que muestra cómo cambian los datos mediante segmentos de recta

line plot [līn plot] A number line with marks or dots that show frequency

diagrama de acumulación Recta numérica con marcas o puntos que indican la frecuencia

lower quartile [lou'ər kwôr'tĭl'] The median of the lower half of a set of data

cuartil inferior La mediana de la mitad inferior de un conjunto de datos

M

markdown [märk′doun′] The amount of decrease in a price

margen de descuento Cantidad en la que disminuye un precio

markup [märk′ŭp′] The amount of increase in a price

margen de aumento Cantidad en la que aumenta un precio

mean [mēn] The sum of the items in a set of data divided by the number of items in the set; also called *average*

media La suma de todos loselementos de un conjunto de datos dividida entre el número de elementos del conjunto. También se llama *promedio*

mean absolute deviation (**MAD**) [mēn ăb′sə-lōot′ dē′vē-ā′shən] The mean distance between each data value and the mean of the data set

desviación absoluta media (DAM) Distancia media entre cada dato y la media del conjunto de datos

measure of central tendency [mĕzh′ər ŭv sĕn′trəl tĕn′dən-sē] A measure used to describe the middle of a data set; the mean, median, and mode are measures of central tendency

medida de tendencia dominante Medida que describe la parte media de un conjunto de datos; la media, la mediana y la moda son medidas de tendencia dominante

My Vocabulary Summary

median [mē′dē-ən] The middle number, or the mean (average) of the two middle numbers, in an ordered set of data

mediana El número intermedio, o la media (el promedio), de los dos números intermedios en un conjunto ordenado de datos

minuend [mĭn′yoo-ĕnd′] The first number in a subtraction sentence

minuendo El primer número en una oración de resta

mixed number [mĭkst nŭm′bər] A number made up of a whole number that is not zero and a fraction

número mixto Número compuesto por un número cabal distinto de cero y una fracción

mode [mōd] The number or numbers that occur most frequently in a set of data; when all numbers occur with the same frequency, we say there is no mode

moda Número o números más frecuentes en un conjunto de datos; si todos los números aparecen con la misma frecuencia, no hay moda

multiple [mŭl′tə-pəl] The product of any number and any nonzero whole number is a multiple of that number

múltiplo El producto de un número y cualquier número cabal distinto de cero es un múltiplo de ese número

Interactive Glossary

Multiplication Property of Equality
[mŭl′tə-plĭ-kā′shən prŏp′ər-tē ŭv ĭ-kwŏl′ĭ-tē] The property that states that if you multiply both sides of an equation by the same number, the new equation will have the same solution

Propiedad de igualdad de la multiplicación Propiedad que establece que puedes multiplicar ambos lados de una ecuación por el mismo número y la nueva ecuación tendrá la misma solución

Multiplication Property of Zero [mŭl′tə-plĭ-kā′shən prŏp′ər-tē ŭv zîr′ō] The property that states that for all real numbers a, $a \times 0 = 0$ and $0 \times a = 0$

Propiedad de multiplicación del cero Propiedad que establece que para todos los números reales a, $a \times 0 = 0$ y $0 \times a = 0$

Multiplicative Inverse Property [mŭl′tə-plĭ-kā′shən ĭn-vûrs′prŏp′ər-tē] The product of a nonzero number and its reciprocal, or multiplicative inverse, is one

Propiedad inversa de la multiplicación El producto de un número distinto a cero y su recíproco, o inverso multiplicativo, es uno

mutually exclusive [myōō′chōō-əl-lē ĭk-sklōō′sĭv] Two events are mutually exclusive if they cannot occur in the same trial of an experiment

mutuamente excluyentes Dos sucesos son mutuamente excluyentes cuando no pueden ocurrir en la misma prueba de un experimento

N

net [nĕt] An arrangement of two-dimensional figures that can be folded to form a polyhedron

plantilla Arreglo de figuras bidimensionales que se doblan para formar un poliedro

© Houghton Mifflin Harcourt Publishing Company

My Vocabulary Summary

numerator [noo′mə-rā′tər] The top number of a fraction that tells how many parts of a whole are being considered

numerador El número de arriba de una fracción; indica cuántas partes de un entero se consideran

obtuse angle [ŏb-toos′ ăng′gəl] An angle whose measure is greater than 90° but less than 180°

ángulo obtuso Ángulo que mide más de 90° y menos de 180°

order of operations [ŏr′dər ŭv ŏp′ə-rā′shəns] A rule for evaluating expressions: first perform the operations in parentheses, then compute powers and roots, then perform all multiplication and division from left to right, and then perform all addition and subtraction from left to right

orden de las operaciones Regla para evaluar expresiones: primero se hacen las operaciones entre paréntesis, luego se hallan las potencias y raíces, después todas las multiplicaciones y divisiones de izquierda a derecha y, por último, todas las sumas y restas de izquierda a derecha.

outcome [out′kŭm′] A possible result of a probability experiment

resultado Posible resultado de un experimento de probabilidad

outlier [out′lī′ər] A value much greater or much less than the others in a data set

valor extremo Un valor mucho mayor o menor que los demás de un conjunto de datos

P

parallel lines [păr′ə-lĕl′ līns] Lines in a plane that do not intersect

líneas paralelas Líneas que se encuentran en el mismo plano pero que nunca se intersecan

Interactive Glossary

parallelogram [păr′ə-lĕl′ə-grăm′] A quadrilateral with two pairs of parallel sides

paralelogramo Cuadrilátero con dos pares de lados paralelos

percent change [pər-sĕnt′ chănj] The amount stated as a percent that a number increases or decreases

porcentaje de cambio Cantidad en que un número aumenta o disminuye, expresada como un porcentaje

percent decrease [pər-sĕnt′ dĭ-krēs′] A percent change describing a decrease in a quantity

porcentaje de disminución Porcentaje de cambio en que una cantidad disminuye

percent error [pər-sĕnt′ ĕr′ər] A special case of percent change in which the amount over or under an expected amount is expressed as a percent of the expected amount

porcentaje de error Caso especial de porcentaje de cambio en que la cantidad esperada por encima o por debajo se expresa como un porcentaje de la cantidad esperada

percent increase [pər-sĕnt′ ĭn-krēs′] A percent change describing an increase in a quantity

porcentaje de incremento Porcentaje de cambio en que una cantidad aumenta

My Vocabulary Summary

perimeter [pə-rĭm´ĭ-tər] The distance around a polygon

perímetro Distancia alrededor de un polígono

---

perpendicular lines [pər-pən-dik´yōo-lər līnz] Two lines that intersect to form four right angles

rectas perpendiculares Dos rectas que se intersecan y forman cuatro ángulos rectos

---

pi (π) [pī] The ratio of the circumference of a circle to the length of its diameter; $\pi \approx 3.14$ or $\frac{22}{7}$

pi (π) Razón de la circunferencia de un círculo a la longitud de su diámetro; $\pi \approx 3.14$ ó $\frac{22}{7}$

---

plane [plān] A flat surface that has no thickness and extends forever

plano Superficie plana que no tiene ningún grueso y que se extiende por siempre

---

population [pŏp´yə-lā´shən] The entire group of objects or individuals considered for a survey

población Grupo completo de objetos o individuos que se desea estudiar

Interactive Glossary

precision [prĭ-sĭzh′ən] The level of detail of a measurement, determined by the unit of measure

precisión Detalle de una medición, determinado por la unidad de medida

prime factorization [prīm făk′-tər-ĭ-zā′shən] A number written as the product of its prime factors

factorización prima Un número escrito como el producto de sus factores primos

prime number [prīm nŭm′bər] A whole number greater than 1 that has exactly two factors, itself and 1

número primo Número cabal mayor que 1 que sólo es divisible entre 1 y él mismo

principal [prĭn′sə-pəl] The initial amount of money borrowed or saved

capital Cantidad inicial de dinero depositada o recibida en préstamo

prism [prĭz′əm] A polyhedron that has two congruent polygon-shaped bases and other faces that are all parallelograms

prisma Poliedro con dos bases congruentes con forma de polígono y caras con forma de paralelogramo

probability [prŏb′ə-bĭl′ĭ-tē] A number from 0 to 1 (or 0% to 100%) that describes how likely an event is to occur

probabilidad Un número entre 0 y 1 (ó 0% y 100%) que describe qué tan probable es un suceso

probability of an event [prŏb′ə-bĭl′ĭ-tē ŭv ən ĭ-věnt′] The probability of an event is the ratio of the number of outcomes in the event to the total number of outcomes in the sample space

probabilidad de un evento Razón del número de resultados del evento con respecto al número total de resultados del espacio muestral

product [prŏd′əkt] The result when two or more numbers are multiplied

producto Resultado de multiplicar dos o más números

proportion [prə-pôr′shən] An equation that states that two ratios are equivalent

proporción Ecuación que establece que dos razones son equivalentes

proportional relationship [prə-pôr′shə-nəl rĭ-lā′shən-shĭp′] A relationship between two quantities in which the ratio of one quantity to the other quantity is constant

relación proporcional Relación entre dos cantidades en que la razón de una cantidad a la otra es constante

Interactive Glossary

pyramid [pĭr′ə-mĭd] A polyhedron with a polygon base and triangular sides that all meet at a common vertex

pirámide Poliedro cuya base es un polígono; tiene caras triangulares que se juntan en un vértice común

Q

quadrilateral [kwŏd′rə-lăt′ər-əl] A four-sided polygon

cuadrilátero Polígono de cuatro lados

quartile [kwôr′tĭl′] Three values, one of which is the median, that divide a data set into fourths. See also *first quartile, third quartile*

cuartiles Cada uno de tres valores, uno de los cuales es la mediana, que dividen en cuartos un conjunto de datos. Ver también *primer cuartil, tercer cuartil*

quotient [kwō′shənt] The result when one number is divided by another

cociente Resultado de dividir un número entre otro

R

radius [rā′dē-əs] A line segment with one endpoint at the center of a circle and the other endpoint on the circle, or the length of that segment

radio Segmento de recta con un extremo en el centro de un círculo y el otro en la circunferencia; o bien la longitud de ese segmento

My Vocabulary Summary

random sample [răn′dəm săm′pəl] A sample in which each individual or object in the entire population has an equal chance of being selected

muestra aleatoria Muestra en la que cada individuo u objeto de la población tiene la misma oportunidad de ser elegido

range (in statistics) [rănj] The difference between the greatest and least values in a data set

rango (en estadística) Diferencia entre los valores máximo y mínimo de un conjunto de datos

rate [rāt] A ratio that compares two quantities measured in different units

tasa Una razón que compara dos cantidades medidas en diferentes unidades

ratio [rā′shō] A comparison of two quantities by division

razón Comparación de dos cantidades mediante una división

rational number [răsh′ə-nəl nŭm′bər] Any number that can be expressed as a ratio of two integers

número racional Número que se puede escribir como una razón de dos enteros

real number [rē′əl nŭm′bər] A rational or irrational number

número real Número racional o irracional

My Vocabulary Summary

reciprocal [rĭ-sĭp′rə-kəl] One of two numbers whose product is 1

recíproco Uno de dos números cuyo producto es igual a 1

---

rectangular prism [rĕk-tăng′gyə-lər prĭz′əm] A polyhedron whose bases are rectangles and whose other faces are parallelograms

prisma rectangular Poliedro cuyas bases son rectángulos y cuyas caras tienen forma de paralelogramo

---

regular polygon [rĕg′yə-lər pŏl′ē-gŏn′] A polygon with all sides of the same length and all angles of the same measure

polígono regular Un polígono con todos los lados de la misma longitud y todos los ángulos de la misma medida

---

regular pyramid [rĕg′yə-lər pĭr′ə-mĭd] A pyramid whose base is a regular polygon and whose lateral faces are all congruent

pirámide regular Pirámide que tiene un polígono regular como base y caras laterales congruentes

---

representative sample [rĕp′rĭ-zĕn′tə-tĭv săm′pəl] A sample that has the same characteristics as the population

muestra representativa Muestra que tiene las mismas características de la población

---

retail price [rē′tāl′ prīs] The amount an item is sold for after a company adds a markup

precio de venta al por menor Cantidad en la que se vende un artículo después que una compañía le agrega un aumento de precio

rhombus [rŏm′bəs] A parallelogram with all sides congruent

rombo Paralelogramo en el que todos los lados son congruentes

---

right angle [rīt ăng′gəl] An angle that measures 90°

ángulo recto Ángulo que mide exactamente 90°

---

right triangle [rīt trī′ăng′gəl] A triangle containing a right angle

triángulo rectángulo Triángulo que tiene un ángulo recto

S

---

sales tax [sāl tăks] A percent of the cost of an item that is charged by governments to raise money

impuesto sobre la venta Porcentaje del costo de un artículo que los gobiernos cobran para recaudar fondos

---

sample [săm′pəl] A part of the population that is chosen to represent the entire group

muestra Una parte de la población que se elige para representar a todo el grupo

Interactive Glossary

sample space [săm′pəl spās] All possible outcomes of an experiment

espacio muestral Conjunto de todos los resultados posibles de un experimento

---

scale [skāl] The ratio between two sets of measurements

escala La razón entre dos conjuntos de medidas

---

scale drawing [skāl drô′ĭng] A drawing that uses a scale to make an object smaller than or larger than the real object

dibujo a escala Dibujo en el que se usa una escala para que un objeto se vea mayor o menor que el objeto real al que representa

---

scale factor [skāl făk′tər] The ratio used to enlarge or reduce similar figures

factor de escala Razón que se usa para agrandar o reducir figuras semejantes

simple interest [sĭm′pəl ĭn′trĭst] A fixed percent of the principal. It is found using the formula $I = Prt$, where P represents the principal, r the rate of interest, and t the time

interés simple Un porcentaje fijo del capital. Se calcula con la fórmula $I = Cit$, donde C representa el capital, i, la tasa de interés y t, el tiempo

simulation [sĭm′yə-lā′shən] A model of an experiment, often one that would be too difficult or too time-consuming to actually perform

simulación Representación de un experimento, por lo regular de uno cuya realización sería demasiado difícil o llevaría mucho tiempo

slope [slōp] A measure of the steepness of a line on a graph; the rise divided by the run

pendiente Medida de la inclinación de una línea en una gráfica. Razón de la distancia vertical a la distancia horizontal

solution of an equation [sə-lōō′shən ŭv ən ĭ-kwā′zhən] A value or values that make an equation true

solución de una ecuación Valor o valores que hacen verdadera una ecuación

solution of an inequality [sə-lōō′shən ŭv ən ĭn′ĭ-kwŏl′ĭ-tē] A value or values that make an inequality true

solución de una desigualdad Valor o valores que hacen verdadera una desigualdad

Interactive Glossary

sphere [sfîr] A three-dimensional figure with all points the same distance from the center

esfera Figura tridimensional en la que todos los puntos están a la misma distancia del centro

Subtraction Property of Equality [səb-trăk′shən prŏp′ər-tē ŭv ĭ-kwŏl′ĭ-tē] The property that states that if you subtract the same number from both sides of an equation, the new equation will have the same solution

Propiedad de igualdad de la resta Propiedad que establece que puedes restar el mismo número de ambos lados de una ecuación y la nueva ecuación tendrá la misma solución

subtrahend [sŭb′trə-hĕnd′] The number that is subtracted from another number in a subtraction sentence

sustraendo el número que se resta de otro número en una oración de resta

supplementary angles [sŭp′lə-mĕn′tə-rē ăng′gəls] Two angles whose measures have a sum of 180°

ángulos suplementarios Dos ángulos cuyas medidas suman 180°

surface area [sûr′fəs âr′e-ə] The sum of the areas of the faces, or surfaces, of a three-dimensional figure

área total Suma de las áreas de las caras, o superficies, de una figura tridimensional

© Houghton Mifflin Harcourt Publishing Company

G34 Interactive Glossary

T

term (**in an expression**) [tûrm (ĭn ən ĭk-sprĕsh′ən)] The parts of an expression that are added or subtracted

término (**en una expresión**) Las partes de una expresión que se suman o se restan

theoretical probability [thē′ə-rĕt′ĭ-kəl prŏb′ə-bĭl′ĭ-tē] The ratio of the number of possible outcomes in the event to the total number of possible outcomes in the sample space

probabilidad teórica Razón entre el número de resultados posibles de un suceso y el número total de resultados posibles del espacio muestral.

third quartile [thûrd kwôr′tĭl′] The median of the upper half of a set of data; also called *upper quartile*

tercer cuartil La mediana de la mitad superior de un conjunto de datos. También se llama *cuartil superior*

tip [tĭp] Another word for gratuity, a monetary percentage that is given or paid in addition to the price of a service

propina Otra palabra para gratificación, que es un porcentaje de dinero que se da o se paga adicionalmente al precio de un servicio

trapezoid [trăp′ĭ-zoid′] A quadrilateral with at least one pair of parallel sides

trapecio Cuadrilátero con al menos un par de lados paralelos

Interactive Glossary

tree diagram [trē dī′ə-grăm′] A branching diagram that shows all possible combinations or outcomes of an event

diagrama de árbol Diagrama ramificado que muestra todas las posibles combinaciones o resultados de un suceso

---

trial [trī′əl] Each repetition or observation of an experiment

prueba Una sola repetición u observación de un experimento

---

triangular prism [trī-ăng′gyə-lər prĭz′əm] A polyhedron whose bases are triangles and whose other faces are parallelograms

prisma triangular Poliedro cuyas bases son triángulos y cuyas demás caras tienen forma de paralelogramo

U

---

unit rate [yo͞o′nĭt rāt] A rate in which the second quantity in the comparison is one unit

tasa unitaria Una tasa en la que la segunda cantidad de la comparación es la unidad

---

upper quartile [ŭp′ər kwôr′tīl′] The median of the upper half of a set of data

cuartil superior La mediana de la mitad superior de un conjunto de datos

V

My Vocabulary Summary

variable [vâr′ē-ə-bəl] A symbol used to represent a quantity that can change

variable Símbolo que representa una cantidad que puede cambiar

vertex [vûr′tĕks′] On an angle or polygon, the point where two sides intersect

vértice En un ángulo o polígono, el punto de intersección de dos lados

vertical angles [vûr′tĭ-kəl ăng′gəls] A pair of opposite congruent angles formed by intersecting lines

ángulos opuestos por el vértice Par de ángulos opuestos congruentes formados por líneas secantes

volume [vŏl′yo͞om] The amount of space enclosed within a three-dimensional region; or the number of cubic units needed to fill that space

volumen La cantidad de espacio dentro de una región tridimensional; o la cantidad de unidades cúbicas necesarias para llenar ese espacio

Interactive Glossary

***x*-axis** [ĕks-ăk′sĭs] The horizontal axis on a coordinate plane

eje *x* El eje horizontal del plano cartesiano

***y*-axis** [wī-ăk′sĭs] The vertical axis on a coordinate plane

eje *y* El eje vertical del plano cartesiano

Index

compass, 293–295, 317–319
complement of an event, 449
complementary angles, 251, 253, 254, 256, 258, 259
complex fractions, 190
  comparing scales, 45, 48
  computing unit rates involving, 19–26
composite figures, 446
  area of, 349–354
  surface area of, 420
  volume of, 380, 420
compound events
  experimental probability of, 455–462
  simulations in testing, 499–508
  theoretical probability of, 483–490
computers
  in generating trials of random numbers, 501, 506
cones
  bases of, 342
  cross sections of, 342, 344
conjectures
  making, 130, 138, 166, 303
  using, 166
constant of proportionality, 12–18, 22, 30–34, 51, 62
  markup rate as, 66, 68
constant rates, 7, 8, 9, 10, 12, 19, 20, 22, 32, 34, 38, 42, 141
constant ratio, 30, 32
coordinate plane
  ordered pairs on, 4
  polygons in the, 291, 292
cross sections, 342, 360, 385
  describing and analyzing, for circular solids, 341–348, 358
  describing and analyzing, for prisms and pyramids, 359–364
cubes
  deriving and applying formula for surface areas of, 365–370
cylinders
  bases of, 342
  cross sections of, 341–348

D

data
  collecting statistical, 390, 440
  comparing center and spread of, when displayed
    in box plots, 421–426
    in dot plots, 415–420
  comparing means using mean absolute deviation and repeated sampling, 427–434
  mean of, 414

  median of, 414
  range in, 414
  sample, 428
  using statistics and graphs to compare, 413–438
data points
  cluster of, 416, 418, 420
decagon, 299
  perimeter of, 233
decimals, 97
  addition of, 128
  converting mixed numbers to, 210
  division of, 164
  multiplication of, 164
    by whole numbers, 54
  subtraction of, 128
  writing fractions as, 179–186
  writing mixed numbers as, 182
  writing probability as, 477, 485
  writing rational numbers as, 181
denominator, 190
density
  as a unit rate, 25
diagrams. *See under* represent
diameter, 294, 296, 297, 299, 323, 328, 329, 330, 332, 335, 336, 337, 338, 339, 340, 342, 343, 344, 347
differences, 100, 128. *See also* subtraction
  for integers, 137–144
  for rational numbers, 145–152
discounts, 63–70
Distributive Property, 167, 170, 200, 222, 231, 232, 233, 234, 235
dividends, 168, 193. *See also* division
division
  with decimals, 164
  in finding unit rate, 21
  with fractions and mixed numbers, 4, 164
  of integers, 179–186
  as inverse operation with multiplication, 168
  long, 180, 181
  of rational numbers, 165–172, 187–192, 196
  in writing fractions as decimals, 179–186
divisor, 168, 193. *See also* division
dot plots, 414. *See also under* represent
  comparing center and spread of data displayed in, 415–420
  range of, 416
  shapes of, 416, 418
Dougherty, Michelle, 97
drawings
  of circles and other figures, 293–300
  scale, 43–50, 296

E

equality
  Addition Property of, 170, 245
  Division Property of, 245, 246
  Subtraction Property of, 246
equations, 219. *See also under* represent
  modeling with, 15, 17
  one-step, 4, 222, 326
  for proportional relationships, 13, 14, 15, 16, 17, 29, 30, 31, 33, 35, 36, 37, 38, 43, 44
  solution of, 244
  for taxes and gratuities, 71–78
  two-step, 237–242
    in finding angle measures, 251–258
    in problem solving, 243–250
    writing for situations, 237–242
equilateral triangles, 231, 241, 379
equivalent fractions, 180
equivalent ratios, 3, 23, 390
  proportional reasoning in writing, 440
estimates
  in checking reasonableness, 203–208, 211
  over-, 203, 206, 207
  under-, 203, 206, 207
events
  complement of, 449
  compound
    experimental probability of, 455–462
    simulations in testing, 499–508
    theoretical probability of, 483–490
  simple
    experimental probability of, 441–446
    finding experimental probability of, 447–454
    simulations in testing, 499–508
    theoretical probability of, 475–482
experimental probability, 439–472, 473, 474, 507
  comparing to theoretical probability, 478–482, 498, 507
  conducting simulations to test, 450–454, 499–506
  of events, 441–446
    compound, 455–462
    simple, 447–454
  and proportional reasoning in making predictions, 463–470
  understanding, 441–446
experiments, 443
expressions, 219. *See also under* represent
  algebraic, evaluating, 326
  linear
    adding, subtracting, and factoring, with rational coefficients, 223–228

Index

right prisms
  deriving and applying formulas for surface areas of, 365–370
  surface area of, 367
square prisms, 386
square pyramids, 359, 362
squares, 291, 318, 325, 326
  sides in, 231, 240
trapezoidal prisms, 380–382
triangles, 291, 292, 302, 319, 320, 322, 324
  area of, 62, 326
  drawing and constructing given angle measures, 309–316
  drawing and constructing given side lengths, 301–308
  equilateral, 231, 241, 379
  inscribing in circles, 294, 296, 299
  isosceles, 238, 368, 385
  right, 294, 318, 380, 426
triangular prisms, 359, 360, 361, 363, 368–370, 373–376, 379, 380, 384–386, 486
vertical angles, 252–260
volume
  exploring, 358
  of rectangular prisms, 371–376
  solving multi-step problems with surface area and, 377–384
Glossary, G2–G38
graphic organizers, 287
graphs. *See also under* represent
  dashed lines in, 29
  origin in, 27–34
  proportional relationships in, 27–34
  solid lines in, 28, 29
gratuities
  equations in determining, 71–78, 95

H

hexagonal prisms, 368, 383
  height of, 373
  surface area of, 370, 380
  volume of, 373, 375, 380, 386
hexagonal pyramids, 361, 363
hexagons, 229, 248, 295, 296, 300
Hinerfeld, Daniel, 97

I

Identity Property of Addition, 130, 170
Identity Property of Multiplication, 170, 198
inequalities, 219

interpreting, writing, and graphing, 258, 262, 308, 322, 470
problem solving using, 261–290
  one-step, 263–270
  two-step, 271–288
inferences, 217
  from random samples, 397–404
  repeated, 405–410
integers, 217
  addition of, 129–136
    with different signs, 132
    with same signs, 132
  division of, 179–186
  negative, 97, 125
  positive, 97, 125
  subtraction of, 137–144
    negative, 109–116, 140
    positive, 101–108, 140
interest
  proportional reasoning in calculating simple, 87–96, 124, 136, 202
interquartile range, 413, 414, 421–426, 436
Inverse Property of Multiplication, 198
isosceles triangles, 238, 368, 385

L

layers, 372
Learning Mindset
  challenge-seeking, 438, 444, 452, 460, 480, 488
  perseverance, 2, 8, 16, 24, 32, 142, 170, 184, 290, 298, 306, 314, 330, 338, 346, 362, 368, 374
  resilience, 150, 220, 226, 234, 240, 248, 268, 276, 388, 394, 402
  strategic help-seeking, 98, 106, 114, 134, 176, 190
like terms
  grouping, 224, 230–234
linear expressions
  adding, subtracting, and factoring, with rational coefficients, 229–236
  writing, for situations in different forms, 223–228
long division, 180, 181

M

MAD. *See* mean absolute deviation (MAD)
manipulatives and materials
  algebra tiles, 244
  compass, 293–295, 317–319
  graph paper, 371, 375

grid paper, 333, 349, 352, 353
number cubes, 442–445, 450, 451, 453, 454, 456, 458, 459, 461, 462, 471, 478, 479, 481, 488–491, 495–498, 508
protractor, 309, 317
maps, 419
markdowns, 259
  proportional reasoning in calculating, 63–70, 95
markups
  as constant of proportionality, 66, 68
  proportional reasoning in calculating, 63–70
mathematical expressions, 219
Mathematical Practices and Processes
  1. *make sense of problems and persevere in solving them,* occurs throughout. Some examples are 9, 25, 39, 66, 76, 91, 191, 383
  2. *reason abstractly and quantitatively,* in some lessons. Some examples are 9, 15, 23, 68, 76, 105, 107, 114, 121, 141, 157, 184, 199, 227, 235, 284, 337, 346, 362, 423, 444, 504
  3. *construct viable arguments and critique the reasoning of others,* in some lessons. Some examples are 33, 114, 158, 307, 337, 394, 417, 424, 459
  4. *model with mathematics,* in some lessons. Some examples are 15, 31, 39, 49, 169, 241, 247, 277
  5. *use appropriate tools strategically,* in some lessons. Some examples are 115, 170, 199, 201, 299, 300, 311, 314, 502
  6. *attend to precision,* in some lessons. Some examples are 60, 61, 77, 85, 200, 214, 248, 381
  7. *look for and make use of structure,* in some lessons. Some examples are 75, 93, 135, 156, 171, 177, 201, 267, 339, 479
  8. *look for and express regularity in repeated reasoning,* in some lessons. Some examples are 169, 171, 183, 185, 256, 401
Math on the Spot videos. *See* student and parent resources on Ed: Your Friend in Learning
mean, 414, 417, 419
  comparing using mean absolute deviation and repeated sampling, 427–434
mean absolute deviation (MAD)
  comparing means using repeated sampling and, 427–434

© Houghton Mifflin Harcourt Publishing Company

V

variance, 432
Venn diagrams, 217
vertical angles, 252–260
volume. *See also* surface area
 of composite figures, 380, 420, 494
 exploring, 358
 of rectangular prisms, 446
 solving multi-step problems with
  surface area and

W

whiskers of the box plots, 421
whole numbers
 multiplication of decimals by, 54
words
 describing inequalities, 277
 expressing ratios in, 3

Z

Zero
 Multiplication Property of, 170

LENGTH

1 meter (m) = 1,000 millimeters (mm)

1 meter = 100 centimeters (cm)

1 meter ≈ 39.37 inches

1 kilometer (km) = 1,000 meters

1 kilometer ≈ 0.62 mile

1 inch = 2.54 centimeters

1 foot (ft) = 12 inches (in.)

1 yard (yd) = 3 feet

1 mile (mi) = 1,760 yards

1 mile = 5,280 feet

1 mile ≈ 1.609 kilometers

CAPACITY

1 liter (L) = 1,000 milliliters (mL)

1 liter = 1,000 cubic centimeters

1 liter ≈ 0.264 gallon

1 kiloliter (kL) = 1,000 liters

1 cup (c) = 8 fluid ounces (fl oz)

1 pint (pt) = 2 cups

1 quart (qt) = 2 pints

1 gallon (gal) = 4 quarts

1 gallon ≈ 3.785 liters

MASS/WEIGHT

1 gram (g) = 1,000 milligrams (mg)

1 kilogram (kg) = 1,000 grams

1 kilogram ≈ 2.2 pounds

1 pound (lb) = 16 ounces (oz)

1 pound ≈ 0.454 kilogram

1 ton = 2,000 pounds

TIME

1 minute (min) = 60 seconds (s)

1 hour (h) = 60 minutes

1 day = 24 hours

1 week = 7 days

1 year (yr) = about 52 weeks

1 year = 12 months (mo)

1 year = 365 days

1 decade = 10 years

Tables of Measures, Symbols, and Formulas

SYMBOLS

$=$	is equal to	10^2	ten squared
$\neq$	is not equal to	10^3	ten cubed
$\approx$	is approximately equal to	2^4	the fourth power of 2
$>$	is greater than	$|-4|$	the absolute value of -4
$<$	is less than	$\%$	percent
$\geq$	is greater than or equal to	$(2, 3)$	ordered pair (x, y)
$\leq$	is less than or equal to	$\degree$	degree

FORMULAS

Perimeter and Circumference

Polygon	$P = $ sum of the lengths of sides
Rectangle	$P = 2\ell + 2w$
Square	$P = 4s$
Circle	$C = \pi d$ or $C = 2\pi r$

Area

Rectangle	$A = \ell w$ or $A = bh$
Parallelogram	$A = bh$
Triangle	$A = \frac{1}{2}bh$
Trapezoid	$A = \frac{1}{2}h(b_1 + b_2)$
Square	$A = s^2$
Circle	$A = \pi r^2$

Volume

Right Prism	$V = \ell wh$ or $V = Bh$
Cube	$V = s^3$
Pyramid	$V = \frac{1}{3}Bh$

Surface Area

Right Prism	$S = Ph + 2B$
Cube	$S = 6s^2$
Square Pyramid	$S = \frac{1}{2}P\ell + B$